Abraham Valentine Williams Jackson

Avesta grammar

In comparison with Sanskrit

Abraham Valentine Williams Jackson

Avesta grammar
In comparison with Sanskrit

ISBN/EAN: 9783741168659

Manufactured in Europe, USA, Canada, Australia, Japa

Cover: Foto ©Andreas Hilbeck / pixelio.de

Manufactured and distributed by brebook publishing software (www.brebook.com)

Abraham Valentine Williams Jackson

Avesta grammar

AVESTA GRAMMAR

IN COMPARISON WITH SANSKRIT

BY

A. V. WILLIAMS JACKSON

OF COLUMBIA COLLEGE, NEW YORK CITY

PART I

PHONOLOGY, INFLECTION, WORD-FORMATION

WITH AN INTRODUCTION ON THE AVESTA

STUTTGART
W. KOHLHAMMER
1892

Inscribed

to

Professor K. F. Geldner

with gratitude and regard.

Preface.

The present Grammar is a work of no pretensions; it is offered as a small contribution toward advancing the Avesta cause. It is written in part fulfilment of a design formed when I first began to study the Avesta and became deeply interested in the true value and importance of that monument of antiquity.

The end for which the book is intended would perhaps have been better accomplished, however, if the work had been a mere grammatical sketch. This was my first design; and it may at another time be carried out. But as the work grew under my hands, it seemed desirable to enlarge it somewhat further, and to embody additional material which for reference might be serviceable to the general philologist, not to the specialist alone. The linguist may thus find in it useful matter and fresh illustrations, especially in the new readings from Geldner's edition of the Avesta texts.

No attempt, on the other hand, has been made to secure absolute completeness. Numerous minor points have been purposely omitted. These may perhaps later be taken up in a more extended work including also the Old Persian by the side of the Avesta and the Sanskrit. Little of importance, however, it is believed, has been overlooked. A fairly symmetrical development has been aimed at, although at times certain less familiar points have received fuller illustration than those that are well-known. This was intentional. They are chiefly matters that had not as yet been sufficiently emphasized elsewhere, or points which are peculiarly individual to the Avesta. They will easily be recognized.

The method of treatment is based throughout on the Sanskrit grammar; a knowledge of Sanskrit is presupposed. At every step, therefore, references have been made to Whitney's *Sanskrit Grammar* 2 ed. 1889; and it is a pleasure here to express thanks to the author of that work for the abundant suggestions received from it.

In the Grammar it might have been easier and more practical in many respects to use the Avesta type itself instead of employing a transcription. On the whole, however, it seemed best under the circumstances to transliterate. For general reference at present this method appears more convenient, and is useful in showing grammatical formations. The original type, it is expected, will be employed, as hinted above, in a little book *Avesta for Beginners*, planned for a date not far distant.

In regard to the transcription here adopted, my views have already been given in *The Avestan Alphabet and its Transcription*, Stuttgart, 1890. The phonetic and palaeographic character of each of the Avestan letters is there discussed. Reasons are likewise presented for transliterating Av. ɩ, ɩ̣ by the 'turned' ə, ə̣, so familiar in phonetic works. The composite ā̊ (aə) for ᵱᵚ (ɩᵚ) is also there explained (p. 13). The choice of the old Germanic characters ƕ, ȝ, þ, đ for the spirants ƀ, ɉ, ð, ǥ, and for the nasal ƞ (ŋ), as well as the method of transliterating ⱶ (ı+ɯ) by hv (h+v) is defended (pp. 14, 21). The 'tag' (‚) appearing in the letters ţ, ꝑ, ṇ, ḳ, ą is an attempt at systematically representing the 'derivation stroke' (ʟ ʃ by which many of the letters palaeographically are formed. Thus, ⱶ ṭ, ⱳ ꝑ, ⱳ ƀ, ʋ ð, ǥ, ⱶ ṗ, ⱳ ḳ etc. — the dotted line denoting the 'derivation stroke'. See *Av. Alphabet* pp. 16—17. The same 'tag' appears in the transcription of ⱳ (ʟ+ⱳ) by š (ᴤ+š). See *Av. Alphabet* p. 20. In the case of ⱳ ṣ̌ (beside ṣ̌), the 'subscript' tag is merely turned in the opposite direction so as to correspond with the hooked part (ᵥ) of the letter. The threefold differentiation š, ṣ̌, ś for ⱳ, ⱳ, ⱳ, is not necessary, however, except in transliterating a text for purely scientific purposes. In practise, š may everywhere be written. A 'substitute alphabet' to be used in popular articles is offered in the same monograph p. 28. I wish again to repeat my thanks to the authorities there quoted (*Av. Alphabet* p. 7) who so kindly aided me with advice and suggestions in regard to the transcription adopted.

In reference to the transliteration of Sanskrit, the familiar system (cf. Whitney, *Skt. Gram.* § 5) is followed; but be it observed that for comparison with the Avesta it seems preferable to transcribe the palatal sibilant by ś (Whitney ç), the palatal nasal by ń (Whitney ñ), the guttural nasal by ŋ (Whitney ṅ).

A word may now be added in regard to my manifold indebtedness in the present book. The general grammatical works from the early contribution of Haug (*Essays*, 1862), through Hovelacque (*Grammaire*, 1868) down to the present date have been on my table. Justi's *Handbuch der Zendsprache* (1864) was of course consulted continually. Constant reference has been made also to Bartholomae's *Altiranische Dialekte* (1883) and to his other admirable grammatical contributions. Spiegel's *Vergl. Gram. der altéran. Sprachen* (1882) was often opened, and will be specially acknowledged with others under the Syntax (Part II). C. de Harlez' *Manuel de l'Avesta* (1882), Darmesteter's *Études Iraniennes* (1883), W. Geiger's *Handbuch der Awestasprache* (1879) furnished more than one good suggestion, for which I am much indebted.

Acknowledgment is also due to some special contributions on grammatical subjects. In the Phonology, selections were made from the rich material collected by Hübschmann in *Kuhn's Zeitschrift* xxiv. p. 323 seq. (1878). My indebtedness to that well-known standard work Brugmann's *Grundriss der vergl. Gram.* (= *Elements of Compar. Grammar of the Indg. Languages*. English translation by Wright, Conway, Rouse, 1886 seq.) may be noticed from the citations below. Under Declension, frequent reference was made to Horn's *Nominalflexion im Avesta* (1885) and Lanman's *Noun-Inflection in the Veda* (1880). Under Verbal Inflection, in addition to Bartholomae's contributions below cited, acknowledgments are due to other authors to be mentioned in connection with Syntax (Part II). Caland's *Pronomina im Avesta* (1891) unfortunately came too late for the Inflections, but is cited under the Syntax of the Pronouns. I also regret that the work of Kavasji Edalji Kanga,

A Practical Gram. of the Av. Language (1891) was not received in time. My indebtedness to Whitney's *Skt. Gram.* is noticed above. For grammatical training in Sanskrit, moreover, I shall always thank my teachers in America and Germany—Professors Perry, Hopkins, and Pischel.

To my honored instructor and friend, Professor K. F. Geldner of Berlin, I owe, as I have owed, a lasting debt of gratitude. The book was begun when I was a student under his guidance; since I returned to America it has progressed with the aid of his constant encouragement, suggestion, and advice. He has been kind enough, moreover, not only to read the manuscript, as it was sent to Stuttgart, but also to look through the proof-sheets before they came back to me in America. The work I may call a trifling expression of the inspiration he gave me as a student. Let what is good in it count as his; the faults are my own.

It is a pleasure to add my cordial thanks to the publisher, Herrn W. Kohlhammer, for the characteristic interest which, with his usual enterprise, he has taken in the work. Special praise is due to his compositor, Herrn A. Säuberlich, whose accuracy is in general so unfailing that I fear I must say that the misprints which may have escaped notice are probably due to original slips of the author's pen, and not to inaccuracies on the part of the type-setter—a thing which cannot always be said. I should like also to express to Messrs. Ginn & Co., of Boston and New York, my appreciation of their willing co-operation in advancing the Iranian as well as other branches of the Oriental field in America.

Preface.

The present part of the Grammar (Part I) is confined to the Introduction, Phonology, and Morphology. The prefatory sketch of the Avesta and the Religion of Zoroaster may perhaps prove not without use. The second volume (Part II), a sketch of the Syntax, with a chapter also on Metre, is already half in print, and is shortly to appear. The numbering of sections in the second part will be continued from the present part; the two may therefore be bound together as a single volume if preferred.

With these words and with the suggestion to the student to observe the Hints for using the Grammar, given below, and to consult the Index, the book is offered to the favor of Oriental scholars. Any corrections, suggestions, or criticisms, which may be sent to me, will be cordially appreciated and gladly acknowledged.

October 1891.

A. V. Williams Jackson
Columbia College
NEW YORK CITY.

INTRODUCTION.

Avesta: The Sacred Books of the Parsis.[1]

The Avesta as a Sacred Book.

§ 1. The Avesta, or Zend-Avesta, as it is more familiarly, though less accurately called, is the name under which, as a designation, we comprise the bible and prayer-book of the Zoroastrian religion. The Avesta forms to day the Sacred Books of the Parsis or Fire-Worshippers, as they are often termed, a small community living now in India, or still scattered here and there in Persia. The original home of these worshippers and of their holy scriptures was ancient Iran, and the faith they profess was that founded centuries ago by Zoroaster (Zarathushtra), one of the great religious teachers of the East.

§ 2. The Avesta is, therefore, an important work, preserving as it does, the doctrines of this ancient belief and the customs of the earliest days of Persia. It represents the oldest faith of Iran, as the Vedas do of India. The oldest parts date back to a period of time nearly as remote as the Rig-Veda, though its youngest parts are much later. The religion which the Avesta presents was once one of the greatest; it has, moreover, left ineffaceable traces upon the history of the world. Flourishing more than a thousand years before the Christian era, it became the religion of the great Achæmenian kings, Cyrus, Darius, and Xerxes, but its power was weakened by the conquest of Alexander, and many of its sacred books were lost. It revived again during the first centuries of our own era, but was finally broken by the Mohammedans in their victorious invasion. Most of the Zoroastrian worshippers were then compelled through persecution to accept the religion of the Koran; many, however, fled to India for refuge, and took with them what was left of their sacred writ-

---

[1] This sketch, with additions and some alterations, is reprinted from my article AVESTA, simultaneously appearing in the *International Cyclopaedia*, for which courtesy I am indebted to the kindness of the Editor, my friend, Professor H. T. Peck, and that of the Publishers, Messrs. Dodd, Mead & Co., New York.

ings. A few of the faithful remained behind in Persia, and, though persecuted, they continued to practise their religion. It is these two scanty peoples, perhaps 80,000 souls in India, and 10,000 in Persia, that have preserved to us the Avesta in the form in which we now have it.

§ 3. The designation *Avesta*, for the scriptures, is adopted from the term *Avistāk*, regularly employed in the Pahlavi of the Sassanian time. But it is quite uncertain what the exact meaning and derivation of this word may be. Possibly Phl. *Avistāk*, like the Skt. *Vēda*, may signify 'wisdom, knowledge, the book of knowledge'. Perhaps, however, it means rather 'the original text, the scripture, the law'. The designation 'Zend-Avesta', though introduced by Anquetil du Perron, as described below, is not an accurate title. It arose by mistake from the inversion of the oft-recurring Pahlavi phrase, *Avistāk va Zand* 'Avesta and Zend', or 'the Law and Commentary'. The term *Zand* in Pahlavi (cf. Av. *azaiṇti-*), as the Parsi priests now rightly comprehend it, properly denotes 'understanding, explanation', and refers to the later version and commentary of the Avesta texts, the paraphrase which is written in the Pahlavi language. The proper designation for the scriptures, therefore, is *Avesta*; the term *Zand* (see below) should be understood as the Pahlavi version and commentary.

Allusions to the Avesta; its Discovery and History of Research.

§ 4. Of the religion, manners, and customs of ancient Persia, which the Avesta preserves to us, we had but meagre knowledge until about a century ago. What we did know up to that time was gathered from the more or less scattered and unsatisfactory references of the classic Greek and Latin, from some allusions in Oriental writers, or from the later Persian epic literature. To direct sources, however, we could not then turn. Allusions to the religion of the Magi, the faith of the Avesta, are indeed to be found in the Bible. The wise men from the East who came to worship our Saviour, the babe in Bethlehem, were Magi. Centuries before that date, however, it was Cyrus, a follower of the faith of Zoroaster, whom God called his anointed and his shepherd (Isaiah 45.1,13; 44.28; 2 Chron. 36.22,23; Ezra 1.1—11) and who gave orders that the Jews be returned to Jerusalem from captivity in Babylon. Darius, moreover (Ezra 5.13—17; 6.1—16), the worshipper of Ormazd, favored the rebuilding of the temple at Jerusalem as decreed by Cyrus. Allusions to the ancient faith of the Persians are perhaps contained in Ezek. 8.16; Is. 45.7,12. See also Apocryphal New Test., The Infancy, 3.1—10.

§ 5. The classical references of Greek and Roman writers to the teachings of Zoroaster, which we can now study in the Avesta itself, may be said to begin with the account of the Persians given by Herodotus

(B. C. 450) in his History I.131—141. To this account may be added references and allusions, though often preserved only in fragments, by various other writers, including Plutarch 'On Isis and Osiris', and Pliny, down to Agathias (A. D. 500).

§ 6. After the Mohammedan conquest of Persia, we have an allusion by the Arabic writer, Masūdi (A. D. 940), who tells of the *Avesta* of Zeradusht (Zoroaster), and its commentary called *Zend*, together with a *Pazend* explanation. The *Abasta* (Avesta) is also mentioned several times by Al-Bīrunī (about A. D. 1000). The later Mohammedan writer, Shahrastani (A. D. 1150), sketches in outline the creed of the Magi of his day. An interesting reference is found in the Syriac-Arabic Lexicon of *Bar-Bahlūl* (A. D. 963) to an *Avastāk*, a book of Zardusht (Zoroaster), as composed in seven tongues, Syriac, Persian, Aramaean, Segestanian, Marvian, Greek, and Hebrew. In an earlier Syriac MS. Commentary on the New Testament (A. D. 852) by 'Isho'dād, Bishop of Ḥadatha, near Mosul, mention is made of the Abhāsta as having been written by Zardusht in twelve different languages. These latter allusions, though late, are all important, as showing the continuity, during ages, of the tradition of such a work as the Avesta, which contains the teachings of Zoroaster, the prophet of Iran. All these allusions, however, it must be remembered, are by foreigners. No direct Iranian sources had been accessible.

§ 7. From this time, moreover, till about the 17th century we find there was little inquiry into the sacred books of the Persians. One of the first series of investigations into the Greek and Roman sources seems then to have been undertaken by a European, Barnabé Brisson, *De Persarum Principatu* (Paris 1590). The Italian, English, and French travelers in the Orient next added some information as to the religion and customs of the Persians. Among them may be mentioned the works of Pietro della Valle (1620), Henry Lord (1630), Mandelso (1658), Tavernier (1678), Chardin (1721), Du Chinon. Most important, however, was the work of the distinguished Oxford scholar, Thomas Hyde (1700). It was written in Latin, and entitled *Historia Religionis veterum Persarum*. Hyde resorted chiefly to the later Parsi sources; the original texts he could not use, although an Avesta MS. of the Yasna seems to have been brought to Canterbury as early as 1633. Hyde earnestly appealed to scholars, however, to procure MSS. of the sacred books of the Parsis, and aroused much interest in the subject. In 1723 a copy of the Vendidād Sādah was procured by an Englishman, George Boucher, from the Parsis in Surat and was deposited as a curiosity in the Bodleian Library at Oxford.

§ 8. No one, however, could read these texts of the Avesta. To a young Frenchman, Anquetil du Perron, belongs the honor of first deciphering them. The history of his labors is interesting and instructive. Happening, in 1754, to see some tracings made from the Oxford MS., and sent to Paris as a specimen, du Perron at once conceived the spirited idea of going to Persia, or India, and obtaining from the priests themselves the knowledge of their sacred books. Though fired with zeal and enthusiasm, he had no means to carry out his plan. He seized the idea of enlisting as a soldier in the troops that were to start for India, and in November, 1754, behind the martial drum and fife this youthful scholar marched out of Paris. The French Government, however, recognizing at once his noble purpose, gave him his discharge from the army and presented him his passage to India. After countless difficulties he reached Surat, and there after innumerable discouragements, and in spite of almost insurmountable obstacles, he succeeded in winning the confidence and favor of the priests, with whom he was able to communicate after he had learned the modern Persian. He gradually induced the priests to impart to him the language of their sacred works, to let him take some of the manuscripts, and even to initiate him into some of the rites and ceremonies of their religion. He stayed among the people for seven years, and then in 1761, he started for his home in Europe. He stopped at Oxford before going directly to Paris, and compared his MSS. with the one in the Bodleian Library, in order to be assured that he had not been imposed upon. The next ten years were devoted to work upon his MSS. and upon a translation, and in 1771, seventeen years from the time he had first marched out of Paris, he gave forth to the world the results of his untiring labors. This was the first translation of the Avesta, or, as he called it, Zend-Avesta (*Ouvrage de Zoroastre*, 3 vols., Paris 1771), a picture of the religion and manners contained in the sacred book of the Zoroastrians.

§ 9. The ardent enthusiasm which hailed this discovery and opening to the world of a literature, religion, and philosophy of ancient times was unfortunately soon dampened. Some scholars, like Kant, were disappointed in not finding the philosophical or religious ideas they had hoped to find; while others missed the high literary value they had looked for. They little considered how inaccurate, of necessity, such a first translation must be. Though Anquetil du Perron had indeed learned the language from the priests, still, people did not know that the priestly tradition itself had lost much during the ages of persecution or oblivion into which the religion had fallen. They did not sufficiently take into account that Anquetil was learning one foreign tongue, the Avesta, through another, the modern Persian; nor did they know how little accurate and scientific training du Perron had had. A discussion as to the authenticity of the work arose. It was suggested that the so-called Zend-Avesta was not the genuine work of Zoroaster, but was a forgery. Foremost among the detractors, it is to be regretted, was the distinguished Orientalist, Sir William Jones. He claimed, in a letter published in French (1771), that Anquetil had been duped, that the Parsis had palmed off upon him a conglomeration of worthless fabrications and absurdities. In England, Sir William Jones was supported by Richardson and Sir John Chardin; in Germany, by Meiners. In France the genuineness of the book was universally accepted, and in one famous German scholar, Kleuker, it found an ardent supporter. He translated Anquetil's work into German (1776, Riga), for the use of his countrymen, especially the theologians, and he supported the genuineness of those scriptures by classical allusions to the Magi. For nearly fifty years, however, the battle as to authenticity, still raged. Anquetil's translation, as acquired from the priests, was supposed to be a true standard to judge the Avesta by, and from which to draw arguments; little or no work, unfortunately, was done on the texts themselves. The opinion, however, that the books were a forgery was gradually beginning to grow somewhat less.

§ 10. It was the advance in the study of Sanskrit that finally won the victory for the advocates of the authenticity of the Sacred Books. About 1825, more than fifty years after the appearance of du Perron's translation, the Avesta texts themselves began to be studied by Sanskrit scholars. The close affinity between the two languages had already been noticed by different scholars; but in 1826, the more exact relation between the Sanskrit and the Avesta was shown by the Danish philologian, Rask, who had travelled in Persia and India, and who had brought back with him to the Copenhagen library many valuable MSS. of the Avesta and of the Pahlavi books. Rask, in a little work on the age and authenticity of the Zend-Language (1826), proved the antiquity of the language, showed it to be distinct from Sanskrit, though closely allied to it, and made some investigation into the alphabet of the texts. About the same time the Avesta was taken up by the French Sanskrit scholar, Eugène Burnouf. Knowing the relation between Sanskrit and Avestan, and taking up the reading of the texts scientifically, he at once found, through his knowledge of Sanskrit, philological inaccuracies in Anquetil's translation. Anquetil, he saw, must often have misinterpreted his teachers; the tradition itself must often necessarily have been defective. Instead of this untrustworthy French rendering, Burnouf turned to an older Skt. translation of a part of the Avesta. This was made in the 15th century by the Parsi Naryosangh, and was based on the Pahlavi version. By means of this Skt. rendering, and by applying his philological learning, he was able to restore sense to many passages where Anquetil had often made nonsense, and he was thus able to throw a flood of light upon many an obscure point. The employment of Skt., instead of depending upon the priestly traditions and interpretations, was a new step; it introduced a new method. The new discovery and gain of vantage ground practically settled the discussion as to authenticity. The testimony, moreover, of the ancient Persian inscriptions deciphered about this time by Grotefend (1802), Burnouf, Lassen, and by Sir Henry Rawlinson, showed still more, by their contents and language so closely allied to the Avesta, that this work must be genuine. The question was settled. The foundation laid by Burnouf was built upon by such scholars as Bopp, Haug, Windischmann, Westergaard, Roth, Spiegel —the two latter happily still living—and to day by Bartholomae, Darmesteter, de Harlez, Hübschmann, Justi, Mills, and especially Geldner, including some hardly less known names, Parsis among them. These scholars, using partly the Sanskrit key for the interpretation and meaning of words, and partly the Parsi tradition contained in the Pahlavi translation, have now been able to give us a clear idea of the Avesta and its contents as far as the books have come down to us and we are enabled to see the true importance of these ancient scriptures. Upon minor points of interpretation, of course, there are and there always will be individual differences of opinion. We are now prepared to take up the general division and contents of the Avesta, and to speak of its Pahlavi version.

Contents, Arrangement, Extent, and Character.

§ 11. The Avesta, as we now have it, is but a remnant of a once great literature. It has come down in a more or less fragmentary condition; not even a single manuscript contains all the texts that we now have; whatever we possess has been collected together from various codices. All that survives is commonly classed under the following divisions or books:

1. *Yasna*, including the *Gāthās*
2. *Vispered*
3. *Yashts*
4. Minor texts, as *Nyāishes*, *Gāhs* etc.
5. *Vendidād*
6. Fragments, from *Hādhōkht Nask* etc.

§ 12. In the first five divisions two groups are recognized. The first group (i) comprises the Vendidad, Vispered, and Yasna; these as used in the service of worship are traditionally classed together for liturgical purposes and form the Avesta proper. In the manuscripts, moreover, these three books themselves appear in two different forms, according as they are accompanied, or not, by a Pahlavi version. If the books are kept separate as three divisions, each part is usually accompanied by a rendering in Pahlavi. On the contrary, however, these three books are not usually recited each as a separate whole, but with the chapters of one book mingled with another for liturgical purposes, on this account the MSS. often present them in their intermingled form, portions of one inserted with the other, and arranged exactly in the order in which they are to be used in the service. In this latter case the Pahlavi translation is omitted, and the collection is called the Vendidād Sādah or 'Vendidād pure' i. e. text without commentary. (ii) The s e c o n d group comprising the minor prayers and the Yashts which the MSS. often include with these, is called the *Khordah Avesta* or 'small Avesta'. Of the greater part of the latter there is no Pahlavi rendering. The contents and character of the several divisions, including the fragments, may now be taken up more in detail.

§ 13. (1) The *Yasna,* 'sacrifice, worship', is the chief liturgical work of the sacred canon. It consists principally of ascriptions of praise and prayer, and in it are inserted the *Gāthās,* or 'hymns', verses from the sermons of Zoroaster, which are the oldest and most sacred part of the Avesta. The Yasna (Skt. *yajñá*) comprises 72 chapters, called *Hā, Haiti.* These are the texts recited by the priests at the ritual ceremony of the Yasna *(Izashne).* The book falls into three nearly equal divisions. (a) The first part (chap. 1—27) begins with an invocation of the god, Ormazd, and the other divinities of the religion; it gives texts for the consecration of the holy water, *zaothra,* and the *baresma,* or bundle of sacred twigs, for the preparation and dedication of the Haoma, *haoma,* the juice of a certain plant — the Indian Soma — which was drunk by the priests as a sacred rite, and for the offering of blessed cakes, as well as meat-offering, which likewise were partaken of by the priests. Interspersed through this portion, however, are a few chapters that deal only indirectly with the ritual; these are Ys. 12, the later Zoroastrian creed, and Ys. 19—21, catechetical portions. — (b) Then follow the Gāthās lit. 'songs', 'psalms' (chap. 28—53), metrical selections or verses containing the teachings, exhortations, and revelations of Zoroaster. The prophet exhorts men to eschew evil and choose the good, the kingdom of light rather than that of darkness. These Gāthās are written in meter, and their language is more archaic and somewhat different from that used elsewhere in the Avesta. The Gāthās, strictly speaking, are five in number; they are arranged according to meters, and are named after the opening words, Ahunavaiti, Ushtavaiti etc. The Gāthās comprise 17 hymns (Ys. 28—34: 43—46: 47—50; 51, 53), and, like the Psalms, they must later have been chanted during the service. They seem originally to have been the texts or metrical headings from which Zoroaster, like the later Buddha, preached. In their midst (chap. 35—42) is inserted the so-called Yasna of the Seven Chapters (*Yasna Haptanghāiti*). This is written in prose, and consists of a number of prayers and ascriptions of praise to Ahura Mazda, or Ormazd, to the archangels, the souls of the righteous, the fire, the waters, and the earth. Though next in antiquity to the Gāthās, and in archaic language, the Haptanghāiti represents a somewhat later and more developed form of the religion, than that which in the Gāthās proper was just beginning. Under the Gāthās also are included three or four specially sacred verses or formulas. These are the Ahuna Vairya or Honovar (Ys. 27.13), Ashem Vohu (Ys. 27.14), Airyama Ishyo (Ys. 54.1) and also the Yenghe Hātām (Ys. 4.26), so called from their first words, like the Pater Noster, Gloria Patri, etc., to which in a measure they answer.—(c) The third part (chap. 52, 55—72) or the 'latter Yasna' (*aparō yasnō*) consists chiefly of praises and offerings of thanksgiving to different divinities.

§ 14. (2) The *Vispered* (Av. *vīspe ratavō*) consists of additions to portions of the Yasna which it resembles in language and in form. It comprises 24 chapters (called *Karde*), and it is about a seventh as long as the Yasna. In the ritual the chapters of the Vispered are inserted among those of the Yasna. It contains invocations and offerings of homage to 'all the lords' (*vīspe ratavō*). Hence the name Vispered.

§ 15. (3) The *Yashts* (Av. *yešti* 'worship by praise') consist of 21 hymns of praise and adorations of the divinities or angels, *Yazatas* (*Izads*), of the religion. The chief Yashts are those in praise of Ardvi-Sura, the goddess of waters (Yt. 5), the star Tishtrya (Yt. 8), the angel Mithra, or divinity of truth (Yt. 10), the Fravashis, or departed souls of the righteous (Yt. 13), the genius of victory, Verethraghna (Yt. 14), and of the Kingly Glory (Yt. 19). The Yashts are written mainly in meter, they have poetic merit, and contain much mythological and historical matter that may be illustrated by Firdausi's later Persian epic, the Shāh Nāmah.

§ 16. (4) The minor texts, *Nyāishes, Gāhs, Sīrozahs, Āfringāns*, consist of brief prayers, praises, or blessings to be recited daily or on special occasions.

§ 17. (5) The *Vendīdād*, or 'law against the daevas, or demons' (*vīdaēva dāta*), is a priestly code in 22 chapters (called *Fargard*), corresponding to the Pentateuch in our Bible. Its parts vary greatly in time and in style of composition. Much of it must be late. The first chapter (Farg. 1) is a sort of an Avestan Genesis, a dualistic account of creation.

Chap. 2 sketches the legend of Yima, the golden age, and the coming of a destructive winter, an Iranian flood. Chap. 3 teaches, among other things, the blessings of agriculture; Chap. 4 contains legal matter — breaches of contract, assaults, punishments; Chap. 5 - 12 relate mainly to the impurity from the dead; Chap. 13—15 deal chiefly with the treatment of the dog; Chap. 16—17, and partly 18, are devoted to purification from several sorts of uncleanness. In Chap. 19 is found the temptation of Zoroaster, and the revelation; Chap. 20—22 are chiefly of medical character. In the ritual, the chapters of the Vendidad are inserted among the Gāthās.

§ 18. (6) Besides the above books there are a number of fragments, one or two among them from the *Hadhōkht Nask*. There are also quotations or passages from missing Nasks, likewise glosses and glossaries. Here belong pieces from the *Nīrangistān*, *Aogemadaēca*, *Zand-Pahlavi Glossary*, and some other fragments. These are all written in the Avesta language, and are parts of a once great literature. Under the Zoroastrian religious literature, moreover, though not written in Avesta, must also be included the works in Pahlavi, many of which are translations from the Avesta, or contain old matter from the original scriptures.

§ 19. From the above contents, it will be seen that our present Avesta is rather a Prayer-Book than a Bible. The Vendidād, Vispered, and Yasna were gathered together by the priests for liturgical purposes. It was the duty of the priests to recite the whole of these sacred writings every day, in order to preserve their own purity, and be able to perform the rites of purification, or give remission of sins to others. The solemn recital of the Vendidād, Vispered, and Yasna at the sacrifice might be compared with our church worship. The selections from the Vendidād would correspond to the Pentateuch when read; the preparation, consecration, and presentation of the holy water, the Haoma-juice, and the meat-offering, described in the Yasna and Vispered would answer to our communion service; the metrical parts of the Yasna would be hymns; the intoning of the Gāthās would somewhat resemble the lesson and the Gospel, or even the sermon. In the Khordah Avesta, the great Yashts might perhaps be comparable to some of the more epic parts of our Bible; but as they are devoted each to some divinity and preserve much of the old mythology, they really have hardly a parallel, even in the apocryphal books.

§ 20. Such, in brief outline, is the contents of the books known to-day as the Avesta; but, as implied above, this is but a remnant of a literature once vastly greater in extent. This we can judge both from internal and from historical evidence. The character of the work itself in its present form, sufficiently shows that it is a compilation from various sources. This is further supported by the authority of history, if the Parsi tradition, going back to the time of the Sassanidæ, be trustworthy. Pliny (*Hist. Nat.* 30.1,2) tells of 2,000,000 verses composed by Zoroaster. The Arab historian, Tabari, describes the writings of Zoroaster as committed to 12,000 cowhides (parchments); other Arabic references by Masudi, and Syriac allusions to an Avesta, which must have been extensive, have been noted above § 6. The Parsi tradition on the subject is contained in the Rivāyats, and in a Pahlavi book, the Dinkard. The Dinkard (Bk. 3) describes two complete copies of the Avesta. These each comprised 21 Nasks, or Nosks (books). The one deposited in the archives at Persepolis, as the Arda Viraf says, perished in the flames when Alexander burned the palace in his invasion of Iran. The other copy, it is implied, was in some way destroyed by the Greeks. From that time the scriptures, like the religion under the Græco-Parthian sway, lived on, partly in scattered writings and partly in the memories of the priests, for nearly 500 years.

§ 21. The first attempt again to collect these writings seems to have been begun under the reign of the last Arsacidæ, just preceding the Sassanian dynasty. Pahlavi tradition preserved in a proclamation of King Khusro Anoshirvān (6th cent A. D.), says it was under King Valkhash, probably Vologeses I., the contemporary of Nero, that the collection was begun of the sacred writings as far as they had escaped the ravages of Alexander, or were preserved by oral tradition. Valkhash was among the last of the Arsacidæ. The Sassanian dynasty (A. D. 226) next came to the throne. This house were genuine Zoroastrians and warm upholders of the faith, and they brought back the old religion and raised it to a height it had hardly attained even in its palmiest days. The first Sassanian monarchs, Artakhshir Pāpakān (Ardeshir Babagān, A. D. 226—240) and his son Shahpuhar I. (A. D. 240—270), eagerly continued the gathering of the religious writings, and the Avesta again became the sacred book of Iran. Under Shahpuhar II. (A. D. 309—380) the final revision of the Avesta texts was made by Atur-pāt Māraspend, and then the king proclaimed these as canonical, and fixed the number of Nasks or books.

§ 22. Of these Nasks, 21 were counted, and a description of them, as noted, is found in the Rivāyats, and in the Dinkard; each received a name corresponding to one of the twenty-one words in the Ahuna-Vairya (Honovar), the most sacred prayer of the Parsis. Each of these Nasks contained both Avesta and Zend, i. e. original scripture and commentary. This tradition is too important to be idly rejected. Its contents give an idea of what may have been the original extent and scope of the Avesta. The subjects said to have been treated in the 21 Nasks may practically be described in brief, as follows: Nask 1 (twenty-two sections), on virtue and piety; 2 (likewise twenty-two sections), religious observance; 3 (twenty-one sections), the Mazdayasnian religion and its teachings; 4 (thirty-two sections), this world and the next, the resurrection and the judgment; 5 (thirty-five sections), astronomy; 6 (twenty-two sections), ritual performances and the merit accruing; 7 (fifty sections before Alexander, thirteen then remaining), chiefly political and social in its nature; 8 (sixty sections before Alexander, twelve after remaining), legal; 9 (sixty sections before Alexander, fifteen later preserved), religion and its practical relations to man; 10 (sixty sections before Alexander, only ten afterwards surviving), king Gushtâsp and his reign, Zoroaster's influence; 11 (twenty-two sections originally, six preserved after Alexander), religion and its practical relations to man; 12 (twenty-two sections), physical truths and spiritual regeneration; 13 (sixty sections), virtuous actions, and a sketch of Zoroaster's infancy; 14 (seventeen sections), on Ormazd and the Archangels; 15 (fifty-four sections), justice in business and in weights and measures, the path of righteousness; 16 (sixty-five sections), on next-of-kin marriage, a tenet of the faith; 17 (sixty-four sections), future punishments, astrology; 18 (fifty-two sections), justice in exercising authority, on the resurrection, and on the annihilation of evil; 19, the Videvdâd, or Vendidâd (twenty-two sections, still remaining), on pollution and its purification; 20 (thirty sections), on goodness; 21 (thirty-three sections), praise of Ormazd and the Archangels.

§ 23. During the five centuries after the ravages of Alexander much, doubtless, had been lost, much forgotten. The Parsi tradition itself acknowledges this when it says above, for example, that the seventh Nask consisted originally of 50 sections, but only 13 remained 'after the accursed Iskander (Alexander)'. So says the Dînkard and so the Rivâyats. Like statements of loss are made of the eighth, ninth, tenth, eleventh Nasks. The loss in the five centuries from the invasion of Alexander, however, till the time of the Sassanian dynasty, was but small in comparison with the decay that overtook the scriptures from the Sassanian times till our day. The Mohammedan invasion in the seventh century of our era, and the inroad made by the Koran proved far more destructive. The persecuted people lost or neglected many portions of their sacred scriptures. Of the twenty-one Nasks that were recognized in Sassanian times as surviving from the original Avesta, only one single Nask, the nineteenth — the Vendidâd — has come down to us in its full form. Even this shows evidence of having been patched up and pieced together. We can furthermore probably identify parts of our present Yasna and Vispered with the Staot Yasht *(staota yesnya)* or Yasht *(yesnya)*, as it is also called. The two fragments Yt. 21 and 22 (as printed in Westergaard's edition) and Yt. 11, in its first form, are recognized in the MSS. as taken from the 20th, or Hadhokht Nask. The Nirangistān, a Pahlavi work, contains extensive Avestan quotations, which are believed to have been taken from the Husparam, or 17th Nask. Numerous quotations in Pahlavi works contain translations from old Avestan passages. The Pahlavi work, Shāyast-lā-Shāyast, quotes briefly from no less than thirteen of the lost Nasks; the Bundahish and other Pahlavi works give translations of selections, the original Avesta text of which is lost. Grouping together all the Avesta texts, we may roughly calculate that about two-thirds of the total scriptures have disappeared since Sassanian times.

§ 24. The present form of the Avesta belongs to the Sassanian period. Internal evidence shows that it is made up of parts most varied in age and character. This bears witness to the statement that during that period the texts, as far as they had survived the ravages of Alexander, and defied the corrupting influence of time, were gathered together, compiled, and edited. According to the record of Khusro Anoshirvan (A. D. 531—579), referred to above, King Valkhash, the first compiler of the Avesta, ordered that all the writings which might have survived should be searched for, and that all the priests who preserved the traditions orally should contribute their share toward restoring the original Avesta. The texts as collected were re-edited under successive Sassanian rulers, until, under Shahpuhar II. (A. D. 309—379) the final redaction was made by his prime minister, Atur-pāt Māraspend. It is manifest that the editors used the old texts as far as possible; sometimes they patched up defective parts by inserting other texts; occasionally they may have added or composed passages to join these, or to complete some missing portion. The character of the texts, when critically studied, shows that some such method must have been adopted.

§ 25. Parts of the Avesta, therefore, may differ considerably from each other in regard to age. In determining this the text criticism by means of **metrical restoration** is most instructive. Almost all the oldest portions of the texts are found to be metrical; the later, or inserted portions, are as a rule, but not always, written in prose. The **grammatical test** also is useful; the youngest portions generally show a decay of clear grammatical knowledge. The metrical Gāthās in this respect are wonderfully pure. They are, of course, in their form the oldest portion of the text, dating from Zoroaster himself. The longer Yashts and metrical portions of the Yasna contain much that is very old and derived doubtless from the ancient faith of Iran; but in their form and in general composition, they are probably some centuries later than the Gāthās. The Vendidād is in this regard most incongruous. Some parts of it are doubtless of great antiquity, though corrupted in form; other parts, like younger portions also of the Yashts, may be quite late. The same is true of formulaic passages throughout the whole of the Avesta, and some of the ceremonial or ritual selections in the Vispered and Nyāishes, etc. Roughly speaking, the chronological order of the texts would be somewhat as follows:

i. Gāthās (Ys. 28—53), and the sacred formulas Ys. 27.13,14, Ys. 54, including also
ii. Yasna Haptanghāiti (Ys. 35—42) and some other compositions, like Ys. 12, 58, 4.26, in the Gāthā dialect.
iii. The metrical Yasna and Yashts, as Ys. 9, 10, 11, 57, 62, 65; Yt. 5, 8, 9, 10, 13, 14, 15, 17, 19; portions of Vd. 2, 3, 4, 5, 18, 19, and scattered verses in the Vispered, Nyāishes, Afringāns, etc.
iv. The remaining prose portions of the Avesta.

In the latter case it is generally, but not always, easy to discover by the style and language, where old material failed and the hand of the redactor came in with stupid or prosaic additions.

§ 26. Considerable portions, therefore, of our present Avesta, especially the Gāthās, we may regard as coming directly from Zoroaster himself; still, additions from time to time must have been made to the sacred canon from his day on till the invasion of Alexander. The so-called copy of the Zoroastrian Bible which it is claimed was destroyed by that invader, doubtless contained much that was not directly from the founder of the faith, but was composed by his disciples and later followers. The Parsis, however, generally regard the whole work as coming directly from Zoroaster; this is a claim that the Avesta itself hardly makes. The Gāthās, however, undoubtedly came directly from the prophet; the Avesta itself always speaks of them as 'holy' and especially calls them the 'five Gāthās of Zoroaster'. We may fairly regard many other portions of the Avesta as direct elaborations of the great teacher's doctrines, just as the Evangelists have elaborated for us portions of the teachings of our Lord.

§ 27. In regard to the locality in which we are to seek the source of the Avesta and the cradle of the religion, opinions have been divided. Some scholars would place it in the West, in Media; the majority, however, prefer to look to the East of Iran, to Bactria. Both views probably have right on their side, for perhaps we shall not be amiss in regarding the Avesta as coming partly from the East, and partly from the West. The scene of most of it doubtless does belong in the East; it was there that Zoroaster preached; but the sacred literature that grew up about the Gāthās made its way, along with the religion to the West, toward Media and Persia. Undoubtedly some texts, therefore, may well have been composed also in Media. The question is connected also with that of Zoroaster's home which may originally have been in the West. On the native place of Zoroaster, see Jackson in *Amer. Or. Society's Journal*, May 1891 pp. 222 seq. The language itself of the texts, as used in the church, became a religious language, precisely as did Latin, and therefore was not confined to any place or time. We may regard the Avesta as having been worked upon from Zoroaster's day down to the time of the Sassanian redaction.

Religion of the Avesta.

§ 28. The religion contained in the Avesta is best called Zoroastrianism, a name that gives due honor to its founder and which is thus parallel with Christianity, Buddhism, Mohammedanism. Other designations are sometimes employed. It has often been termed Mazdaism, from its supreme god; or again Magism, from the Magi priests; sometimes we hear it styled Fire-Worship, or even Dualism, from certain of its characteristic features. The designation Parsiism, from the name of its modern followers, is occasionally applied.

§ 29. Beyond our own Bible, the sacred books perhaps of hardly any religion contain so clear a grasp of the ideas of right and wrong, or present so pure, so exalted a view of the coming of a Saviour, a resurrection and judgment, the future rewards and punishments for the immortal soul, and of the life eternal, as does the Avesta, the book of the scriptures of ancient Iran.

§ 30. In Zoroastrianism, however, as in other religions, we recognize a development. In the older stage of the Gāthās, we have the faith in its purity as taught by Zoroaster (Zarathushtra) himself, more than a thousand years perhaps before our Lord. But later, and even before the invasion of Alexander had weakened the power of the religion, we find changes creeping in. There was a tendency, for example, to restore many of the elements of the primitive faith of Iran, which Zoroaster had thrown into the background. Traces of the different stages are plainly to be recognized in the Avesta.

§ 31. The most striking feature of Zoroaster's faith, as taught in the Gāthās, is the doctrine of Dualism. There are two principles, the good and the evil, which pervade the world. All nature is divided between them. These principles are primeval. Good and evil have existed from the beginning of the world. Ahura Mazda, the Lord of Wisdom (the later Persian Ormazd) is Zoroaster's god: Angra Mainyu, or the Spiritual Enemy (the later Persian Ahriman) is the devil. The evil spirit is also called Druj 'Deceit, Satan'. The good spirit and the evil are in eternal conflict. The good, Zoroaster teaches, however, will ultimately triumph. Man, a free agent, will bring the victory by choosing right and increasing the power of good. Evil shall be banished from the world. This will be the coming of the 'kingdom' or 'the good kingdom' — *vohu kšaþra* — as it is called. To the right choice Zoroaster exhorts his people. The question whence Zoroaster derived his idea of dualism, and how far he was a reformer, will not here be entered into.

§ 32. According to the prophet's teaching, Ahura Mazda, the god of good, is not without the aid of ministering angels. These are called Amesha Spentas, 'Immortal Holy Ones', the later Persian Amshaspands. They correspond in a measure to our idea of Archangels. They are six in number and constitute, with Ahura Mazda, the heavenly host. Their names are personifications of abstractions or virtues, Righteousness, Goodness, or the like. The seven-fold group, or celestial council, is as follows.

<blockquote>
Ahura Mazda
aided by
Vohu Manah
Asha Vahishta
Khshathra Vairya
Spenta Armaiti
Haurvatāt
Ameretāt
also
Sraosha.
</blockquote>

These abstractions or personifications may be noticed more in detail.

§ 33. Vohu Manah (lit. 'good mind', Plutarch εὔνοια) is the personification of Ahura Mazda's good spirit working in man and uniting him with God. In the later development of the religion, this divinity was specialized into the good mind or kindliness that is shown toward cattle. He thus became the guardian genius of the flocks.

§ 34. Asha Vahishta (lit. 'best righteousness, Plutarch ἀλήθεια) is the next divinity in the celestial group and is the personification of right (Skt. *r̥ta*), the divine order that pervades the world. In the heavenly court Asha stands almost in the relation of prime minister to Ormazd. To live 'according to Asha' (Right, or the Law of Righteousness e. g. Ys. 31.2) is a frequent phrase in the Avesta. The attribute *Ashavan* is the regular designation of 'the righteous', as opposed to *Dregvant* 'the wicked', or one that belongs to Satan or the Druj. In later times Asha Vahishta came to preside as guardian genius over the fire, a symbol of perfect purity.

§ 35. Khshathra Vairya or Vohu Khshathra (lit. 'the wished-for kingdom, the good kingdom', Plutarch εὐνομία) is the personification of Ahura Mazda's good rule, might, majesty, dominion, and power, the Kingdom which Zoroaster hopes to see come on earth. The establishment of this kingdom is to be the annihilation of evil. In later times, Khshathra Vairya, as a divinity, came to preside over metals. The symbolic connection may have been suggested by the fact that the coming of the Kingdom (khshathra) was presumed to be accompanied by a flood of molten metal, the fire that should punish and purge the wicked, and which should purify the world. The metals thus became emblematic of Khshathra.

§ 36. Spenta Armaiti (lit. 'holy harmony, humility', Plutarch σοφία) is the harmony, peace, and concord that should rule among men. She is represented as a female divinity; the earth is in her special charge. She plays an important part at the resurrection. The earth is to give up its dead

§ 37. Haurvatāt (Plutarch πλοῦτος) literally means 'wholeness, completeness, the saving health, the perfection', toward which all should strive, in short 'Salvation', with which word it is etymologically cognate. This divinity is always mentioned in connection with Ameretāt. In the later religion, Haurvatāt came to preside as guardian angel over the health-giving waters.

§ 38. Ameretāt literally means 'immortality', and is always joined with Haurvatāt. In later Zoroastrianism, Ameretāt presides over the trees. The pair of Haurvatāt and Ameretāt together seem to symbolize the waters of health and the tree of life.

§ 39. To the number of the celestial council also is to be added the divinity Sraosha (lit. 'obedience'). This genius completes the mystic number seven when Ahura Mazda is excepted from the list (cf. also Ys. 57.12). Sraosha is the angel of religious obedience, the priest god, the personification of the divine service that protects man from evil.

§ 40. Beside the above divinities in the Gāthās, mention is also made of Geush Tashan, the creator of the cow, and Geush Urvan, the personified soul of the kine. We sometimes also find Spenta Mainyu, the Holy Spirit of Ormazd, the will of God, represented practically as a distinct personage. Lastly, the Fire, Atar, is personified in the Gāthās as one of God's ministering servants, and is a sacred emblem of the faith.

§ 41. Such is the heavenly hierarchy, and such the faith of Ormazd in which Zarathushtra exhorts the people to believe. The faithful are called Ashavans 'righteous', or later more often Mazdayasnians i. e. 'worshippers of Mazda'. This is the true religion in contradistinction to the false. The false religion is the worship of the Daevas 'demons' (Av. *daēva* opposed to Skt. *dēva* 'god'). The Daeva-worshippers are misguided and live in error. They are the wicked Dregvants (lit. 'belonging to the Druj, Satan'), 'the children of the wicked one' (St. Matt. xiii. 38 – 43). The two religions themselves are a part of the dualism.

§ 42. In juxtaposition to Ahura Mazda, Zoroaster sets the fiend Druj 'Deceit, Satan' or Angra Mainyu (Ys. 45.2). The spirit of evil in co-existent with Ormazd (Ys. 30.3), but is less clearly pictured in the Gāthās. In later times, to carry out the symmetry of dualism, Angra Mainyu is accompanied by a number of Arch-Fiends, in opposition to the Archangels of Ormazd. The number of the infernal group is not sharply defined, but the chief members are

>   Angra Mainyu
>   aided by
>   Aka Manah
>   Indra
>   Saurva
>   Taro-maiti
>   Tauru
>   Zairica
>   also
>   Aeshma.

Each is the opponent of a heavenly rival. Aka Manah or 'Evil Mind' is the antagonist of Vohu Manah; Taro-maiti, the demon of 'Presumption', is the opponent of Armaiti or humility; Aeshma, 'Fury, Wrath', the foe of Sraosha or holy obedience. The antagonism in the case of the others is less marked, and the connection somewhat more mechanical.

§ 43. In the final struggle between the two bands, the powers of light and the powers of darkness, the good eventually shall triumph. That was an ethical idea which Zoroaster inculcated. But the warfare that rages in the world between the two empires and between the true religion and the false, the belief in Mazda and the Daeva-worship, pervades also the soul of man and leaves the way uncertain. Yet on his choice the ultimate triumph of right or of wrong depends. Each evil deed which man commits, increases the power of evil (e. g. Ys. 31.15); each good deed he does, brings nearer the kingdom of good. As Ahura Mazda's creature, man should choose the right. Zoroaster's mission, as shown in the Gāthās (e. g. Ys. 31.2 et al.), is to guide man's choice. A summary of the prophet's moral and ethical teachings may best be given in the triad, so familiar later, 'good thoughts, good words, good deeds'. This forms the pith of the whole teaching. Purity alike of body and soul, and the choice of the good Mazda-religion rather than the wicked Daeva-worship, are inculcated. Zoroaster enjoins also the care of useful animals, especially the cow, and commends the good deeds of husbandry. He is the teacher of a higher and nobler civilization, as may be judged from the Avesta creed Ys. 12.1 seq.

§ 44. Man's actions, according to Zoroaster, are all recorded in Ormazd's sight as in a life-book (e. g. Ys. 31 13 14. Ys. 32.6). By his own actions man shall be judged, and rewarded or punished. The doctrine of a future life, the coming of the Kingdom, the end of the world, forms a striking feature in the teachings of the Avesta. This is the tone that Zoroaster himself constantly strikes in the Gāthās. This very doctrine, and a belief also in a resurrection of the body characterises the entire Persian faith. The resurrection is to be followed by a general judgment when evil shall be destroyed from the world. This general division and new dispensation is called the Vīdāiti (*vi* + √*dā* 'dispose').

§ 45. The views in regard to a future life, though incomplete in the Gāthās, are carried out in the Younger Avesta, and are fully given in the Pahlavi books. That the belief in a resurrection and a life hereafter was common among the Persians, some centuries before our Saviour, we have evidence in the early Greek writers, such as Theopompus, Herodotus, etc. The belief in an immediate judgment of the soul after death, the weighing in the balance, the leading of the soul across the Cinvat Bridge and through the mansions of paradise to bliss, or through the grades of hell to torment, or again in special cases to an intermediate state to await the final judgment—are all to be recognized in the Zoroastrian books and have their prototypes in the Gāthās.

§ 46. In the Yasna of the Seven Chapters, though not much later than the Gāthās, we find in some respects a slight descent from the lofty level on which the religion had been placed by its founder. There is a tendency to revive ancient ideas and forms from the old worship, in which nature had played a prominent part. The elements, earth, air, fire, and water, receive adoration; the Fravashis, or guardian angels of the righteous, are worshipped and praised together with Ahura Mazda and the Amesha Spentas. The deity Haoma, the divinity of the plant which produced the intoxicating Soma drink, again finds place in the religious rites.

§ 47. In the Younger Avesta, especially in the Yashts, we find still further restorations or innovations. The gods of the ancient mythology, like Mithra, Verethraghna, once more appear in honor by the side of the supreme deity; the divinities of the stars, moon, and sun have their share of pious worship. In the later parts of the Yasna, the sacrifice is developed into a somewhat elaborate ritual. The Zoroaster presented in certain portions of the Vendidad, moreover, is evidently no longer a living, moving personage as in the Gāthās; he has become a shadowy figure, around whom time has thrown the aureola of the saint. These passages differ widely from the old hymns; they show unmistakeable signs of lateness. They present a religion codified in the hands of the priests; superstitious beliefs and practices have found their way into the faith; intricate purifications in particular are enjoined to remove or to avoid the impurity arising from contact with the dead. The spirit of the Gāthās is gone. It is only here and there that passages in late texts are old and have the genuine Zoroastrian ring. They must not be overlooked. In general, a distinction must be drawn between what is old and what is young. We must recall, as above (§ 27), that the Avesta was probably worked upon from Zoroaster's own day down to the time of the Sassanian redaction.

The Pahlavi Version of the Avesta.

§ 48. To the period of the Sassanian editing of the texts belongs the Pahlavi translation and interpretation of the Avesta. At the date when the texts were compiled and edited (§ 21), the general knowledge of the Avesta and the understanding of the sacred texts was far from perfect. The preparation of a translation or version became necessary. Accordingly, the great body of the texts was rendered into Pahlavi, the language used in Persia at the time of the Arsacidæ and Sassanidæ. The Pahlavi version and interpretation of the entire Yasna, Vispered, and Vendidad, with some portions of the other texts, has been preserved. We have not as yet a thorough enough understanding of this version, as the Pahlavi question is still a vexed one; but as our knowledge of this translation increases, we see more and more its importance. Owing to a somewhat imperfect knowledge of the Avesta texts at the time when the version was made, and owing to the unskilfull and peculiar manner in which the Pahlavi translation is made, this version abounds in numerous errors and inaccuracies. Its renderings, however, are often of the greatest value in interpreting allusions, particularly also in giving hints for the meanings of obscure words, and in such matters it is many times our best and only guide. When more fully understood and properly used in connection with the 'comparative method', referring to the Sanskrit in interpreting the sacred texts, the 'traditional method' or native explanation is destined to win great results. The 'traditional' and the 'comparative' methods must go hand in hand.

Manuscripts of the Avesta.

§ 49. The manuscripts of the Avesta are quite numerous. Some of our specimens were copied down over five hundred years ago. They are written on parchment. The oldest was copied about the middle of the 13th century. From that date onward we have a considerable number of codices still extant. They come to us from India and from Yezd and Kirman in Persia. A number of the manuscripts are deposited in the libraries at Copenhagen, Oxford, London, Paris, Munich. The Parsi priests, especially the Dasturs, Dr. Jamaspji Minocheherji and also Peshotanji Behramji, have shown princely generosity in aiding Western scholars in editing texts by putting valuable MSS. in their possession. It is thus that the new edition of the Avesta texts by Professor Geldner of Berlin, is able to be presented in so critical a manner. No codex is complete in containing all the texts (§ 11). The different MSS. themselves, moreover, show certain variations in reading; but these chiefly affect the form and construction of single words, rather than entire passages and the sense. As a rule, the older the MS. is, the better is its grammar; and the later, the more faulty. Notable exceptions, however, must be made, especially in favor of some later MSS. from Persia.

Importance of the Avesta.

§ 50. The importance of the Avesta, as stated above (§ 2), lies not alone in the field of philology, ethnology and early literature, but especially also is it of importance from the standpoint of comparative religion. Resemblances to Christianity in its teachings become significant when we consider the close contact between the Jews and the Persians during the Babylonian captivity. These are beginning more and more to attract the attention of students of the Bible.

Language of the Avesta,
Grammatical Summary.

§ 51. The language in which the Avesta is written belongs to the Iranian branch of the Indo-Germanic tongues. With the Ancient Persian of the inscriptions it makes up the Old Iranian division. The later Iranian languages, New Persian, Kurdish, Afghan, Ossetish, Baluchi, Ghalcha, and some minor modern dialects, complete the younger division. The intervening Pahlavi and Pâzand, or Parsi, do not quite complete the link between the divisions. The extent of its relationship with the Armenian is not yet defined with sufficient exactness. On the positive kinship between the language of the Avesta and Sanskrit, see below § 55.

§ 52. The language in which the Avesta is written may best be termed *Avesta* or *Avestan*. The designation *Avesta* for the language, as well as the book, is in keeping with the Pahlavi *Avistāk*, which is used both of the tongue and of the scriptures. The term *Avestan*, both for the language and as an adjective, is preferred by some scholars, in order to distinguish the speech from the work itself. This is sometimes found very convenient. The term *Zend* for the language, as noted above (§ 3), is a misnomer. The designation Old Bactrian, occasionally used for the tongue, has little to recommend it.

§ 53. The alphabet in which the Avesta is written is far younger than the language it presents. The characters are derived from the Sassanian Pahlavi, which was used to write down the oral tradition when the texts were collected and edited under the dynasty of the Sassanidæ. The writing is read from right to left. What the original Avestan script was we do not know.

§ 54. Two dialects may be recognized in the Avesta: one the 'Gāthā dialect' or the language of the oldest parts, the Gāthās, or metrical sermons of Zoroaster; the other 'Younger Avesta' or the 'classical dialect'. This latter is the language of the great body of the Avesta. The Gāthā dialect is more archaic, standing in the relation of the Vedic to the classical Sanskrit, or the Homeric Greek to the Attic. Possibly the Gāthā language may owe some of its peculiarities noticed below, also to an original difference of locality. The Gāthā dialect was the speech of Zoroaster and his followers. Its grammatical structure is remarkably pure. The younger Avesta, but only in its late compositions, owing to linguistic decay, shows many corruptions and confusions in its inflections. All that is old or is written in meter, however, is correct and accurate. Inaccuracies that have there crept in, we must generally attribute to the carelessness of the scribes. In its forms, as a rule, the Avesta is extremely antique; it stands in general on the same plane as the Vedic Sanskrit, and occasionally, though not often, it even shows more ancient forms.

§ 55. The language of the Avesta is most closely allied to the Sanskrit, though individually quite distinct from the latter. Together they may be classed as making up an Indo-Iranian group. Almost any Sanskrit word may be changed at once into its Avestan equivalent, or vice versa, merely by applying certain phonetic laws. As example may be taken the metrical stanza Yt. 10.6 in the Avesta:

tǝm amavaṇtǝm yazatǝm
sūrǝm dāmōhu savištǝm
miϑrǝm yazāi zaoϑrābyō — —

'Mithra that strong mighty angel, most beneficent to all creatures, I will worship with libations' — becomes when rendered word for word in Sanskrit:

tam ámavantam yajatám
śúram dhā́masu sáviṣṭham
mitrám yajāi hótrābhyaḥ.

§ 56. In its **phonology** the Avesta agrees with the Sanskrit in its vowels in general, but the Avesta shows a greater variety in using *e-* and *o-*sounds instead of *a*. Final vowels, except *ō*, are shortened as a rule. The Skt. diphthong *ē* appears in Av. as *aē*, *ōi*, *ē* (final). Thus Av. *vaēnōiṗe* 'they two are seen' = Skt. *vḗn-ē-tē*. Skt. *ō* appears as Av. *ao*, *ɔu*, *ō* (final), thus Av. *aojō* 'strength' = Skt. *ōjō*, *ōjas*; Av. *hratōuš* 'of wisdom' = Skt. *krátos*. A striking peculiarity in Av., moreover, is the introduction of epenthetic vowels and help sounds, giving rise to improper diphthongs, Av. *bavaiti* 'he becomes' = Skt. *bhávati*; Av. *haurva-* 'whole' = Skt. *sárva-*; Av. *vaḣdra-* 'word' = Skt. *vaktra-*; Av. *hvarə-* 'sun' = Skt. *svàr*. The Skt. voiceless stops *k*, *t*, *p* generally become spirants *ḣ*, *ṗ*, *f* in Av. before consonants. Thus, Av. *ḣṡapra-* 'rule, kingdom' = Skt. *kṣatrá-*; Av. *fra* 'forth' = Skt. *pra*. The original voiced aspirates *gh*, *dh*, *bh*, become in Av. simply voiced stops *g*, *d*, *b*. They are so preserved in the old Gāthā dialect; the younger dialect commonly resolves them again before consonants and between vowels into voiced spirants. Thus, GAv. *adā*, YAv. *aδa* 'then' = Skt. *ádha-t*. Similarly spirantized in YAv. the voiced stops YAv. *uγra-*, GAv. *ugra-* 'mighty' = Skt. *ugrá-*. The sibilant *s*, when initial in Skt., becomes Av. *h*, as in Greek. Thus, Av. *hapta* 'seven' = Skt. *saptá*. When internal, Skt. *s* may also appear as *ṇh*. Thus, Av. *vaṇhana-* 'vesture' = Skt. *vásana-*. Final *-as* of Skt. appears regularly as *-ō*. Thus Av. *aspō* 'horse' = Skt. *áśvas*.

§ 57. The Gāthā dialect regularly lengthens all final vowels. It frequently inserts the anaptyctic vowels: GAv. *frā*, YAv. *fra* = Skt. *pra*. Original *ns* appears in GAv. as *ṇg*. Thus GAv. *daēvə̄ṇg* (acc. pl.), YAv. *daēvąn* 'demons' = Skt. *dēvā́n*; GAv. *məṇghāi* 'I shall think' = Skt. *maṃsāi*.

§ 58. In **inflection** the Avesta shows nearly the richness of the Vedic Sanskrit. There are three genders, masculine, neuter, feminine; likewise three numbers, singular, dual, plural. The dual is not extensively used. There are eight well-developed cases of the **noun** and the **adjective**; the normal endings are: Singular. Nom. *-s*; Acc. *-əm*; Instr. *-ā*; Dat. *-e*; Abl. *-at*; Gen. *-ō (-as)*; Loc. *-i*; Voc. —. Dual. Nom., Acc., Voc. *-ā*; Instr., Dat., Abl. *-byā*; Gen. *-ā̊*; Loc. *-ō*, *-yō*. Plural. Nom., Voc. *-ō (-ās)*, *-a*; Acc. *-ō (-ās, -ns)*, *-ā*; Instr. *-bīš*; Dat *-byō (-byas)*; Gen. *-ąm*; Loc. *-su*, *-hu*, *-šva*. The classes of declension agree exactly with the

Sanskrit; the method of forming comparison of adjectives likewise corresponds. The numerals answer to Skt. forms, except Av. *aēva-* 'one', opposed to Skt. *ēka-*, Av. *baēvar-* '10,000', but Skt. *ayúta*. The Av. pronouns closely resemble the Skt., but show also individual peculiarities. Noteworthy is the remote demonstrative Av. *ava, hāu* 'that, yonder', contrasted with Skt. *amú, asāu*. The verbal system in Av. and in Skt. are in general identical. The roots are chiefly monosyllabic and are subject to the same modifications as in Skt. In voice, mode, and tense, and in their conjugation-system the two languages quite agree. The endings show equal antiquity with the Sanskrit. The primary active endings in Av. are: Sing. 1, *-mi*, 2, *-hi*, 3, *-ti;* Dual. 1, *-vahi*, 3, *-tō, -ṗō;* Plur. 1, *-mahi*, 2, *-ṗa*, 3, *-ṇti*. The other endings also are parallel with the Sanskrit.

§ 59. The Av. possesses like facility with the Sanskrit in forming words by means of prefixes, and by adding suffixes of primary and secondary derivation. The same classes of compounds may be recognized in both tongues. The rules of external Sandhi, or joining together of words in a sentence, so universal in Skt., are almost wanting in Avesta. The Avesta separates each word by a dot. The vowels are fully expressed as in Greek etc., by individual letters. No diacritical points or accents are written in the texts. The meters in which the Gāthās are composed have analogies in the Veda. Almost all the metrical parts of the younger Avesta are in eight-syllable lines. The syntax, however, differs from the Sanskrit in certain points, and shows some marked individualities, especially in the later portions.

Specimens of the Avesta Text.

I. From the Gathas.

Yasna 45.1—2.

Zoroaster preaches upon The Two Spirits.

[Avestan script text, lines 1–2]

Ys. 45.1 translated.

Now shall I preach, and do you give ear and hear,
Ye who hither press from near and from afar,
Therefore lay ye all these things to heart as clear
Nor let the wicked teacher your second life destroy—
The perverted sinner your tongues with his false faith.

Transliteration of the same.

(See opposite page.)

1 aṯ fravaḵṣyā nū gūṣōdūm nū sraotā
yaēcā asnāṯ yaēcā dūrāṯ iṣapā
nū im vispā ciþrō zī mazdāṅhōdūm
nōiṯ daibitīm duš.sastiš ahūm mᵊrąṣyāṯ
akā varᵃnā dragvā̊ hizvā̊ āvarᵊtō.

2 aṯ fravaḵṣyā aṅhōuš ma¹nyū poᵘruyē
yayā̊ spanyā̊ ūiti mravaṯ yȝm aṅgrᵊm
nōiṯ nā manā̊ nōiṯ sᵊṅghā nōiṯ ḫratavō
nacdā varᵃnā nōiṯ uḫdā nacdā šyaopᵃnā
nōiṯ daēnā̊ nōiṯ ᵘrvąnō hacaintē.

Ys. 45.2 translated.

Now shall I preach of the world's Two primal Spirits
The Holier One of which did thus address the Evil:
'Neither do our minds, our teachings, nor our concepts,
Nor our beliefs, nor words, nor do our deeds in sooth,
Nor yet our consciences, nor souls agree in aught.'

II. FROM THE YOUNGER AVESTA.

a. **Yasna** 9.5 (metrical).
The Golden Age of Yima.

5 yimahe hšaθre aurvahe
noiṭ aotəm åŋha noiṭ garəməm
noiṭ zaurva åŋha noiṭ mərəθyuš
noiṭ arəsko daēvō.dātō:
paṇca.dasa fracaroiθe
pita puθrasca raodaēšva kataraseiṭ
yavata hšayōiṭ hvāθwō
yimō vīvaŋhatō puθrō.

In the reign of princely Yima
There was neither cold, nor heat
Old age was not, death there was not,
Nor disease, the work of Demons.
But the son walked with the father
Fifteen years old each in figure,
Long as Vivanghvat's son, Yima
The good shepherd, ruled as sovereign.

b. **Vendidad 6.44—45** (prose).
Disposal of the Dead.

44
[.*ratādā* .*mqnapēag* .*mqnitiavtsa* .*muāša*]
dātarə *gaēþanąm* *astva¹tinąm* *ašāum*
O Creator of beings material O holy One

[.*avk* .*mqran* .*mqnatsiri* .*mūnat* .*amārah* .*aruha*]
kva *narąm* *iristanąm* *tanūm* *barāma* *ahura*
where of men dead (gen.) body shall-we-bear O Ahura

45
[.*adzam* .*avk* .*amāpadin* .*āat* .*toarm* .*ōruha*]
mazda *kva* *nidaþāma* *āat* *mraot* *ahurō*
Mazda where deposit Then spake Ahura

[.*ōdzam* .*barezištačšvaca* .*acavšeatšizvab* .*atiap* .*acavšutāg*]
mazdā̊ *barezištačšvaca* *paiti* *gātušvaca*
Mazda the heights upon and-on-beds

[.*amatips* .*artšuparaz* .*tiōday* .*mid* .*matšidiāb*]
spitama *zaraþuštra* *yadōit* *dim* *bāidištəm*
O Spitama Zarathushtra where it always

[.*mqnazava* .*ōnus* .*āv* .*ōraḥ.šfarək* .*ōyav* .*āv*]
avazanąn *sūnō* *vā* *kərəfš.ḥarō* *vajō* *vā*
may-see dogs either corpse-eating birds or

[.*ōraḥ.šfarək*]
kərəfš.ḥarō
corpse-eating.

TRANSCRIPTION OF AVESTAN ALPHABET

(Compared with Justi, *Handbuch der Zendsprache*).[1]

A. Vowels.

Short ..	ᴧ *a*	*i*	*u*	*ə*	*c*	*o*		
	a	*i*	*u*	(*e*)	(*e*)	*o*		
Long	*ā*	*ī*	*ū*	*ə̄*	*c̄*	*ō*	*ō̄*	*q*
	ā	*ī*	*ū*	(*ē*)	*e*	*ō*	(*ao*)	(*å*)

B. Consonants.

Guttural	*k*	*kh*	*g*	*ġ*	
	k	(*kh*)	*g*	(*gh*)	
Palatal	*c*	—	*j*	...	
	c		*j*		
Dental	*t*	*þ*	*d*	*ḍ*	*t̰*
	t	(*th*)	*d*	(*dh*)	(*t*)
Labial	*p*	*f*	*b*	*w*	
	p	*f*	*b*	*w*	
Nasal	*n* · *ṇ*	*n*	*ṅ*	*m*	
	(*n*)	(*n*)	*n*	(*ṅ*)	*m*
Semivowel and Liquid	(*y*), *y̌* (*i*)[2]	*r*	(*w*), *v̌* (*u*)[2]		
	y		*r*	*v*	
Sibilant	*s*	*š*	*š̌*[3]	*ṣ̌*[3]	*z* *ž*
	(*c*)	(*s*)	(*sh*)	(*sk*)	*z* (*zh*)
Aspiration	*h*	*ḣ*			
	h	(*q*)			
Ligature	*h*				
	(*ç*)				

---

[1] Forms in parentheses ( ) show where Justi has been deviated from.

[2] The signs *i̯*, *u̯* need only be employed for purely scientific purposes; the letters *y*, *v* for both initial and internal *y*, *v*, answer fully for practical purposes.

[3] The differentiation *š*, *š̌*, *ṣ̌* need only be made in scientific articles. The single sign *š* is ordinarily quite sufficient for the three *š*, *š̌*, *ṣ̌*.

SUGGESTIONS.

The following hints may be helpful to the student in using the Grammar. The chief points on which stress should be laid, and which it will be sufficient for the beginner to acquire, are:

1. In the Preface, the remarks on Transcription, pp. vi—vii.
2. In the Introduction, the sketch of the language of the Avesta, pp. xxx—xxxiii.
3. Throughout the Grammar, the large print alone need be studied. Every thing marked 'GAv.' (Gāthā Avesta), and all that is in small type, may be practically disregarded.
4. Under Phonology, only the sections (§§) referred to in the Résumé pp. 60—61.
5. Under the Declension of Nouns and Adjectives, the following sections should suffice: §§ 236, 243, 251, 262, 279, 291, 300, 322, 339, 362, 363.
6. Under Numerals, note merely the Cardinals § 366.
7. Under Pronouns, compare the Av. and Skt. forms in the case of §§ 386, 390, 399, 409, 417, 422, 432. No attempt need be made to commit the paradigms to memory.
8. Under Verbs, the following sections relating to the Present-System are important: §§ 448, 466, 469, 470, 478—481, 483—488. The remaining conjugations, and the Perfect, Aorist, Future, etc., may be learned as needed.
9. The rest of the book may be overlooked by the beginner.
10. In consulting the Grammar, the Index will be found of service for reference.

A FEW OF THE BOOKS MOST NECESSARY FOR THE BEGINNER.

The following list contains a few books that the beginner will find most useful. The list is very brief; the student as he advances will see how rapidly it may be enlarged.

a. Texts.

GELDNER — *Avesta, or the Sacred Books of the Parsis.* — Stuttgart 1885 seq.
    The new standard edition.

WESTERGAARD — *Zendavesta, or the Religious Books of the Zoroastrians.* — Copenhagen.
    Hard to procure, but useful until Geldner's edition is complete.

W. GEIGER — *Aogemadaēča, ein Pārsentract in Pazend, Altbaktrisch und Sanskrit.* — Erlangen 1878.
    Useful for the brief Av. fragment it contains.

SPIEGEL — *Die altpersischen Keilinschriften,* im Grundtexte mit Übersetzung, Grammatik und Glossar. 2. Aufl. — Leipzig 1881.
    Good for comparative purposes.

b. Dictionary.

JUSTI — *Handbuch der Zendsprache,* Altbaktrisches Wörterbuch. — Leipzig 1864.
    The only dictionary at present, and indispensable for reference. Possible to obtain second-hand.

c. Translation.

DARMESTETER AND MILLS — *The Zend-Avesta* translated, in the *Sacred Books of the East,* ed. by F. Max Müller, vols. iv, xxiii, xxxi. — Oxford 1883-7.
    This translation is complete. Translations of separate portions are to be found in the works mentioned under (d) and (e).

d. Grammar and Exegesis,
including also Translations of selected portions.

(Books specially mentioned above in Preface, are not repeated here.)

BARTHOLOMAE—*Arische Forschungen* i-iii.—Halle 1882-7.
    Grammatical and metrical investigations, with translations of selected Passages.

GELDNER — *Ueber die Metrik des jüngeren Avesta.*— Tübingen 1877.
    A useful treatise on Metre. Also contains translations.

— *Studien zum Avesta.*—Strassburg 1882.
    Grammatical contributions, and numerous translations.

— *Drei Yasht aus dem Zendavesta* übersetzt und erklärt.—Stuttgart 1884.
    Translation of Yt. 14, 17, 19, with Commentary.

SPIEGEL.— *Commentar über das Avesta.* Bd. i-ii.—Wien 1864-8.
    Useful for occasional reference.

e. Literature, Religion, Antiquities.

DARAB PESHOTAN SANJANA—*Civilisation of the Eastern Iranians.* Vols. i-ii; being a translation from the German of W. Geiger's *Ostiranische Kultur im Alterthum.*—London 1885-6.
    Useful for reference.

GELDNER—*Zend-Avesta, Zoroaster,* articles in the *Encyclopaedia Britannica.* Ninth edition.—1888.
    By all means to be consulted.

HAUG AND WEST— *Essays* on the Sacred Language, Writings, and Religion of the Parsis. 3 ed.—London 1884.
    Contains much useful information.

FIROZ JAMASPJI—Casartelli's *Mazdayasnian Religion under the Sassanids.*—Bombay 1889.
    Treats fully of the later development of Zoroastrianism.

RAGOZIN.—*Media, Babylon and Persia.* (Story of Nations' Series.)—New York 1888.
: A good and readable book.

WINDISCHMANN.—*Zoroastrische Studien,* herausgegeben von Fr. Spiegel.—Berlin 1863.
: Contains much good material.

Beside the above works the student will find abundant and valuable contributions on the Avesta and kindred Iranian subjects in the philological journals and periodicals of the last few years. Reference need only be made to the names Bartholomae, Bang, Bezzenberger, Caland, Casartelli, Darmesteter, de Harlez, Geiger, Geldner, Horn, Hübschmann, Fr. Muller, Mills, Pischel, Spiegel, Wilhelm, and some others, in the following:

> *Bezzenberger's Beiträge;*
> *Kuhn's Zeitschrift;*
> *Zeitschrift der deutschen morgenländischen Gesellschaft;*
> *Brugmann und Streitberg's Indogermanische Forschungen;*
> *Le Muséon;*
> *American Oriental Society's Proceedings;*
> *American Journal of Philology;*
> *Babylonian and Oriental Record.*

Table of Contents

OF

PART I.

(The Numbers refer to the Sections §§.)

Section		Page
	PREFACE	v—x
	INTRODUCTION: THE AVESTA AND ZOROASTER	xi—xxxiii
	SPECIMENS OF THE AVESTA TEXT	xxxiv—xxxviii
	SUGGESTIONS, AND BOOKS RECOMMENDED	xxxix—xlii
	CONTENTS, AND ABBREVIATIONS	xliii—xlviii

GRAMMAR.
PHONOLOGY.
ALPHABET AND PRONUNCIATION.

§ 1. 1-3. The Av. characters.—4. Punctuation.—5-7. Pronunciation of Vowels and Diphthongs.—8-13. Sounds of the Consonants . . . . 1—4

SYSTEM OF VOWELS.

§ 14. **Simple Vowels.** 14. The Av. and Skt. Vowel-Systems.—15. Agreement both in Quality and Quantity between Av. and Skt. Vowels.—16-22. Agreement in Quality, Difference in Quantity.—23-26. Rules for Quantity of Vowels in Av.—27-46. Difference in Quality between Av. and Skt. Vowels.—47-49. Original *r* in Av.—50-52. Concurrence of Vowels, Euphonic Rules, Contraction, Resolution, Hiatus . . . . 4—15

§ 53. **Diphthongs.** 53. Proper, Improper Diphthongs; Reduction and Protraction Diphthongs.—54-59. The diphthongs Av. *aē, ōi; ao, ǝu; ōi, āu*.—60. Vowel-Strengthening, Guṇa and Vṛddhi.—61. Changes in *y*- or *v*-Syllables.—62. Vocalization of *y* and *v*.—63-68. Reduction and Abbreviation in *y*- or *v*-Syllables.—69-72. Epenthesis, Prothesis, Anaptyxis . . . . 15—27

SYSTEM OF CONSONANTS.

§ 73. **General Rules for Consonants.** 74. Voiceless and Voiced (Surd and Sonant). — 75. Remarks on Sandhi. — 76. Tenues, Av. *k, t, p.* — 77-80. Voiceless (Surd) Spirants, Av. *ḱ, ṗ, f.* — 81. The character of Av. *f.* — 82-88. Mediae, Av. *g, d, b, j* and the Voiced (Sonant) Spirants, Av. *ǰ, δ, w.* — 89-90. Bartholomae's Law for original aspirate mediae + *t* or + *s.* — 91-93. Semivowels, Av. *y (i̯), v (u̯).* — 94-99. Original *v* in combination with Consonants. 100. Liquid, Av. *r.* — 101-105. Nasals, Av. *n, ṇ, ń, ŋ, m.* — 106-107. Sibilants, Av. *s, š, ś, ṣ̌, z, ž.* — 108-110. Original *s,* how represented in Av. — 111-124. Original *as, ās,* how represented in Av. — 125-129. Original *us.* — 130. Original *sv.* — 131-144. Original *sy, sr, sm, sk₁, ts, ps.* — 145-150. Older palatal *ś* (Skt. *ś̱*), how represented in Av. — 151-153. Developed Av. *s.* — 154-166. Av. *š, ś̱, š̌.* — 167-175. Av. *z.* — 176-183. Av. *ž.* — 184. Aspiration, Av. *h, ḣ, ḫ* 27-57

§ 185. **Special Rules for Consonants.** — 185. Assimilation. — 186. Double Consonants reduced in Av. 187. Consonant dropped. — 188-190. Consonants added or substituted. 191. Metathesis. — 192-193. Final Consonants in Av. — 193 Note. MS.-Fluctuations in writing certain Consonants and certain Vowels. — 194. Repetition of same sound avoided in Av. . . . . 57—60

RÉSUMÉ OF PHONOLOGY.

§ 195. 195-201. Differences between Av. and Skt. Vowels. — 202-203. Av. and Skt. Diphthongs compared. — 204-206. Origin of the Consonants in Av. — 207-218. Representation of various Skt. Consonants in Av. . . . . 60—61

INFLECTION.

DECLENSION OF NOUNS AND ADJECTIVES

§ 219. Synopsis of the Declension of Nouns and Adjectives. — 220. Case, Number, Gender. 221. Table of Case-Endings. — 222-227. Remarks on the Endings. — 228-231. General Plural Case in Av. — 232. Interchange of Neuter with Feminine Forms. — 233. Interchange of Cases in their Functions. — 234. Transition in Declension. — 235. Stem-Gradation (Strong and Weak Forms). — 236-250 Declension of Stems in *a, ā.* — 251-261. Stems in *i, ī.* — 262-276. Stems in *u, ū.* — 277-278. Diphthongal Stems

Section	Page
in *āi*, *āu*.—279-283. Stems without Suffix. - 284-288. Strong and Weak Stems. 289-298. Derivative Stems in *ayt*, *mayt*, *vayt*. — 299-315. Derivative Stems in *an*, *man*, *van*. — 316. Derivative Stems in *in*. — 317-318. Radical *n*- and *m*-Stems.—319-337. Stems in original *r*.—338-360. Stems in original *s*.— 361-362. Feminine Formation.—363-365. Comparison	62—105

DECLENSION OF NUMERALS.

§ 366. 366-374. Cardinals and Ordinals. — 375-376. Numeral Derivatives	106—108

DECLENSION OF PRONOUNS.

§ 377. 377-384. General Remarks and Synopsis of the Pronouns.— 385-398. Personal.—399-405. Relative.—406-407. Interrogative. — 408. Indefinite. — 409-433. Demonstrative. — 434-443. Other Pronominal Words and Derivatives, Possessive, Reflexive, Adjectives, Adverbs	109—126

CONJUGATION OF VERBS.

§ 444. 444-447. General Synopsis, Voice, Mode, Tense, Person, Number. — 448. Table of Personal Endings. - 449-458. Remarks on the Endings.- 459-464. Mode-Formation, Subjunctive, Optative. - 465-466. Reduplication and Augment.— 467. Vowel-Variation (Strong and Weak Forms)	127—137
§ 468. **Present-System.** —469-470. Classes of Verbs.— 471. Transfer of Conjugation.— 472-477. The *a*-Conjugation (thematic).—478. Cl. 1 (*a*-class. s t r. root).- 479. Cl. 6 (*a*-class, u n s t r. root).— 480. Cl. 4 (*ya*-class).— 481. Cl. 10 (*aya*-class).— 482-506. Paradigms of *a*-Conjugation.— 507-515. The non-*a*-Conjugation (unthematic).— 516-539. Cl. 2 (root-class). — 540-553. Cl. 3 (reduplicating class).— 554-565. Cl. 7 (nasal class).—566-575. Cl. 5 (*nu*-class). — 576-582. Cl. 8 (*u*-class).— 583-591. Cl. 9 (*nā*-class)	137—167
§ 592. **Perfect-System.** 592-596. Perfect Formation.— 597-601. Table of Perfect Endings and Remarks.—602. The Pluperfect (Preterite).—603-604. Mode-Formation of the Perfect.— 605-619. Paradigms of the Perfect-System. — 620-622. Absence of Reduplication. - 623. Periphrastic Perfect	167—176
§ 624. **Aorist-System.** 624-625. Form and Classification of Aorists. — 626. Augment and Endings. — 627. Modes of the Aorist.— 628-652. Non-Sigmatic Group, (1) Root-	

Section		Page
	Aorist, (2) Simple Aorist, (3) Reduplicated Aorist.—653-666. Sigmatic Group, (4) h- (or s-) Aorist, (5) ha-(ia-) Aorist, (6) $iš$-Aorist, (7) $hiš$-Aorist.—667-668. Aorist Passive Third Singular	176—186
§ 669.	**Future-System.** 669. Future Formation.—670-671. Modes of the Future.—672. Paradigms	186—187
§ 675.	**Secondary Conjugation.** 675-683. Formation of the Passive.—684-694. Causative.—695-696. Denominative.—697-698. Inchoative.—699-701. Desiderative.—702-707. Intensive	187—195
§ 708.	**Verbal Abstract Forms.** 709-715. Active, Middle, and Passive Participles.—716-718. Gerundive and Gerund.—719-721. Infinitive	195—199
§ 722.	**Periphrastic Verbal Phrases.** 722-723. Periphrases instead of a tense-stem.—724. Periphrastic Expressions and Circumlocutions	199—200

INDECLINABLES.

§ 725.	725-733. Adverbs.—734-737. Prepositions.—738-740. Conjunctions.—741-742. Interjections	201—206

WORD-FORMATION.

FORMATION OF DECLINABLE STEMS.

§ 743.	Morphology in general.—744-745. Suffixless Formation.—746. Derivation by Prefix and Suffix.—747-754. Nominal and Verbal Prefixes.—755. Derivation by Suffix.—756-823. Primary Suffixes.—824-857. Secondary Suffixes	207—236

FORMATION OF COMPOUND STEMS.

§ 858.	Noun and Verb Compounds.—859-860. Noun-Composition.—861-877. Euphonic Laws in the Union of the Members of Compounds.—878. Classes of Compounds.—879. Copulative Compounds.—880-882. Determinative Compounds.—883-889. Secondary Adjective Compounds, Possessive Compounds and Adjective Compounds with governed Final Member.—890-894. Other Compounds, Numeral, Adverbial, Loose.—895-900. Sandhi in Compounds and Encliticis	236—247
	INDEXES	249—271
	ADDITIONS AND CORRECTIONS	272—273

ABBREVIATIONS.

adj. = adjective	Afr. = Afringan
advl. = adverbial	Av.[1] = Avesta
etc. = *et cetera*	GAv.[2] = Gatha Avesta
et al. = *et alia*	Ind. Iran. = Indo-Iranian
fr. = from	Indg. = Indogermanic
indecl. = indeclinable	MS. = manuscript
infin. = infinitive	MSS. = manuscripts
nom. propr. = *nomen proprium*	Ny. = Nyaish
num. = numeral	Phl. = Pahlavi
orig. = original, originally	Sir. = Sirozah
opp., opp. to = opposed to	Skt. = Sanskrit
pret. = preterite	Vd. = Vendidad
ptcpl. = participle	Vsp. = Vispered
str. = strong	Wg. = Westergaard
subst. = substantive	YAv.[3] = Younger Avesta
v. l. = *varia lectio*	Ys. = Yasna
var. = variant	Yt. = Yasht
wk. = weak.	ZPhl. Gloss. = Zand-Pahlavi Glossary.

The other abbreviations require no remark.

Observe.

1. Av. (Avesta) prefixed to a word indicates that the word or form in question is either found in both GAv. and YAv. or has nothing peculiar about it which would prevent its occurence in both.

2. GAv. (Gatha Avesta) is prefixed (1) when the word, or form, or construction is peculiar to the Gatha dialect and is not found in YAv.; (2) to contrast a Gatha form with a younger form (YAv.) which may stand beside it; (3) to emphasize the fact that the form in question is found even in the Gathas, e. g. *stavas* § 1.43.

Under GAv. are comprised the usual 17 hymns and the sacred formulas (Introd. p. xxiii, § 25), the Yasna Haptanghaiti, and those portions, such as Ys. 12, that are written in the Gāthā dialect even including some possible later imitations, e. g. Ys. 58, 4.20.

3. YAv. (Younger Avesta) comprises everything that is not written in the dialect of the Gāthās. For its usage see preceding note.

4. The sign (°) is placed before a form to denote that the first part of the word is omitted.

5. In the paradigms under Inflection, the forms in parentheses () do not actually occur, but are made up after the form in small print which stands beside them. See § 236 foot-note. Thus Loc. *(yasnaēṣu) vīraēju*.

GRAMMAR.

PHONOLOGY.

Alphabet.

§ 1. The Avesta is written in the following characters

A. Vowels.

Short . .	*a*	*i*	*u*	*ə*	*e*	*o*			
Long . .	*ā*	*ī*	*ū*	*ə̄*	*ē*	*ō*	*ā̊*	*ą*	

B. Consonants.

Guttural .	*k*	*x*	*g*	*j*	
Palatal	*c*	--	*j*	--	
Dental . . .	*t*	*p*	*d*	*đ*	*t*
Labial .	*p*	*f*	*b*	*w*	
Nasal . . .	*ŋ*	*ŋ́*	*n*	*ń*	*m*
Semivowels and Liquid . . .	*w, (ᵘ)*	*y*	*r*	*y, (ⁱ)*	*v*
Sibilant . . .	*s*	*š*	*ṣ̌*	*š́*	*z*	*ž*
Aspiration . .	*h*	*h́*			
Ligature . . .	*hv*				

§ 2. The writing runs from right to left. The vowels are fully expressed by individual letters as in Greek

---

Note. The epenthetic and anaptyctic vowels (§§ 70, 72) will be expressed in transcription, in the Grammar only, by a small vowel slightly raised: e. g. Av. *aᵘruša-* 'white' = Skt. *aruṣá-;* Av. *antarᵊ* 'within' = Skt. *antár*.

etc.; there are no diacritical points; nor are any accents written in the Avesta texts.

§ 3. In the manuscripts numerous **ligatures** occur; these except ꭥ *št* are generally resolved in printing. Observe that ꭦ *hr* is different from ꭧ *hv*. Many MSS. have a sign ꭨ *m̊* interchanging with ꭩ *hm*.

§ 4. In Avesta, all **words** except some enclitics are written **separately** and each is followed by a point (.); the compounds even are mostly written separately in the MSS.; but in printed texts these are written together, a point (.) being used to divide the members.

§ 5. The **punctuation** in the MSS. is meagre, mostly arbitrary and quite irregular; the following symbols borrowed from the MSS. have been adopted to correspond to our signs, namely ⁖ for colon or semicolon; ⁘ a full stop; ⁙ a larger break; ⁙⁙ the end of a chapter; • symbol of abbreviation.

Pronunciation.

§ 6. **Vowels.** ꭪ *a*, ꭫ *ā*, ꭬ *i*, ꭭ *ī*, and ꭮ *u*, ꭯ *ū* are pronounced as ordinarily in Sanskrit, but *a, ā* perhaps duller. — ꭮ *ə* is most probably obscure like the short indefinite vowel familiar in English, 'gard*e*ner', 'm*e*asuring', 'hist*o*ry', 'sach*e*m'; it often corresponds to the vulgar 'chim^{e}ney', 'rheumatis^{u}m'. In the combination ꭰ *arə*, cf. Skt. *r̥*, much like English 'pretty' (when pronounced 'p^{e}r^{e}tty'), e. g. ꭱ *pərəsaṭ* 'he asked', cf. Mod. Persian *pursīdan* 'to ask'; Av. *mərəja-* 'bird', Skt. *mr̥ga-*, Mod. Pers. *murj*. See above, Introduction, on Transcription. — ꭮ *ə̄* is the corresponding long vowel to ꭮ *ə*. — ꭲ *e* and ꭳ *ē*, both narrow, about as English 'let, veil', French 'été'. — ꭴ *o* and ꭵ *ō* probably somewhat muffled. — ꭶ *ā̊*, as English 'extra*o*rdinary, f*au*lt, fa*wing*', i. e. approaching '-aw' in 'saw'. — ꯘ *q*, nasalized *a*, or *ā*, French 'sans', likely rather dull.

§ 7. **Diphthongs.** ᷛ *āi* and ᷜ *āu* are pronounced as in Sanskrit. — ꯙ *ōi* as a Gk. ωι. — ꯚ *aē*, ꯛ *ao* and ꯜ *au* as a union of the two elements *a i* etc. — ꯝ *ae* as forming two distinct sounds.

§ 8. **Tenues** ꯞ *k*, ꯟ *t*, ꯠ *p*, and **Mediae** ꯡ *g*, ꯢ *d*, ꯣ *b*, as ordinarily. — ꯤ *c*, ꯥ *j*, as in Sanskrit, English 'church, judge'.

§ 9. **Spirants.** ꯦ *ḫ*, as *ch* in Scotch 'loch', Mod. Gk. χ. — ꯧ *j̇*, a roughened *g*, guttural buzz, cf. (often) Germ. 'Tage', Mod. Gk. γ. — ꯨ *þ*, as English 'thin', surd. — ꯩ *d*, as English 'then', sonant. — ꯪ *t*, apparently a spirant, § 81. — ꯫ *f*, as in English. — ꯬ *w*, corresponding sonant, Germ. *w*, Mod. Gk. β (cf. Eng. *v*). — ꯭ *s*, sharp as in 'sister'. — ꯮ *z*, corresponding sonant, English 'zeal'. — ꯯ *š*, as English *sh* in 'dash'. — ꯰ *ž*, corresponding sonant, English 'pleasure, azure'. — ꯱ *ṣ́*, a more palatal *sh*, generally before *y*. — ꯲ *ś*, apparently a variety *sh*, differing little from ꯯ *š*; etymologically it most often equals original *rt*.

§ 10. **Nasals.** ꯳ *ṅ*, guttural = Skt. *ṅ*. — ꯴ *ñ*, a modification of the preceding, -mouillé; the two (꯳ *ṅ* and ꯴ *ñ*) respectively perhaps as in Eng. 'longing'. — ꯵ *n*, as Eng. 'nun'. — ꯶ *ṇ* (modified from *an*), a variety of *n*. — ꯷ *m*, as ordinarily.

§ 11. **Semivowels and Liquid.** ꯸ *y* (initial), probably spirant as Eng. 'youth'; — ꯹ *y* (internal), probably semivowel, *i*, English 'many a man'. — ꯺ *v* (initial), probably spirant as Eng. 'vanish'; — ꯻ *v* (internal), probably semivowel, *u*, cf. Eng. 'lower, flour'. — ꯼ *r* is a liquid vigorously pronounced. Observe *l* is wanting.

Note. On ꯻ in *uvuēbya*, see Vocabulary after ꯽ *u*.

§ 12. **Aspiration.** ⱶ *h*, as ordinarily. — ḥ *ḥ*, a modification of *h* before *y*, possibly stronger.

§ 13. **Ligature.** ⱶ *hr*, perhaps more vigorous than ⱶ *hv*, and possibly already shading towards the later Pers. *ḫv*.

Sounds.
SYSTEM OF VOWELS.

§ 14. **General Remark.** The Avesta presents a greater variety than the Sanskrit in its vowel-system, especially through the frequent presence of *e*- and *o*-sounds instead of *a*.

Simple Vowels.
A. Agreement in Quality between Avesta and Sanskrit Vowels.

Av. ⱶ, ⱶ, ⱶ, — ⱶ, ⱶ, ⱶ.
a, i, u, — ā, ī, ū.

i. Agreement in both Quality and Quantity.

§ 15. The Av. vowels *a, ā, i, ī, u, ū*, agree in general with the corresponding vowels in Sanskrit.

(1) Av. *a* = Skt. *a*;—Av. *ā* = Skt. *ā*.

Av. *asti* 'is' = Skt. *ásti*; Av. *mātarō* 'mothers' = Skt. *mātáras*; Av. *vātāiš* 'with winds' = Skt. *vátāis*.

(2) Av. *i* = Skt. *i*;—Av. *ī* = Skt. *ī*.

Av. *cistiš* 'wisdom' = Skt. *cittis*; Av. *hiṇcaiti* 'he sprinkles' = Skt. *siñcáti*; Av. *jīvyąm* 'living, fresh' (acc. f.) = Skt. *jívyām*.

(3) Av. *u* = Skt. *u*;—Av. *ū* = Skt. *ū*.

Av. *uta* 'also' = Skt. *utá*; Av. *dā^uru* 'wood' = Skt. *dáru*;— Av. *būrōiš* 'of richness' = Skt. *bhū́rēs*; Av. *būmīm* 'earth' = Skt. *bhū́mim*.

Simple Vowels.

ii. Agreement in quality; difference in quantity.

§ 16. As to the relation between long and short quantity, the Avesta and the Sanskrit do not always coincide with each other. This is probably due in part to shifting of accent, partly to deficiencies or inaccuracy in Avesta writing, partly to dialectic peculiarities.

§ 17. (1) Av. a = Skt. a.

GAv. *nanā* 'differently' = Skt. *nānā;* GAv. *mavaite* 'to one like me' = Skt. *māvatē;* YAv. *°kasat̰* 'looked' = Skt. *kāśat;* YAv. *bajina* 'dishes' = Skt. *bhājana-;* YAv. *dvarəm* 'door' = Skt. *dvāram;* YAv. *urvaranqm* 'of trees' = Skt. *urvārāṇām*.

§ 18. (2) Av. $ā$ = Skt. a.

Av. *varəzānāi* 'for the community' = Skt. *vṛjánāya;* Av. *yatārō* 'which of two' = Skt. *yataràs;* Av. *āþrava* (nom. sg.) 'priest' = Skt. *átharvā*.

Note 1. The manner of writing the same word or form in the Av. itself, sometimes varies between *a* and *ā*. — Av. *hāmō* beside *hamō* 'same' = Skt. *samás;* Av. *ayu-* beside *āyu* 'age' = Skt. *āyu-;* Av. *hutāštəm, hutāštəm* 'well-formed' = Skt. *sútaṣṭam;* Av. *yazamaide* 'we worship' beside (rarer) *barāmaide* 'we carry' (Yt. 11.7) = Skt. *yájāmahe, bhárāmahē;* Av. *uštanəm* beside *uštānəm* 'vital power'; YAv. *adwānəm* (but GAv. *advānəm*) 'way' = Skt. *ádhvānam;* GAv. *ayār³* beside YAv. *ayar³* 'days'. — Especially does the preposition *ā*, Av. *ā (a)*, vary: Av. *avazaiti* 'he rides to' = Skt. *ā-vahati;* GAv. *akā-* beside *ēkā-* 'judgment'.

Note 2. A part of the differences between *a* and *ā* in Av. and Skt., as well as the variation in the Av. itself, may be explained, as said (§ 16), by vowel-gradation: e. g. Av. *-mna-, -mana-,* ptcpl. pres. mid. = Skt. *-māna-*. The treatment of the old vowel-gradation must be sought in the comparative grammar, cf. Brugmann, *Grundriss der vergl. Gram.* § 307. Examples in Avesta are

Lower-grade	Higher-grade
apqm 'of waters'	*āpō* 'waters'
(1) *da-də-maide* 'we give', (2) *daþra-* 'gift'	*dātar-* 'giver'
ha^urva-fš-u- 'with full flocks'	*pasu* 'flock, sheep'
(1) *fra-bd-a-* 'fore-foot', (2) *paδō* (acc. pl.)	*pāda* (acc. du.)
caþru-gaoša- 'four-eared'	*caþwar-aspa-, caþwārō.*

See also under *guṇa* and *vṛddhi* § 60.

Phonology.

Note 3. On the relation, Av. *hātąm* 'of beings' = Skt. *satām*; or GAv. *dręgvātē* 'for the wicked', cf. YAv. *drvataṭ*, see Bartholomae, in *B.B.* x. 278 seq.; *K.Z.* xxix. p. 543 = *Flexionslehre* p. 124.

§ 19. Similarly (§ 18 Note 1) in Av. itself, internal *a* often takes the place of *ā*, when *ca* etc. is suffixed or the word otherwise grows by increment:

(a) Av. *katārō* 'which' but *katarasciṭ*; Av. *dahāka* 'dragon' but *dahākaca*; Av. *ābyō* 'with these' but *aēwyasca* (initial *ā*); GAv. *dəmā́nəm* 'house' (acc.) but (gen.) *dəmānahyā*; Av. *bipaitiṣtānəm* 'biped' (acc.) but *bipaitiṣtānayā̊* Yt. 13.41.—(b) Likewise a lightening of *ā* to *a* in ablative *-āṭ* occurs before enclitic *haca*: Av. *yimaṭ haca* 'from Yima'; *apaḵtaraṭ haca naēmāṭ* 'from northern region'; *huš-hąm.bərətaṭ haca ḡaētāṭ* 'from well-collected possessions'.

§ 20. (3) Av. *ī*, *ū* = Skt. *i*, *u*.

Very often, Av. *ī* and *ū* are found where the Skt. has *i*, *u*. The long vowel *ī*, occurs most frequently in the vicinity of *v*; the long vowel *ū*, chiefly when followed by epenthetic *i* § 70.

Av. *sīṣāiṭ* 'might direct, teach', cf. Skt. *śiṣyāt* ($\sqrt{śās}$-, *śiṣ*-); Av. *vīspəm* 'all' = Skt. *viśvam*; Av. *vītastim* 'a span length' = Skt. *vitastim.*—Av. *sūnō* 'of a dog' = Skt. *śúnas*; Av. *yūṣmaṭ*, *yūṣmākəm* 'from, of you' = Skt. *yuṣmát*, *yuṣmākam*; Av. *srūtā* 'heard' = Skt. *śrutás*; Av. *°drūta*- 'run' = Skt. *drutá*-; Av. *stūtō* 'of praise' = Skt. *stutás.*—Av. *āhūiriš* (but gen. *āhurōiš*) 'Ahurian' = Skt. *ásuris*; Av. *azūitiš* (but gen. *āzutōiš*) 'oblation' = Skt. *āhutis*; Av. *stūitiš* 'praise' = Skt. *stutis*; Av. *stūidi* 'praise thou' = Skt. *stuhi*; Av. *yūidyeiti* 'he fights' = Skt. *yúdhyati*.

§ 21. (4) Av. *i*, *u* = Skt. *ī*, *ū*.

Sometimes Av. *i* and *u* are found where the Skt. shows *ī*, *ū*.

Av. *isyeiti* 'he seeks', cf. Skt. *īhate*; Av. *ainikəm* 'face' = Skt. *ānīkam*; Av. *isānəm* 'having power' = Skt. *īśānam*; Av. *hunavō* 'sons' = Skt. *sūnávas*; Av. *tanunąm* 'of bodies' = Skt. *tanūnām*.

Note 1. In general as to *i*, *ī* and *u*, *ū*, the MSS. themselves often vacillate between the long and the short in the same passage, or in the same word at different places: — e. g. at times Av. *srīra*- written instead of *srira*- 'fair'; Av. *mišti* and *mīšti* 'with moisture'; Av. *vispəm* for *vīspəm* 'all'; Av. *miždəm* and *mīčdəm* 'reward'.—Av. *aura-* written for *dūra-* 'far'; Av. *drvjō* and *drujō* 'of the Druj'; Av. *yuḫta-* and *yuḫtu-* 'yoked'.

§ 22. GAv. shows everywhere an overwhelming preference for long vowels, especially for ɪ *ā*.

GAv. *azǝ̄m* 'I', YAv. *azǝm* = Skt. *ahám:* GAv. *apǝ̄ma-* 'last', YAv. *apǝma-* = Skt. *apamá-;* GAv. *jǝ̄myāṯ* 'might come', YAv. *jamyāṯ* = Skt. *gamyā́t;*—GAv. *-cīṯ, īṯ,* particles, YAv. *-ciṯ, iṯ* = Skt. *cid, -id;* GAv. *dǝ̄jīṯ-* 'victorious', YAv. *jiṯ-;* GAv. *ratū́š* 'chief, Ratu' (nom. sg.) beside *ratuš.*

Note. Similarly, GAv. *-bīš* (pada-ending) compared with YAv. *-biš* or *-bīš,* Skt. *-bhis;* but GAv. *cīš* etc. No rule for lengthening is laid down.

Principal Rules for Quantity of Vowels.

§ 23. (1) In Avesta, original *i* and *u* are regularly lengthened before final *m*.

Av. *paitīm* 'lord' (acc.) = Skt. *pátim;* Av. *dāhīm* 'creation' = Skt. *dhāsím;*—Av. *tāyūm* 'thief' = Skt. *tāyúm;* Av. *pitūm* 'food' = Skt. *pitúm.*

Note. Likewise *i* arising from reduction of *ya,* § 63 is lengthened; but the *u,* arising from reduction of *va,* appears mostly short before *m:*—Av. *maiδim* 'middle' (acc.) = Skt. *mádhyam;* but often Av. *priṯum* beside *priṯūm* (from *priṯ-va-m) 'third'.

§ 24. (2) Monosyllables ending in a vowel show regularly the long vowel.

Av. *zī* 'for' = Skt. *hí;* Av. *nī* 'down' = Skt. *ní;* Av. *nū* 'now' = Skt. *nú, (nū́);* Av. *frā* 'forth' = Skt. *prá.*

Note. The enclitic *-ca,* as united with the preceding word, does not regularly fall under this law.

§ 25. (3) Polysyllables in YAv. shorten as a rule all final vowels except *ō*.

YAv. *haēna* 'army' (nom. sg. fem.) = Skt. *sénā;* YAv. *pita* 'father' = Skt. *pitā́;* YAv. *para* 'before' = Skt. *párā.* —YAv. *āfriti* 'blessing' (instr. f.), cf. Skt. *dhītī́* 'with devotion'; YAv. *nāiri* 'woman' = Skt. *nārī́.* —YAv. *sūre* 'O mighty one' (fem.) = Skt. *śū́re;* YAv.

baraite 'he carries' = Skt. *bharatē*.—YAv. *dahyu* 'two nations', cf. Skt. *dásyū*, YAv. *dva ərəzu* 'two fingers' = Skt. *dvā ṛjū*.

Note. Exceptions occur: YAv. *pāyū* 'two protectors' = Skt. *pāyū*; YAv. *mainyā* beside *mainyu* 'two spirits', cf. Skt. *manyū*, YAv. *asrū* 'tears'; etc.

§ 26. (4) In GAv. all final vowels are l o n g without exception.

(a) GAv. *ahurā* 'O Ahura, Lord' = YAv. *ahura*, Skt. *ásura*; GAv. *utā* 'also' = YAv. *uta*, Skt. *utá*; GAv. *kuþrā* 'whither' = YAv. *kuþra*, Skt. *kútra*.— GAv. *ahī* 'thou art' = YAv. *ahi*, Skt. *ási*.—GAv. *yaēṣū* 'among whom' = Skt. *yéṣu*.—(b) Even the anaptyctic vowel (§ 72), with trifling exceptions, is lengthened: GAv. *ā̊ŋharə* 'they have been' = YAv. ā̊ŋharə, cf. Skt. *āsúr*; GAv. *vadarə* 'weapon' = YAv. *vadarə*, Skt. *vádhar*; GAv. *aṇtarə* (but also *aṇtarə*) 'within' = YAv. *aṇtarə*, Skt. *antár*.

Note. Before *-cā* 'que' in GAv. a vowel is sometimes found lengthened, sometimes again shortened: — e. g. GAv. *yehyācā* 'and of which'; *vacahicā* 'and in word'; —*ašicā* 'and Ashi' (fem. *i*); *vohucā manavhā* beside *vehū manavhī* 'with the Good Mind'.—Similar fluctuations are to be observed in YAv. also.

B. Differences in Quality between Avesta and Sanskrit Vowels.

Av. ɩ, ʃ, ʮ, ʯ, ᴝ, ᴝ,—ᵆ, ᵮ.
ə, ɟ, ɛ, ē, o, ō,—ω, ą.

§ 27. The above vowels are found under special conditions as representatives of Skt. *a* and *ā*.

§ 28. **Summary.** The Av. *e* answers oftenest to Skt. *a* before *n* or *m*, also occasionally before *v*. It is commonly the anaptyctic vowel.—The corresponding long is ɟ very frequent in GAv., more rare in YAv.—The letter ɩᴜ e is commonly a shading from a after y.—The corresponding long is ꭙ ē.—Avesta ∽ o and ∻ ō stand sometimes for a under influence of a labial, u, v.—Av. ᴩᴍ ą̄ is either Skt. ās, or it answers to Skt. ā before n plus stop-sound.—Av. ɤ ą is nasalization of a, ā before m, n; it often answers to Skt. a with anusvāra.

Av. ɩ ə.

§ 29. Av. ə often corresponds to Skt. a before n or m—regularly so before the latter when final; occasionally also before v.

Av. vində̄n 'they found' = Skt. ávindan; Av. hə̄ntə̄m 'being' = Skt. sántam; Av. upəməm (beside upaməm) 'highest' = Skt. upamám;—GAv. evistī 'by ignorance', cf. Skt. ávittī; Av. ma͡inyə̄vīm 'spiritual' beside Av. ma͡inyavō; Av. səvišta- 'most mighty, beneficent' (beside savō) = Skt. śáviṣṭha-; Av. hvaphəvīm 'blessed life' Ys. 53.1 (acc. from hvaphavya-).

Note. The MSS. sometimes vary between ə and a: e. g. Av. barəṇtū beside barəṇtu 'carrying'; jasə̄ṇtu beside jasəṇtu 'let them come'; vazəṇti beside vazəṇti 'they drive'; etc.

§ 30. The ə (§ 29) arising from a before m or n, is often palatalized to i when either y, c, j or ž, immediately precedes.

Av. yim 'whom' = Skt. yám; Av. vācim 'voice' beside vācəm = Skt. vācam; Av. drujim beside drujəm 'Deceit, Fiend' = Skt. drúham; Av. būjim beside būjəm 'absolution'; Av. bajina 'dishes' = Skt. bhājana-; Av. dražimnō 'holding' beside Av. dražəmnō.

§ 31. In GAv., ə appears sometimes to be written (as a kind of dissimilation) for u or i, when in the following syllable an u (v) or i stands. The epenthetic vowel is written beside it, according to rule § 70. Thus is to be explained GAv. *drəgvaṇt-* 'wicked' (= **drugvaṇt-* to Av. *druj-*); GAv. *bəzvaṇt-* 'advantageous' (= **bazvaṇt-* to Skt. √*bhuj-*); GAv. *ušǝ̄uru-* 'zeal' (?) see Ys. 34.7. cf. *ušuruyō* Ys. 32.16; GAv. *hušǝ̄iti-* 'well-being'; GAv. *jnǝ̄iti-* Ys. 30.11; GAv. *āskǝ̄iti-* Ys. 44.17.

Note. This interchange of *ǝ* with *u* and *i* may be added as a further suggestion in regard to the intermediate character of Av. *i ə*, before suggested.

Av. | ā.

§ 32. Av. *ā* is the corresponding long vowel to *ə*; it is especially common in GAv.—answering to YAv. *ə*, *a* and sometimes to YAv. *ō*, *ą*.

GAv. *azə̄m* 'I' = YAv. *azəm*, Skt. *ahám*; GAv. *yə̄m* 'whom' (beside GAv. *yim*) = YAv. *yim*, Skt. *yám*; GAv. *āmavaṇtəm* 'strong' = YAv. *amavaṇtəm*, Skt. *ámavantam*; GAv. *āhmā* 'of us' Ys. 43.10 beside YAv. *ahmā*, cf. Skt. *asmákam*;—GAv. *yə̄* 'who' = YAv. *yō*, Skt. *yás*; GAv. *nə̄* 'us' = YAv. *nō*, Skt. *nas.*—Sometimes, GAv. *starə̄m* 'of stars' = YAv. *strąm*; GAv. *hə̄m* 'with, together' = YAv. *hąm*, Skt. *sám.*—Also GAv. *hvarə* 'sun' = YAv. *hvarə*, Skt. *svàr*; GAv. *vadarə* 'weapon' = YAv. *vadarə*, Skt. *vádhar*.

Note. On GYAv. *ā* in *aməṣ̌ā spəṇtā*, and GAv. *āŋg* (final), *āŋh* (internal) from original *ans*, see §§ 128, 129.

§ 33. In YAv., *ā* (not common) is used apparently often without fixed rule, perhaps being borrowed from GAv.; it occurs most often for *an*, *ah* before *b*, also for *ā*.

YGAv. *spə̄ništa-* 'holiest'; YGAv. *aməṣ̌ā spəṇtā* 'Immortal Holy Ones'; YAv. *yazatā* beside *yasata* 'divinities'; YAv. *draomə̄byō* 'from assaults'; YAv. *avə̄biš* 'with helps'; YAv. *raocə̄byō* 'to light'; YAv. *haēnə̄byō* (!) abl. 'from enemies' Yt. 10.93;—as contraction YAv. *frə̄rənaot* (i. e. *fra-ərənaot*) 'he offered'.

Av. ю e.

§ 34. Av. *e* generally answers to Skt. *a, ā,* after *y,* if *i, ī, e, ē* or *y* follows in the next syllable.

YAv. *raocayeiti* 'lights up' = Skt. *rōcáyati;* GAv. *x̌šayehī* 'thou rulest' = Skt. *kṣáyasi;*—YAv. *ayeni,* GAv. *ayenī* 'I shall go' = Skt. *áyāni;*—YAv. *yesne,* GAv. *yesnē* 'in worship' = Skt. *yajñé;*—YAv. *yeŋhā̊* 'of whom' (f.) = Skt. *yásyās;* GAv. *yehyā* 'of whom' (m.) = Skt. *yásya.*

Note. Observe, however, that *y* does not always thus change *a* to *e:* e. g. *māzdayasniš* 'Mazdayasnian'; *yave* 'for ever'; *yahmi, yahmī, yahmya* 'in which'. Sometimes the MSS. vary.

§ 35. YAv. *e* answers to Skt. *ē* only when final. See §§ 54 α, 25.

YAv. *avaŋhe* 'for help' = Skt. *ávasē;* YAv. *yazaite* 'he worships' = Skt. *yájatē.*

Note 1. On Av. *e* for *ya* in reductions, see § 67.
Note 2. In the MSS. final *e* often interchanges with *i.*

Av. ю ē.

§ 36. Av. *ē,* the corresponding long to *e,* stands:—
(1) in the combination Av. *aē* = Skt. *ē;* (2) at the end of monosyllables § 24; (3) everywhere when final in GAv. § 26.

(1) GYAv. *daēva-* 'demon'.—(2) GYAv. *mē* 'me', *hē* 'him'.—(3) GAv. *yazaitē* 'he worships' (opp. to YAv. *yazaite*): GAv. *ārmaitē* 'O Armaiti' (opp. to YAv. *sūre* 'O mighty one' fem.).

Note. See Geldner, in *K.Z.* xxvii. p. 259.

Av. ⸺ o.

§ 37. Av. *o* occurs chiefly in the combination Av. *ao* = Skt. *ō,* see § 57.

§ 38. Av. *o* rarely corresponds to Skt. *a* when followed by *u.* Labialization.

Phonology.

Av. *rohu* 'good' = Skt. *vásu*; Av. *mošu* 'quickly' = Skt. *makṣú*; Av. *vohuṇąm* 'of good things' = Skt. *vásūnām*.

Av. ⇀ ō.

§ 39. Av. *ō* often corresponds to Skt. *a*, *ā* when followed by a labial vowel *u*, *ū*, *o*; rarely before *r* plus consonant.

Av. *dāmōhu* (beside *dāmahva*) 'among creatures' = Skt. *dhámasu*; GAv. *gūṣōdūm* 'may ye hear', beside GAv. *gūṣahvā* 'hear thou'; GAv. *vǝrǝzyōtū* 'let him do', beside Av. *vǝrǝzyaṇtō*.—Av. *astō.vīdōtuš* 'Bone-divider', beside *vīdātaoṯ* = Skt. -*dhātus*.—GAv. *bahṣō-hvā* 'share thou' = Skt. *bhákṣasva*; Av. *aojōnhvaṇtąm*, beside *aojahvaṇtąm* 'mighty' = Skt. *ōjasvantam*; Av. *hṣapōhva* 'in nights, at night' = Skt. **kṣápasu*; so locatives Av. *yavōhva* 'in granaries' variant *yavahva*; *garǝmōhva* 'jaws', *karǝšvōhu* 'regions', *ravōhu* 'freedom' (*au*-stems).—GAv. *uzǝmōhī* 'we may respect', influence of labial *m*.—YAv. *pwōrǝštāra* (dual) 'deciders', beside YAv. *pwarštahe*; GAv. *cōrǝṯ* 'he made' = Skt. *ákar* (for *ákart*); GAv. *frōrǝti*-, beside YAv. *frāreti*- 'forth-coming'.

Note. Observe GAv. *vōtōyōtū* 'let him make known' = Skt. *vītáyatu*; GAv. *aḣtōyōi* 'for sickness' (for -*ayōi*), the first *ō* being due to the influence of the following *ō*.

§ 40. On Av. *ō* = Skt. *as*, see § 120.

§ 41. On Av. *ō* in compounds, see under Composition.

§ 42. Av. *ō* (final) sometimes answers to Skt. *āu*.

Av. *garō* 'on a mountain' = Skt. *girāu*; Av. *dva yaska aciśtō* 'the two worst sicknesses'.

Av. ⇋ *w̄*.

Av. *w̄* = Skt. *ās*.

§ 43. (1) On Av. *w̄* answering to Skt. *ās*, see § 121 seq.

Simple Vowels.

Av. ā̃ = Skt. ā.

§ 44. (2) Av. ā̃ also corresponds to Skt. ā before *nt*.
Av. *mazā̃ntəm* 'great' = Skt. *mahā́ntam*; Av. *pā̃ṇtō* 'guarding', pres. ptcpl. nom. pl. = Skt. *pā́ntas*.

Note. Similarly, Av. *vīrō.nyā̃ṇçim* 'striking men down' = Skt. *nyáñcam*.

Av. ą̇ ą.

§ 45. (1) Av. ą presents a nasalization of *a, ā* before Av. *m* or *n*.

Av. *hąm* 'with, together' = Skt. *sám*; Av. *mąm* 'me' = Skt. *mā́m*;—Av. *ayąn* 'they may go' = Skt. *áyan*; Av. *daēvąn* 'demons' = Skt. *dēvā́n*; Av. *ᵘrvąnō* 'souls' beside Av. *ᵘrvānəm* (acc. sg.).

Note 1. In the MSS., *ā̃* often stands as variant beside *ą*: e. g. Av. *dąmi, dā̃mi* 'creature', et al.

Note 2. Defective writing:—instances often occur in endings where the final nasal after *ą* is omitted:—e. g. *imą haomą* 'these haoma-offerings' = Skt. *imā́n sómān*; Av. *yą* 'quos' = Skt. *yā́n*.

Note 3. Pleonastic writing:—a pleonastic *n* is sometimes introduced after *ą* before *m*: e. g. *dąnmahi* 'we shall give' Ys. 68.1 (variant) cf. Skt. *dā́ma*; Av. *hvąnmahī* variant *hvąmahī* 'we put foward'; Av. *fryąnmahī* variant *fryąmahī* 'we bless'.

§ 46. (2) Av. *ą* is often a union of *a (ā)* with nasal before Av. sibilants (cf. Skt. anusvāra); also before Av. spirants.

Av. *apąš* 'backward' = Skt. *ápāṅ*; Av. *hąs* 'being' (*haṇt-*) = Skt. *sán*; GAv. *mąstā* 'he thought' = Skt. *ámąsta*; Av. *ąsayā̃* 'of two parties = Skt. *ąsayós*; Av. *ązō* 'distress' = Skt. *ąhas*; Av. *bązaiti* 'he supports' = Skt. *bąhate*.—Av. *mąprəm* 'word, spell' = Skt. *mántram*; Av. ᵒ*dąprəm* 'tooth'; Av. *ą̊nā̃* 'reins'.

Original *r* (*r*-sonant).

Av. *ər*ᵊ, (*ar*ᵊ) = Skt. *r̥*.

§ 47. The Skt. *r̥* is represented in Av. by *ər*ᵊ or often *ar*ᵊ.

Av. kerənaoiti 'he makes' = Skt. kr̥nṓti; Av. marə-
byuš 'death' = Skt. mr̥tyús; Av. hakərəṯ 'at once' =
Skt. sakŕ̥t.— Av. anarətāiš 'with the untrue' = Skt.
anr̥tāis; Av. varəšəm 'wood' = Skt. vr̥kṣám; Av.
arštiš 'spear' = Skt. r̥ṣṭís.

Note. The MSS. vary, often writing arə for ərə. The new edition
of the Avesta has restored many instances of ərə: e. g. frasrərəta- (where
Westergaard frasturəta-).

§ 48. Av. ar, ər (also arə, ərə, air, aur) often = (orig. r̥)
Skt. ir, ur;— sometimes = (orig. r̥̄) Skt. īr, ūr. See Brugmann, Grundriss der vergl. Gram. 1. § 288 seq., 306 seq.

Av. zaranyehe 'of golden' = Skt. hiraṇyasya; Av.
gairiš 'mountain' = Skt. giris; Av. ā̊ṅhar (GAv.
ā̊ṅharə) 'they have been' = Skt. āsúr; Av. taurva-
yeiti 'he overcomes' = Skt. √turv-, tū́rv-; Av. darə-
ɣəm 'long' = Skt. dīrghám.— So sometimes Av. ərə, ra
= Skt. ra, r̥:— Av. ərəzatəm 'silver' = Skt. rajatám;
Av. ratu- 'chief, point of time', cf. Skt. r̥tú-.

§ 49. Av. ərq may represent original r + n.
GAv. nərąš (acc. pl.) 'men', cf. nr̥̄́s cyautnū́ RigVeda 10.50.4;
GAv. mātərąšca (acc. pl.) 'mothers', cf. Skt. mātr̥̄́n RV. 10.35.2.

Concurrence of vowels.
Contraction and Resolution.

§ 50. **General Remark.** In Avesta, the rule for the
union of two vowels within a word or in composition, corresponds in general to the Sanskrit. (1) Two similar vowels
coalesce into their corresponding long (sometimes short).
(2) Two dissimilar vowels, when the first is *a* unite in
giving guṇa § 60. (3) Before dissimilar vowels, the
i- or *u*-vowel (simple or in diphthongs), passes over into
the corresponding semi-vowel. (4) In Avesta compounds,
however, hiatus is often allowed to remain.

§ 51. The following are instances of **contraction of similar vowels**.

Av. $a, \bar{a} + a, \bar{a} = \bar{a}$: Av. *parāzəṇti* 'they drive away' = *para* + *az°*;
$i, \bar{i} + i, \iota = \bar{i}$: Av. *nīre* 'I let go down' = *ni* + *ire*;
$u, \bar{u} + u, \bar{u} = \bar{u}$: Av. *hūḥtāiš* 'by good words' (*hu* + *u°*) = Skt. *sūktāis*.
$a + q = q$: Av. *nqmyqsuš* 'with pliant branches' = *nqmya qsuš* § 46.

Note 1. Instead of the long vowel in contractions, the short vowel is often written: e. g. Av. *frapayemi* 'I shall attain to' (= *fra* + *ap°*); Av. *paititəm* 'atoned' (= *paiti* + *i°*); Av. *anuḥtēe* 'speak after' (= *anu* + *uḥti-*).

Note 2. Hiatus sometimes remains in compounds: Av. *ava-ajnaoiti* 'he attains'; GAv. *ciprā-avavhəm* Ys. 34.4, beside YAv. *cipravavhąm* Ny. 3.10 'manifestly aiding'; Av. *ḥṣviwi-iṣuš* 'having darting arrows'.

Note 3. Metrically, contractions of like vowels are often to be resolved in reading. See Geldner, *Metrik*, p. 13 seq.

§ 52. Av. *i*- and *u*-vowels, simple or in diphthongs, before dissimilar vowels, pass over into *y* or *v*.

(a) Av. *vyānō* 'pursued' ($\sqrt{vī}$-) = Skt. *vyānās*; Av. *ḥjayehi* 'thou rulest' ($\sqrt{ḥji}$-); Av. *vīdōyąm* 'anti-demoniac' (*daēva-*; on *ōi* = *aē* § 56); *uityaojanō* 'thus speaking' beside *uiti aojanō*; *paityāpəm* 'up stream' (*paiti* + *āp°*); *nmānaya* (loc. °*aē* + *a* postpos.) 'in a house' beside *nmāne*. — (b) *tanvō* 'of body' (*tanu-as*); *hāvana* 'haoma-mortars' ($\sqrt{hu}$); *hvaspəm* 'well-horsed' (*hu* + *aspəm*); *anajraēṣva* 'among the infinite' (loc. -*ṣu* + *a*). — (c) With lengthening after the semi-vowel: Av. *aiwyāmaṇąm* 'of the over-mighty' (*aiwi* + *am°*); *aiwyā-vavha* 'with protection' (*avavh-*); *aipyūḥda* 'interrupted in speaking mispronounced' (*uḥda-*).

Note 1. In compounds the hiatus often remains: e. g. Av. *tiži-arštim* 'sharp-speared'; Av. *āśu-aspəm* 'swift horsed' = Skt. *āśvāśvam*.

Note 2. Metrically, the resulting semi-vowel *y*, *v* is often to be restored as vowel or read *iy*, *uv*.

Diphthongs.

§ 53. **General Remark.** The Avesta vowel-combinations (diphthongs with triphthongs) are of four-fold origin, and may conveniently be divided and designated as follows:

i. Proper diphthongs, corresponding to Sanskrit *guṇa* (more rarely *vṛddhi*) in its two-fold sense: (1) vowel-strengthening, (2) the result of contraction of two dissimilar vowels. See § 60 seq.

ii. Reduction-diphthongs, resulting from reduction by contraction of two syllables. See § 64 seq. Metrically often dissyllabic.

iii. Improper diphthongs (and triphthongs) arising from epenthesis. See § 70 seq.

iv. Protraction-diphthong *āa*, a peculiar extension of *a* or *ā* into *āa* in ablative singular before *-ca* 'que'; likewise in *āat̰* 'then' (abl. as adv.), GAv. *bāat̰* 'verily' Ys. 35.5. Cf. Av. *daēvāat̰ca* 'and from the Demon' (*daēva-*); *apāat̰ca* beside *apat̰* 'from water', etc.

Proper Diphthongs.

Av. ᵍ—, ᵍ—ᵍ, ᵍ — ᵍ, ᵍ
aē, ōi — ao, āu — āi, āu.

§ 54. The above are real diphthongs when they correspond to the Skt. diphthongs. The relation between the Av. and the Skt. diphthongs is concisely this:

α. Skt. *ē* is represented in Av.
(1) chiefly by *aē*, (2) less often by *ōi*, (3) again by *ē*, only when final, but there regularly.

β. Skt. *ō* is represented in Av.
(1) chiefly by *ao*, (2) more rarely by *āu*, (3) again by *ō*, only when final, but there regularly.

γ. Skt. *āi* and *āu* are represented in Av. by *āi* and *āu*.

Note. In some instances Skt. *āu* (final) seems to be represented in Av. by *ō*, § 42.

Av. *aē* = Skt. *ē*.

§ 55. The diphthong Av. *aē* (very common) answers to Skt. *ē* (old *ai*), initial or internal; likewise as ending in first member of a compound, or again before enclitic *-ca* 'que'

Av. *aētaṯ* 'this' = Skt. *etát:* GAv. *vaēdā*, YAv. *vaēda* 'knows' = Skt. *vḗda*. — Av. *fraēṣyeiti* 'he drives forth' (*fra* + *iš-*) = Skt. *prḗṣyati*. — Av. *dūraēdars* 'far-seeing' (loc. *dū're*) = Skt. *dūrē.dŕ́s-*; Av. *raθaēštā-rəm* 'warrior in chariot' = Skt. *rathēṣṭhā́m* (loc. *ráthē*).

Note 1. Observe that in gen. *aṣaheca* 'and of righteousness', the *e* is reduction-vowel (= *ya*), therefore of course no *aē* appears.

Note 2. On reduction-diphthong *aē*, see § 64.

Av. *ōi* = Skt. *ē*.

§ 56. Av. *ōi*, as real diphthong, also answers to Skt. *ē* (old *ai*). It interchanges often with Av. *aē*, being of like etymological value; but *ōi* occurs perhaps oftenest in monosyllables and in declensional endings generally. It is especially frequent in GAv.

GAv. *vōistā* 'thou knowest' = Skt. *véttha;* YAv. *sōire* 'they lie' = Skt. *śére;* Av. *hṣōiθni* (fem.) 'shining, princely', beside Av. *hṣaētō* (masc.); Av. *maidyōi.paiti-štāna-* 'to middle (loc.) of foot', beside Av. *dūraē.sruta-* 'far (loc.) renowned'. — GYAv. *yōi* 'who' (beside *yaē-ca*) = Skt. *yé;* GYAv. *kōi* 'who' (interrog.) = Skt. *ké*. — YAv. *ažōiš* 'of Dragon' = Skt. *áhēs;* GAv. *būrōiš* 'of richness' = Skt. *bhū́rēs;* GYAv. *barōiṯ* 'he might carry' = Skt. *bháret;* Av. *pairi.vaēnōiθe* 'they two are seen' = Skt. *vḗnēthē*. — GAv. *gavōi* 'for the cow', YAv. *gave* = Skt. *gávē;* GAv. *zastōibyā* 'with both hands' = YAv. *zastaēibya;* GAv. *hṣaθrōi* 'in the kingdom', YAv. *hṣaθre* = Skt. *kṣatré*.

Av. *ao* = Skt. *ō*.

§ 57. Av. *ao* as real diphthong answers to Skt. *ō* (old *au*), initial and internal.

Av. *aojō* 'strength' = Skt. *ójas;* Av. *raodənti* 'they grow' = Skt. *róhanti;* Av. *tāyaoš* 'of a thief' = Skt.

tayós. — Av. *fraoḵtō* 'pronounced' (*fra + uč*) Skt. *prōktás.*

Note. On reduction-diphthong *ao*. see § 64.

Av. ə̄u = Skt. ō.

§ 58. The diphthong Av. ə̄u (as strengthening of *u*), also sometimes answers to Skt. *ō*, internal. It occurs in the genitive of *u*-stems, and in a very few words. Observe the pair ə̄u and *ao* as *ōi* and *ač*.

Av. *hratə̄uš* 'of wisdom' = Skt. *krátōs*; Av. *vaŋhə̄uš* 'of the good' = Skt. *vásōs*; Av. *mainyə̄uš* 'of spirit' = Skt. *manyós.*—Also in *dōuš.sravaḥ* 'things of ill-repute', cf. *haosravaŋha*; *dōuš.manahya-* 'evil-minded', cf. *haomanaŋha-*; GAv. *gə̄ušāiš* 'with ears' = Skt. *ghóṣāis.*

Av. āi = Skt. āi;—Av. āu = Skt. āu.

§ 59. Av. *āi*, *āu* when they are real diphthongs (i. e. not epenthetic or reduction) correspond to Skt. *āi*, *āu*.

Av. *mąþrāiš* 'with words' = Skt. *mántrāis*; Av. *gāuš* (nom.) 'cow' = Skt. *gāús*.

i. Vowel-Strengthening — *a*-Vowel Contraction.

§ 60. **Guṇa and Vṛddhi.** The terms *guṇa* and *vṛddhi* are conveniently borrowed from the Sanskrit Grammar for the Avesta. In Avesta, as in Sanskrit, guṇa- and vṛddhi-vowels in the fullest sense have a double origin: (1) vowel-strengthening in vowel-gradation;[1] (2) contraction of two dissimilar vowels whether in composition or in inflection.

---

[1] Brugmann, *Grundriss der vergl. Gram.* § 307 seq.

Guṇa in Avesta, owing to the greater richness in the vowel system, has a greater variety than in Sanskrit.— The vṛddhi-increment, however, is comparatively rare, and is not so regularly carried out as in Sanskrit; nor are the instances always certain (cf. § 18 Note 1); but vṛddhi is not to be denied to the Avesta.

Synopsis of Guṇa and Vṛddhi modelled after the Sanskrit.

Avesta.

Simple Vowel	a, ā	i, ī	u, ū	ərə
Guṇa	—	aē (ay), ōi (ōy), -ē	ao (av), āu, -ō	arə (ar)
Vṛddhi	ā	āi (āy)	āu (āv)	ārə (ār)

(The forms in parentheses appear before vowels. On the interchange of aē, ōi, see § 56).

Strengthening:
a-vowel.

Vṛddhi: Av. *āhurōiš* 'of the Ahurian' *(ahura-)* cf. Skt. *ásures*; GAv. *vācī*, *avācī* 'is spoken' (aor. pass.) = Skt. *ávāci*; Av. *dāhyumə̄* (var. *dāhyumə̄*) 'belonging to the region' *(dahyu-)*; Av. *hācayene* 'I may cause to follow' (√*hac-*); Av. *tācayeinti* 'they cause to run' (√*tac-*); Av. *rāmayeiti* 'he makes content' = Skt. *rāmáyati*.—Cf. also the patronymics in Yt. 13.97 seq.

Strengthening:
i-vowel.

Guṇa:—Av. *daēsayən* 'they showed' (√*diš-*), *daēdōišt* 'he showed' (intens. √*diš-*); *saēte* 'he lies down', *sōire* 'they lie down' (√*sī-*); *ḫšayehe* 'thou rulest' (√*ḫši-*); *vīdōyūm* 'anti-demoniac' (acc. fr. *vīdaēva-*, fr. √*div-*). —Vṛddhi:—Av. *dāiš* 'thou sawest' (aor. √*di-*); *staomáyō* 'praises' (fr. *staomi-*); *ϑrāyō* 'three' (fr. *ϑri-*, but cf. § 18 Note 1), *nāismī* Ys. 12.1.

Contraction:

Av. *upaēta-* 'approached' *(upa + √i-)*: YAv. *ḫšaϑre*, GAv. *ḫšaϑrōi* 'in the kingdom' *(ḫšaϑra-)*; Av. *upāisayən* 'they might seek' *(upa + √is-)*;—*upōiti* 'he approaches'

Phonology

Strengthening: *u*-vowel.

Guṇa: — Av. *haomǝm* 'haoma' ($\sqrt{hu}$-); *zaotārǝm* title of priest, cf. Skt. Hotar ($\sqrt{zu}$-); *staomi* 'I praise', *stavanō* 'praising' ($\sqrt{stu}$-); *vaŋhave, vaŋhāuš* 'for, of the good' (*vaŋhu*-); *daiŋhavō* 'countries' (*daiŋhu*-): *dōuš.sravā* 'having evil repute' (*duš*).—Vṛddhi:—Av. *srāvayōiš* 'shouldst recite' ($\sqrt{sru}$-); GAv. *srāvī* 'he was heard' ($\sqrt{sru}$-); *vaŋhāu* 'in good' (*vaŋhu*-); *daiŋhāvō* 'countries' (*daiŋhu*-); *ujra.bāzāuš* 'strong-armed' (*bāzu*-); *fraṣāupayeiti* 'he propels' Yt. 8.33.

Contraction:

Av. *fraoḥtō* 'pronounced' (*fra + uḥta-*) = Skt. *pröktás*; so also Av. *vaocaṭ* (redupl. aor.) 'he spoke' = Skt. *vōcat*, cf. Av. *vaokuṣe* = Skt. *ūcuṣe* pf. act. ptcpl. $\sqrt{vakle}$, weak form *ukle*.

Strengthening: *r*-vowel.

From Av. *vǝrǝprajna-* 'victory', *vǝrǝprajni-* 'victorious'; so Av. *karǝnǝm* 'I cut', *karǝtǝm* 'knife' (acc.), *karanǝm* 'limit, dividing line' (acc.), *kārayeiti* 'he cuts'. But see § 47 Note.

Note. (a) The Avesta sometimes has guṇa where the Skt. has a long vowel: Av. *staorǝm* 'bullock' = Skt. *sthūrám*; Av. *gaozaiti* 'he hides' = Skt. *gūhati*.—(b) Conversely, the Av. sometimes has a long vowel where the Skt. shows guṇa: Av. *yūḳtar-* 'yoker' = Skt. *yoktár-*; GAv. *ūrūpayeiṇti* 'they cause pain' = Skt. *rōpáyanti*; GAv. *ūrūdōyatō* 'he made lament' = Skt. *rōdáyati*.—(c) The Av. has sporadically guṇa where the Skt. has vṛddhi: Av. *haomanuvhǝm* 'well-minded' = Skt. *sāumanasām*; Av. *syaoþna-* 'deed' = Skt. *cyáutna-*; Av. *haēnyǝ* 'belonging to the army' = Skt. *sainyás*.—(d) Sporadically, Av. vṛddhi, where Skt. guṇa: Av. *gāvyanǝm* beside *gavya-* 'belonging to the cow' (§ 18) = Skt. *gavyá-*.—(e) Observe Av. *dúš.sravah-* 'ill-famed'; *dúš.manahya-* 'evil-minded' opp. to Skt. *duḥ:qsa*.

ii. Changes in *y*- or *v*-Syllables.

§ 61. **General Remark.** The syllables containing internal *ǝ y* and *ǝ v* often suffer reduction and abbreviation. This is partly old and due to the vowel character of *y* (*i̯*) and *v* (*u̯*); in part it is young and is to be explained from the character of the writing—the close graphic resemblance of ‿ *i* to ‿‿ *y* (*ii*) and ، *u* to ،، *v* (*uu*) often producing awkward accumulations of signs which are avoided.

(a) Vocalization of *y* and *v*.

§ 62. In the combinations original internal *vy*, *vn*, *vr*, *yv*, the first element is generally vocalized to *u*, *i*. When *a* immediately precedes this *u*, the two are contracted according to § 60 into *ao*. For *ao* an *āu* is frequently found in GAv.

(1) Orig. *vy* = Av. *uy;—yv* = Av. *iv*.

Av. *vaṅhuyā̊* 'of the good' (fem.) = Skt. *vásvyās*; GAv. *poᵘruyō* 'first' = Skt. *pūrvyás*; Av. *marṣuyā̊* 'of the belly' (stem *marǰvī-*); Av. *snāuya-* 'made of sinew', cf. Skt. *snā́van-*.—Av. *maⁱnivā̊* 'of the two Spirits' (for *maⁱnyvā̊* § 68, b).

(2) Orig. *avy* = Av. *aoi;—avn* = Av. *aon (āun);— avr* = Av. *aor*.

Av. *haoyą̇m* 'the left' = Skt. *savyā́m*; Av. *gaoyaoⁱ- tīš* 'cow-pastures' = Skt. *gávyūtīs*.—Av. *vaonarᵊ* 'they have won', cf. Skt. *vavné*; Av. *raonąm* 'of valleys' *(ravan-)*; Av. *ašaonō* 'of the righteous' *(ašavan-)*, cf. Skt. *maghónas*.—GAv. *vāunuš* 'having striven', ptcpl. pf. √*van-*; GAv. *ašāunē* 'to the righteous' = Skt. *r̥tā́vnē* (cf. Note 1); Av. *apaᵘrun-* wk. stem of *ā́pravan-* 'priest' = Skt. *átharvan-*.—Av. *fraoⁱrisaⁱti* 'he comes forward' (for orig. *fra-vris-aⁱti*), cf. *fraoᵘrvaēsayeni*; Av. *fraorᵊṇta* 'they confessed', cf. Skt. *ávr̥ṇīta*; Av. *fraorᵊt* (i. e. **pravr̥t*) 'prone, ready'.

Phonology.

Note 1. Often in YAv. *aṣ̌aun-* is found in the formulaic connection *aṣ̌aunąm fravašayō*. The original difference is to be explained thus: *āu* = orig. *āv*, and *ao* = orig. *av*, cf. Av. *aṣ̌āvan* = Skt. *r̥távan-*.

Note 2. In YAv., *paoiryō* is written for GAv. *pouruyō* 'first' above.

Note 3. A like vocalization of Av. *v* = Av. *w* (orig. *bh*) § 87 may take place — e. g. Av. *taipaoryo* (for *tbāewō*, *twyō*, *θbyō*) from plagues; Av *adaoyo* (for *adawyo*) 'undeceived' = Skt. *ádābhyas*; Av. *nuruyō aṣ̌avaovō* (for *twyō*, *twyō*, *θwō*) 'to righteous men' Yt. 10.55. Av *rasmaovō* (for *twyō*, *twyō*, *θbyō*) 'to the ranks'. Perhaps Av. *aoi*, beside *avi* (for Av. *aiwi*) = Skt. *abhi*.

(b) Reduction and Abbreviation.

a. Reductions.

§ 63. The syllables *ya* and *va* before *m* or *n*, especially when final, are generally reduced to *i (ī)*, or *u (ū)* respectively — a kind of samprasāraṇa.

Old *ya* = Av. *i (ī); va* = Av. *u (ū)* — before *m, n*.

Av. *zaranim* 'golden' (acc.) = Skt. *híraṇ-ya-m;* Av. *uẋšin* 'they increased' (for **uẋš-ya-n*), Av. *mainimna* 'thinking' (fem.) = Skt. *mán-ya-mānā;* Av. *paiβimnō* 'possessing' = Skt. *pát-ya-mānas;* Av. *iriθinti* 'they die' (for *irih-ya-ṇti*). — GAv. *asrūždūm* 'ye were heard of' Ys. 32.3 = Skt. *áśrodh-va-m;* Av. *daēum* 'demon' = Skt. *dē-vá-m;* Av. *þrišum* 'third' (for *þriš-va-m);* Av. *mōurum* 'Merv' (for **mar-va-m); —* Av. *təmavhuṇtəm* 'dark' = Skt. *támas-vant-;* Av. *harənavhuṇtəm* 'glorious' beside *harənamhaṇtə* for *harənavh-va-ṇtəm*.

Note 1. In the acc. sg. of *-va*-stems, *ūm* instead of *ǔm* is mostly written.

Note 2. Av. *-ava-* commonly becomes *-ava-* before *m* (cf. §§ 60, 52 a): Av. *vidōyūm* 'anti-demoniac' acc. to *vīdaēva-* (but also Av. *daēum*); Av. *harō-yūm* 'Haraeva', cf. Anc. Pers. *haraiva-;* Av. *hayūm* 'seaevum', if stem *haēva-*.

Note 3. Instead of *i* (= *ya*), an *ə* appears in Av. *madəma-* 'midmost' = Skt. *madh-ya-má-*.

§ 64. On the same principle as § 63, the syllables *aya* and *ava*, reduced before *m* or *n*, give rise to diphthongs, *aē* and *ao* (*āu* §§ 62, 195).

Old *aya* = Av. *aē*; *ava* = Av. *ao* (also *āu* § 195)—
before *m*, *n*.

Av. *aēm* 'this' (nom.) = Skt. *ayám*; Av. *vīdāraēm*
'I upheld' = Skt. *-dhārayam*; Av. *cikaēn* 'they atoned'
(i. e. *cikayan) cf. Av. *cikayat*.—Av. *yaom* 'grain' =
Skt. *yávam*; Av. *mainyaom* 'spiritual', acc. to *mai-
nyava-*; Av. *mraom* 'I spake' = Skt. *ábravam* —Av.
nāumō also *naomō* 'ninth' = Skt. *navamás*; Av. *kər*-
nāun (var. *kərənaon*) 'they made' = Skt. *kŗņávan*; Av.
bāun also *baon* 'they were' = Skt. *ábhavan*.

Note. Similarly, Av. *raōi-ca* Ys. 68.11 cf. instr. *raya* 'splendor'

§ 65. The syllables internal *āya*, *āva* likewise reduced
§ 64, give rise to the diphthongs *āi*, *āu*.

Orig. *āya*, *āva* = Av. *āi*, *āu*—before *m*, *n*.

Av. *dasa.gāim* 'space of ten steps' = Skt. °*gāyam*;
Av. *avāin* 'they came down' = Skt. *avāyan*; Av. *nasāum*
'corpse' (i. e. *nasāvam*).

Note. Metrically the reduced syllables *aəm*, *aom*, *āum*, *aən*, *āin*
(§§ 63, 64) are dissyllabic.

§ 66. Final *aye* is reduced to Av. *ǯe*,—metrically
dissyllabic.

Av. *apaigatǯe* 'for going away' = Skt. *gátayē*;
Av. *paitištātǯe* (beside *paitištātayaē-ca*) 'to withstand'
= Skt. *sthítayē*; Av. *ārmatǯe* 'to Piety'; Av. *zaņtu.patǯe*
'for the lord of a town'.

§ 67. Final *ya* in polysyllables appears in YAv. as *e*
(GAv. shows *yā*).

YAv. *kahe* 'of which' (GAv. *kahyā*) = Skt. *kásya*;
YAv. *gayehe* 'of life' (GAv. *gayehyā*) = Skt. *gáyasya*;
YAv. *ašahe* 'of Righteousness' (GAv. *ašahyā*) = Skt.
ŗtásya; YAv. *aire* (for *airya*, nom. pl.) 'the Aryans';
YAv. *fraņrase* (for °*sya*, nom. sg.) 'Franrasyan' cf.
acc. °*syānəm*; YAv. *maire* (for °*rya*, nom. sg. fem.)

'deadly', cf. gen. *mairyayā̊*; YAv. *bāzuve* 'with both arms' (§ 85 a, end), beside YAv. *bāzubya*.

Note. Isolated is internal *e (= ya)* in *vahehiš* 'better' (fem. pl.) cf. § 137 = Skt. *vásyasis*.

β. Abbreviated Writing.

Av. „ *y* (*i*) = *iy*; „ *v* (*u*) = *uv*.

§ 68. To avoid awkward combinations of letters, the original syllables *iy* (graphically Av. „„ *iii*) and *uv* (graph. Av. „„ *uuu*) are respectively abbreviated in writing „ *y* (graph. *ii*) and „ *v* (graph. *uu*). See § 61. Metrically, to such *y* or *v* the syllabic value *iy* or *uv* is generally to be restored.

(a) Av. „ for „„.

(1) In composition:—Av. *paityantu* 'let them come to' = Skt. *prátiyantu*; Av. *pryaḥštīš* 'three twigs' (for *pri-yaḥštīš*) cf. *panca-yaḥštīš*.—(2) Internal:—Av. *fryō* 'friend' (graphically *friiō* for *friiiō*) = Skt. *priyás*; Av. *yasnyō* 'worshipful' = Skt. *yajñyas*.—(3) Initial: —Av. *yeyąn* (written *iieiiąn* for orig. *iyáyān); GAv. *yadacā* 'and here' Ys. 35.2 (written *iiadā* for Av. *iiiadā*).

(b) Av. „ for „„.

(1) In composition:—Av. *hvacaṇham* 'having good words' = Skt. *svádcasam*; Av. *hvidātā̊* 'well-built (houses)' Yt. 17.8 (i. e. *hu-vidāta-* cf. Ys. 57.21); Av. *vohvarə̄z-* 'doing good' (i. e. *vohu + v*).—(2) Internal: —Av. *yvānəm* 'juvenem' = Skt. *yúvānam*; Av. *drvahe* 'firm' (gen.) = Skt. *dhruvásya*;—Av. *hva-* 'suus' (metrically *huva-*) cf. Skt. *svá-*. See Geldner, *Metrik*, p. 20 seq.

Note 1. Similarly when *v* (*v*) stands for *w* (= *bh*) § 87: Av. ᙕᙕ *uuacibya* for *uuuacibya* for *uwacibya* cf. GAv. *ubōibyā* 'with both' = Skt. *ubhābhyām*.

Note 2. Instances of Av. *v* (*v*) equal Skt. *iv, iv* may be found: Av. *jvanti* 'they live' = Skt. *jīvanti*; Av. *cvat* 'quantum' = Skt. *kívat*; Av. *vīdidvå̄* 'looking around' ($\sqrt{di}$) = Skt. *dīdivān;* perhaps Av. *jaɣnvā̊* 'having smitten' cf. Skt. *jaghnivān.*

Note 3. Internal *ay, av* are sometimes found written as an extension of *y, v* (i. e. *iy, uv*): Av. *nāvaya-* 'navigable, flowing' = Skt. *nāvyà;* Av. *aspaya-* (cf. acc. *aspaēm* § 64) 'belonging to a horse' = Skt. *áśvya-;* Av. *hava-* (cf. gen. f. *hᵃoyā̊*) 'suus' = Skt. *svá-;* Av. *kava* variant for *kva* 'where' = Skt. *kvà.*

iii. Epenthesis, Prothesis, and Anaptyxis.

Cf. Brugmann, *Grundriss der vergl. Grammatik* § 637 seq.; § 623 seq.

§ 69. Two of these viz. Epenthesis, Prothesis (and certain cases of Anaptyxis like *sᵘrunvata*)—may be considered fundamentally the same, as each consists in the introduction of an anticipatory parasitic sound. For convenience, however, in the following, Epenthesis and Prothesis will be distinguished thus: (1) Epenthesis—an anticipatory vowel attached internally to a vowel; (2) Prothesis—an anticipatory vowel attached initially before a consonant.

§ 70. **Epenthesis** is one of the characteristic sound-phenomena of the Avesta. It consists in the insertion of a light anticipatory *i* or *u*, when in the following syllable respectively an *i, ī, e, ē, y,* or an *u, v* stands.—Epenthesis of *i* takes place before *r, n, ṇt, t, þ, þr, d̃, p, b, w,* also before *ŋh* (= orig. *sy*).—Epenthesis of *u* takes place only before *r*.

Note. The epenthetic vowel attaches itself parasitically to diphthongs as well as to the simple vowels including *a*-privative. In the MSS., the law of epenthesis is not always consistently carried out; many times it is omitted: e. g. *manyōuš* beside *maⁱnyōuš* 'of the Spirit'.

Epenthetic *i*.

Av. *bavaⁱti* 'he becomes' = Skt. *bhávati;* Av. *aēⁱti* (GAv. *aēⁱtī*) 'he goes' = Skt. *éti;* Av. *inaoⁱti* 'he forces, drives' = Skt. *inóti;* Av. *aⁱpi* 'unto, in' = Skt. *ápi;* Av. *baraⁱṇti* 'they carry' = Skt. *bháranti;* Av. *aⁱnikəm* 'face' = Skt. *ánīkam;* Av. *būⁱri* 'fullness' = Skt. *bhūri;* Av. *aⁱrištəm* 'unhurt' = Skt. *áriṣṭam.*—GAv.

‚āiti 'with offering' = Skt. *ráti* GAv. *aibi* (YAv. *aiwi*) 'unto, to' = Skt. *abhi*; YAv. *maiδīm* 'middle' (acc. sg.) = Skt. *mádhyam*;-- Av. *bairyeṇte* 'they are brought' = Skt. *bhrīyántē*; Av. *nirōiryeite* 'is confined' (√*var*-); Av. *niurudyāt̰* 'should flow' (√*rud*-). — Av. *airyō* 'Aryan' = Skt. *aryás*; Av. *nairyqm* 'manly' (acc. fem.) = Skt. *náryām*; Av. *mainyuš* 'Spirit' = Skt. *manyús*.— With vanishing of the *y* which caused the epenthesis, *aiŋhå* gen. sg. fem. of *aēm* 'this' = Skt. *asyás*.

Epenthetic *u*.

Av. *aurvaṇtō* 'swift steeds' = Skt. *árvantas*; Av. *auruna*- 'wild, fiery', cf. Skt. *aruṇa*-: Av. *auruṣō* 'bright, white' = Skt. *aruṣas*; Av. *paurvata* 'two mountains' = Skt. *parvatau*; Av. *taurunəm* 'young' = Skt. *táruṇam*; Av. *haurvəm* 'whole' = Skt. *sárvam*; Av. *pouru*- (also *paouru*-) 'many', for *paru*-.

Note 1. Epenthetic *i* is even attached to the anaptyctic vowel (§ 72): Av. *həm.varətim* 'courage' Vsp. 7.3; GAv. *mərəṇgəidyāi* 'to destroy' Y. 46.11; *fraorəitim* 'confession' Ys. 13.8.

Note 2. Epenthetic *u* is found also before *v* for *w* (§ 87): *gəurvayeite* 'he seizes' (√*garw*- = Skt. √*grabh*-)

§ 71. **Prothesis.** As intermediate between Epenthesis and Anaptyxis, we may distinguish Prothesis, which consists in the similar introduction of an anticipatory *i* or *u* initially before a consonant. It takes place regularly before *r* followed by *i* or *u* (*v*). An instance is found also before *p*.

Av. *irinaḣti* 'he lets go, drives' = Skt. *riṇákti*; Av. *irišyeiti* 'is hurt' = Skt. *risyati*; GAv. *urūpayeiṇtī* 'they cause pain' = Skt. *rōpáyanti*; Av. *urune* 'for the soul', *urvan*- 'soul' (i. e. for *ruvan* § 68 = Mod. Pers. *ruvān*).—Before *p*, Av. *ipyejō* 'destruction' = Skt. *tyájas*.

§ 72. **Anaptyxis.** An irrational vowel (Anaptyxis), which does not count in the metre, is often developed in Avesta between two consonants, especially if one be r, and regularly after final r. The anaptyctic vowel is generally ǝ (ə), more rarely a, i or ö. In GAv., anaptyxis is still more common than in YAv.

Av. vahᵊdra- 'word' = Skt. vaktrá-; Av. nafᵊdraṯ 'offspring' (abl. from naptar-); Av. zᵊmō 'of earth'; GAv. dadᵊmahī 'we give' = Skt. dadmási; Av. garᵊmō 'hot' = Skt. gharmás; GAv. fᵊrā 'forth', YAv. frā § 24 = Skt. prá; GAv. aēṣᵊmō 'fury' = YAv. aēṣmō; GAv. rachᵊnanhō 'of share' = Skt. réknasas.—GAv. dᵊbāvayaṯ 'he deceived'.—YAv. aṇtarᵊ 'within', GAv. aṇtarᵊ = Skt. antár; YAv. hvarᵊ 'sun', GAv. hvarᵊ = Skt. svàr.—GAv. šyaopᵊna- 'deed', YAv. šyaoṯna- = Skt. cyáutná-; GAv. marᵊka- 'death', YAv. mahrka- = Skt. marká-.—GAv. yezᵢvī 'young' = Skt. yahvī; YAv. nisᵢrinaoiti 'he delivers over'.—YAv. māvᵊya 'to me' = GAv. maibyā; YAv. hāvᵊya- 'left' = Skt. savyà-; GAv. dužazᵊbō 'maledictus'. —YAv. sᵘrunvata (instr.) 'worthy of being heard'.

Note. Anaptyxis occurs sometimes between the members of a compound: e. g. GAv. dušᵊḳšaṯra- 'evil-ruling'; GAv. hᵊmᵊfraštā 'he questioned with'; YAv. usᵊhišṯaṯ 'he stood up'.—More rarely in the few instances of sandhi: YAv. haṯpaipyaōsᵊ tanvō 'of his own body'; YAv. yasᵊ tē 'who to thee'.

SYSTEM OF CONSONANTS.

§ 73. **General Remark.** Viewing the Av. and the Skt. system of consonants side by side, it may be noted: (1) The Av. palatal series is incomplete — the Av. possesses only c and j. (2) The Skt. cerebral series is entirely wanting in the Avesta. (3) The Av. has no aspirates, their place being in part taken by the corresponding spirants. (4) The nasals are only in part identical. (5) The

Av. is richer than the Skt. in sibilants, especially through the presence of the sonant sibilants z and $ž$.

§ 74. Surd and Sonant (Voiceless and Voiced). For the distinction between **surd** and **sonant** (voiceless and voiced), we may refer to the Sanskrit. The law, moreover, that in internal combination, **surd** (voiceless) consonants stand before **surd** consonants, and **sonant** (voiced) before sonants, has in general the same extent as in Sanskrit.[1] Observe that n and in part m are at times treated as surd.[2]

§ 75. Sandhi between words (§ 4) is wanting in Avesta, except in case of some enclitics and compounds.

Tenues — Surd Spirants.

Av. ?, ?, ? and ? — ?, ?, ? — ?.
k, t, p and c — h, p, f — $ſ$.

Av. k, t, p and c.

§ 76. The Av. tenues k, t, p and c agree mostly with the corresponding tenues in the Sanskrit.

Av. *katārō* 'which of two' = Skt. *kataras*; Av. *tāpayeiti* 'makes hot' = Skt. *tāpáyati*; Av. *patanti* 'they fly' = Skt. *pátanti*.—Av. *caraiti* 'he moves' = Skt. *cárati*; Av. *cakana* 'has been pleased' = Skt. *cākana*.

Note. In the distinction between guttural and palatal k/c, the Av. and the Skt. do not always agree: Av. *paskāt* 'from behind, behind' = Skt. *paścāt*, cf. Av. *pascu*; Av. *cicihwā* 'through the wise one' = Skt. *cikitvā*; Av. *frajo.corətar-* 'converter' = Skt. *°kartar-*, cf. Av. *frajo.kərəti-*; Av. *vaokuše* dat. sg. pf. ptcpl. √*vak/c* = Skt. *ūcuṣē*.

Av. h, p, f.

§ 77. The surd spirants h, p, f in Av. are of two-fold origin:—(1) they are the representatives

---
[1] Cf. Whitney, *Sanskrit Grammar*, § 156 seq.; Stenzler, *Elementarbuch der Sanskritsprache*, § 44 seq.
[2] See Sievers, *Grundzüge der Phonetik*, pp. 114, 133.

Tenues—Surd Spirants.   29

of the old surd aspirates *kh, th, ph;* or (2) they have arisen from the tenues *k, t, p* regularly changed before most consonants in Av. to corresponding *ẖ, ṗ, f*. Observe that *f* has in general the treatment of a spirant § 81.

(1) Av. *ẖ, ṗ, f* = Skt. *kh, th, ph*.

Av. *ẖā̊* 'fountains' = Skt. *khā́s*; Av. *ẖarəm* 'ass' = Skt. *kháram*; Av. *haẖa* 'friend' = Skt. *sákhā*.— Av. *haptapəm* 'seventh' = Skt. *saptátham*; Av. *gāpā̊* 'hymns' = Skt. *gā́thās*; Av. *arəpa-* 'part, portion' = Skt. *ártha-*.—Av. *safanhō* 'hoofs' = Skt. *śaphā́sas*; Av. *kafəm* 'foam, slime' = Skt. *kapham*.

(2) Av. *ẖ, ṗ, f* = Skt. *k, t, p*.

Av. *ẖratuš* 'wisdom' = Skt. *krátus*; Av. *irinaẖti* 'he lets go, drives' = Skt. *riṇákti*; Av. *taoẖma* 'seed' = Skt. *tókma*; Av. *ẖšapram* 'rule, kingdom' = Skt. *kṣatrám*.—YAv. *šyaoṗnāiš*, GAv. *šyaoṗənāiš* 'by deeds' = Skt. *cyā́utnāis*; Av. *haiṗyō* 'true' = Skt. *satyás*.—Av. *drafšō* 'spear, banner' = Skt. *drapsás*; Av. *ẖafnəm* 'sleep' = Skt. *svápnam*; YAv. *frā*, GAv. *fərā* 'forth, before' = Skt. *prá*; Av. *fraviɉtō* 'pronounced' = Skt. *próktás*.

Note 1. In Av., we sometimes find *ẖ* prefixed to *š*, initial or internal, apparently without etymological value: e. g. *ā-ẖšnuš* 'up to knee', cf. Skt. *abhi-jñu*. See Bartholomae, *A.F.* iii. 19 seq., and § 188 below.

Note 2. In Av., *ṗ* sometimes takes the place of *s* (Skt. *s*): e. g. Av. *ṗamnōuhvaṇt-* 'healing' from √*ṗam-* = Skt. √*sam-* 'to heal', cf. also Av. *sāma-*; Av. *aiwiṗyō* 'over-sleeping' (nom. pl.) with √*si-* = Skt. √*si-* 'lie, sleep'; Av. *aiwiṗārō* 'very mighty', beside Av. *sūrō* 'mighty' = Skt. *śúras*; Av. *anaṗaẖtąm* (fem.) 'whose time of delivery is not come', beside *frasaẖtahe* (masc.) 'whose time is come, dead' √*sac-*.

Note 3. Original *th* (Iranian *þ*) becomes *d* after *ẖ* and *f*: e. g. GYAv. *uẖda-* 'spoken, word' = Skt. *ukthá-*; Av. *frafəda-* 'satisfied' = Indo-Iran. **tramptha-*; Av. *anaiwi.druẖdō* 'not to be deceived' Yt. 10.5. See Bartholomae, *K.Z.* xxix. 483, 502 = *Flexionslehre* pp. 63, 82.

Note 4. On Av. *f* apparently for earlier *pr*, see § 95.

§ 78. (a) Exception. The change of *k, t, p*, to *χ, þ, f*, before consonants § 77, does not take place when a sibilant or a written nasal (not *ą*) immediately precedes; nor under these circumstances, are *χ, þ, f*, as answering to older aspirate § 77, allowed. In all such cases, simple *k, t, p* are employed.

Av. *uštrəm* 'camel' (-*štr*-) as opposed to *kəhrpa* 'where' (-*þr*-) = Skt. *úṣṭram, kṛ́tra*; Av. *xrafstrāiš* 'with noxious creatures'; Av. *pištrəm* 'bruising, wound'; Av. *zaṇtvō* 'in this (*ahmi*) tribe' (-*ṇtv*- § 94) as opposed to *haozaϑwa* (-*aþwa*-).—Av. *staorəm* 'bullock' = Skt. *sthūrám* (-*th*-); Av. *sparat* 'he darted' = Skt. *ásphurat*, § 48; Av. *skarayaṇt*- 'springing, turning' (in nom. propr.) cf. Skt. *skhalayati*; perhaps Av. *skarəna*- 'turning, active' = Skt. *skhalana*-.—Av. *paṇtānəm* 'path' (beside Av. *paþō* acc. pl.) = Skt. *pánthānam, patháś*.

§ 79. (b) Exception. (1) Similarly *pt* remains unchanged; but (2) not original *ptr* which becomes (with assimilation) *fədr* as original *ktr* becomes *xdr*, in both GAv. and YAv.

(1) Av. *hapta* 'ἑπτά' = Skt. *saptá*; Av. *supti*- 'shoulder' = Skt. *súpti*-.—But (2) Av. *nafədrō apąm* 'of offspring of waters', cf. Skt. *náptrē*; Av. *rafədrəm* 'aid' cf. Av. *rap-aṇtəm, rap-akō*; Av. *apaxdre* 'in north', beside *apāxtara*-; Av. *yaoxdra*- 'girdle' = Skt. *yōktra*-.

Note. Some further exceptions occur: Av. *dāiϑya*- 'lawful', *priṭya*- 'third', *biṭya*- 'second', see § 92 Note 1. Observe especially *ātrəm* 'fire', and *trəfyāṯ* 'may steal' for *tarəfyāṯ, tərəfyāṯ* see variants - an abbreviated writing.

§ 80. On *þw* for original *tv* see § 94.

Av. ẓ *f*.

§ 81. There can be little doubt that Av. *f* has in general a spirant value. It seems to occupy a position intermediate between *t, d* and *þ, đ.* It is both surd and sonant (voiceless and voiced); to find a distinction palaeographically when it appears as surd or as sonant is not warranted by the MSS. It occurs chiefly as final for *t,* except when *s* or *š* precede; in that case *t* appears § 192. As initial, surd and sonant, it is found in a few words, *t̰kaēšəm* 'faith, faithful'; *t̰baēšō* 'hatred, harm' = Skt. *dvêṣas.* cf. § 96. As internal it occurs in a few words, compound or in the MSS. treated as compound, and therefore handled as if it were final.

> Av. *ašāt̰* 'from Right' = Skt. *ṛtā́t;* Av. *bavat̰* 'he became' = Skt. *ábhavat;* Av. *yavat̰* 'how much' = Skt. *yā́vat;* Av. *hakərᵊt̰* 'once' = Skt. *sakṛ́t.*—GAv. *haēcat̰.aspa-* nom. propr.; YAv. *aᵘrvat̰.aspa-* 'swift-horsed'; Av. *brvat̰byąm* 'both brows'; Av. *°tat̰kušiš* 'running' (MSS. *°tat̰ kušiš*); Av. *at̰ca* 'atque'.—GYAv. *t̰kaēšəm* 'faith, faithful'; YAv. *t̰baēšō* 'hatred, harm', cf. GAv. *dvaēšaŋhā* = Skt. *dvéṣas.*

Note 1. Sometimes, *t̰* appears as variant of *d* before *k:* e. g. *adkəm* 'robe' (variant *at̰kəm*) = Skt. *átkam.*

Note 2. In *tat̰.āpəm* 'with running water' (adj.), Yt. 13.43, *t̰* stands for final *c,* cf. Av. *taci aᵢpya* 'in running water' (loc.), Vd. 6.26.

Mediae — Sonant Spirants.

Av. 𐬔, 𐬛, 𐬠 and 𐬘 — 𐬖, 𐬜, 𐬡.
g, d, b and *j* — *γ, δ, w.*

§ 82. The mediae *g, d, b,* in Av. have a two-fold value:—(1) they represent old mediae, agreeing with the Skt. *g, d, b;* or (2) they are the representatives of the old sonant aspirates, *gh, dh, bh;* that is to say, originally in Av. the sonant aspirates lost their aspiration and fell together with the mediae. In GAv., the mediae thus arising are regularly preserved unchanged throughout. But see § 82 (a).

The following scheme shows the standpoint of the Gāthās in comparison with the Sanskrit.

```
Skt. . . . . . . . . . g gh      d dh     b bh
                       \/        \/       \/
Original- and GAv.      g         d        b
```

(1) GAv. (old) *g, d, b* = Skt. *g, d, b.*
GAv. *ugrəng* 'mighty' (acc. pl.) = Skt. *ugrấn*;— GAv. *yadā* 'when' = Skt. *yadā*; GAv. *vīdvā̊* 'knowing' = Skt. *vidvấn.*

(2) GAv. *g, d, b* = Skt. *gh, dh, bh.*
GAv. *darəgəm* 'long' = Skt. *dīrghấm*;—GAv. *adā* 'then' = Skt. *ádha*; GAv. *advānəm* 'way' = Skt. *ádhvānam*;—GAv. *ubōibyā* 'both', cf. Skt. *ubhấbhyām*; GAv. *aibī* 'unto' = Skt. *abhí.*

§ 82 a. Observe in connection with this rule § 82 that the sonant spirants appear before *ž*: cf. § 180. GAv. *aojžā* 'thou spakest'; *diwžaidyāi.*—See § 89 Bartholomae's Law.

Note. On the sonant spirants—in GAv. *rujədru-* aid'; *uhla-* 'spoken, word'—arising from old tenues or aspirate tenues, cf § 77 Note 3.

§ 83. (1) In YAv. these mediae *g, d, b* —of double origin § 82—are preserved unchanged when initial; or again when internal, if immediately preceded by a nasal consonant or by a sibilant. (2) Under all other circumstances in YAv. these mediae—whether representing old mediae or old sonant aspirates—are regularly changed to the corresponding sonant spirant (*j, d, w*). Exceptions to the rule are not many. The secondary relation of GAv. to YAv. may thus be tabulated (cf. § 82):

```
GAv.      g          d          b
         /\         /\         /\
YAv.    g  j       d  d       b  w
```

(1) YAv. *g, d, b* (GAv. *g, d, b*) = Skt. *g, d, b*.

YAv. *gąm* 'cow' (GAv. *gąm*) = Skt. *gā́m*; YAv. *grīvā-* 'neck' = Skt. *grīvā́-*; YAv. *aŋguštaēibya* 'toes of both feet', cf. Skt. *aṅguṣṭhā́bhyām*.—YAv. *dūrāṯ* 'from afar' (GAv. *dūrāṯ*) = Skt. *dūrā́t*; YAv. *viṇdāiti* 'may find, receive' = Skt. *vindáti*; YAv. *hazdyāṯ* 'might sit' opt. pf. = Skt. *sasadyāt, sédyāt*.—YAv. *barəzište* 'on the highest' (cf. GAv. *barəzištəm*) = Skt. *bárhiṣṭhē*.

(2) YAv. *g, d, b* (GAv. *g, d, b*) = Skt. *gh, dh, bh*.

YAv. *gaošəm* 'ear' (cf. GAv. *gə̄ušāiš*)=Skt. *ghóṣam*; YAv. *saŋgəm* 'foot' = Skt. *jáṅghām*.—YAv. *dārayaṯ* 'he held fast' (GAv. *dārayaṯ*) = Skt. *dhāráyat*; YAv. *drvahe* 'firm' (gen.) = Skt. *dhruvásya*; YAv. *baṇdəm* 'bond, sickness' = Skt. *baṇdhám*; YAv. *dazdi* 'give thou' = Skt. *daddhi*.—YAv. *būmīm* 'earth' (GAv. *būmīm*) = Skt. *bhū́mim*; YAv *brāta* 'brother' (GAv. *b^arāta*) = Skt. *bhrā́tā*; YAv. *zəmbayadwəm* 'crush ye' = Skt. *jambháyadhvam*.

(3) YAv. *j, d, w* (GAv. *g, d, b*) = Skt. *g, d, b*.

YAv. *ujrəm* 'mighty' (GAv. *ugra-*) = Skt. *ugrám*; YAv. *bajəm* 'portion, lot' (GAv. *baga-*) = Skt. *bhágam*; YAv. *mərəjō* 'bird' = Skt. *mr̥gás*.—YAv. *vīdvā̊* 'knowing' (GAv. *vīdvā̊*) = Skt. *vidvā́n*; YAv. *paidyavuha* 'set foot' = Skt. *pádyasva*.

(4) YAv. *j, d, w* (GAv. *g, d, b*) = Skt. *gh, dh, bh*.

YAv. *darəjəm* 'long' (GAv. *darəgəm*)=Skt. *dīrghám*; YAv. *maējəm* 'cloud' = Skt. *meghám*; YAv. *jajnvā̊* 'having smitten' = Skt. *jaghnivā́n*.—YAv. *ada* 'then' (GAv. *adā*) = Skt. *ádha*; YAv. *adwanəm* 'way' (GAv. *advānəm*) = Skt. *ádhvānam*; YAv. *arədəm* 'side, half' = Skt. *árdham*.—YAv. *aiwi* 'unto' (GAv. *aibī*) = Skt. *abhí*; YAv. *garəwəm* 'foetus' = Skt. *gárbham*; YAv. *awrəm* 'cloud' = Skt. *abhrám*.

§ 84. Exception 1. Initial *j*, not *g*, is found before *ū* YAv. *jnū̆*, *jnā* 'women' (GAv. *ɣnā*) = Skt. *gnās*; YAv. *jnaṇm* 'to smite' inf. to √*jan-* = Skt. √*han-*.

§ 85. Exception 2. Exceptions to the law for internal change are also found.

(a) Commonly in the endings -*biš*, °*byō*, °*bya*:
YAv. *tanūbyō* 'to bodies' = Skt. *tanūbhyas*; YAv. *āfrivanāebiš* 'with blessings', cf. Skt. *samānē-bhis*, etc. But YAv. *aⁱwyas-ca* 'and with these' (fem. abl.) beside *ābyō* Yt. 10.82 = Skt. *ābhyás*; YAv. *bāzuwe* 'with both arms' § 67 cf. Skt. *bāhúbhyām*; YAv. *hinūⁱwyō* 'from fetters' Yt. 13.100 beside YAv. *gātubyō*.

(b) The combination internal *dr* remains generally unchanged:
YAv. *ḣ∫udrāṭ* 'from seed' = Skt. *kṣudrāt*; YAv. *udrəm* 'otter' = Skt. *udrám*; GYAv. *arədra-* 'pious'; GYAv. *sāira-* 'misfortune'; YAv. *dadrāna-* 'being held' √*dar-* = Skt. √*dhar-*.

(c) In some other instances internal *d* remains in YAv. unchanged:
YAv. *vadarə* 'weapon', GAv. *vadarə* = Skt. *vádhar*; YAv. *yazamaide* 'we worship' = Skt. *yájāmahē*, etc.; YAv. *varədapəm* 'growth', beside *varədaya* 'make thou grow' = Skt. *vardháya*.

§ 86. Instead of internal *d* in YAv., *þ* is sometimes written; especially before *u*, *w*.

YAv. *viþuṣi*, *viþuṣīm* 'having knowledge' = Skt. *vidúṣī*, *vidúṣīm*, GAv. *viduṣē*; YAv. *caraþwe* 'ye go' Yt. 13.34 = Skt. *cáradhvē*; YAv. *daþuṣō* 'of creator' = GAv. *daduṣō*; YAv. *arəþwa-* 'uplifted' as variant to *arədwa-*. So YAv. *daþaⁱti* 'he gives' = Skt. *dádati* RV. 2.35.10; YAv. *agaþaⁱti* 'vanishes' beside YAv. *agadaⁱti*; GAv. *vaēþā* Ys. 5.6 'he knows', beside GAv. *vaēdā* = Skt. *vḗda*.

§ 87. Instead of internal YAv. *w*, we sometimes find YAv. *v* written.

YAv. *avarōiṭ* 'should bring out' = Skt. *a-bharēt*; YAv. *ḣṣmāvəya* 'to you', beside GAv. *ḣṣmaⁱbya*. YAv. *yuṣmaoyō* = Skt. *yuṣmábhyam*; YAv. *mavəya* 'to me', GAv. *maⁱbyā*; YAv. *gəurvayeⁱte* 'he seizes' (for *gər-ə-wayeⁱti* § 70 Note 2) = Skt. *gṛbháyati*; YAv. *vaeⁱbya* 'with both' (for *uvačibya* § 68 for *uvaëibya*), cf. Skt. *ubhābhyām*, GAv. *ubōibya;* YAv. *frabavara* 'he brought forth' = Skt. *babhāra*. Perhaps YAv. $a^iṷi > avi > aoi$ 'unto' = Skt. *abhi*.

Note. On Av. *ṗw* for *tv*, *dw* for *dhv*, etc., see §§ 94, 96.

Av. ž, j.

§ 88. From the fact that the original sonant aspirates fell together with the mediae in Avesta, § 82, and also from the two-fold nature of Skt. *j* and *h*—see Brugmann, *Grundriss der vergl. Gram.* §§ 452, 480, 451,—is to be explained the following relation between the Avesta and the Sanskrit.

$$\text{Av. } j < \genfrac{}{}{0pt}{}{\text{Skt.}\ j}{h} > \text{Av. } z$$
$$\phantom{\text{Av. } j < \genfrac{}{}{0pt}{}{}{\text{Skt.}}}$$

(1) Av. *j* = Skt. *j*.

YAv. *jvaṇtəm*, GAv. *jvaṇtō* 'living' = Skt. *jīvantam*, etc. (§ 68 Note 2); YAv. *jaǰnvā̊* 'having smitten' = Skt. *jaghnivān;*—YAv. *jyā̊* 'bowstrings' = Skt. *jyā́s;* GAv. *jyātəuš* 'of life', cf. Skt. *jīvā́tōs;* also GYAv. *aojištō* 'strongest' = Skt. *ójiṣṭhas;* GYAv. *iþyejō* 'destruction' = Skt. *tyájas*.

(2) Av. *j* = Skt. *h*.

YAv. *jaṇtārəm* 'smiter' = Skt. *hantāram;* YAv. *jaiṇti* 'he smites' = Skt. *hánti;* YAv. *arəjaiti* 'is worth' = Skt. *árhati;* GYAv. *drujəm* 'Deceit, Fiend' = Skt. *drúham*.

Note 1. According to § 83, the media *j* when initial should in YAv. pass over into its corresponding sonant spirant, this spirant has in our alphabet fallen together with the sonant sibilant *ž*. Hence the relation §§ 177, 178 below YAv. *ž* = Skt. *j;*—YAv. *ž* = Skt. *h*.

Note 2. Owing to the etymological relation *gh*, we sometimes find Av. *j* = Skt. *g;*— e. g. GYAv. *haṇjumana-* 'assembly' = Skt. *saṃgámana-;*

GYAv. *jasōit* 'he might come' = Skt. *gáchēt*; Av. √*jad-* 'to beseech', cf. Skt. √*gad-*.

Note 3. Av. *j* also sometimes answers to Skt. *gh*:— e. g. Av. *drāj-iṣṭəm* 'longest' = Skt. *drāghiṣṭham*; Av. *drājō* 'length, duration', cf. Skt. *drāghvān-*.

Bartholomae's Law.

See Bartholomae, *A. F.* i. p. 3 seq.; *A. F.* iii. p. 22 Note.

§ 89. The combination, original aspirate mediae + *t* or + *s*, had already in the Indo-Iranian period become media + *dh* or + *zh*; the consonant group thus arising is then treated according to the special laws of the language, Indic or Iranic. In GAv. the law is carried through without exception (but see § 82 a, and Note). In YAv., however, the law shows a number of exceptions § 90.— Examples of the law from GAv. are:

GAv. *aogədā* 'he spake' to √*augh* + ending *ta*, cf. Gk. εὔχομαι, Skt. *ūhatē*; GAv. *cagədō* 'they two grant' to √*kaugh* + -*tas*. — GYAv. *varədа-* 'grown great, mighty', to √*vardh* + -*ta-*, cf. Skt. *vṛddhá-*; GAv. *dazdē* 'he makes', to √*dhā-*, pres. stem *dadh* + -*tē*; GYAv. *mazdāh-*, nom. *mazdā̊* 'wisdom, Mazda', to orig. √*mandh* + -*tas-* = Skt. -*medhás-*.— GAv. *gərədā* 'he complained', to √*gargh* + -*ta*, cf. Skt. *gárhate*.— With orig. *s*, GAv. *aogžā* 'thou spakest', to √*augh* + -*sa*, 2nd. sg. pret. mid.;— GAv. *diwžaidyāi* 'to deceive', to orig. √*dabh* + -*sa-*. infin. desiderative, cf. YAv. *diwžat* 'from deceit', a substantive from desid. stem, cf. Skt. *atpsati*.

§ 90. In YAv., as compared with GAv., this law holds good only in part; as for the rest, the old tenues *t*, or surd sibilant *s*, is restored and assimilation then takes place. Thus:—

YAv. *aoxta* 'he spake', to √*augh* + ending *ta*, beside GAv. *aogədā*; YAv. *druxtō* 'deceived', to √*draugh* + -*ta-*, = Skt. *drugdhás*. — YAv. *daste* 'he makes', to √*dhā-*, pres. stem *dadh* + *tē*, beside GAv. *dazdē*; YAv. *mastim* 'wisdom' to orig. √*mandh* + -*ti-*, beside GAv. *humązdra-*, YAv. *mazdra-*.— YAv. *dapta* 'deceived' nom. f. past ptcpl. to orig. √*dabh*, cf. Skt. *dabdha-*.— With orig. *s*, YAv. *vaṣ̌ata* 'he carried' (*s* restored § 165), 3rd. sg. mid. *sa-* aor. to √*vagh*, beside YAv. *vaẑat* 'he carried'.

Semivowels.

Av. ͽ *y* (initial), ·· *y* (internal); ᛃ *v* (initial), ·· *v* (internal).

§ 91. **General Remark.** The semivowels ͽ *y* and ᛃ *v* were probably spirants; internal ··*y* and ··*v* were apparently sometimes spirant, sometimes vocalic (see § 92 Note 1).

Note. In a few instances ··*y* and ··*v* stand as initial, when representing *iy, uv*: GAv. ⁓⁓ *iyaducā* 'and here' Ys. 35.2 (pron. stem *i*); YAv. ⁓⁓ *uvaēibya* 'with both', Skt. *ubhā́bhyām*—see §§ 87, 68.

Av. *y* = Skt. *y*.

§ 92. Av. *y* (initial and internal) corresponds to Skt. *y*:

Av. *yasnəm* 'worship' = Skt. *yajñám*; Av. *tāyuš* 'thief' = Skt. *tāyús*; GAv. *ahurahyā* 'of Ahura' = Skt. *ásurasya*.

Note 1. (a) A possible test as to when ··*y* is spirant or semivowel, may perhaps be found in the treatment of a preceding *t*, e. g. *haiþya* 'true' (*y* spirant) but *dāitya-* 'lawful' (*y* semivowel *dāit-i-a-*). (b) Moreover the metre shows that *y* is often to be read with vowel value *iy* § 68: GAv. *fryō* 'friend' (read *fr-iy-ō*) = Skt. *priyás*; YAv. *bitya-* 'second' (read *bit-iy-a-*) = Skt. *dvitī́ya-*.—In Yt. 13.99 initial ͽ must be read *iy* in *yaēša* 'he has sought' = Skt. *iyéṣa*.

Note 2. On Av. *y* = Skt. *v*, in *tanuyē* etc., see § 190.

Av. *v* = Skt. *v*.

§ 93. Av. *v* (initial and internal) corresponds to Skt. *v*:

Av. *vastrəm* 'vesture' = Skt. *vástram*; Av. *vātō* 'wind' = Skt. *vā́tas*;—Av. *tūtava* 'he has power' = Skt. *tūtā́va*; Av. *hvaspō* 'with good horses' = Skt. *sváśvas*.

Note 1. Metrically ··*v* is often to be read as a vowel. Thus: Av. *gaēþāhva* 'among beings' Ys. 9.17 (loc. *āhu + a* postpos.); *cipraēšva* 'among seeds', GAv. *tvəm* 'thou' (read *tuəm*) = Skt. *tvám (tuám)*; YAv. *kva* 'where' (read *kua*) = Skt. *kvà (kúa)*.

Note 2. On Av. *v* for *w*, see § 87.
Note 3. On Av. *v* for Skt. *uv* see § 68.

Original *v* in Combination with Consonants.

Av. representative of Skt. *tv*.

§ 94. The combination original *tv* (1) generally becomes Av. *þw*; (2) it remains unchanged when a sibilant

precedes or when *v* preserves its vocalic character *u*.—
When samprasāraṇa with following *a* takes place, *t* remains unaltered.

(1) GYAv. *hrapvā, hrapvō* 'by, of wisdom' = Skt. *krátvā, krátvas;* YAv *hwąm* 'thee' = Skt. *tvám;* Av. *mąpwa-* 'to be thought, thought', for **mantva-;—
(2) Av. *varštva-* 'to be done, act'; Av. *ratvō* 'O Master', *gātvō* 'from the seat' (prob. *rat-u-ō, gāt-u-ō*); GAv. *tvōm* 'thou' *(tuōm).—*YAv. *tūm* 'thou'= Skt. *tvam*.

Original *pv*.

§ 95. The combination original *pv* apparently seems to become *f* in Av.: — e. g. Ys. 57.29 *āfəṇte* 'they are overtaken', for earlier **āpvaṇte* (cl. S), Av. *āfəṇtəm* 'aquosum' for older **āpvaṇtam;* Av. *huſhafa* 'slumbering' nom. sg. from orig. **susvapvan(t)-.*

Original *dv, dhv*.

§ 96. The combination original *dv, dhv* becomes
(1) when initial, GAv. *dv, d^ab;* in YAv. *ʃb, b (dv);—*
(2) when internal, GAv. *dv;* in YAv. *dv, dw (dv).*

(1) Initial.

GAv. *dvaēṣavhā* 'through hatred' (YAv. *ʃbaēṣavha*) = Skt. *dvéṣasā;* GAv. *d^aibiṣəṇtī* 'they hate' (cf. YAv. *ʃbaēṣayāṭ*) = Skt. *dviṣánti;* GAv. *d^aibitīm* 'second' (YAv. *bitīm*) = Skt. *dvitīyam.—*YAv. *ʃbaēṣavha* 'through hatred' = Skt. *dvéṣasā;* YAv. *ʃbaēṣayāṭ* 'may harm through hatred' = Skt. *dvéṣeyāṭ;* YAv. *bitīm* 'second' = Skt. *dvitīyam.—*YAv. *dva* 'two' = Skt. *dvā;* Av. *dvarəm* 'door' = Skt. *dváram;* Av. *dvąsaiti* 'rushes, springs' = Skt. *dhvąsati*.

(2) Internal.

GAv. *advaēṣō* 'without harm' = Skt. *advéṣás;* GAv. *vidva* 'knowing', YAv. *vidvō* = Skt. *vidván;—*GAv. *advānəm* 'path', YAv. *adwanəm* = Skt. *ádhvānam*.

—Av. *didvaēṣa* 'I have hated' = Skt. *didvéṣa*; YAv. *vidvaēštvō* 'foe to harm'.

Note. In YAv. *vīḇaēǰaṇhəm* 'foe to malice' and *vīdvaēštvō* 'foe to harm', the *ṭʰ*, *dv* is treated apparently as initial,—prefix *vi*.

Av. representative of Skt. *sv*.

§ 97. The combination *sv* (Skt.) appears in Av. as *sp*.

Av. *vīspəm* 'all' = Skt. *viśvam*; Av. *aspō* 'horse' = Skt. *áśvas*; Av. *spaētəm* 'white' = Skt. *śvētám*.

§ 98. On Av. representative of *sv* (Skt.), see § 130.

Av. representative of Skt. *hv*.

§ 99. The combination Skt. *hv* appears in Av. as *zb*.

Av. *zbayemi* 'I invoke' = Skt. *hváyāmi*; GAv. *duž-azōbā̆* 'male-dictus' cf. Skt. √*hvā-*.

Liquid.

Av. ↑ *r*.

§ 100. The Av. liquid is *r*; it corresponds to Skt. *r* and *l*, the letter *l* being wanting in Av.

Av. *r* = Skt. *r* (*l*).

Av. *rapəm* 'wagon' = Skt. *rátham*; Av. *narəm* 'man' = Skt. *náram*; Av. *srīrō* 'beautiful' = Skt. *śrī-rás, śrīlás.*—Av. *hukərəpta-* 'well-formed' = Skt. *-kḷptá-*; GAv. *hrapaiti* 'arranges', cf. Skt. *kálpatē*.

Note 1. In Av., *hr* appears instead of simple *r* when immediately followed by *k* or *p*:—YAv. *vəhrkō* 'wolf' = Skt. *vŕkas*; GYAv. *kəhrpəm* 'corpus' = Skt. *kṛ́pam*; YAv. *mahrkō* 'death' = Skt. *markás*, cf. GAv. *mar^dkaē-cā* 'morti-que'; YAv. *kəhrkana-* nomen propr., cf. Skt. *kṛkaṇa-*. See Bartholomae, *A.F.* ii.39; Brugmann, *Grundriss der vergl. Gram.* § 260.

Note 2. On *urv-* (i. e. *ᵘrv-* for *vr-*), see § 191.

Note 3. On *r* in vowel combinations *ar*, *aⁱr*, *aᵘr*, *ər*, see § 48.

Nasals.

Av. ı, ᴇ, ı, ʋ, ɱ.
n, ṅ, ṇ, ñ, m.

§ 101. General Remark. Of the nasals in Av., ɱ corresponds in general to Skt. *m.*—To the Skt. *n* there correspond in Av., ı *n* and ᴇ *ṅ*,—the latter, a modification of ı *n*, stands before stopped consonants.—The letter ı *ṅ* is evidently guttural in Av. *paṅtaṅham* 'fifth' from **paṅktasva.* Otherwise ı *ṅ* stands in the combination *ṅh, ṅuh* derived from orig. *s*-syllable § 108.—The character ʋ *ñ* is palaeographically, from the manuscripts, a modification of ı *ṅ*; it occurs for *ṅ* in connection with *h* when it is preceded by an *i*- or *e*-sound § 118 Note.

§ 102. Av. *n* occurs initial, internal (except before stopped-sounds), and final.

Av. *nāma* 'name' = Skt. *nāma;* — Av. *tanuš* 'body' = Skt. *tanūs;* — Av. *anyō* 'another' = Skt. *anyás;* Av. *vanancm* 'victorious' = Skt. *vanānvān;* Av. *varšnōiš* 'of.a male' = Skt. *vṛṣṇes;* — Av. *baran* 'they carried' = Skt. *ábharan.*

§ 103. Av. *ṅ* occurs before *k, g, c, j, t, d* and *-hya* (for *-dhyo*), *bya.*

Av. *saṅga-* 'upper part of foot' = Skt. *jaṅghā-;* — Av. *paṅca* 'five' = Skt. *páñca;* — Av. *haṅjaiti* 'bestirs, hurries' = Skt. *sahate;* — Av. *aṅtarə* 'inter' = Skt. *antár;* Av. *baraṅti* 'they carry' = Skt. *bháranti;* Av. *barəzəṅbya* 'for the two great ones'.

Note. For *-ṅg* see under Sibilants § 128.

§ 104. On Av. ı *ṅ*, ʋ *ñ*, see above General Remark.

§ 105. Av. *m* occurs initial, internal, final.

Av. *maδəmam* 'midmost' = Skt. *madhyamam.* Av. *amam* 'strength' = Skt. *ámam;* Av. *mraom* 'I spake' = Skt. *ábruvam.*

Note 1. The *m* in Av. √*mru-* (opp. Skt. √*brū-*) is probably the more original.

Note 2. On initial *m* = Skt. *sm*, see § 140.

Sibilants.

Av. ว, ·ʋ, . ꙍ, ⱳ — ʃ, ꙍ.
s, š, ṣ́, ṣ̌ — z, ž.

§ 106. General Remark. Of the sibilants, s, š, ṣ́, ṣ̌ are surd; and z, ž are sonant. In Avesta, s corresponds to both Skt. s and to ś.—Av. š answers in general to Skt. ṣ. The letter Av. ṣ́ is chiefly final after i, u and consonants, also in some ligatures. Av. ṣ̌ is not so common, chiefly before y.

Note. Av. š, ṣ́, ṣ̌ are palaeographically closely related. In most MSS., š and ṣ́ interchange with each other. In the younger Indian MSS., š is the predominant character; the Persian MSS. often (though by no means throughout) show a preference for ṣ́ when the sound answers to orig. rt. In the four oldest MSS., with Pahlavi translation, ṣ́ is the principal character,—š standing as final or in ligatures. This rule is there preserved almost without exception.—In the old Mss. ⱳ š has a double value—(1) as a ligature for š + k, hiški 'dry', et al.; or (2) it is a modification of š, ṣ́ before y, § 162. Younger MSS. write in the (1) first case šk; in the (2) second case they have a special ligature.—See Geldner, *Drei Yasht* p. viii seqq.

Av. s.

§ 107. General Remark. Av. s is of three-fold origin:—
1. = original s,
2. = older palatal ś (Skt. ś),
3. = developed.

---

1. Original s.

§ 108. General Remark. Original s (1) under certain conditions remains s in Avesta (2) but generally otherwise becomes h (ṽh).

i. Original s remains s.

§ 109. Original s remains s in Avesta before initial k, c, t, p, n, or internal before the same letters when it is preceded by a, q, ā.

Av. *skəmbəm* 'scaffold' = Skt. *skambhám*; Av. *yas-karət-* 'making efforts', cf. Skt. *a-yás-*; Av. *skəndəm* 'broken', *scindayeiti* 'breaks asunder', cf. Lat. *scindere*. —Av. *staotārəm* 'praiser' = Skt. *stōtā́ram*; Av. *vaste* 'he clothes' = Skt. *váste*; Av. *āste* 'he sits' = Skt. *ā́ste*; GAv. *məstā* 'he thought' = Skt. *amąsta*; Av. *dąstvąm* 'cunning, skill', cf. Skt. *dąsas-*; GAv. *spərədānī* 'I will strive' = Skt. *spárdhāni*; Av. *manaspaoirya-* 'having the mind pre-eminent'. —Av. *snayaēta* 'should wash' = Skt. *snáyēta*; Av. *āsnatārəm* 'priest who washes the utensils', cf. Skt. *a-snātā́ram* 'dreading water'.

ii. Original *s* becomes *h*.

§ 110. Original *s* becomes *h* in Av., regularly when initial before vowels.

Av. *hapta* 'ἑπτά' = Skt. *saptá*, Lat. *septem*; Av. *haca* 'with, from' = Skt. *sácā*; Av. *haomən* 'Haoma' = Skt. *sómam*; Av. *hō* 'he' = Skt. *sás*; Av. *hūḥtəm* 'good word' = Skt. *sūktám*; Av. *hakərət* 'at one time' = Skt. *sakŕ̥t*.

as.

§ 111. The combination old *as* becomes in Avesta (1) *ah-*, (2) *aṅh-*, *av-*, (3) *-ō* (final).

Old *as-* = (1) Av. *ah-*.

§ 112. α. Old *as-* = Av. *ah-* — regularly before *i, ī*.

YAv. *ahi* 'thou art', GAv. *ahī* = Skt. *así*; GAv. *nəmahī* 'in homage = Skt. *námasi*.

§ 113. β. Old *as-* = Av. *ah-* — before *i, ī*, when the *a* becomes *e*, § 34.

Av. *dārayehi* 'thou holdest fast' = Skt. *dhārāyasi*; Av. *jaidyehi* 'thou askest'; Av. *saduyehi* 'thou appearest' = Skt. *chadáyasi*; Av. *aojyehīš* 'more strong' (acc. pl. fem.) = Skt. *ójyasis*.

§ 114. γ. Old *as-* = Av. *ah-*, generally before *u, ū* and their strengthenings.

Sibilants: Original s.

Av. *azahu* 'in distress' = Skt. *ahasu;* Av. *ahurǝm* 'Ahura, Lord' = Skt. *ásuram;* Av. *ahūm* 'life' = Skt. *ásum.*

§ 115. δ. Old *as-* = Av. *ah-*, the *a* before *u, v* then passing over into *o, ō.*

Av. *vohu* 'good' = Skt. *vásu;* GAv. *bahyōhvā* 'distribute' = Skt. *bhákṣasva.*

§ 116. ε. Old *as-* = Av. *ah-* rarely before *e*, cf. perhaps § 35 Note 2.

Av. *raodahe* 'thou growest' = Skt. *ródhasi;* Av. *pāvhahe* 'thou mayest protect' (aor. subj.) Yt. 8.1 = Skt. *pāsasi.*

Old *as-* = (2) Av. *aṿh-*.

§ 117. ʓ. Old *as-* = Av. *aṿh-*, regularly before *a, ā, ǝ, ǝ̄, ō, ōi, ą.*

Av. *vaṿhanǝm* 'vesture' = Skt. *vásanam;* GAv. *nǝmaṿhā* 'with homage' = Skt. *námasā.*—Av. *vaṿhǝ̄uš* 'of good' = Skt. *vásōs.*—Av. *avaṿhō* 'of help' = Skt. *ávasō.*—GAv. *rāṿhaṿhōi* 'thou mayest offer' (aor. subj.) = Skt. *rāsasē;* Av. *uṣaṿhąm* 'of dawns' = Skt. *uṣásām.*

Note. An exception is Av. *dahākō* 'Dragon', *dahakāca.*

§ 118. β. Old *as-* = Av. *aṿh-*, generally before *e, ē, aē-ca*, but cf. § 116.

YAv. *avaṿhe, avaṿhaē-ca*, GAv. *avaṿhē* 'for help' = Skt. *ávasē;* GAv. *nǝmaṿhē* 'for homage' = Skt. *námasē.*

Note. Here Av. *ṿh-* may appear instead of *ṿh-* when epenthetic *i* precedes it, or when *a* is shaded to *e* after *y* § 34: —YAv. *avaiṿhe* 'for help' beside *avaṿhe* = Skt. *ávasē;* GAv. *didaiṿhē* 'I was made wise' (redupl. aor.).—YAv. *yeṿhe* 'of which' = Skt. *yásya;* GAv. *srāvayeṿhē* 'to make heard'; GAv. *rāṣ̌ayeṿhē* 'to harm'—cf. the Skt. infinitives in *-asē.*

§ 119. γ. Old *as-* = Av. *aṿh-*, seldom before *u:*

Av. *vaṿhuš* 'good' = Skt. *vásus;* Av. *aṿhuš* (beside *ahūm*) 'life' = Skt. *ásus.*

Old -as = (3) Av. -ō.

§ 120. Old -as final = Av. -ō.—(GAv. often has -ə̄ § 32).

Av. puþrō 'son' = Skt. putrás; Av. išavō 'arrows' = Skt. íṣavas; Av. dārayō 'didst hold fast' = Skt. dhārayas.—Cf. GAv. yā̊ 'who' (YAv. yō) = Skt. yás; GAv. vō 'of ye' (YAv. vō) = Skt. vas; GAv. masō̆ 'great' (gen.) = Skt. mahás.

Note. Observe that as is retained before enclitic ca 'que', etc. Av. išavasca 'and arrows' = Skt. iṣavas-ca; Av. iṣavascit̃ 'even the arrows' = Skt. iṣavas-cit; Av. yasca 'and who' = Skt. yás-ca.—Av. nəmas° tē 'homage to thee' = Skt. námas tē; Av. yastat̃ 'qui id' = Skt yás tát.

ās.

§ 121. The combination old ās becomes in Avesta (1) āh-, (2) ā̊ŋh-, (3) -å (final).

Old ās- = (1) Av. āh-.

§ 122. Old ās- = Av. āh- regularly before i, ī, u, ū.

Av. bavāhi 'mayest thou be' = Skt. bhávāsi; Av. pāhi 'thou protectest' = Skt. pā́hi.—Av. dahīm 'creation' = Skt. dhasim; GAv. rāhī 'I offer' (aor.) = Skt. rā́si.—Av. ahurōiš 'of the Ahurian', cf. Skt. ásurēs; GAv. áhū loc. pl. fem. of aēm 'this' = Skt. āsú.

Old ās- = (2) Av. ā̊ŋh-.

§ 123. Old ās- = Av. ā̊ŋh-,—before a, ā, ə, e, ē, ō, ōi, ą.

Av. ā̊ŋha 'has been' = Skt. ā́sa; Av. θrā̊ŋhayeite 'he terrifies' = Skt. trāsáyatē; Av. nā̊ŋhābya 'with both nostrils' = Skt. nā́sābhyam;—Av. mā̊ŋhəm 'moon' = Skt. mā́sam;—GAv. rā̊ŋhē 'I offer' = Skt. rā́sē;—Av. ā̊ŋhō 'of mouth' = Skt. āsás;—Av. dā̊ŋhōit̃ 'creation' (abl.), cf. Skt. dhāsī-;—Av. ā̊ŋhąm 'of these' (fem.) = Skt. āsā́m.

Old -ās = (3) Av. -ā̊.

§ 124. Old -ās final = Av. -ā̊—regularly.

Av. buyā̊ 'mightest be' = Skt. bhūyás; Av. haēnayā̊ 'of an army' = Skt. sénāyās; Av. dā̊ 'thou madest' = Skt. ádhās.

Note. Before enclitics (ca etc.), orig. -ās appears as -ās̊:—Av. gāpāsca 'and the Gathas' = Skt. gā́thāsca; Av. urvarāsca 'and trees' = Skt. urvárāsca; Av. haēnayāsca 'and of the army' = Skt. sénāyāsca;—G.Av. dā̊scā 'and madest', dā̊s-tū 'thou madest' = Skt. ádāsca, etc.

Original ns.

§ 125. The combination old internal -ans- before vowels becomes:—(1) in YAv. -aṇh-, -ǝṇh-, -ąh-;—(2) in GAv. -ə̄ṇgh-, -ə̄h-.

Old -ans- = (1) YAv. -aṇh-, -ǝṇh-, -ąh-.

§ 126. α. Old -ans- internal = YAv. -aṇh-, -ǝṇh- before ā, a, ə, ōi.

YAv. saṇhāni 'I shall proclaim' = Skt. śąsāni; YAv. daṇhaṇha 'with cunning, skill' (Ny. 1.16) = Skt. dąsasā. —YAv. vǝṇhən 'they will struggle' (Yt. 13.154) = Skt. vąsan.—YAv. saṇhōiš 'shouldst proclaim' = Skt. śąsēs. —Similarly YAv. jaṇhəntu 'shall injure' (Vd. 2.22), cf. Skt. hisantu.

§ 127. β. Old -ans- = YAv. -ąh- before i, y.

YAv. dąhištəm 'most cunning, skilled' = Skt. dąsistam; YAv. ząhyamnanąm 'of those who will be born' (√zan- = Skt. √jan-).

Old -ans- = (2) GAv. -ə̄ṇgh-, -ə̄h-.

§ 128. Old -ans- internal = (α) GAv. -ə̄ṇgh- (or ə̄ŋ) before vowels;—and = (β) GAv. -ə̄h- before m.

(a) GAv. sə̄ṇghānī 'I shall proclaim' = Skt. śąsāni; GAv. və̄ṇghaṭ, və̄ṇghən 'shall strive' (aor.) = Skt. vąsat;

GAv. *sɔ̄nghō* 'proclamation, proclaimer' = Skt. *śasas*.
—GAv. *mə̄nghī* (also *mə̄nhī*) 'I thought' = Skt. *masi*.
—GAv. *fṣ̄ənghyō, fṣ̄ənghīm* 'thrifty' = orig. **psansyas*.
—(b) *mə̄hmaidī* 'we thought' (s-aor. from √*man*-).

§ 129. The combination old final -*ans* = (1) YAv. -*ąn*, or -*ą* (-*ąs-ca*), -*ə* (-*əs-ca*);—(2) GAv. -*ə̄ng*, -*ą*.

YAv. *daēvąn*, GAv. *daēvə̄ng* 'Demons' = Skt. *devā́n*.
—GAv. *spəṇtə̄ng aməṣ̄ə̄ng* Ys. 39.3 = YAv. *aməṣ̄ə̄ spəṇtə̄* = YAv. *aməṣ̄ąs-ca spəṇtə̄* = GAv. *aməṣ̄ą spəṇtą* = YAv. *aməṣ̄ąs-ca spəṇtą* (acc. pl.) = Skt. *amŕ̥tān*.—YAv. *aēsmąn, aēsmąs-ca* 'wood', cf. Skt. *aśvān, aśvą́śca*; YAv. *varəsə̄s-ca* 'hair'.

Note. In some of the above examples, it might be suggested that YAv. *ə* is perhaps due to Gatha influence.

Original *sv*.

§ 130. The combination orig. *sv* becomes in Avesta *hv* or *h*.—Sometimes, *sv* when internal, becomes *vuh* (also written *vh*).

(1) Orig. *sv*- initial = Av. *hv*-, *h*-.

GYAv. *hva*-, also *ha*- 'suus' = Skt. *svá*-; GYAv. *hvarə* 'sun' = Skt. *svàr*; YAv. *hvaspō* 'having good horses' = Skt. *sváśvas*.—YAv. *havharəm* 'sister' = Skt. *svásāram*; GYAv. *harəaw* 'splendors', cf. Skt. *svàrvara*-; YAv. *hīsaṭ* 'he sweated', fr. Av. √*hid*- = Skt. √*svid*-.

(2) Orig. -*sv*- internal = Av. -*hv*-, -*h*-, -*vhv*-, -*vuh*-. (Pers. MSS. -*vh*-).

(a) It becomes *hv*,—after *ā*— YAv. *āhva* 'among these' (*āhu* + *a* postpos.) = Skt. *āsú*; YAv. *unāhva* 'in empty holes' = Skt. *ūnásu*; YAv. *vyarəpāhva* 'in separate places' (loc.).—After *a*—GAv. *gūṣahvā* 'hear thou' = Skt. *ghóṣasva*; so YAv. *dāmahva* 'among creatures' (loc. *an*-stem + *a*) = Skt. *dhā́masu*.—After *o* (= *a* § 39)—YAv. *baṣ̌jahva* 'distribute thou' = Skt. *bhákṣasva*.—(b) Becomes *h*,—after *a*—GAv. *nəmahvaitīš* 'full of homage' = Skt. *námasvatīs*; YAv. *harahvaitīm* nom. propr. = Skt. *sárasvatīm*.—So (see below under Composition) YAv. *pairiṣ̌hahtəm* 'surrounded' = Skt. *pariṣvaktam*.—*c*) Becomes -*vvh*-

Sibilants: Original *s*. 47

(*-wh-, -wh^a-*) — GYAv. *vavuhīm* 'good' (fem.), Pers. MSS. *vanhīm* = Skt. *vásvīm;* YAv. *paidyauuha* 'set foot, abide' = Skt. *pádyasva;* YAv. *hunavuha* 'press haoma-juice', cf. Skt. *sunuṣvá;*—YAv. *aojavuhaṇt-*, GAv. *aojōnghvaṇt-*, *aojōnhvaṇt-* 'strong' = Skt. *ōjasvant-*.—YAv. *vauhvqm* 'of good things', beside *vohunqm;* YAv. *hvarᵊnavuhvaṇta* 'glorious', cf. Yt. 15.56, beside *hvarᵊnavuhaṇtəm;* YAv. *varᵊcavhuṇtəm* 'brilliant' Yt. 12.1 = Skt. *varcasvantam*.

Note. In *rāma hvāstrəm* orig. 'having good pastures', *hv* = orig. *su* + *vᵒ* (§ 68).

Original *sy*.

§ 131. This combination, orig. *sy* preceded by a vowel, becomes somewhat complicated in Av., owing to the varied treatment of *y*, as *y* sometimes **remains** after *s* has become an *h*-sound, or *y* sometimes **vanishes**, with or without leaving a trace of epenthesis. In GAv., *y* is generally retained, in YAv. *y* generally vanishes.

(A) *y* remains.

§ 132. Orig. *sy* = (1) Av. *hy* (the *y* remaining);— mostly GAv., more rare YAv.

(a) YAv. *hyāṭ* 'might be' = Skt. *syāt;* YAv. *uzdūhyamnanqm* 'of offerings to be elevated', cf. Skt. *dhā-sy-atē;* YAv. *māhyaᵉibhyō* 'to lords of the month' = Skt. *māsyēbhyas;* YAv. *manahyō* 'spiritual' (nom. sg.) for **manasyas.*—(b) GAv. *ahurahyā* 'of Ahura, Lord' = Skt. *ásurasya;* GAv. *ahyā* 'of this' = Skt. *asyá;* GAv. *vahyō* 'better' = Skt. *vásyas*.

§ 133. Orig. *sy* = (2) Av. *hy*, mostly GAv., rarely YAv.

(a) YAv. *dahyunqm* 'of countries', cf. Skt. *dásyu-;* and YAv. *hyaona-*, *hyaonya-* nom. propr.—(b) GAv. *vahyō* 'melior' = Skt. *vásyān;* GAv. *ahyācā* 'ejus-que' (beside *ahyā*) =: Skt. *asyá*. Cf. Geldner, *Studien zum Avesta* p. 141.

(B) *y* vanishes.

§ 134. Orig. *-sy-* internal = (1) Av. *-wh-*, the *y* vanishing without leaving epenthesis.

YAv. *vavhō* 'melius' = Skt. *vásyas;* YAv. *aēvavhā̊* gen. sg. fem. (orig. *-syās*) from *aēva-* 'one'.

§ 135. Orig. -sy- internal = (2) Av. -iph-, the y vanishes but leaves epenthesis.

YAv. *aiphā* (also *aphā*) 'of this' (fem.) = Skt. *asyās*; YAv. *daiŋh3uš* 'of country', cf. Skt. *dáçyu-*.

§ 136. Orig. -sy- internal = (3) Av. -yh-, the y with a following a becoming e.

(a) With epenthesis – YAv. *aiyhe* 'of this' = Skt. *asyá*. – (b) Without epenthesis — YAv. *yeyhe* 'of whom' = Skt. *yásya*.

§ 137. Orig. -sy- internal = (4) Av. *h*, the y with a following a having become *e*, § 67. Very common in YAv. genitive singular.

YAv. *ahe* 'of this' = Skt. *asya*; YAv. *ahurahe* (beside GAv. *ahurahyā*) 'of Ahura' = Skt. *ásurasya*. — Isolated GYAv. *vahehiš* 'the better ones' (fem.) = Skt. *vasyasīs*.

Original *sr*.

§ 138. Orig. *sr*- initial = (?) Av. *r*- (the instances are uncertain).

GAv. *raoŋhayən* 'they made fall', cf. Skt. *sraṣayan*; YAv. *ravius* 'the lame', cf. Skt. √*sras-, srqs-*; Av. *rāmsm* 'sickness' = Skt. *srâmam*.

§ 139. Orig. -sr- internal = Av. -wr-.

Av. *hazavrəm* 'thousand' = Skt. *sahásram*; Av. *davrō* 'cunning, wise' = Skt. *dasrás*; ZPhl.Gloss. *vavri-, vavra-* 'spring', cf. Skt. *vasantá-*; Av. *aŋrō mainyuš* 'the Evil Spirit'.

Note. In GAv. -*ŋgr*- is also written: GAv. *daŋgra-, aŋgra-*.

Original *sm*.

§ 140. Orig. *sm*- initial = Av. *m*, through loss of *h*.

Av. *mat* 'with' = Skt. *smát*; YAv. *maha*, GAv. *mahi* 'sumus' = Skt. *smási*.

§ 141. Orig. *sm*- internal = Av. *hm*.

Av. *kahmāi* 'to whom' = Skt. *kásmāi*; YAv. *ahmi*, GAv. *ahmī* 'sum' = Skt. *ásmi*.

Original *sk*.

§ 142. Orig. sk_1 = Av. *s* (cf. Skt. *ch*).

Av. *jasaiti* 'he comes' = Skt. *gáchati*, cf. βάσκει; Av. *isaiti* 'he desires' = Skt. *ichắti;* Av. *yasaiti* 'holds' = Skt. *yáchati*.

Original *ts*.

§ 143. Orig. *t* + *s* = Skt. *s* (through intermediate *ss* §§ 185, 186).

GAv. *hšmāvasū* (loc. pl.) 'belonging to you' = Skt. *yuṣmāvatsu;* GAv. *dragvasu* 'among the wicked' (*dragvat* + *su*); YAv. *masyō* 'fish' = Skt. *mátsyas;* YAv. *aṣava.hšnus* 'rejoicing the righteous' (Yt. 13.63 nom. sing. °*t* + *s*), cf. Av. *hšnūtəm* 'joy'; YAv. *h isaṯ* 'he sweated' (°*d* [= *t*] + *s* § 74), cf. Skt. √*svid-;* YAv. *raose* 'thou growest', cf. Av. *raodahe, raosta;* GAv. *stavas* 'praising' (nom. sg. *stavaṇt-*), cf. Lat. *aman(t)s;* GAv. *dasvā* 'give thou' = Skt. *datsva;* GAv. *pišyasū* loc. plur. stem *pišyaṇt-* 'beholding'.

Original *ps*.

§ 144. Orig. *ps* = Av. *fš*, except before *r, tr*.

YAv. *drafšō* 'spear, banner' = Skt. *drapsás;* GAv. *hafšī* 'thou extendest', cf. GAv. *hapti* from √*hap-* = Skt. √*sap-;* GAv. *nafšū* 'among children', cf. *napātəm, naptyaēšū* § 187 (5); YAv. *hangərəfšānē* 'I will seize' (*s*-aor.), beside *gərəptəm,* √*garw-* = Skt. √*garbh-*.

Note 1. Observe *s* remains unchanged before *r, tr:*—Av. *fšaratu-* 'fruit, reward', Av. *hrafstra-* 'noxious creature'.

Note 2. Observe that *s* (= *sk*; cf. § 142) remains unchanged in the examples *tafsaṯ* (YAv.) 'grew warm', *narəfsaiti* (GAv.) 'it wanes'.

2. Older palatal *ś* (Skt. *ś*).

§ 145. General Remark. Older palatal *ś* (Skt. *ś*) commonly appears as Av. *s*. In certain combinations it is changed to *š*.

i. Older palatal ś (= Skt. ś) = Av. s.

§ 146. Older palatal ś (= Skt. ś) = Av. s before vowels, semivowels, and most consonants.

Av. *safå̄vhō* 'hoofs' = Skt. *saphásos*; Av. *qsayå̄* 'of two parties' = Skt. *qśayós*; G.Av. *sāsti* 'he teaches' = Skt. *śā́sti*; Av. *pasūm* 'pecus' = Skt. *paśúm*; Av. *spasō* 'spies' = Skt. *spáśas*;—Av. *nasyeiti* 'he vanishes' = Skt. *náśyati*; Av. *usyāṭ* 'he might wish' = Skt. *uśyāt*; Av. *isvan-* 'having power', cf. Skt. *īśvará*;—Av. *vīspaitiš* 'village-lord' = Skt. *viśpátis*; Av. *usmahi* 'we wish' = Skt. *uśmási*; Av. *sraēšta-* 'fairest' = Skt. *śréṣṭha-*.

Note 1. On Av. *p* instead of Av. *s* (= Skt. *ś*), see § 77 Note 2.
Note 2. On older palatal *ś* retained in Av. before *n*, see § 160 Note.
Note 3. On older palatal *ś* in *tv* = Av. *sp*, see § 97.
Note 4. On Av. *saēna-* 'eagle' = Skt. *śyenā́-*, see § 187 (3).

ii. Older palatal ś = Av. š.

§ 147. Older palatal ś (= Skt. ś) before *t* becomes Av. š (= Skt. *ṣṭ*). For examples see § 159.

§ 148. Older palatal ś (= Skt. ś) before *n* generally becomes Av. š (= Skt. *śn*). For examples see § 160.

§ 149. Older palatal ś (= Skt. ś) after Av. *f* (= orig. *p*) becomes š. For examples see § 161.

iii. Older palatal ś = Av. ž.

§ 150. Older palatal ś (= Skt. ś) becomes Av. ž before sonants. For examples see § 182.

3. Developed Av. s.

§ 151. Av. *s* sometimes results from the dentals *t* (*þ*), *d* (*đ*) becoming *s* before *t*.

Av. *cistiš* 'wisdom' = Skt. *cittis*; Av. *amavastara-* 'stronger' (*amavaṇt*) = Skt. *ámavattara-*; Av. *iristahe* 'of the dead' (√*iriþ-*); Av. *aiwi-sastar-* 'one who sits'

(√*had-*) = Skt. *sáttar-;* Av. *raosta* 'has grown up', cf. Av. *raoδəṇti*,. Skt. √*rudh-*.

Note. Sometimes *t* (*ṯ*) becomes *s* before *c*:—Av. *raēvascipra-* 'of splendid family' (*raēvant-* + *cipra-*); Av. *yasca* 'and when' (*yaṯ* + *ca*).

§ 152. Av. *s* sometimes results from Av. *z* becoming *s* before *m*.

Av. *upasmąm* 'upon earth' (acc. fem.), beside Av. *ząm*, *zəmō*; Av. *rasmanąm* 'of battle ranks', cf. Av. *rāzayeiṇte* 'they arrange in ranks' (√*rāz-* = Skt. √*rāj-*); Av. *maēsmana* 'with urine', cf. Av. *maēzaṇti* 'they make urine' (√*miz-* = Skt. √*mih-*); Av. *barəsmana* 'with barsom', cf. Av. √*barz-* 'grow up, be high, great' (= Skt. √*barh-*).

§ 153. Av. *s* more rarely results from Av. *z* becoming *s* before *n*. See also § 164 Note. 1.

Av. *asnya-* 'belonging to the day' (from *azan-*) = Skt. *tirō-ahnya-* (fr. *áhan-*); Av. *yasnəm* 'worship' (√*yaz-* = Skt. √*yaj-*).

Av. *š*, *ṣ̌*, *š̍*.

§ 154. **General Remark.** Av. *š* (*ṣ̌*, *š̍*) stands either for an original *s* after *i*, *u* and certain consonants; or for an earlier palatal *ś* under special conditions.

Av. *š* (*ṣ̌*, *š̍*) = Skt. *ṣ*.

§ 155. Av. *š* (*ṣ̌*, *š̍*) answers to Skt. *ṣ* after *i*, *u*, and their strengthenings, and after *ḫ* and *r*. Cf. Whitney, *Skt. Gram.* § 180.

Av. *iṣ̌avō* 'arrows' = Skt. *iṣavas;* Av. *vahištō* 'best' = Skt. *vásiṣṭhas;* Av. *raēṣ̌ayāṯ* 'may wound' = Skt. *rēṣáyāt:* Av. *sraēṣ̌yeiti* 'it clings', cf. Skt. *śliṣyati.*—Av. *duš.kərətəm* 'ill-done' = Skt. *duṣ-kṛtam;* Av. *mušti-* 'fist' = Skt. *muṣṭí-;* Av. *gaoš̍əm* 'ear' = Skt. *ghôṣam;* Av. *taoṣ̌ayeiti* 'makes still' (Yt. 10.48) = Skt. *tōṣáyati.*—Av. *uḫṣ̌ānəm* 'bull' = Skt. *ukṣáṇam;* G.Av. *vaḫṣ̌yā*

'I will speak' = Skt. *vakṣyāmi*.— Av. *taršnōiš* 'of a ram' = Skt. *tṛṣṇés*; Av. *taršnō* 'thirst' = Skt. *tṛṣṇā-*.

Note 1. Before *r* we find *s* not *š* though *i* or *u* precede:—GAv. *þwisra-* 'glancing', cf. Skt. *√tviṣ-*: YAv. *husra-, pisra-*. Similarly in Skt. *usra-, tamisra-*, cf. Whitney, *Sanskrit Grammar* § 181 c.

Note 2. Sometimes, *š* is written for *š* before *y*:— GAv. *fraēšyāmahī* 'we send forth' = Skt. *preṣyāmasi*; YAv. *büšyaṇtąm* 'of those to be' : Skt. *bhaviṣyatām*, etc.

§ 156. Av. *-š* from orig. *s*, appears similarly (§ 155) when final after *i-, u-*vowels and their strengthenings, also after *ḥ* and *r*, cf. § 192 (3).

Av. *ažiš* 'Dragon' (nom. sg.); *gairiš* 'mountains' (acc. pl.); *tanūš* 'body'; *vaŋhūš* 'good' (acc. pl.); *rašnaoš* 'of Rashnu, Justice'; *vaŋhǝuš* 'of the good'; *barōiš* 'thou shouldst bear'; *gāuš* 'cow'; *uḥdāiš* 'with words'.—*drukš* 'fiend'; *ānuš.haḥš* 'following'; *parō-darǝš* 'Fore-seer' § 192 (3).

§ 157. On Av. *fš* from orig. *ps*, see § 144.

§ 158. Av. *š* (= older palatal *š + s* Indog. *ḱs*) = Skt. *kṣ*.

Av. *vaši* 'thou wilt' = Skt. *vákṣi* (√*vaś-*); Av. *dīšyāt̰* 'should show' (opt. aor.), cf. Skt. *adikṣat* (√ *diś-*); Av. *nāšǡti* 'may vanish' (aor. subj.), √ *naś-*: Av. *parōdarǝš* 'Fore-seer, the cock' (*-dars + s* nom. sg.); GAv. *nāšū* loc. pl. from *nās-* 'loss, mishap'.—So Av. *šaēti* 'he dwells' = Skt. *kṣéti*; Av. *mošu* 'quickly' = Skt. *makṣú*, cf. Lat. *mox*.—Similarly Av. *dašina-* 'right, dexter' = Skt. *dákṣiṇa-*; Av. √ *taš-* 'to fabricate' = Skt. *takṣ-*.

Note 1. Indog. *ḱs* appears in Av. as *šš*.—In Skt. orig. *ḱs* and *ḱs* fell together in *kṣ*; but Av. still holds them apart as respectively *šš* and *š*. See Hübschmann, *Z.D.M.G.* 38 p. 428. The same distinction between the two original sounds is to be remarked in Prakrit and Pāli as observed by Pischel, *Gött. gel. Anz.* 1881, p. 1322.

Note 2. On *ḥšmākǝm* 'of you' and *āšnąš* 'up to the knees', cf. §§ 77 Note 1, 188.

§ 159. Av. š appears for older palatal ś (= Skt. ś) before t (= Skt. ṣṭ), cf. § 147.

Av. *naštō* 'made to vanish' = Skt. *naṣṭás* (√*naś*-); GAv. *vaštī* 'he wishes' = Skt. *váṣṭi* (√*vaś*-); Av. *daršti-* 'seeing, sight' = Skt. *dṛ́ṣṭi-;* Av. *paršta-* 'question' = Skt. *pṛṣṭá-* (√*praś*-); GAv. *daēdōišt* redupl. aor. 3 sg. mid. Av. √*diš*- 'show' = Skt. √*diś-*.

§ 160. Av. š appears for older palatal ś (= Skt. ś) before n = Skt. *śn,* cf. § 148.

Av. *ašnaoiti* 'he attains' = Skt. *aśnóti;* Av. *frašnō* 'question' = Skt. *praśnás;* Av. *spašnaoṭ* 'he espied' √*spas-* = Skt. √*spaś-*.

Note. Sometimes Av. *s* appears instead of the above š before *n,* cf. § 146, and Note 2:—Av. *snaþa-* 'smiting, wounding', to √*snaþ-* = Skt. *snath-;* Av. *vasna* 'by will', √*vas-* = Skt. √*vaś-*.

§ 161. Av. š appears for old palatal ś (= Skt. ś) after Av. f (= orig. p), cf. similarly, orig. ps (dental) § 144.

Av. *fšǝbiš* 'with fetters', cf. Skt. 2 *pas-* 'to bind'; Av. *haurva-fš-avō* 'having whole flocks' *(pasu-* = Skt. *paśú-).*

Note. On Av. *tafsaṯ, noṛǝfsaiti* see § 144 Note 2.

§ 162. Av. šy (or sometimes simply š) appears for older cy. In GAv. the y is mostly retained; in YAv. the y is mostly dropped.

YAv. *šyaoþnǝm,* GAv. *šyaoþnǝm* 'deed' = Skt. *cyáutnám;* GAv. *ašyō,* YAv. *ašǝ* 'worse', comparat. to *aku-* (superl. *aciš̌ta-*), cf. Skt. *aka-;* YAv. *š̌āvayōiṯ* 'might cause to go' (√*šyu-*) = Skt. *cyāváyēt* (√*cyu-*); GAv. *šyeṇtī* 'they abide, repose', YAv. *š̌aitim* 'repose, joy', cf. Lat. *quies;* GYAv. *fraša-* 'forward, prone, ready' = Skt. *prácyá-;* GAv. *vašyeitē* 'is spoken' = Skt. *ucyátē.* See Hübschmann, Z.D.M.G. xxxviii. p. 431.

§ 163. Av. š (ṣ̌) = Skt. *rt.* See Bartholomae, A.F. ii. p. 39.

Av. *amǝšǝm* 'immortal' = Skt. *amŕ̥tam;* Av. *pǝšanā* 'battles' = Skt. *pŕ̥tanās;* Av. *mašyehe* 'of mortal' = Skt. *mártyasya;* Av. *bāšārǝm* 'rider' = Skt. *bhártāram.* —Likewise Av. *ašavanǝm* 'the righteous' = Skt. *r̥tá-*

vānam; Av. *aṣəm* 'Right, righteousness', beside Av. *an-arətāiš* = Skt. *r̥tām*; Av. *p̄wāṣəm* 'quickly' = Skt. *tūrtām*, et al.

Note. As a rule, Av. *š* = Skt. * árt, r̥t* (observe accent), and Av. *ərət* = Skt. *r̥t* (observe unaccented): — e. g. Av. *marətō* 'dead' = Slt. *mr̥tás*; Av. *bərətəm* 'carried' = Skt. *bhr̥tám*; Av. *fra-barətārəm* title of priest = Skt. *-bhartāram*. Allowing a shift of accent would explain a number of apparent anomalies where the law as to accent appears not to hold.

§ 164. Av. *š* results from Av. *z* changed to *š* before *n*.

Av. *rāšnąm* 'of ordinances', from stem *rāzan-*; Av. *rašnūm* 'Justice', beside *raz-ištəm* 'most just', Skt. *rā́j-iṣṭham*; Av. *barəšnavō* 'heights' beside *bərəz-atō* 'of the high', Skt. *br̥hatás*; Av. *dužvarəšnavhō* 'evil-doers' (*varz-*); Av. *ā-ḷ-šnūš* 'up to the knees', beside *zanva* 'knees', cf. Skt. *abhi-jñú* § 188.

Note 1. Observe however, that sometimes Av. *s* instead of *š* (for Av. *z*) before *n* is found, cf. § 153:—Av. *asni* 'by day' (*azan-*) = Skt. *áhni* (*áhan-*); Av. *paro.asnu-* 'beyond the day, future', cf. Skt. *aparāhṇá-* 'after mid-day'; Av. *yasnəm* 'worship' (beside *yaz-aite*) = Skt. *yajñám*; Av. *āsna-* 'in-born' (*ā* + |ˊ*zan-* 'to bear').

Note 2. Observe *š* in Av. *šnātar-* (|ˊ*zan-* 'know') = Skt. *jñātár*; Av. *žnūm* 'knee', *āžnubyasciṯ* 'even to the knees'.

§ 165. Av. *š* sometimes results from Av. *z* (= Skt. *j* or *h*) being changed to *š* before *s*.—See §§ 185, 186.

GAv. *ərəvāšaṯ* 'shall proceed' (s-aor.), |ˊ*vraz-* = Skt. *vraj-*; GAv. *vərəžaiti* 'may do' (s-aor.), |ˊ*varz-*, cf. Skt. |ˊ*varj-*; GAv. *varəš-cā* 2 sg. aor. (*ə* + *s*); Av. *hvarəš* 'well-doing' nom. sg. (*ə* + *s*); Av. *harəšyamna-* 'about to be imbrued' (*ə* + *s* |ˊ*harz-* = Skt. *sarj-*).

Note. Perhaps here Av. *ažaēta* 'might be led' beside Av. *azaiti*, Skt. *ájati*.

§ 166. Av. *š* sometimes results from Av. *z* (= Skt. *j*) being changed to *š* before *t* (cf. Skt. *ṣṭ*).

Av. *°maršta* 'rubbed' (|ˊ*marz-*) = Skt. *°mr̥ṣṭás* (|ˊ*marj-*); Av. *°haršta-* 'imbrued' (|ˊ*harz-*) = Skt. *°sr̥ṣṭá-* (|ˊ*sarj-*); Av. *yaštar-* 'worshipper' (|ˊ*yaz-*) = Skt. *yaṣṭar-* (|ˊ*yaj-*).

Av. z.

§ 167. General Remark. Av. z appears either as the representative of Skt. j or h, see § 88; or it is the corresponding sonant to s, §§ 106, 74.

§ 168. Av. z = Skt. j.

Av. zaošəm 'wish' = Skt. jóṣam; Av. zātō 'born' = Skt. jātás; Av. zəmbayadwəm 'ye knock together' = Skt. jambháyadhvam; Av. zināṭ 'may take violently' = Skt. jināt; Av. zrayō 'sea' = Skt. jráyas. — Av. azaiti 'he drives' = Skt. ájati; Av. yazaite 'he worships' = Skt. yájatē; Av. harəzaṇti 'they send forth' = Skt. sṛjánti; Av. vazrəm 'club' = Skt. vájram.

§ 169. Av. z = Skt. h.

Av. zasta- 'hand' = Skt. hásta-; Av. zarōiš 'of the golden' = Skt. hárēs; Av. zī 'for' = Skt. hí. — Av. azəm 'ἐγώ' = Skt. ahám; Av. mazištō 'μέγ-ιστος' = Skt. máhiṣṭhas; Av. bāzuš 'πῆχυς' = Skt. bāhús; Av. bərəzaṇtəm 'great, high' = Skt. bṛhántam; Av. maēzaṇti 'mingunt' = Skt. méhanti; Av. izyeiti 'he seeks', cf. Skt. thatē.

§ 170. Av. z results often from s being sonantized before sonant consonants.

Av. azgatō 'unmatched, unconquered' Yt. 13.107, √hag-, orig. sag- = Skt. √sagh-; Av. vaṇhazdā̊ 'giving the best' (comparat. to vaṇhu- + √dā), cf. Anc. Pers. vahyasdāta- nom. propr.; Av. māzdrājahya- 'a month long', cf. Skt. más-; Av. azdəbīš 'with bones' = (stem ast-); GAv. zdī 'be thou', cf. Av. as-ti 'he is'. Cf. Brugmann, Grundriss der vergl. Gram. §§ 589 seq.

§ 171. Av. z (similarly § 170) in combination zd = Skt. (i)dh, (ā)dh. See above (Bartholomae's Law) § 89; and Brugmann, Grundriss der vergl. Gram. §§ 476, 591.

Av. mazdāh- 'wisdom, Mazda' = Skt. °mēdhās; GAv. þrāzdūm 'ye protected' (s-aor. from √þrā-) = Skt. trādhvam; et al.

Original Av. z changed to s, š.

§ 172. Av. z before n becomes s (š), see §§ 153, 164 for examples.
§ 173. Av. z before m becomes s, see § 152 examples.
§ 174. Av. z before t becomes š, see § 166 examples.
§ 175. Av. z before s becomes š, see § 165 examples.

Av. ž.

§ 176. **General Remark.** Av. ž is the corresponding sonant to š as Av. z is to s. Sometimes (though more rarely) it answers like z to Skt. j, h.

§ 177. Av. ž (more rarely) = Skt. j. See § 88 Note 1.

Av. *taēžm 'sharpness, edge', cf. Skt. tējas ($\sqrt{tij}$-); Av. bažat 'he distributed, offered' = Skt. bhājat.

§ 178. Av. ž (more rarely) = Skt. h. See § 88 Note 1.

Av. aži 'Dragon' = Skt. áhis; Av. dažaiti 'it burns' = Skt. dáhati.

§ 179. Av. ž most commonly results from Av. š being sonantized before sonant consonants.

GAv. asrūždūm 'ye were heard of' (Ys. 32.3, s-aor. mid.-pass. $\sqrt{sru}$-) = Skt. asrōdhvam, beside Av. sᵊraožānē, sraoša-; Av. snaipižbya 'with two weapons' from stem Av. snaipiš-; Av. awždāta- 'laid in the waters', beside Av. afścipra- 'having the seed of waters'; Av. yaoždapəṇtəm 'making pure', beside Av. yaoš = Skt. yós. — Av. dužūhtəm 'ill-spoken' = Skt. duruktám; Av. dužvacavhō 'ill-speaking', beside Av. duškərətəm 'ill done' = Skt. durvacas, duṣkṛtám; Av. dušmanavhe 'to the evil-minded' (here m-surd) = Skt. durmanasē.

Note. Exceptions occur: GAv. ərəžvacō 'true-speaking' et al.; cf. Bartholomae, B.B. xiii. p. 77.

§ 180. Av. wž (= orig. bh + s) = Skt. ps. See § 89.

YAv. diwžaf 'from deceit', GAv. diwžaidyāi 'to deceive', cf. Skt. dipsati.

§ 181. YAv. ž (= Av. z [= Skt. h] + s) = Skt. kṣ. Cf. § 165.

YAv. us-važat 'he carried forth' (s-aor. from $\sqrt{vaz}$-) = Skt. vákṣat ($\sqrt{vah}$-).

Note 1. On *š* in GAv. *ažǝ̄nvamnǝm* 'unharmed' cf. Skt. √*kṣan*-, see § 89.
Note 2. GAv. *āžuš* Ys. 53.7 is uncertain. Uncertain also GYAv. *ižačal*, 'striving' to √*iz*- = Skt. √*īh*- (?).

§ 182. Av. *ž* appears for old palatal *j* (= Skt. *s*) before sonants.

GAv. *āždyāi* 'to attain', √*as*- = Skt. √*aś*-; GYAv. *vižibyō* 'to, from villages' (*vīs*-) = Skt. *viḍbhyás* (*vís*-).

§ 183. Av. *žd* = Skt. *ḍh*, or *ḍ*. See Brugmann, *Grundriss* § 591.

Av. *miždǝm* 'μισθόν' = Skt. *mīḍhám*; Av. *mǝrǝždikǝm* 'mercy' (if from √*marž*-, cf. § 179) = Skt. *mṛḍīkám*. Here again GAv. *asrūždūm* Ys. 32.3 (§ 179) = Skt. *asrǝḍhvam*.

Aspiration.

Av. *ʋ*, *ϛ*, *ᵽ*.
h, *ḣ*, *hv*.

§ 184. These are all derived from an original *s*-sound, and have been treated, in particulars, under the sibilants § 110 seqq.

Some Additional Rules as to Consonants.

§ 185. In Av., **assimilation** of consonants is sometimes found.

YAv. *nmānǝm* 'house' = GAv. *dǝmānǝm*; Av. *kamnǝm* 'few' (for **kabnǝm* or *kambuǝm* § 186), cf. *kambištǝm*.— Total assimilation, Av. *bunǝm* 'foundation' (for *bunnǝm* § 186) = Skt. *budhnám*; Av. *sanaṯ* 'it appeared' Yt. 14.7 (i. e. *sannaṯ, sad-naṯ*).

§ 186. In Av., **double consonants** (i. e. the same consonant repeated) are not allowed. If owing to total assimilation § 185 they should occur, the combination is then reduced in writing to a single consonant.

Av. *masyō* 'fish' (for *massyō* § 185) = Skt. *mátsyas*; Av. *usnāiti*- 'ablution' (for *ussnāiti*-, i. e. *ud-snāiti*- § 185, cf. Av. *us tanūm snayaēta*); Av. *dušiti*- 'distress' (i. e. *duš-šiti*-, cf. Skt. *sukṣiti*-); Av. *hōmipyaṯ* from hǝm + √mip- 'to change', Ys. 53.9; GAv. drǝgvasū 'among the wicked' (for drǝgvassu); Av. uṣahva 'at dawn' (for nṣah-hva); Av. ajāvarǝš 'evil-doing' (nom. sg. varǝz-š, from √varz- § 165); Av. huuǝm § 185 end.

§ 187. A consonant sometimes falls out. See § 186.

(1) g before v falls out in YAv.

YAv. drīvyās-ca 'poor' (gen. fem.), beside YAv. drijaoš (gen. masc. drijū-); YAv. drvaṇtǝm 'wicked', beside GAv. drǝgvaṇtǝm, cf. Skt. drúhvan-; YAv. hvōvā nomen propr. beside GAv. hvōgvō.

(2) d between consonants falls out.

Av. bǝrǝzaṇhya 'great' (dat. dual for older ·aṇdbhyǝ·).

(3) y after initial older š-palatal (= Skt. ś) sometimes falls out.

Av. sāmahe 'of black' = Skt. śyāmásya; Av. saēnō 'eagle' = Skt. śyenás.

(4) h (= original s) is dropped before m (initial) and r §§ 140, 138 seq.

(5) k (ḵ) seems sometimes to fall out.

Av. tūirya- 'quartus' for *kturya- cf. ā-ḵtūirya- 'four times'; Av. avajata 'he spake', if these forms are from √vac-.

(6) t seems sometimes to fall out.

GAv. nafšū loc. pl. for *naptsu from Av. napāt-, napt- 'offspring', cf. § 185 seq.

§ 188. Av. ḵ is sometimes introduced before š.

Av. āḵšnūš 'knee-high', cf. Skt. abhi-jñu; Av. ḵšmā-kǝm, ḵšmaṭ 'of, from you'.

§ 189. On s (= Skt. ś, s) retained before ·ca etc., see §§ 120 Note; 124 Note; 129.

§ 190. In Av., y takes the place of v between u and e.

Av. dnyē 'two' = Skt. dvé, Av. upa.mruyē 'I invoke' = Skt. upa-bruvé; Av. tanuyē 'for the body' = Skt. tanvé; Av. ·buye 'to be' = Skt. bhuvé.

Note. Similarly Av. uve ·both· (for *uvǝ, uwe § 68 Note 1) = Skt. ubhé.

§ 191. In Av., metathesis of *r* often takes place; —Skt. *vr (vl)* becomes with prothesis § 71, Av. *ᵘrv*.

Av. *āprava* 'priest' = Skt. *átharvā*; Av. *caprudasō* 'fourteenth' = Skt. *caturdaśás*; Av. *brātūiryō* 'uncle' (for *brātvryō* § 62) = Skt. *bhrā́tṛvyas*; Av. *ᵘrvātāiš* 'with doctrines', cf. Skt. *vrátāiš*; Av. *ᵘrvapō* 'faithful, friend' (√ *var*-).

§ 192. As final consonants in Av., the following may stand: (1) nasal, *n* and *m*, (2) dental *t̰* (or *t* when preceded by developed *s* or by *š*), (3) sibilant *š* and *s*.— Two consonants may stand in the case of *ḫš, fš, št, st* and GAv. *ng*.

(1) *barən* 'they carried'; *azəm* 'I'; (2) *pərəsat̰* 'he asked'; *amavat̰* 'strong'; (3) *hizubīš* 'with tongues'; *tanuš* 'body'; *haᵘrvatās* 'perfection' (nom. sg. -*tāt-s*); *ḫšayąs* 'ruling' (nom. sg. -*ant-s*). — *druḫš* 'fiend, Druj'; *āfš* 'water'; *kərəfš* 'corpse'; *cōišt* 'he promised, announced'; *aⁱbī.mōist* 'he turned toward'.— GAv. *mašyə̄ng* 'mortals' acc. pl.

Note. When orig. *s* precedes final *t̰* the latter is dropped:—e. g. Av. *ās* (i. e. **ās-t̰*) 'was' = Skt. *ā́sīt*; Av. *cinas* (i. e. *cinast § 109) 'thou didst promise', opp. to *cōišt* or to *mōist (mip-)*.

§ 193. Av. *m* appears instead of final *n* in vocatives of *an*-stems.

Av. *ašāum* 'O righteous one' = Skt. *ṛ́tāvan*; Av. *āpraom* 'O priest' = Skt. *átharvan*; Av. *yum* (for *yuvən) 'O youth' = Skt. *yúvan*; Av. *θrizafəm* 'O triple-jawed' (cf. acc. *θrizafanəm*).

Note 1. The MSS. often fluctuate between final *m* and *n* in endings, *ą, ąn, ąm*, e. g. *huoma, haomąn, haomąm* 'haoma-offerings' (acc. pl.) Yt. 10.92 = Skt. *sómān*, cf. § 45 Note 2.— So apparently, Av. *cašmąm* 'in eye', cf. Skt. *jánman*.

Note 2. Observe other MS. fluctuations (cons. and vowel): — *c ǰ; j z; þ d; ā ǣ; ə̄ āu; ə̄ āṯ; ai aə; ə u — daţqm, dadqm; mazdā, mazdə̄, hratā̊ ᵒtāu; vastrā ᵒtrāt̰.*

§ 194. Av. avoids generally a repetition of the same syllable.

Av. *maiḍyāiryehe* 'of Mid-Year' (for *maiḍya-yāiryehe*); *huyāiryā* 'of good harvest' (for *huyāiryaya*); Av. *frazinte, frazinṭa* 'they are, were plundered' (for **frazinante, *frazinaṇṭa*), cf. Skt. *prajināte*; Av. *harəna hacimnō* for **harənanha hacimnō* attended with glory Yt. 10.121.

Resumé.
Principal differences between Sanskrit and Avesta in Phonology.
Vowels.

§ 195. GAv. lengthens all final vowels, YAv. lengthens them in monosyllables, shortens them in polysyllables (§§ 24—26).

§ 196. Original ī and ū are lengthened before final m in Av. (§ 23).

§ 197. Av. ẹ ọ generally answers to Skt. a before m or n. — Av. ṃ (aṇ) = Skt. r̥ (§§ 29, 47).

§ 198. Av. e, commonly a modification of internal a after y. — Sometimes equals final ya (§§ 34, 67).

§ 199. Av. ō chiefly equals final Skt. as (o) § 120.

§ 200. Av. å chiefly equals Skt. ās; — more rarely Skt. ā + stop-sound (§§ 121—124, 44).

§ 201. Av. ą q is a nasalization of a (ā) before m or n. It often equals Skt. a with anusvāra (§§ 45, 46).

Diphthongs.

§ 202. The Skt. e is represented by Av. aē, ōi, or (when final) e; the Skt. o by Av. ao, āu, or (when final) ō (§§ 55—58, 35, 41).

§ 203. A striking peculiarity in Av. is Epenthesis (§ 70) and Anaptyxis (§ 72) and the frequent Reductions (samprasāraṇa etc.) § 63 seq.

Consonants.

§ 204. The voiceless spirants Av. h, þ, f are chiefly sprung from old tenues k, t, p before consonants; — sometimes they represent old voiceless aspirates (§ 77 seq.).

Resumé of principal Phonetic Laws.

§ 205. The original voiced aspirates *gh, dh, bh* fell primarily together with the mediae in Av. (§ 82).

§ 206. The voiced spirants Av. *j, d, w* are developments from these earlier two-fold mediae (§ 83).

§ 207. Skt. *j* is often represented by Av. *z* (§ 168).

§ 208. Skt. *h* is represented sometimes by Av. *j*, sometimes by Av. *z* (§§ 88, 169).

§ 209. Skt. *s* generally becomes *h* in Av. (§ 110 seq.).

§ 210. Skt. *as* (internal) becomes *avh, ah;* or (final) *ō* (§§ 111—120).

§ 211. Av. *ðs* (internal) becomes *ðvh, ðh;* or (final) *ð* (§§ 121—124).

§ 212. Skt. *ś* is represented in Av. by *s* (§ 146).

§ 213. Skt. *sv* is represented in Av. by *sp* (§ 97).

§ 214. Skt. *ch* is represented in Av. by *s* (§ 142).

§ 215. Dentals before dentals are changed to *s* in Av. (§ 151).

§ 216. Av. *z* and *s* (= Skt. *ś*) before voiceless consonants generally become *š* (§§ 164—166, 160).

§ 217. Skt. *rt* is often represented in Av. by *š* (§ 163).

§ 218. Skt. *kṣ* is represented by Av. *hš* or *š* (§ 158 Note 1).

INFLECTION.
DECLENSION,
NOUNS AND ADJECTIVES.

§ 219. Nominal declension includes nouns and adjectives; these may be conveniently taken together in Avesta and divided into two great classes of declension—(a) the **vowel class**, and (b) the **consonant class**—according as the stem ends in a vowel or in a consonant.

For a summary of Avesta declension in a tabular form, see opposite page.

§ 220. **Case, Number, Gender.** The Avesta agrees with the Sanskrit in its **eight cases**, nominative, accusative, instrumental, dative, ablative, genitive, locative, vocative; **three numbers**, singular, dual, plural; and in the **three genders**, masculine, feminine, and neuter.

The uses of the cases are in general the same as in Skt., but see § 233. The Av. dual is interesting as showing a distinct form for the locative case, see §§ 223, 236, 262. In Avesta, a substantive has commonly the same gender that it has in Sanskrit.

Note 1. As to gender, however, some individual peculiarities occur, as a few words in Av. show a **different gender** from that which they have in Skt.:—e. g. Av. vāc- (masc.) 'vox' = Skt. vāc (fem.)—but observe the compound paitivac- is fem.; Av. taršna- (masc.) 'thirst' = Skt. tṛṣṇā- (fem.); Av. zaṅga- (masc.) 'leg' = Skt. jaṅghā- (fem.); Av. sti- (fem.) 'existence, creation' = Skt. sti- (masc.)—This occasional phenomenon is sometimes important to observe in the matter of exegesis.

Note 2. On fem. and neut. plur. forms interchanging with each other, see § 232.

SYNOPSIS OF DECLENSION.

A. Vowel Stems.

1. Stems in *a*.
2. Stems in *ā* { a. Derivative stems in *-ā*.
                  b. Radical stems in *-ā*.
3. Stems in *i* and *ī* { a. Derivative stems in original *-i*.
                          b. Derivative stems in original *-ī*.
                          c. Radical stems in original *-ī*.
4. Stems in *u* and *ū* { a. Derivative stems in original *-u*.
                          b. Derivative stems in original *-ū*.
                          c. Radical stems in original *-ū*.
5. Diphthongal stems { a. Stems in *-ai*.
                       b. Stems in *-āu*.

B. Consonant Stems.

6. (A) Stems without suffix.
7. (B) Derivative stems in *-ant, -mant, -vant*.
8. (C) Derivative stems in *-an, -man, -van*.
9. (D) Derivative stems in *-in*.
10. (E) Radical stems in *-u* and *-n*.
11. (F) Stems in original *r* { a. Derivative stems in original *-tar, -ar*.
                                 b. Radical stems in original *-r*.
                                 c. Neuters (derivative) in original *-ar*.
12. (G) Stems in original *s* — { α. *-ah*.
                                  β. *-ih*.
                                  γ. *-uh*.
   b. Radical stems in *-h* (original *-s*) — { α. *-āh*.
                                                 β. *-īh*.
                                                 γ. *-ūh*.
   c. Derivative stems in *-īh, -ūh*.
   3. Those resembling them.

§ 221. **Endings.** Here may be enumerated the normal endings which are added to the stem in formation of the various cases. The stem itself, moreover, sometimes varies in assuming these endings, as it often appears in a stronger form in certain cases, and in a weaker form in others. Connecting elements as in Skt. seem at times to be introduced between stem and ending.

The normal endings (but observe §§ 25, 26) are:

i. MASCULINE — FEMININE.

Singular:

	Av.		cf. Skt.
N.	-s (-š), — .	.	-s, —
A.	-(a)m . . .	.	-(a)m
I.	-ā .	.	-ā
D.	-ē		-ē
Abl.	-(a)ṯ		-aṯ
G.	(-as°) -ō; -s (-š); -hv, -hyā .		-as; -s; -sya
L.	-i		-i
V.	— .	.	—

Dual:

N.A.V.	-ā .	. .	-ā (Ved.)
I.D.Abl.	-byā .		-bhyām
G.	-ā̊ .	.	-ōs
L.	-ō	. .	see gen.

Plural:

N.V.	(-as°) -ō, ā		-as
A.	(-ns°), (-as°) -ō; ā . .		(-ns) -as
I.	-biš		-bhis
D.	(-byas°) -byō .		-bhyas
G.	-ąm . .		-ām
L.	-su, šu, hu .		-su

ii. NEUTER (Separate Forms).

Sg.	N.A.V.	—, -m .	. . .	—, -m
Du.	N.A.V.	—, -ī .		-ī
Pl.	N.A.V.	—, -i . .		-i

General Remarks on the Endings.
I. MASCULINE—FEMININE.

§ 222. Singular:—

Nominative: The typical ending -s is disguised by entering into euphonic combinations with vowels and consonants; it assumes especially often the form -š, § 156.—Often it is wanting—e. g. cf. derivative stems in orig. ā and ī.

Accusative: The typical ending -m appears after vowels; the ending -əm (= -am = -ṃm) after consonants. Cf. also § 23.

Instrumental: Regularly ā, a, § 25.—This is sometimes disguised by combining with a preceding y to e, § 67.—The fem. ā-declension, as in Skt., shows a fuller form, making the case end in -uyā (-nya) beside the simpler normal form in ā.

Dative: YAv. -e (orig. -ai), GAv. -ē, -ōi, § 56.—Notice of course Av. -āē-ca.—In the a-declension, the ē (orig. ai) unites with the stem vowel into āi, cf. Gr. ῳ, § 60.—The feminine derivative ā-stems and ī-stems show a fuller ending āi, which in the ā-stems is preceded by a y, as in Skt. also.

Ablative: The typical ending is -t, or -(a)t (consonant decl.), -āt (in a-decl.). Observe, this is not confined, as in Skt., simply to the a-declension, but appears in all the declensions (ā, ī, ū and cons.). Instances of interchanges between -at and -āt are not infrequent.—Observe before -ca, the form -āatca, § 53 iv.—The ending -(a)t is often followed by the enclitic postposition a, thus giving -(a)ta.—In GAv., the t-ablative is found, as in Skt., only with the a-declension, e. g. hyapiāt, akāt; otherwise, as in Skt., the genitive is used with ablative force.—The feminine ā- and ī-stems, unlike the Skt., both show -āt which in the ā-stems is preceded by y.

Genitive: The common ending, as in Skt., is ō, -asca; it occurs chiefly in the consonant declension.—The ending, simple (s) š is also found, e. g. throughout the i- and u-stems, the stem vowel being generally strengthened before it.—In the a-stems, the ending -hē (Skt. -sya, § 67), GAv. -hyā, -hyācā (on h cf. § 133) is regularly found.—In feminine ā- and ī-stems a fuller ending -ō, -āsca (= Skt. ās) is found, which in the ā-declension is preceded by y as in Skt.,—see dative above.

Locative: The normal form, as in Skt., is -i.—In the a-declension, this coalesces with the stem vowel to -e, -āē-ca.—Sometimes the loc. is without ending—the stem being simply strengthened, e. g. cf. u-stems and some an-forms.—To the locative ending, an enclitic postpositive a is often attached, giving rise to forms in -ya (-aya),

-a̅ca.—The feminine ā-stems show -aya (perhaps orig. instr., or ya-suffix advl.) answering to Skt. -āyām.

Vocative: Commonly, simple stem without ending. — Often the nom. stands instead of the vocative.

§ 223. Dual:—

Nom. Acc. Voc.: The prevailing form for the consonant and the a-declension is ā (a), cf. Vedic Skt. ā.—The ā-stems show ē (e).—The masc. fem. i- and u-stems simply lengthen (then YAv., cf. § 25 and Note, shorten) their stem vowels.

Instr. Dat. Abl.: The normal ending in Av. is -byā (-byō).—The form -byąm, which exactly corresponds to Skt. -bhyām, is only once found, in Av. brvaṯbyąm 'both brows'.—Instead of YAv. -bya, the form written -we (§§ 67, 87) often appears.

Genitive: Regularly -ā̊, -ā̊sca answering to Skt. -ōs—a preceding vowel being treated as in Skt.

Locative: The ending ō occurs in zastayō (YAv.) from zasta- 'hand', in ubōyō (GAv.) from uba- 'both', and aṅhvō (GAv.) Ys. 41.2 from aṅhu- 'world, life'.

§ 224 Plural:—

Nom. Voc.: The typical form orig. as occurs both in the vowel and the consonant classes of declension.—But beside this, in the masculine of both classes the ending ā (a) is common, especially in YAv.—Its occurrence in the consonant. declension is probably due to borrowing from the a-decl.—In the a-declension, the normal orig. -as unites, as in Skt., with the stem vowel, thus giving -ā̊ (= orig. -ās, § 124) which is, however, less common than the ending ā (a).—Often the a-stems have -ā̊ṅhō, cf. Vedic Skt. -āsas.—In the i-stems, the usual nom. pl., as in Vedic Skt., is -iš instead of -yō, -yasca.

Accusative: The original ending -ns (seen in -qsca from a-stems) appears in the consonant stems as -ō, -as° (i. e. orig. -ns).—Beside this, in the masculine of both classes the ending ā (a) is found, cf. nom. above.—In the a-declension the normal orig. -ns combines with the a of the stem into YAv. -q(n), -qsca, GAv. -ə̄ṅg, -qsca—sometimes also YAv. -š, -šca.—The fem. ā-stems show -ā̊, -ā̊sca.—The masc. fem. i- and u-stems show generally -īš, -ūš.

Instrumental: Everywhere the ending -biš, -bīš (§ 21 Note), except in the a-stems which show -āiš.

Dat. Abl.: The regular form is -byō, -byasca, or written -ayō, -aya, -uyō, §§ 83 (4), 87, 62 Note 3.

Genitive: Universally -ąm, which is often dissyllabic as in Vedic Skt. —In the vowel stems an n is usually inserted before this -ąm.

Remarks on the Endings, Cases and Forms. 67

Locative: The normal form is *-hu, -ju.*—To this ending, an **enclitic postpositive** *a* in YAv. is often attached, thus giving *-hva, -jva,* cf. Skt. *vánĕṣv ā* RV. 9.62.8.

ii. NEUTER (Separate Forms).

The neuter shows in general the same endings as the masculine. Its special forms, however, are worthy of note in the following cases:

§ 225. **Singular:**—
Nom. Acc. Voc.: In general no ending — the case is simply the bare stem in its weak form, if the stem have a weak form. The *a*-stems have *m* as in the accusative masculine.

§ 226. **Dual:**—
Nom. Acc. Voc.: The ending orig. *-ī* is to be recognized in the *a*-stems, where it is combined with the stem vowel preceding it, into *e,* e. g. *duy-e saiṫ-e* 'two hundred'.—Sometimes the simple stem (or like nom. sing.) seems to be used, e. g. *va, dąma* Yt. 15.43, *aṣi* 'two eyes' Yt. 11.2.

§ 227. **Plural:**—
Nom. Acc. Voc.: Commonly the ending is wanting i. e. the case-form is the simple stem, or if consonantal it is the strongest form of the stem (cf. *afsmanivąn* i. e. orig. *vānt;* or again *manå* from *ah*-stem). —Seldom the ending is *-i: nāmąni,* cf. Skt. *nāmāni.*—Sometimes in the consonant declension, the endings *-a, -å* of the vowel (*a-* or *ā-*) declension are found, cf. § 234, e. g. *daēmāna, masanå, maēsma* to stems *daēman-* 'eye, glance', *masan-* 'greatness', *maēsman-* 'urine', but see § 308.

§ 228. **General Plural Case.**
The plural in Av. occasionally shows a certain instability which is exhibited in the transfer or rather generalization of some of its case-forms. This is especially true of the neuter plural; and in general it may be added that the tendency to fluctuation increases in proportion to the lateness of the text.—See also, Johannes Schmidt, *Pluralbildungen der indogermanischen Neutra* pp. 259 seq., 98 seq.

§ 229. (1) The instrumental plural in *-biš, -āiš* is occasionally used in YAv. as general plural case, e. g. *azdbīš* (as acc. neut. Vd. 6.49)— *vīspāiš* (nom. Yt. 8.48), *sraēštāiš* (Yt. 22.9), *hufstrāiš* (as acc. Ys. 19.2), etc.

§ 230. (2) The *an*-stems have also the neuter plural in *ą(n)* sometimes used as general plural case, see § 308.

§ 231. (3) An ending *-īš, -āš* (like orig. fem. pl.) is sometimes employed in nouns and adjectives as general plural case, acc. as well as instr., e. g. GYAv. *nāmąnīš* (as acc.) Yt. 1.11 and (as instr.) Ys. 51.22

= Ys. 15.2, YAv. *afuonīš* Vsp. 21.3, *aēuuhutīš* Vd. 19.37 *auhāš* Vsp. 6.1, GAv. *avaŋhāš* (as instr.) Ys. 12.4, *jaīāš* Ys. 12.4.

§ 232. Interchange of Neuter with Feminine forms. Closely connected with this instability in the plural (especially neuter) is the interchange between neuter and feminine forms, as the neuter plural (occasionally also the singular) often shows the closest analogy to the feminine. Instances of this interchange are abundant, e. g. *a*-decl. *nmānəm* (nom. acc. sg. neut.) 'house', beside which *nmānα* (acc. pl., cf. fem.), *nmānāhu* (loc. pl., cf. fem.); *aēvrəm* (nom. acc. sg. neut.) 'cloud', *aēvra* (nom. pl., cf. fem.).—*ah*-stem *avaŋhō* (gen. sg.) 'of aid', GYAv. *avaŋhāi* (dat. sg. fem.).—Similarly stem *barəzah*- (neut.) beside *barəzā*- 'height', et al.—Adjective combinations *tišarō sata* 'three hundred', *vīspāhu karšvōhu* 'in all climes', *s^urascəintīš harəpō* 'steaming viands'. See also, Johannes Schmidt, *Pluralbildungen* p. 29 seq.

§ 233. Interchange of cases in their functions. The cases in their usage are not always so sharply distinguished in YAv. as in Sanskrit. Sometimes a case may take upon itself the functions that belong properly to another, e. g. dative in genitive sense, etc. A discussion of the question, however, belongs to Syntax.

§ 234. Transition in Declension. Transfers of inflection in parts of some words from one declension to another, especially in general from the consonant declension to the *a*-declension, are not infrequent in Avesta. A word may thus follow one declension in the majority of its cases, but occasionally make up certain of its forms quite after another declension. Examples are numerous and are of two kinds.

(a) The simple unchanged stem is used, but given the endings of another declension — much the commonest case, e. g. stem *jaidyan^t*- 'imploring' with dat. sg. *jaidyantāi* (*a*-decl.) instead of *jaidyaitē; *tacintąm* acc. sg. f., et al.

Vowel Class: — (1) Stems in *a*. 69

(b) The stem itself is remodelled and made to conform to another declension, thus really giving a new stem, e. g. *sravah-* 'word' with instr. pl. *sravāiš* (stem *srava-*) instead of *sravōbiš cf. gen. pl. *sravaŋhąm*. The case is much less common.

§ 235. **Stem-gradation.** In Avesta, as in Sanskrit— cf. Whitney, *Skt. Gram.* § 311—the stem of a noun or adjective, especially in the consonant declension, often shows **vowel-variation**, strongest, middle or strong, and weak forms,

ā, a, —,
-āy-, -ay-, -i-;
-āu-, -ao-, -u-;
-ārᵊ-, -arᵊ-, -r-, -ǝrᵊ-;
-ānt-, -ǝnt-, -at- [= n̥t̪];
-ān-, -ǝn-, -n-; etc. (cf. § 60).

The strong and strongest forms appear commonly in Singular Nom. Acc. Loc., in Dual Nom. Acc., and in Plural Nom., of the Masc. and Fem., and in the Plural Nom. Acc. of the Neuter. The remaining cases are weak, but there is much overlapping in this matter of stem-gradation. The distinctions are not always so sharply drawn as in Sanskrit.

A. STEMS IN VOWELS.
1. Stems in *a*.
Masculine and Neuter (cf. Whitney, *Skt. Gram.* § 330).

I. MASCULINE.

§ 236. Av. ⟨yasna⟩ *yasna-* m. 'worship, sacrifice' = Skt. *yajñá-*.

Av. *mazda-yasna-*,[1] *daēva-yasna-*[1] 'worshipper of Mazda, of Demons'; *ahura-* 'Lord, Ahura'; *vīra-* 'man'; *haoma-* 'haoma-plant'.

---

[1] The forms with e. g. °*yasna* are from *mazda-yasna-*, *daēva-yasna-*. The forms in parentheses do not actually occur, but are made up after the forms beside them — so throughout below.

Inflection: Declension of Nouns and Adjectives.

	Av.	Singular:	cf. Skt.
N.	yasn-ō .		yajñ-ás
A.	yasn-ǝm		yajñ-ám
I.	yasn-a .		yajñ-á (Ved.)
D.	yasn-āi		yajñ-áya
Abl.	yasn-āṭ		yajñ-át
G.	yasn-ahe .		yajñ-ásya
L.	yesn-e[1] . . .		yajñ-é
V.	(yasn-a) ahura . .		yájñ-a

Dual:

N.A.V.	(yasn-a) vīra . . .	yajñ-á (Ved.)
I.D.Abl.	(yasn-aēibya) vīraēibya .	yajñ-ábhyām
G.	(yasn-ayā̊) vīrayā̊ . .	yajñ-áyōs
L.	(yasn-ayō) zastayō .	—

Plural:

N.V.	•yasn-a	yajñ-ás
	•-ā̊ŋhō .	-ā́sa(Ved.)
A.	(yasn-ą) haomą	yajñ-án
I.	yasn-āiš .	yajñ-āis
D.Abl.	•yasn-aēibyō	yajñ-ébhyas
G.	yasn-anąm . .	yajñ-ánām
L.	(yasn-aēšu) vīraēšu .	yajñ-éṣu
	•-aēšva . .	—

ii. NEUTER (Separate Forms).

§ 237. Av. vastra- 'garment' = Skt. vástra-; Av. havuharǝna- 'jaw'.

	Av.	cf. Skt.
Sg. N.A.V.	vastr-ǝm . . .	vástr-am
Du. N.A.V.	(vastr-e) havuharǝne .	vástr-e
Pl. N.A.V.	vastr-a	vástr-ā (Ved.)

Forms to be observed in GAv. and YAv.

§ 238. In general, GAv. has the same forms as above, with long final vowel, cf. § 26.

---

[1] cf. § 34.

i. MASCULINE.

§ 239. Singular:—

Nom.: YGAv. *yasnas-ca*.—Quite late, the forms of nom. sg. in *-a*, *-e* Yt. 1.8,12 seqq. and occasionally in the Vd.

Acc.: YAv. also *maṣ̌īm* 'mortal' (i. e. *-ya-m*, § 63); *daēūm* 'demon' (i. e. *-va-m* § 63).—GAv. also *maṣ̌īm* 'mortal' (i. e. *-ya-m*); also *anyəm*, §§ 32, 29, beside *ainīm* 'alium'; *fraṣ̌īm* 'proue, ready'.

Instr.: YAv. also *hvaēpaipe* 'with own' (*-e = -ya*, § 67).

Abl.: YAv. *yasnāaṱ-ca* (§ 53 iv).—Also *miþrāda* 'from Mithra' (*-āṱ + a*, § 222) Yt. 10.42; *sraošaḍa* 'from obedience'; *xšaþrāda* 'by the sovereignty' Ys. 9.4.—Also *huþaxtāṱ haca θanvanāṱ* 'from well-drawn bow' § 19.

Gen.: YAv. *vāstryehe* 'of a husbandman' (§ 34).—GAv. has only *-hyā* e. g. *yasnahyā, vāstryehyō*, or *-hyā* (before *-ca* 'que' § 133) e. g. *ašahyā-cā*.

Loc.: YAv. *zqθaē-ca* 'and in birth' (§ 55).—With postpos. *a* § 222, *nmānaya* 'in the house' (*-aē + a*).—Also (sporadic) *raiþya* 'in a chariot' Yt. 17.17. —Again (rare) *maiδyōi* 'in medio' Vd. 15.47;—but (often in compounds § 56) *maiδyōi°*.—GAv. *yesnē*, as above.—Also (common) *zqθōi* 'in birth' § 56.

§ 240. Dual:—

N.A.V.: YAv. also (but not common) *gavō* 'both hands', *yaskō* 'two sicknesses', § 42.

I.D.Abl: YAv. also *gaošaiwe* beside *gaošaēwe* 'with both ears' (§§ 85, 67), *pāδave* 'with both feet' (§§ 87, 67).—GAv. *rānōibyā* 'with both allies'.

Gen.: YAv. *hāvanayās-ca* 'of both haoma-mortars'.

§ 241. Plural:—

Nom.: YAv. also (not common) *aməšā* 'immortals' (*-ā = Skt. -ās*).—Observe YAv. *aire* 'Aryans' (*-e = -ya*, § 67).

Acc.: YAv. *yasnqs-ca;* also *daēvqn* 'Demons'.—Sometimes *yazatā* 'divinities' (§ 33); *daēvās-ca* 'and Demons'.—Again like nom. *yazata* 'divinities', *mąþrā̊* 'words'.—GAv. (regularly) *mašyəng* 'mortals'; also *yasnqs-cā* 'and sacrifices'. Like nom. (rare) *mąþrā̊* 'words'.

Instr.: YAv. also (rare) *āfrivanāibiš* 'with blessings'.

Dat. Abl.: YAv. *mazdayasnaēibyas-ca*.—GAv. also *yasnōibyō* 'with sacrifices'.

Gen.: YAv. also (isolated) *mašyąnqm* 'of mortals' (*ā*).—Occasionally without inserted *n varəsqm* 'of hairs' (*°qm* for *°anqm*), *suxrqm, muþrqm*.

Loc.: GAv. (only *ū*) *mašyaēšū* 'among mortals'.

ii. NEUTER (Separate Forms).

§ 242. Plural:—

N.A.V.: YAv. also *vastrā̊* (*ā*-decl., § 232).

Loc.: YAv. also *nmānāhu* 'in houses' (*ā*-decl., § 232).

2. Stems in ā.

Feminine (cf. Whitney, *Skt. Gram.* § 364).

§ 243. Av. -𐬛𐬀𐬉𐬥𐬁- *daēnā-* f. 'conscience, religion'.
Av. *urvarā-* 'tree', *grīvā-* 'neck', *nāirikā-* 'woman', *gāθā-* 'hymn'.

A. Derivative Stems in ā.

FEMININE.

	Av. Singular:	cf. Skt.
N.	*daēn-a*	*sēn-ā*
A.	*daēn-ąm*	*sēn-ām*
I.	*daēn-aya*	*sēn-ayā*
D.	*daēn-ayāi*	*sēn-āyāi*
Abl.	(*daēn-ayāt̃*) *urvarayāt̃*	see gen.
G.	*daēn-ayā̊*	*sēn-āyās*
L.	(*daēn-aya*) *grīvaya*	*sēn-āyām*
V.	*daēn-e*	*sēn-e*

Dual:

N.A.V.	(*daēn-e*) *urvaire*	*sēn-e*
I.D.Abl.	(*daēn-ābya*) *gāθwābya*	*sēn-ābhyām*
G.	(*daēn-ayā̊*) *nāirikayā̊* [1]	*sēn-ayos*

Plural:

N.V.	*daēn-å*	*sēn-ās*
A.	*daēn-å*	*sēn-ās*
I.	*daēn-ābīš*	*sēn-ābhis*
D.Abl.	*daēn-ābyō*	*sēn-ābhyas*
G.	(*daēn-anąm*) *urvaranąm*	*sēn-ānām*
L.	(*daēn-āhu*) *urvarāhu*	*sēn-āsu*
	-*āhva gāθāhva*	—

Forms to be observed in GAv. and YAv.

§ 244. In general, GAv. has the same forms as above, with the long final vowel, cf. § 26.

§ 245. Singular:—
Nom.: YAv. also *nāire* 'manly' (fem. adj., -*e* = -*ya*, § 67) = Skt. *náryā*.—

---

[1] See Haug, *Zand-Pahlavi Glossary* p. 100 l. 23.

Vowel Class: — (2) Stems in $\bar{a}$.

Again some adjs. and nouns, like the pronominal declension, have -e for -a: Av. nāirike (nom.) beside nāirika 'woman', aparənāyūke 'maiden', parəne 'plena' beside acc. parənam. — GAv. also barəhδ̄ 'dear, welcome'.

Instr.: YAv. also daēna. — Also (isolated) suwrya 'with a ring' beside acc. suwrəm, cf. Skt. śubhráyā, śubhrám. — GAv. duenā; — also sāsnayā 'by command'.

Dat.: YAv. also (rare) gaēþyāi 'for the world' Ys. 9.3 seq.

Abl.: In GAv. wanting — its place supplied by gen.

Gen.: YAv. daēnayās-ca § 124 Note. — GAv. (exceptional) vairyā̊ Ys. 43.13 from vairya- 'desirable' (for vairyayā̊ § 104 trissyllabic).

Voc.: GAv. pōurucistā 'O Pourucista', spəṇtā 'O holy one'.

§ 246. Dual: —

Acc.: YAv. (rare) vąpwa 'flocks' (a-decl.).

§ 247. Plural: —

N.A.V.: YGAv. duenā̊s-ca.

Dat. (Abl.): YAv. urvarā̊byas-ca 'and from trees'. — Also gaēþāvyō 'from beings', vōignāuyō 'from plagues' Ys. 68.13, § 62 Note 3. — Again (but uncommon) haēnābyō 'from hosts' Vt. 10.93 (analogy to the following word draomǎbyō).

Gen.: YAv. (not common) jənąnąm 'of woman' (-ą- § 45). — Without inserted n (-ąm for -anąm) nāirikąm 'of woman'.

Loc.: GAv. (only -hū) adāhū 'in rewards'.

B. Radical Stems in $\bar{a}$.

§ 248. Stems with radical $\bar{a}$, so far as they have not gone over to the ordinary a, $\bar{a}$ declension, are represented by a few forms (a) masculine and neuter, (b) feminine.

(i) **Masculine and Neuter** (cf. Lanman, *Noun Inflection in the Veda* p. 443 seq.).

§ 249. Declension of Av. raþaēštā- m. 'warrior standing in chariot' = Skt. rathēṣṭhá- (part of its forms, however, are from the stem raþaēštar-, cf. Skt. sūryeṣṭhár-). — The forms from radical raþae-štā- are: — **Singular**. Nom. raþaēštā̊; Acc. raþaēštąm; Dat. raþōište (cf. Skt. dhiyą-dhḗ, and on ōi cf. § 56), raþaēštāi (a-decl., cf. Skt. rathēṣṭháyā); Gen. raþaēštā̊. — **Plural**. Acc. raþaēštā̊s-cā.

Note 1. The forms from stem raþaēštar- are enumerated at § 330.

Note 2. Similar, dat. sg. neut. pōi 'for protecting'; cf. also vōi.

(ii) **Feminine** (cf. Whitney, *Skt. Gram.* § 351).

§ 250. Here belong a few forms:—Singular. Nom. *jā̊* 'joyous', *ākā̊* 'judgment'; Acc. *mqm* 'measure' Vd. 5.61; Yt. 5.127; Instr. *jya* 'with bowstring'.—Plural. Nom. *jyā̊* 'bowstrings'.

3. Stems in *i* and *ī*.

Masculine, Feminine and Neuter (cf. Whitney, *Skt. Gram.* §§ 339, 364).

A. Derivative Stems in original *i*.

i. MASCULINE—FEMININE.

§ 251. Av. ࢽࣞ *ga͡iri-* m. 'mountain' = Skt. *giri-*. Av. *ax̌ti-* f. 'sickness', *paitištāiti-* f. 'opposition', *nmānō.paiti-* m. 'lord of house', *aẽpra.paiti-* m. 'teacher', *aši-* f. 'Rectitude, Blessing', *aši-* n. 'eye'.

	Av.	Singular:	cf. Skt.
N.	*ga͡ir-iš*	.	*gir-is*
A.	*ga͡ir-īm*	.	*gir-im*
I.	*(ga͡ir-i) ax̌ti* . .		*gir-i* (Ved.)
D.	*(gar-ǰe) paitištāite*		*gir-áyē*
Abl.	*gar-ōit̰*		see gen.
G.	*gar-ōiš* .		*gir-és*
L.	*gar-a*		*gir-á* (Ved.)
V.	*(ga͡ir-e) nmānō.paite* . .		*gir-e*
	-i aši . .		—

Dual:

N.A.V.	*(ga͡ir-i) aẽpra.paiti* . .		. .	*gir-í*
I.D.Abl.	*(ga͡ir-ibya) ašibya* . .		.	*gir-ibhyām*

Plural:

N.	*gar-ayō* .	. . .		*gir-áyas*
A.	*ga͡ir-īš* .			*gir-īn* m., *-īs* f.
D.Abl.	*ga͡ir-ibyō* .	. . .		*gir-ibhyó*
G.	*ga͡ir-inqm*	.	.	*gir-īṇā́m*

ii. NEUTER (Separate Forms).

§ 252. Av. *bāiri-* n. 'richness', *zarap̌uštri-* (adj.) 'Zoroastrian'.

Sg. N.A.V.	*būir-i*	. cf. Skt.	*bhūr-i*
Pl. N.A.V.	*(būir-i) zarap̌uštri*	.	*bhūr-i*

Forms to be observed in GAv. and YAv.

§ 253. In general, GAv. has the same forms as above, with the long final vowel, cf. § 26.

§ 254. Singular:—

Acc.: In metrical passages, *-īm* (cf. § 23) is sometimes dissyllabic, cf. Geldner, *Metrik* p. 15.

Dat.: YAv. *paitištātayaē-ca* 'and for withstanding'.—GAv. has *-ayōi* (= YAv. *-aye-* § 56) e. g. *aħtōyōi* 'for sickness' (on *ō* see § 39 Note).—Also from weak stem GAv. *paipyaē-cā* (YAv. *paipē* Yt. 17.58) 'and to the husband' = Skt. *pátyē*, cf. Lanman, *Noun Inflection* p. 400.—Also inf. GAv. *mrūitē* 'to speak', *stōi* 'for being', YAv. *stē* 'for being', *tarōidītē* and *tarōidīti* 'for despising'.

Abl.: In GAv. wanting i. e. its place supplied by gen.

Gen.: YAv. seldom *āhityō* 'of sickness' (like *ī*-decl., but variant *āhitayō*). — Also *darŋyōiš* 'of daring' Yt. 14.2.

Loc.: YAv. likewise *garō* 'on the mountain' Vd. 21.5 = Skt. *girāu* (on *ō* see § 42).—GAv. regularly *vīdātā* 'at the judgment'.

§ 255. Plural:—

Nom.: YAv. also (from strongest stem) *staomāyō* 'praises'.

Acc.: YAv. also (*-īš* for *-īš*, § 21 Note 1) *īštīš-ca* 'and wishes' et al.—Also (from middle stem) *garayō*. — GAv. also (from middle stem) *ārmatayō* —likewise (with *-īš*) *uštīš* 'desires'.

Gen.: YAv. also (from weak stem without inserted *n*) *kaoyąm* (i. e. *kav-y-ąm, § 224) 'of Kavis'.

§ 256. Observe also the declension of *haħi-* m. 'friend' = Skt. *sákhi-*, cf. Whitney, *Skt. Gram.* § 343 a.—Strong stem *-āy-*, mid. st. *-ay-*, wk. st. *-y-*.

    Singular. Nom. *haħa*; Acc. *°haħāim* (i. e. *-āyəm*, § 65) Ys. 46.13; Instr. *haša* (§ 162); Dat. *haše*.—Dual. N.A.V. *haša*.—Plural. Nom. *haħayō*, *haħaya*; Acc. *haħayō*, *haħaya*; Gen. *hašąm* (§ 162).

Note. Transfers from the *i*-declension to the *a*-declension occur: e. g. from Av. *vi-* m. 'bird' = Skt. *ví-*, Du. Instrum. *vayaēibya*.— Pl. Abl. *vayaēibyas-ca*; Gen. *vayanąm* (beside the regular *i*-decl. forms *viš*, *viš* nom. sg. Yt. 13.3; Vd. 2.42; *vayō* nom. pl. and *vayąm* gen. pl.).

B. Derivative Stems in original *ī*.
(Cf. Whitney. *Skt. Gram.* § 364.)

FEMININE.

§ 257. Av. اشــاونـي *aṣ̌aonī-* fem. to *aṣ̌avan-* 'righteous'.

Av. *ərəjaiti-* f. 'dark, dreadful' *(ərəjaiti-)*, *barəfri-* f. 'bearer, mother', *fṣ̌aonī* f. 'fatness', *āzīzanāiti* f. 'giving birth', *ḫṣ̌apri-* f. 'female'.

	Av.	Singular:	cf. Skt.
N.	*aṣ̌aon-i*	. .	*dev-ī*
A.	*aṣ̌aon-īm*	. .	*dev-īm*
I.	(*aṣ̌aon-ya*) *ərəjaitya* . .		*dev-yā*
D.	*aṣ̌aon-yāi*	. .	*dev-yāi*
Abl.	(*aṣ̌aon-yāṭ*) *barəfryāṭ*	.	see gen.
G.	*aṣ̌aon-yā̊*	. . .	*dev-yās*
L.	*aṣ̌avan-aya* (?)[1]		*dev-yām*
V.	*aṣ̌aon-i*	.	*dev-i*

Dual:

N.A.V.	(*aṣ̌aon-i*) *fṣ̌aoni* . . .	*dev-ī* (Ved.)
I.D.Abl.	(*aṣ̌aon-ibya*) *fṣ̌aonibya* .	*dev-ībhyām*

Plural:

N.	*aṣ̌aon-īš* . . .	*dev-īs* (Ved.)
A.	*aṣ̌aon-īš* . . .	*dev-īs*
I.	(*aṣ̌aon-ibiš*) *āzīzanāitibiš*	*dev-ībhis*
D.Abl.	*aṣ̌aon-ibyō*	*dev-ībhyas*
G.	*aṣ̌aon-inąm* . . .	*dev-īnām*
L.	(*aṣ̌aon-iṣu*) *ḫṣ̌apriṣu* . .	*dev-īṣu*
	-*iṣva ḫṣ̌apriṣva* . .	--

Forms to be observed in GAv. and YAv.

§ 258. In general, GAv. has the same forms as above, with the long final vowel, cf. § 26.

§ 259. Singular:—

On varying *ī, i* see § 21 Note 1.

Nom.: GAv. has *aṣ̌āunī* Ys. 53.4.

Instr.: So GAv. *vaŋhuyā* 'with good', *vahehyā* 'with better', and *mainyā* 'with thought', cf. Dat. *mainyāi* Ys. 43.9.

---

[1] Yt. 5.54. uncertain, cf. § 68 Note 3.

Vowel Class: — (4) Stems in *u* and *ū*. 77

Gen.: YAv. *drəgvatąs-ca* 'and of the wicked' (fem.); — also *astvaibyō* 'of the corporeal' (according to cons. decl.).
Voc.: VAv. sometimes (*e* according to *i*-decl.): *ašaone; ahurāne* 'O Ahuran'.

§ 260. Plural: —
Nom. Acc.: YAv. also *-īš* (cf. § 21 Note) *barəntīš* 'bearing' Yt. 8.40, *hrvi-jyeitīš* 'havocking, bloody' Yt. 10.47. — Also (like Skt. *devyàs*) *tištryenyō, tištryenyas-ca* 'wives of Tishtrya'.
Gen.: YAv. *vanuhīnąm* 'of the good' (observe *ī*) is sometimes written.

C. Radical Stems in original *ī*.

Feminine Nouns and Adjective Compounds m. f. n. (cf. Whitney, *Skt. Gr.* §§ 351, 352).

§ 261. Here belong a few words chiefly monosyllables — mostly mere roots: Singular. Nom. *barəzui-dīš* 'high-spirited', *ərəžu-jīš* 'right-living'; Acc. *yavae-jīm* 'ever-living'; Instr. *sraya* 'by beauty'; Dat. *ərəžu-jyōi* 'for the right-living'; Gen. *srayǡ* 'of beauty', *h̀ivō, h̀śyas-ca* 'of destruction'; Loc. *ayaoz-dya* (?) 'in impurity'. — Plural. Nom. *fryō* 'blessings'; Acc. *varšn-jīš* (m.) 'buds', *yavae-jyo* 'ever-living'; Dat. *yavae-jibyō*.

4. Stems in *u* and *ū*.

Masculine, Feminine and Neuter (cf. Whitney, *Skt. Gr.* § 341, 364).

A. Derivative Stems in original *u*.

I. MASCULINE—FEMININE.

§ 262. Av. ⟨⟩ *mainyu-* m. 'Spirit' = Skt. *manyú-*.
Av. *zantu-* m. 'tribe', *ratnu-* m. 'justice', *vaŋhu-* 'good', *pasu-* m. 'small cattle', *aiiu-* m. 'life', *barəšnu-* f. 'head, top', *gātu-* m. 'place, bed'.

	Av.	Singular:		cf. Skt.
N.	*mainy-uš*	.		*many-úš*
A.	*mainy-ūm*	. .		*many-úm*
I.	(*mainy-ū*) *zantū*			*many-únā, -vā*
D.	*mainy-ave*			*many-áve*
Abl.	*mainy-aoṱ*		.	see gen.
G.	{ *mainy-ōuš* .	. }		*many-ōs*
	{ *-aoš rašnaoš* . . . }			
L.	(*mainy-āu*) *vaŋhāu* (GAv.) .			*many-ā́ā*
V.	*mainy-ō*			*mány-ō*

Inflection: Declension of Nouns and Adjectives.

	Av.	Dual:	cf. Skt.
N.A.V.	maińy-ū, -u .		many-ā́
I.D.Abl.	(maińy-ubya) pasubya		many-ā́bhyām
G.	maini-vā̊¹	. .	many-vṍs
L.	(maini-vō) avhvo (GAv.) .		—

Plural:

N.	(maińy-avō) barẹnavō	.	many-ā́vas
A.	(maińy-ūš) barṣnuš	.	many-ū́n m., -ū́š f.
D.Abl.	(maińy-ubyō) gātuṣyō		many-ū́bhyes
G.	(maińy-unąm) zaṇtunąm		many-ū́nām
L.	(maińy-ušu) vaṇhušu		many-ū́ṣu
	-ušva barẹnušva .		—

ii. NEUTER (Separate Forms).

§ 263. Av. vohu- 'good' = Skt. vásu-.   cf. Skt.
Sg. N.A.V. voh-u .   vás-u
Pl. N.A.V. voh-u .   vás-u, -ū

Forms to be observed in GAv. and YAv.

§ 264. In general, GAv. has the same forms as above, with the long final vowel, cf. § 26.

i. MASCULINE—FEMININE.

§ 265. Singular:—

Nom.: YAv. also (from strongest stem) uγrabāzāuš 'strong-armed' Yt. 10.75; darẹjō.bāzāuš 'long-armed' Yt. 17.22.

Acc.: YAv. also (from strongest stem) nasāum (i. e. -āvm̥, § 65) 'corpse', garᵊmāum 'heat'; — again (from strong stem) daⁱŋhaom (i. e. -avṃ, § 64) 'nation, country'.

Instr.: Less common instr. (weak stem +) ending ā: YA. ḥrapwa, GAv. ḥrapwā 'by wisdom'; YAv. parⁱpwa Vd. 9.2; GAv. cicipwā 'through the wise one' = Skt. cikitvā́ (fr. cikitu-). — Also (orig. gen. or cf. § 39) YAv. ḥrⁱ.adrvō 'with spear of havoc'; rašnvō 'with Rashnu' Yt. 14.47.

Dat.: YAv. also (from weak stem) rapwe, rapwaē-ca 'to the Master';— observe (also from weak stem) YAv. awuhe (i. e. orig. *asv-ē) 'for

¹ See §§ 68 b, 62.

Vowel Class: — (4) Stems in *u* and *ū*.   79

life' Ys. 55.2, GAv. *ahuyē* (i. e. orig. *asu-i-ē*, § 190) 'for life' Ys. 41.6.
— Observe also GAv. *haēṭaovē* variant *haēṭaoē* Ys. 53.4 beside *haēṭavō* Ys. 46.5, cf. YAv. variant *haēṭaoe* beside *haēṭave* 'for kindred' Ys. 20.1, cf. § 61.

Abl.: In GAv. wanting — i. e. its place is supplied by the gen. as in Skt.
Gen.: (a) Also (from strongest stem) YAv. *bāzāuš* 'of the arm', GAv. *mərəθyāuš* 'of death'. — Again (from strongest stem +) ending *ō*: YAv. *nasāvō* 'of a corpse'; — and (from weak stem + *ō*) YAv. *rapwō* 'of the Master'.
— (b) The interchange in the gen. ending -*ōuš*, -*aoš* is connected perhaps with an original difference of accent: e. g. observe Av. *vaŋhəuš*, *aŋhəuš* = Skt. *vásōs*, *ásōs* (unaccented ultima), and Av. *tāyaoš*, *garənaoš* = Skt. *tāyós*, *gṛdhnós* (accented ultima) et al. Exceptions depend perhaps upon a shift of the accent.

Loc.: (a) The above loc. in -*āu* is Gatha locative, cf. also Ys. 62.6 *vaŋhāu* (Gatha reminiscence). — Similarly, GAv. *pərətō* 'at the bridge' Ys. 51.13; *hratō* 'in judgment' Ys. 48.4. The regular YAv. loc. is formed in *ō* (weak stem + *ō*, orig. gen.?), e. g. *ahmi zaytvō* 'in this tribe' Ys. 9.28, *gātvō* 'on a couch', *daiŋhvō* 'in the country', *aŋhvō* 'in the world'.
— (b) Observe Vsp. 12.5 *daiŋhō* = Skt. *dasyāu*, cf. § 42 (but see variants), Av. *haētō* 'at the bridge' = Skt. *sétāu*; Av. *varətafšō* Vd. 8.4 — and GAv. *pərətō* Ys. 51.12. — With postpositive *a* and strong stem: YAv. *anhava* 'in the world' Yt. 6.3; *gātava* 'in place' Ys. 65.9.

Voc.: YAv. occasionally *ratvō* 'O Master', *ərəzvō* 'O righteous one', *rašnvō* 'O Rashnu, Justice'.

§ 266. Dual: —

I.D.Abl.: YAv. also *bāzuwe* 'with both arms', cf. §§ 67, 85 a.

§ 267. Plural: —

Nom.: YAv. also with ending *a*, § 224 (from strong stem) *gātava* 'couches'.
— With regular ending *ō* (from strongest stem) *nasāvō* 'corpses', (from weak stem) *pasvas-ca* 'small cattle'. — Observe Yt. 14.38 *dušmainyuš* 'enemies' (nom. pl.).

Acc.: YAv. also (-*ūš*, § 21 Note 1) *barš̌nuš* 'heights'; *pauruš* 'many' Yt. 8.49; *daiŋhuš* 'countries' Yt. 8.9. — Again with ending *a*, § 224 (from strong stem) *barš̌nava*. — Ending *ō* like nom. (from strongest stem) *nasāvō* 'corpses', (from strong stem) *gātavō* 'places', (from weak stem) *pasvō* 'small cattle'.

Dat. Abl.: YAv. *hinūiwyō* 'from fetters' Yt. 13.100 = Yt. 19.86.

Gen.: YAv. also (without inserted *n*) *vaŋhvąm* 'of the good', *rapwąm* 'of Masters'; *yāpwąm* 'of sorcerers'. — Observe the variant -*ūnąm* for -*nnąm* (§ 21 Note 1) occurs, e. g. variant *vohūnąm* Ys. 65.12 etc.

Loc.: GAv. (only -*ū*) *pouruṣū* 'among people'.

ii. Neuter.

§ 268. Plural: — N.A.V. YAv. with ā: *asrū* 'tears'. — Also *zanvą* 'knees' occurs. — Observe *ā* in *asrū* 'tears' Yt. 10.38, cf § 25 Note.

§ 269. Occasional transfers to the *a*-declension are found:
— e. g. **Sg.** Gen *gātvahe* 'of the place'; Dat. *hiškrāi* 'for the dry'.

§ 270. Declension of Av. *daiŋ́hā-*, *daŋ́vu-* f. 'nation, country', cf. Skt. *dásyu-* §§ 135. 133 — **Singular.** Nom. *daiŋ́hā*; Acc. *daiŋ́haom* (i. e. *-avəm* § 64), *dahyūm* (GYAv.); Instr. *daiŋ́ha*; Dat. *daiŋ́have*; Abl. *daiŋ́haoṭ*; Gen. *daiŋ́hōuš* (YAv.), *dahyə̄uš* (GAv.); Loc. *daiŋ́hvō*. — **Dual.** Nom. *daiŋ́hu* (Yt. 10.8,47), *dahyu* (Yt. 10.107). — **Plural.** Nom. Voc. *daiŋ́hā̊*, *daiŋ́havō*; Acc. *daiŋ́huš*, *daiŋ́hāvo*; Gen. *dahyunąm* (GYAv.).

B. Derivative Stems in original *ū*.

(Cf. Whitney, *Skt. Gram.* § 356.)

These are not sharply to be distinguished from A in Avesta, nor are they numerous. As example may be taken

FEMININE.

§ 271. Av. tanū̆ f. 'body' = Skt. *tanū̆-*.

	Av.	Singular:	cf. Skt.
N.	*tan-uš*	. . . .	*tan-ūs*
A.	*tan-vąm* (GAv.), *tan-ūm* (GYAv.)	.	*tan-vām, tan-ūm*
I.	*tan-va*[1]	. . . .	*tan-vā*
D.	*tan-āve* (GYAv.)		*tan-vē*
Abl.	*tan-vaṭ*	.	see gen.
G.	*tan-vō*	.	*tan-vas*
		Plural:	
N.A.	*tan-vō*	. . . . .	*tan-vās*
I.	*(tan-ubīš) hizubīš* (GAv.)	.	*tan-ūbhis*
D.Abl.	*tan-ubyō*	. . .	*tan-ūbhyas*
G.	*tan-unąm*	. .	*tan-ūnām*
L.	*tan-ušu*	.	*tan-ūṣu*

Forms to be observed in GAv. and YAv.

§ 272. Metrically, the *v* in *tanvām* etc. is to be resolved into *u* as in Sanskrit.

---

[1] See *Aogəmadaēčā* 48 p. 25 ed. W. Geiger.

Vowel Class: — (5) Diphthongal Stems.   81

§ 273. Singular:—
Dat.: Observe *tanvaē-ca* Haug, *Zand-Pahlavi Glossary* p. 52. 9.
Abl.: YAv. a'so *tanaoţ* like *u*-decl.
Gen.: G(V)Av. *tanvas-cit̰;* — also GAv. *hizvō* 'of the tongue' Ys. 45.1, cf.
    Skt. *vadhvas*.
§ 274. Plural:—
N.A.V.: YAv. *tanvas-ca*.

C. Radical Stems in original *ū*.
Masculine Nouns and Adjective compounds (cf. Whitney, *Skt. Gram.*
§ 355 c end, § 352.)

§ 275. Here belong a very few root words:—Singular. Nom. (without *s*) *ahū* (GAv.), *ahu* (YAv.) 'Lord'; *āyū* (neut. GAv.) 'duration'; Acc. *ahūm*.—Plural. Acc. *anhvas-cā* (GAv.). — Similarly (nom. sg. without *s*) *aparənāyū* 'youth', *framrū* or °*mrū* 'pronouncing'. — Add dative -*buye* 'to become'.

§ 276. Declension of *yū* n. 'duration, ever':—Singular. Instr. (adv.) *yavē* (YAv.), *yavā* (GAv.); Dat. *yave*, *yavaē-ca* (YAv.), *yavē* or *yaove*, *yavōi* (GAv.); Gen. *yāuš*.

5. Diphthongal Stems.
(Cf. Whitney, *Skt. Gram.* § 360 seq.)

i. Stems in *āi*.

§ 277. Av. *rāi, raē-* f. 'splendor' = Skt. *rāi-*.
Singular. Acc. *raēm* (i. e. *ray-əm* § 64); Instr. *raya*.—Plural. Acc. *rāyō* (GAv.), also *raēš-ca* (YAv. § 64 Note); Gen. *rayąm*.

ii. Stems in *āu*.

§ 278. Av. *gāu-, gao-* m. f. 'cow' = Skt. *gāu-*.
Singular. Nom. (Voc.) *gāuš, gaoš;* Acc. *gąm*, or rare *gāum, gaom* (i. e. *gāv-əm* §§ 64, 65); Instr. *gava;* Dat. *gave* (YAv.), *gavōi* (GAv.); Abl. *gaoţ;* Gen. *gəuš*.—Dual. N.A.V. *gavā* (GAv.); Gen. °*gavā̊*.— Plural. Nom. *gavō*[1]; Acc. *gā̊;* Instr. *gaobīš;* Gen. *gavąm*.

Note. Similarly Sg. Nom. *hipāuš*, Acc. *hipąm* 'ally' Ys. 48.7, 34.10.

---

[1] See *Aogəmadaēcā* 84 p. 28 ed. W. Geiger.

B. STEMS IN CONSONANTS.
6. (A) Stems without Suffix.
Root-words and those inflected like them.

Masculine, Feminine and Neuter (cf. Whitney, *Skt. Gr.* §§ 383, 391).

§ 279. Av. -ʙνϙ *vīs*- f. 'village' = Skt. *viś-*.

Av. *spas*- m. 'spy', *amərətāt*- f. 'Immortality', *ast*- n. 'bone', *nās-* 'misfortune'.

	Av.	Singular:	cf. Skt.
N.V.	(*vīš*) *spaš* .		*vít*
A.	*vīs-əm* . . .	.	*viś-am*
I.	*vīs-a*	.	*viś-ā*
D.	*vīs-e*		*viś-ē*
Abl.	*vīs-aṭ* .	.	see gen.
G.	*vīs-ō* . .	. .	*viś-ás*
L.	*vīs-i* .	.	*viś-í*

		Dual:	
N.A.V.	(*vīs-a*) *amərətāta* .	.	*viś-āu*
I.D.Abl.	(*vīži-bya*) *amərətadbya*		*vid-bhyām*
G.	(*vīs-ww*) *amərətātw*		*viś-ós*

		Plural:	
N.V.	(*vīs-ō*) *spasō* . .	. .	*viś-as*
A..	*vīs-ō* . . .		*viś-as*
I.	(*viži-bīš*) *azdibīš* . .		*vid-bhís*
D.	*viži-byō*		*vid-bhyás*
G.	*vīs-qm* . . .		*viś-ām*
L.	(*vīšu*) *nąṣu* (GAv.)		*vikṣú*

Forms to be observed in GAv. and YAv.

§ 280. In general, GAv. has the same forms as above, with the long final vowel, cf. § 26.

§ 281. Singular:—

Nom.: GYAv. *druxš* 'Fiend' § 192, *haurvatās* 'Perfection, Salvation' (-*tās* i. e. -*tāt-s* § 192); *āθrəš* title of priest (-*t + s*), Nirangistan.

Acc.: YAv. also *drujim* 'Fiend' (-*im* = -*əm* § 30).—GAv. also *drujim* § 30 and *kəhrpəm* 'body' (-ə- § 32).

Dat.: YAv. *yavaētātaē-ca* 'and for eternity'.—GAv. also (*-ōi* more common than *-ē* § 56) *mazōi* 'for the great'.
Abl.: In GAv. wanting—i. e. its place supplied by the gen. as in Skt.
Gen.: GAv. also *mazā* 'of the great' (*-ā* = orig. *-as* § 32).
Loc.: YAv. also *aipya* 'in water' (*aipi* + *a* § 222), *uštatāitya* 'in the word *ušta*' (*ºtāiti* + *a* § 222).—GAv. has simply *ī: amərətāitī* 'in Immortality'.

§ 282. Dual:—
I.D.Abl.: Solitary YAv. *brvaṯbyąm* 'both brows'.

§ 283. Plural:—
Nom. Acc.: YAv. also (with ending *-a* § 224) *vāca*, *vaca*. Neut. pl. acc. *asti* 'bones' Yt. 13.11 (variant *asta*, but see § 283 Note).
Loc.: GAv. as above *nāfū* and (§ 26 Note) *nafšu-cā* 'among descendants'.

Note. Transfers to the *a*-decl. are numerous:—e. g. Sg. Nom. *hvarə.darəs-ō* 'sun-like', Skt. *svar-dṛ́ś;* Acc. (neut.) *ast-əm* 'bone'; Abl. *vīsāṯ* or *vīsāda* 'from a village' Yt. 13.49.— Pl. Acc. (neut.) *asta* 'bones'; Loc. like *ā*-decl. *barəzāhu* 'on the heights'.

With stem-gradation (Strong and Weak).

Cf. Whitney, *Skt. Gram.* § 385 seq.

§ 284. The strong and weak forms are distinguished by a variation in the quantity of the stem-vowel (as long or short) or by its elision, again by the presence (strong) or absence (weak) of a nasal. For examples see the following declensions.

§ 285. (i) Declension of Av. *vak/c-* m. 'voice, word' (strongest stem *-ā-*, strong *-a-*) = Skt. *vák/c-* f. (no vowel variation), cf. Whitney, *Skt. Gram.* § 391:—

Singular. Nom. *vāḵš;* Acc. *vācəm, vācim;* Instr. *vaca;* Gen. *vacō* (Ys. 31.20).—Dual. *vājäibyā-ca.*—Plural. Nom. *vācō, vaca* (ending *a* cf. vowel decl. § 224); Acc. *vācō, vacus-ca, vāca;* Dat. Abl. *vājži-byō;* Gen. *vacąm*.

Note. (a) The dat. du. and pl. (pada-endings) seem to derive their *s* (ž) from the nom. sg. *vāḵš*.—(b) Observe the form *vāḵš* as gen. Ys. 8.1.

§ 286. (ii) Declension of Av. *ap-* f. 'water' (strongest stem *āp-*, strong stem *ap-*) = Skt. *áp-* f. (stems *āp-*, *ap-*) Whitney, *Skt. Gram.* § 393:—

Singular. Nom. *áfš;* Acc. *apəm, apəm-ca* § 19; Instr. *apā-ca;* Abl. *apat, apātat-ca* (a-decl.); Gen. *apō, apas-ca, āpō;* Loc. *aipya* (-*i* + *a* § 222). — Dual. *āpa, āpō* (Gah 4.5 *ā*-decl.). — Plural. Nom. *āpō, apas-ca* § 19; Acc. *apō, apas-ca, āpō;* Dat. *aiwyō;* Gen. *apqm.* Note. The dat. pl. *aiwyō* is for orig. **abbhyás* § 186.

§ 287. (iii) Declension of *aṇc*-stems (cf. Whitney, *Skt. Gram.* §§ 408, 409):—

Singular. Nom. *frąš* 'forward'; Acc. *ənyāṇcəm* 'down'; Instr. *fraca* (? Yt. 10.118 *fraca āiti* [√*i-* + *ā*] cf. Skt. *prā:ā*), *tarasca* 'across', cf Skt. *tirascā* instr. advbl. (Whitney § 309 d), *pairivqṇca* 'advancing'; etc.

§ 288. Av. *pap-* m. 'path' = Skt. *path-* belongs partly here and partly under *an*-stems § 310—which see.

---

7. (B) Derivative Stems in *aṇt, maṇt, vaṇt*.

Participial Adjectives and Possessives (see Bartholomae, in *KZ.* xxix. p. 487 seq. = *Flexionslehre* p. 68 seq.—Whitney, *Skt. Gram.* § 441 seq., § 452 seq.)

§ 289. This subdivision of consonant stems includes: —(i) participial (and adjective) stems in *aṇt;* and (ii) possessive adjective stems in *maṇt, -vaṇt*. They are masculine and neuter; the corresponding feminine is made in *ai(ṇ)tī-*. The stem shows vowel-gradation, strong stem *aṇt,* weak stem *at* (from *ṇt;* also GAv. *āt,* see § 18 Note).

§ 290. As to stem-gradation, (1) the adjective *aṇt-*stems generally show *at* in the weak (= Skt. weak) cases, (2) the participial (thematic) *aṇt*-stems show *aṇt* in almost all forms. (3) The *maṇt-, vaṇt*-stems agree with the adjective stems in showing *at* in the weak cases. A number of interchanges, however, between all three occur—these interchanges are found chiefly in YAv. e. g. dat. du. *bərəzaṇbya* (from str. st.) Ys. 1.11; 3.13.

i. MASCULINE.

§ 291. (1) Adjective, Av. ⟨script⟩ *bərəzaṇt-* 'great' = Skt. *bṛhánt-;* (2) Participial, Av. ⟨script⟩ *fšuyaṇt-*

Consonant Class: — (7) Derivative Stems in *aṇt, maṇt, vaṇt.* 85

'thrifty, raising cattle'; (3) Possessive, Av. ⟨⟩ *astvaṇt-* 'possessing bones, corporeal'; ⟨⟩ *drəgvaṇt-* (GAv.) 'belonging to the Druj, follower of Satan'.

(1—2) *aṇt-*stems: Av. *haṇt-* 'being'; *stavaṇt-* 'praising'; *ḃišyaṇt-* 'hating'; *aṣaohṣayaṇt-* 'increasing Righteousness'; (3) *maṇt-, vaṇt-* stems: *drəgvaṇt-* (GAv.), *drvaṇt* (YAv.) 'belonging to the Druj', *pwāvaṇt-* 'like thee', *amavaṇt-* 'mighty', *satavaṇt-* 'hundred-fold', *pourumaṇt-* 'multitudinous', *daēvavaṇt-* 'belonging to the Daevas', *cazdonnhvaṇt-* 'wise-in-heart'.

(a) *aṇt-*Stems.

(1) Adjective.   (2) Participial.

	Av.	Singular:	cf. Skt.
N.	1. *bərəz-ō* 2. *fṣ̌uy-ąs* -*as* *slav-as*		*bṛh-án*
A.	*bərəz-aṇt-əm*		*bṛh-ántam*
I.	*bərəz-ata*		*bṛh-atā*
D.	1. *bərəz-aite* 2. *fṣ̌uy-aṇte*		*bṛh-até*
Abl.	1. (*bərəz-ataṭ*) 2. (*fṣ̌uy-aṇtaṭ*) *ḃišyaṇtaṭ*		see gen.
G.	1. *bərəz-atō* 2. *fṣ̌uy-aṇtō*		*bṛh-atás*
V.	*berəz-a*		*bṛ́h-an*

Dual:

N.A.V.	*bərəz-aṇta*		*bṛh-ántā* (Ved.)
I.D.Abl.	1. *bərəz-aṇbya*		*bṛh-ádbhyām*
G.	2. (*fṣ̌uy-aṇtā̊*) *aṣaohṣayaṇtā̊*		*bṛh-atós*

Plural:

N.V.	*bərəz-aṇtō*		*bṛh-ántas*
A.	1. (*bərəz-atō*) *hatō* 2. *fṣ̌uy-aṇtō*		*bṛh-atás*
I.	(*bərəz-adbīš*) *hadbīš*		*bṛh-ádbhis*
D.Abl.	1. (*bərəz-adbyō*) 2. (*fṣ̌uy-aṇbyō*) *ḃišyaṇhyō*		*bṛh-ádbhyas*

Inflection: Declension of Nouns and Adjectives.

G. { 1. *b·rəz-atąm* .
{ 2. *(fṣuy-aṇtąm) fbiṣyaṇtąm* . } *br̥h-atām*
L. (*bərəz-asu*) *fṣuyasū* (GAv.) *br̥h-átsu*

(b) *maṇt-, vaṇt*-Stems.
(3) Possessives.

	Av.	Singular:	cf. Skt.

N.	{ *ast-vå̄* . . . . .
	    -vąs *pwārąs*
	    -va *amava* .
			} *bhága-vān*

A.	*ast-vaṇtəm* . .		*bhága-vantam*
I.	(*ast-vata*) *satavata*		*bhága-vatā*
D.	*ast-vaite* . .		*bhága-vate*
Abl.	*ast-vataṯ* . .		see gen.
G.	*ast-vatō* . .		*bhága-vatas*
L.	{ *ast-vaiṇti* . . *-maiti* *paurumaiti* .		} *bhága-vati*
V.	(*ast-vō*) *drvō*		*bhága-van*

Plural:

N.V.	*drəg-vaṇtō*		*bhága-vantas*
A.	*drəg-vatō*		*bhága-vatas*
I.	*drəg-vōdəbīš* and *daēvavaṯbīš* . .		*bhága-vadbhis*
D.Abl.	*drəg-vōdəbyō* and *cazdōṇuhvadəbyō*		*bhága-vadbhyos*
G.	*drəg-vatąm* . .		*bhága-vatām*
L.	*drəg-vasū*		*bhága-vatsu*

ii. NEUTER (Separate Forms).

§ 292. Av. *haṇt-* 'being', *astvaṇt-* 'corporeal', *afsmanvaṇt-* 'metrical'.

Sg. N.A.V. (a) *haṯ* (b) *ast-vaṯ* . . cf. Skt. *bhága-vat*
Pl. N.A.V. — *afsmani-vąn*   *bhága-vanti*

Forms to be observed in GAv. and YAv.

§ 293. In general, GAv. has the same forms as YAv., with the long final vowel, cf. § 26.

§ 294. (a) According to § 29, *-aṇt-* or (after palatals § 30) *-iṇt-* may be found instead of *-aṇt-*:—Av. *pat-əṇt-əm* 'falling', *druž-int-əm* 'deceiving', *raoc-int-aṱ* (abl.) 'shining' et al. — (b) According to § 63, -*int*-, -*unt*- may be found instead of -*yant*-, -*vant*-: — Av. *varəz-int-əm* beside *varəz-yant-ō* 'working', *harənaṷh-unt-əm* 'glorious', *təmaṷh-unt-əm* 'dark' Yt. 5.82, cf. Skt. *támasvantam*.

I. MASCULINE.

§ 295. Singular:—

Nom.: In YAv., the *ant*-stems generally have nom. -*ō*, and the *vant*-stems have nom. -*vā̊* or -*va* or sometimes -*vō*. In GAv. the nom. is -*qs* or -*as* (for -*at-s*). — Observe YAv. *perənavō, astuvō* 'possessing a feather, possessing a bone' Yt. 14.36; also *hą* 'being' Yt. 13.129, *vyqsca* 'driving'. — GAv. *f̌šuyąs* 'thriving, prospering', *staras* 'praising', *ϑβāvąs* 'like thee'. — On *təmavuhā̊* 'dark', *harənavuhā̊* 'glorious' (for orig. -*sv*-) see § 130 (2) c.

Instr.: GAv. also *drəgvātā* (observe *ā* § 18 Note 3) 'with the wicked'.
Dat.: GYAv. also *drəgvāite, drvāite* (observe *ā* § 18 Note 3) 'for the wicked' Ys. 31.15 etc., Ys. 71.13. — On GAv. *drəgvātaē-cā*, see § 19.
Gen.: On *harənavuhatō* 'of the glorious', see § 130 (2) c.
Loc.: Sometimes variant *astvaiti*. See furthermore below § 297.
Voc.: YAv. *drvō* above is like nom. (see Nom.).

§ 296. Plural:—

Nom.: YAv. with ending *a* § 224: *barəzaṇta* 'great' Yt. 5.13, *yātumaṇta* 'belonging to sorcery';—also (isolated) weak stem nom. pl. *mrvatō* 'speaking' Ys. 70.4.
Acc.: YAv. also (observe strong stem) *barəzaṇtō* 'great'.
Gen.: YAv. also (2 from weak stem) *ϑβišyatąm* 'of those hating' Yt. 10.76. — Also GYAv. *hātąm* 'of beings' (observe *ā*) § 18 Note 3.

§ 297. Transfers to the *a*-declension are not infrequent. Here belong:

I. MASCULINE. Singular. Nom. *barəzō* above in paradigm, also Voc. *barəza;* Dat. *zbayaṇtāi* 'for him invoking'; Abl. *saošyaṇtāṱ* 'from Saoshyant'; Gen. *raēvaṇtahe* 'of the radiant'; Loc. *barəzaṇtaya* or *barəzaṇtaᵃya* (uncertain see § 257) Yt. 5.54,57. — Plural. Dat. Abl. *saošyaṇtaēibyō* 'for the Saoshyants', *drvataēibyō* 'from the wicked'. —
II. NEUTER. Singular. Acc. *varəcaṷhaṇtəm* et al. Yt. 19.9.

§ 298. Declension of Av. *mazaṇt*- 'great' = Skt. *mahánt*-. This word shows a strongest stem *mazāṇt*-, like Skt. *mahā́nt*-. I. MASC. Singular. Nom. *maza*, Acc. *mazāṇtəm;* II. NEUT. *mazaṱ*, cf. Skt. *mahā́n, mahā́ntam, mahát*, Whitney, *Skt. Gram.* § 450 b.

8. (C) Derivative Stems in *an, man, van.*

Masculine, (Feminine) and Neuter (cf. Whitney, *Skt. Gr.* § 420 seq.).

§ 299. The stem has a triple form:—strongest stem *ān*, strong stem *an*, weak stem *n* (before vowels) or *a* (= *n̥*) before consonants. Cf. Brugmann, *Grundriss der vergl. Gram.* ii. § 113.—The strong and weak forms do not always agree with the Sanskrit in its sharp division; cf. also Whitney, *Skt. Gram.* § 425 f.

(a) *an-, man-*Stems.
i. MASCULINE.

§ 300. Av. ⟨airyaman-⟩ *airyaman-* m. 'friend' = Skt. *aryamán-* m.

Av. *maēsman-* n. 'urine', *x̌ṣapan-* f. 'night', *maretan-* m. 'mortal', *čašman-* n. 'eye', *priẓafan-* 'triple-jawed', *ašavan-* 'righteous', *asan-* m. 'stone', *rasman-* m. 'rank, column', *dāman-* n. 'creature', *aršan-* m. 'male', *vyāxman-* n. 'council'.

	Av. Singular.	cf. Skt.
N.	*airyam-a*	*aryam-ā́*
A.	*airyam-anəm*	*aryam-áṇam*
I.	*airyam-na* *-ana maēsmana*	*aryam-ṇā́*
D.	*(airyam-aine)*[1] *-ne x̌ṣafne*	*aryam-ne*
Abl.	*(airyam-naṭ) marəθnəṭ* *-anaṭ čašmanaṭ*	see gen.
G.	*(airyam-nō)*[2] *-anō*[3]	*aryam-ṇás*
L.	*(airyam-aini) čašmainī* (GAv.)	*aryam-áṇi*
V.	*airyam-a* *-əm priẓafəm* § 194	*áryam-an*
	Dual:	
N.A.V.	*airyam-ana*	*aryam-aṇā́* (Ved.)
I.D.Abl.	*(airyam-anā)* *čašmanā*	*áryam-aṇōs*

[1] See Vd. 22.13. — [2] Thus, metrically *airyamnas-cā* Ys. 33.4; 46.1. — [3] Vsp. 1.8 etc.

Consonant Class: — (8) Derivative Stems in *an, man, van*. 89

Plural:

N.V. (aⁱryam-anō) *aṣavanō* . . *aryam-āṇas*

A. { (aⁱryam-nō) *hạfnō* . . . } *aryam-uás*
 { -anō *rasmanō* . }

I. (aⁱryam-ōbīš) *dāmōbīš* . *aryam-ābhis*

D.Abl. (aⁱryam-abyō) *dāmabyō* . . *aryam-ābhyas*

G. { (aⁱryam-nąm) *arīnqm* . . } *aryam-ṇām*
 { -anąm *rasmanąm* }

L. { (aⁱryam-ōhu) *vyāhmōhu*[1] . } *aryam-āhu*
 { -ōhva *dāmōhva* . . }

ii. NEUTER (Separate Forms).

§ 301. Av. *nāman*- n. 'name', *cinman*- n. 'attempt'.

Sg. N.A.V. *nąm-a* . *nām-a*

Pl. N.A.V. { *nām-ą(n)* . }
 { *nām-ōni* . . . . } *nām-āni*
 { *cinm-ānī* (GAv.)[2] . }

Forms to be observed in GAv. and YAv.

§ 302. In general, GAv. has the same forms as above with the long final vowel, see § 26.

§ 303. Occasionally (1) instead of Av. *ā* we find *ą* before the *n* (§ 45) or (2) instead of *a* we find GAv. *ō* (§ 32): — e. g. (1) Av. *urvąnō* 'souls'; — (2) GAv. *mazōnā* 'with greatness'; GAv. *asōnō* 'stones, heavens'.

§ 304. On the interchange of strong (*an*) and weak (*n*) forms see § 299.

i. MASCULINE.

§ 305. Singular: —

Nom.: YAv. *fravrase* 'Franrasyan' (= *ṣya* cf. § 67, acc. *franrasyānəm*).

Acc.: YAv. also (from strongest stem) *hāvanānəm* title of priest; and (from weak stem) *arīnəm* 'male'.

Instr.: GAv. also *mazōnā* § 303.

Dat.: Similar (-*aine*) infin. dat. n. YAv. *hṣnūmaine* 'to rejoice', *staomaine* 'for praise'; GAv. *hṣṇmōnō* 'to be content' § 303. — Observe *aiwi.ǰōipne* Vd. 3.24. — From strongest stem YAv. *puþrāne* 'having a child'.

Gen.: GYAv. also (from strongest stem) *marətānō* 'of mortal', *hāvanānō*.

---

[1] Yt. 13.16, cf. § 39. — [2] Ys. 12.3.

Abl.: YAv. isolated (undeclined abl.) *barəsman* (neut.) 'with barsom'.
Loc.: YAv. also (from weak stem) *asni* 'by day' § 164 Note 1;—and (from strongest stem) *husravāni* 'in good word' (?) Ny. 4.8.—GAv. also *cašmə̄ṇg*, *caš́maṇ* (neut.) 'in eye' Ys. 31.13; Ys. 50.10, cf. Whitney, *Skt. Gram.* § 425 e.
Voc.: YAv. *airyama* (cf. Vd. 22.9) above in paradigm is like nom. or after *a*-decl.

§ 306. Dual:—
N.A.V.: YAv. also (from strongest stem § 314 Note 1 b) *spāna* 'two dogs'.

§ 307. Plural:—
Nom.: YAv. also (from strongest stem) *asā́nō* 'stones'. With ending *a* § 224 (from strongest stem) *arṣ̌āna* 'males', and (from weak stem) *asna* 'stones'.
Acc.: YAv. also (from strongest stem) *asā́nō* 'stones'; GAv. *asə̄ṇg* Ys. 30.5 cf. § 303.—With ending *a* § 224 (from strongest stem) *arṣ̌āna* 'males'.
Dat. Abl.: YAv. also *draomō̆byō* 'from assaults' § 33.

ii. NEUTER.
§ 308. Plural:—
Nom. Acc.: The common ending is *q(n)* § 45 Note 2: Av. *nāmq(n)*, *dāmqn*, *dāmqm* cf. Ys. 48.7, 46.6, etc.—Less frequent is the ending -*āni* (-*ə̄ni*), cf. Skt. -*āni*.—Observe as dual and plural (like sing.) *dq̇ma* Yt. 15.43; Ys. 71.6.—Perhaps here belong likewise *maēsma* Vd. 8.11,12, et al., cf. Johannes Schmidt, *Neutra* pp. 89, 316, but see § 227 above.

As general plural case, *qn* is also used: e. g. (as instr.) Av. *srīrāiš nāmqn* 'by fair names' Ys. 15.1, Vsp. 6.1; so *dāmqn* (as nom. pl.) Yt. 8.48, (as gen. pl.) Ys. 57.2, (as instr. pl.) Yt. 22.9.—As acc. pl. and gen. loc. singular *aγqn*.

As general plural case, *īš* (§§ 228, 331) is also used: e. g. (as instr.) *hāiš nāməniš* 'by their own names' Ys. 15.2.

§ 309. Transfers to the *a*-declension are found. Here belong:

Singular. Dat. *syāvarṣ̌ānāi* 'to Syavarshan'; Gen. *arṣ̌ānahe* 'of a male'; Abl. *xšafnāaṭca* 'night'.—Plural. Loc. *asānaēṣ̌va* m. 'on stones'.

§ 310. Declension of Av. *paṇtan-*, *paθ-* m. 'path' = Skt. *pánthan-*, *path-* m. cf. Whitney, *Skt. Gram.* § 433. This word follows partly the *an*-declension (strongest stem *paṇtān-*, strong stem *paṇtan-* § 299), partly the suffixless consonant declension (weak stem *paθ-* § 288).

Consonant Class: — (8) Derivative Stems in *an, man, van.*

Singular. Nom. *paṇta, paṇtā̊* Ys. 72.11; Acc. *paṇtānəm, paṇtąm;* Instr. *papa;* Abl. *paṇtaṭ;* Gen. *papō;* Loc. *paiṗi* (GAv.). — **Plural.** Nom. *paṇtānō;* Acc. *papō, papa;* Gen. *papąm.*

Note. Transfers to the *ā*-declension (fem.) are **Sg.** Acc. *papąm;* Gen. *papayā̊.* — **Pl.** Acc. *papā̊.*

§ 311. Often, a neuter stem in *an* stands parallel with one in *ar*, see § 237, and Brugmann, *Grundriss der vergl. Gram.* ii. § 118.

(b) *van*-Stems.

§ 312. The *van*-stems are declined like those in *an*, *man*, but in the weak case-forms the *va* becomes (by samprasāraṇa § 63) *u*, which coalesces with a preceding *a* into *ao* (*āu* § 62) or with a preceding *u* into *ū* (*u* § 51 Note 1).

§ 313. (i) Declension of Av. *ašavan-* m. 'righteous' = Skt. *r̥tā́van-* shows in weak cases *ašaon-, ašāun* (i. e. GAv. and cf. § 62 Note 1).

Singular. Nom. *ašava;* Acc. *ašavanəm;* Dat. *ašaone, ašaonaē-ca, ašāunē* (GAv. § 62 Note 1); Abl. *ašaonaṭ;* Gen. *ašaonō, ašaonas-cā* (GAv.), *ašāunō* (GAv.); Voc. *ašāum* § 193. — **Dual.** Nom. Acc. Voc. *ašavana;* Gen. *ašaonā̊.* — **Plural.** Nom. *ašavanō;* Acc. *ašavanō* (str. stem YAv.), *ašāunō* (wk. stem GAv.), *ašavana* (ending *a* § 224); Dat. *ašavabyō* (GYAv.), *ašavaoyō* (YAv. § 62 Note 3); Gen. *ašaonąm, ašāunąm* (§ 62 Note 1).

Note 1. Similar to *ašavan-* is (a) the declension of GAv. *magavan-* (str. st.), *magāun-* (wk. st.) m. 'member of the community', cf. Skt. *maghávan-, maghôn-* Whitney, *Skt. Gram.* § 428; —and (b) the declension of Av. *āθravan-* (str. st.), *aθaurun-* (wk. st. §§ 62, 191) m. 'priest' = Skt. *átharvan-*. Observe Av. voc. sg. *āθraom* § 193.

Note 2. Transfers to the *a*-decl. are not infrequent: e. g. Dat. Du. *ašavanaēibya.*

§ 314. (ii) Declension of Av. *urvan-* (i. e. *uruvan-* §§ 68 b and 71 end) m. 'soul'. This has in weak case-forms *urun-* (*ū* § 51 Note 1).

Singular. Nom. *urva;* Acc. *urvānəm;* Instr. *uruna;* Dat. *urune, urunaē-ca;* Gen. *urunō.* — **Plural.** Nom. *urvąnō* (§ 45); Acc. *urunō, urunas-cā* Ys. 63.3, *urvąnō* (str. st.); Dat. *urvōibyō* (a-decl.).

Note 1. (a) Similar to *urvan-* is the declension of Av. *yvan-* (i. e. *yuvan-* § 68 b, str. st.), *yūn-* (wk. st.) m. 'youth' = Skt. *yúvan-, yū́n-* m., cf. Whitney, *Skt. Gram.* § 427.—Observe Av. voc. sg. *yūm* opp. to Skt. *yúvan* (§ 193).—(b) Similar also in Av. *span-* (triple stem *spān-, span-, sūn-* § 20) m. 'dog' = Skt. *śvān- (śvān-, śvan-, śūn-)* m., cf. Whitney, *Skt. Gram.* § 427.—(c) Likewise Av. *zrvan-* n. 'time', dat. sg. *zrūne* Yt. 5.129.

Note 2. Transfers to the *a*-decl. are found:—e. g. gen. sg. *sūnahe* beside *sūno;* again gen. sg. *zrvānahe* (stem *zrvāna-*), loc. *zrūne* Vd. 19.9 (stem *zrūna-*, but cf. § 35 Note 2 or § 233). So above dat. pl. *urvōibya* (variant *urvōibyō*, after *a*-decl. instead of **urvabyō*).

§ 315. (a) Forms to be observed are: YAv. nom. sg. *taurvā* (vanstem) 'overpowering', cf. Bartholomae, in *K.Z.* xxix. p. 561 = *Flexionslehre* pp. 141, 142. So sg. nom. *þrtafā*, acc. *°anəm*, voc. *°əm* (stem orig. **zapvan-* § 95.— GAv. nom. sg. *advā* (variant *advā*) m. 'way'.—(b) As general plural case with ending *-qn* §§ 230, 308: YAv. *karfvqn* 'climes'.—As general plural case with ending *-īš* §§ 231. 308: Av. *afaonīš* (as acc. pl. neut. Vs. 71.6 *dāma afaonīš;* as instr. pl. masc. Vsp. 21.3).

9. (D) Derivative Stems in *in*.

Masculine, Feminine and Neuter, (derivative adjectives), cf. Whitney, *Skt. Gram.* § 438 seq.

§ 316. The *in*-stems (few in number) are declined like those in *an;* cf. Brugmann, *Grundriss der vergl. Gram.* ii. § 115:—e. g. Av. *kainin-* f. 'maiden', et al.

i. MASCULINE—FEMININE. Singular: Nom. *kaini;* Acc. *kaininəm;* Dat. *parənine* 'having a feather'; Gen. *kainīnō, kainīnō.*—Dual: Nom. *hąmina* 'belonging to summer'.—Plural: Nom. *kainīnō, kainīnō, kainina;* Acc. *afštacinō* 'having running waters'; Dat. *kainibyō;* Gen. *drujinąm* 'belonging to the Druj' Yt. 4.7.—ii. NEUTER. Sg. Nom. Acc. *raoķini* 'shining'.

Note. On the interchange of *i, ī,* see § 21 Note 1.

10. (E) Radical *n-* and *m-*Stems.

§ 317. Here belongs the root *jan-* 'slay' as final element of a compound: Av. *vərəþrajan-* 'victorious' = Skt. *vṛtrahán-,* cf. Whitney, *Skt. Gram.* § 402. The stem shows triple forms *-jān-, -jan-, -jn-.*

Singular: Nom. *vərəþraja, vərəþrəmjā* (GAv.), *vərəþrajā* (i. e. *-ā* [= *an*] + *s* § 222); Acc. *vərəþrajanəm;* Abl. *vərəþrajnat;* Gen. *vərəþrajnō, vərəþrājanō.*—Plural: Nom. *vərəþrājanō;* Acc. *afava-janō.*

§ 318. Radical *m*-stem is Av. *zam- zᵊm-* f. 'earth' = Skt. *kṣā́m- jm-*, cf. Brugmann, *Grundriss der vergl. Gram.* ii. § 160.

Singular: Nom. *zā̊*; Acc. *zqm*; Instr. *zᵊmā* (§ 24); Dat. *zᵊmē* (cf. also § 233); Abl. *zᵊmat̰*, *zᵊmāδa* Yt. 7.4 (§ 222, *a*-decl.); Gen. *zᵊmō*; Loc. *zᵊmi*. — Plural: Nom. *zᵊmō*; Acc. *zᵊmō*, *zᵊmas-ca*; Gen. *zᵊmqm*.

Note 1. The nom. sg. *zā̊* is *zā* (= ? *zam-* = *zm̥*) + *s* § 223; similarly acc. *zqm* (= ? *zm̥* + *m*).

Note 2. Similar to *zᵊm-* is Av. *zyam-* m. 'hiems', Sg. Nom. *zyā̊*, *zyā̊s-cit̰*; Acc. *zyqm*; Gen. *zimō*; cf. Brugmann, *Grundriss* ii. § 160. Likewise Av. *dam-* 'domus', cf. GAv. gen. sg. *dňg*, loc. sg. *dqm* — see Brugmann, *Grundriss* ii. § 160.

11. (F) Stems in original *r*.

Masculine (Feminine and Neuter), cf. Whitney, *Skt. Gram.* § 369 seq.

§ 319. Here belong a limited number of nouns: (a) Derivative stems in orig. *-tar, -ar* — nouns of agency and nouns of relationship; (b) Radical stems in orig. *-ar*; (c) Derivative stems (indeclinable) in orig. *-ar*.

§ 320. Strong and weak case-forms. — Nouns of this declension show three stem-forms: strongest stem *ār*, strong stem *ar*, weak stem *r* (before vowels), *ᵊrᵊ* (before consonants). The (1) nouns of agency show the strongest form *ār* in acc. sg., nom. du., and nom. pl.; the (2) nouns of relationship show simply the strong form *ar* in those cases. — The strong and weak case-forms, however, do not always agree with the Skt. in its sharp division, cf. also Lanman, *Noun-Inflection in the Veda* p. 420 fin.

(a) Derivative Stems in *-tar, -ar*.

§ 321. These are divided with reference to the acc. sg., nom. du., and nom. pl. *ār* or *ar* into two classes:

1) Nouns of Agency. — 2) Nouns of Relationship.
Chiefly Masculine (cf. Whitney, *Skt. Gram.* § 373).

§ 322. 1) Av. ⟨script⟩ *dātar-* m. 'giver, creator' = Skt. *dātár-, dhātár-*. 2) Av. ⟨script⟩ *patar-* m. 'father' = Skt. *pitár-*.

94   Inflection: Declension of Nouns and Adjectives.

Av. *frabərətar-* m. title of priest, *ātar-* m. 'fire', *nar-* m. 'man', *nipātar-* m. 'protector', *zāmātar-* m. 'son in law', *sātar-* m. 'persecutor'.

	Av.	Singular:	cf. Skt.
N.	*dā-ta*	. . .	*dā-tā́*
A.	1. *da-tārəm* . . .		*dā-tā́ram*
	2. *pi-tārəm*		*pi-tā́ram*
I.	(*dā-θra*) *āpıā* (GAv.) .		*dā-trā́*
D.	(*dā-θre*) *frabərəθre*		*dā-tré*
Abl.	(*dā-θraṯ*) *āpraṯ* .	. . .	see gen.
G.	*dā-θrō* . .	. . .	*dā-túr*
L.	(*dā-tari*) *naⁱri* .		*dā-tári*
V.	*dā-tarə* .	. . .	*dā-tar*

Dual:

N.A.V.	1. (*dā-tāra*) *nipātārō* . .	*dā-tárā* (Ved.)
	2. (*pi-tāra*) *zāmātara* . .	*pi-tárā* (Ved.)
I.D.Abl.	(*dā-tərəbya*) *nərəbya* .	*dā-tṛ́bhyām*
G.	(*dā-θrā̊*) *narā̊* . . .	*dā-trós*

Plural:

N.	1. *dā-tārō*	*dā-tā́ras*
	2. *pi-tārō* .	*pi-tā́ras*
A.	1. *dā-tārō* . .	*dā-tṛ́n*
	2. *fə-drō*	*pi-tṛ́n*
D.Abl.	(*dā-tərəbyō*) *ātərəbyō* .	*dā-tṛ́bhyas*
G.	(*dā-θrąm*) *sāθrąm* .	*dā-tṝṇā́m*

Forms to be observed in GAv. and YAv.

§ 323. In general, GAv. has the same forms as above, with the long final vowel, see § 26.

§ 324. On the occasional interchange of strong *(ar)* and weak *(r, ərə)* case-forms see § 320, and § 47 Note.

§ 325. Singular:—

Nom.: YGAv. observe *pita, pitā, ptā* 'father'.

Acc.: YAv. also (from weak stem) *brāθrǝm* 'brother'.—Observe Av. *havhāram* 'sister' opp. to Skt. *svásāram* (-*ār-*).—GAv. also (*in* §§ 22, 32) *pitarǝm* 'father'.

Gen.: YAv. *sāθras-cit̰* 'of the persecutor'.—Also (isolated) from strong stem + *s, sāstors* 'of the tyrant' Ys. 9.31, like gen. *narš* § 332

Dat.: GAv. also *fəðroi* 'father' (i. e. -*oi* = -*e*, § 56) Ys. 53.4.

Consonant Class: — (11) Stems in original *r*.

§ 326. Dual:—
N.A.V.: YAv. also (from weak stem) *brāpra* 'two brothers'.

§ 327. Plural:—
Nom.: YAv. also *dātāras-ca* see § 19.—Also ending *a: vaŝtāra* 'coursers'.
Acc.: YAv. also acc. pl. in *-ǰuš, -ǰš* (like *strǰuš, strǰš, nərǰuš*, §§ 329, 332) *pairi.aētrǰuš* Vd. 9.38, cf. Skt. *paryətār-*, see *American Journal of Philology* x. p. 346.— GAv. also (from strong stem) *mātarō* 'mothers'.
—Also *mātərąš-cā* § 49.
Dat.: YAv. observe *ptərəbyō* 'for fathers' Vd. 15.12.

§ 328. Transfers to the *a*-decl. occur: e. g.:
Singular. Gen. *sāstrahe* 'of the persecutor' (i. e. stem *sāstra*-beside *sāstar*-).—Plural. Gen. *sāstranąm* 'of persecutors'.

(α) Like nouns of agency.

§ 329. (i) Declension of Av. *star*- m. (strongest stem *stār*-, strong stem *star*-, weak stem *str*-, *stərə*-) = Skt. *stár*- (cf. Whitney, *Skt. Gram.* § 371):—
Singular. Acc. *stārəm*; Gen. *stārō*.—Plural. Nom. Acc *stārō, staras-ca* (§ 19 on *ā*), *strǰuš* (acc. YAv. cf. § 327); Dat. Abl. *stərəbyō*; Gen. *strąm, stārąm, starǰm-cā* (GAv.).

§ 330. (ii) Declension of Av. *rapaēštar*- 'warrior standing in charriot'.— This word shows also a parallel stem *rapaēštā* according to the radical *ā*-decl., see § 249. The forms from stem *rapaēštar*- are:—
Singular. Acc. *rapaēštārəm*; Gen. *rapaēštārahe* (*a*-decl.); Voc. *rapaēštāra* (*a*-decl.).—Plural. Nom. *rapaēštārō*; Acc. *rapaēštārǰs-ca* (§ 327, or perhaps here *a*-decl. § 129).
Note. The forms from stem *rapaēštā*- are enumerated at § 249.

(β) Like nouns of relationship.

§ 331. (iii) Declension of Av. *ātar*- m. 'fire' (strong stem *ātar*-, wk. st. *āpr*-, *ātr*- [§ 79 Note], *ātərə*-):—
Singular. Nom. *ātarš* (= str. st. +*s*); Acc. *ātrəm* (YAv.), *ātrām* (GAv.); Instr. *āprā* (GAv.); Dat. *āpre, āprasˊ-ca*; Abl. *āpraṯ*; Gen. *āprō, āpras-ca*; Voc. *ātarə* (YAv.), *ātarš* (GAv.), *ātarš* (YAv. same as nom.).—Plural. Acc. *ātarō*; Dat. Abl. *ātərəbyō*; Gen. *āprąm*.

§ 332. (iv) Declension of Av. *nar*- m. 'man' = Skt. *nár*- (cf. Whitney, *Skt. Gram.* § 371):—

Inflection: Declension of Nouns and Adjectives.

Singular: Nom. *nā*; Acc. *narəm*; Dat. *naire* (YAv.), *narōi* (GAv.); Abl. *nərəṯ* Phl. Version at Vd. 3 42; Gen. *narš* (YAv.), *narəš* (GAv.); Loc. *nairi*; Voc. *narə*.—Dual: Nom. *nara*; I.D.Abl. *nərəbyō*; Gen. *narā̊*.—Plural: Nom. Voc. *narō, naras-ca, nara* (§ 224); Acc. *nərąš* (GAv. Ys. 40.3 see § 49), *nərūš* (acc. YAv. cf. § 327); Dat. Abl. *nərəbyō, nərəbyas-ca, nəruyō, nuruyo, nərəyo* (§ 62 Note 3, and § 31 Note); Gen. *narąm* (YAv.), *narə̄m* (GAv.) Ys. 30.2, see § 32.

Note 1. GAv. *nərąš* at Ys. 45.7 is apparently used as gen. sg. rather than acc. pl., see Gah 3.6 *narš* citation, cf. Skt. *nr̥n*, Pischel-Geldner, *Vedische Studien* p. 43.

Note 2. Transfers to the *a*-declension, stem *nara-* occur:— Singular: Nom. *narō*; Gen. *narahe*; etc.

(b) Radical Stems in original *r*.

§ 333. Here belong a very few nouns and their (adjective) compounds, e. g.:—

§ 334. (i) Av. *hvar-* n. 'sun' = Skt. *svàr-* (cf. Whitney, *Skt. Gram.* § 388 d):— Singular: Nom. Acc. *hvarə* (YAv.), *hvarə̄* (GAv.); Gen *harō* or *hū* (YAv.), *hə̄ng* (GAv. i. e. *hvan-s*, cf. §§ 337, 318 Note 2).

§ 335. (ii) GAv. *sar-* f. 'association unity':—Singular: *sarəm, sarə̄m*; Dat. *sarōi*; Gen. *sarə̄* (Ys. 49.3); Loc. *sairi* (Ys. 35.8).—Plural: Acc. *sarō* (Ys. 31.21).

(c) Neuters (derivative) in original *ar*.

§ 336. These neuters (indeclinable) in *arə, arə̄* (GAv.) are used chiefly as acc. sg., but they may supply other cases.

Singular: Nom. Acc. *vadarə* (YAv.), *vadarə̄* (GAv.) 'weapon' (= Skt. *vádhar*); as Dat. (and acc.) *dasvarə* 'strength' Ys. 68.2; as Gen. (and acc.) *karšvarə̄* 'clime' Vsp. 10.1.—Dual: N.A.V. (and acc. sg.) *danarə* 'two D. measures'.—Plural: Acc. (beside acc. sg.) *ayārə̄* (GAv.).

Note. These neuters rarely show declined cases:—e. g. Sg. Instr. *dasvara* 'with strength' (Ys. 55.3); Pl. Instr. *baēvarəbīš* 'with thousands'.— Like *a*-decl., Dat. sg. *ba.varāi*.

§ 337. These *ar*-neuters commonly show parallel *an*- stems with which they unite in forming a declension: e. g. Av. *karšvar-, karšvan-* n. f. 'clime, zone'; *ayar-, ayan-* n.

'day'; *zafar-, zafan-* n. 'jaw'; *panvar-, panvana-* (a-decl.) n. 'bow'. See § 311 and Brugmann, *Grundriss der vergl. Gram.* ii. § 118.

12. (G) Stems in original *s*.

(a) Derivative Stems in -*h* (= orig. *s*).

(α) Stems in -*ah* (= orig. Ind.-Iran. -*as*).

§ 338. These very common stems in -*ah* (= orig. -*as*) are chiefly n e u t e r nouns; but as adjectives (compound or with original accent on the ending, cf. Whitney, *Skt. Gram.* § 417) they may likewise be m a s c u l i n e or f e m i n i n e. A feminine substantive *uṣah-* (see § 357 for declension) also occurs.—Cf. Horn, *Nominalflexion im Avesta* p. 26 seq.; and Whitney, *Skt. Gram.* §§ 414, 418.

i. MASCULINE—FEMININE (ADJECTIVE).
NEUTER (SUBSTANTIVE).

§ 339. Av. ⸺ *hvacah-* (adj. m. f.) 'well-speaking' = Skt. *suvā́cas-*. Av. ⸺ *vacah-* n. 'word' = Skt. *vā́cas-*; Av. ⸺ *duš-vacah-* (adj.) 'evil-speaking' = Skt. *durvacas-*.

Av. *anaocah-* (adj.) 'hostile', *raocah-* n. 'light', *sarah-* n. 'head' (= Skt. *śiras-* n.), *zrayah-* n. 'sea', and m. nom. propr. 'Zrayah', *arəzah-* n. 'daylight'.

	Av.	Singular:	cf. Skt.
N.	*hvac-ā̊*		*suvā́c-ās*
A.	*hvac-aŋhəm*		*suvā́c-asam*
I.	*vac-aŋha*		*vā́c-asā*
D.	*vac-aŋhe*		*vā́c-ase*
Abl.	*vac-aŋhaṭ*		see gen.
G.	*vac-aŋhō*		*vā́c-asas*
L.	*vac-ahi*		*vā́c-asi*
V.	*hvac-ō*		*súvāc-as*

Dual:
N.A.V. (*hvac-aŋha*) *anaocaŋhō* (G.Av.) . *suvā́c-asā* (Ved.)
G. (*vac-aŋhā̊*) *zrayaŋhā̊* . *vā́c-asos*

	Av.	Plural:	cf. Skt.
N.V.	dužvac-aŋhō	. .	suvā́c-asas
A.	dužvac-aŋhō .		suvā́c-asas
I.	vac-ə̄biš¹ .	.	vā́c-ōbhis
D.Abl.	(vac-ə̄byō) raocə̄byō¹		vā́c-ōbhyas
G.	vac-aŋhąm .		vā́c-asām
L.	(vac-ahu) sarahu	vā́c-asu
	-ahva arəzahva		—

ii. NEUTER (Separate Forms).

| Sg. | N.A.V. vac-ō . . . . | vā́c-as |
| Pl. | V.A.N. vac-ā̊ . . . . | vā́c-ąsi |

Forms to be observed in GAv. and YAv.

§ 340. In general, GAv. has the same forms as above with the long final vowel, see § 26.

i. MASCULINE—FEMININE—NEUTER.

§ 341. Singular:—

Nom.: YAv. also uncompounded adj. (see § 338) *aojō* 'strong' Ys. 57.10 beside substantive *aojō* n. 'strength', GAv. *dvaēšō* 'hating' beside *θραēšō* n. 'hatred', cf. Skt. *yaśās* 'beauteous' (observe accent) beside *yáśas* n. 'beauty'.—Add *harənas-ca* n. 'and glory'.

Acc.: On *ušaŋhəm*, *ušąm* f. 'dawn', see § 357.

Dat.: YAv. *rafnaŋhas-ca* 'and for support'.—GAv. infin. dat. *srāvayeŋhē* 'to announce' (see § 118 Note on *-ye- = -va-*).

Abl.: YAv. also (+ postpositive *a* § 222) *zrayaŋhaδa* 'from the sea' Yt. 8.47. —After *o*-decl. (+ postpos. *a* § 222) *təmaŋhaδa* 'from darkness'.

Gen.: YAv. *harənaŋhas-ca* 'and of glory'.

Loc.: YAv. peculiar *zraya* (Yt. 5.38; 8.8), *zrayī* (Ys. 65.4), *zrayāi* (Yt. 5.4; 8.31) 'in the sea'.— See also § 357 Note 2.

§ 342. Plural:—

Nom.: YAv. *framanaŋhas-ca* 'kindly-minded'.

Instr.: YGAv. also (with variant *-biš* § 21) *vacə̄biš*.

Loc.: YAv. also (*-ōhv-, -ohva* § 39) *ravohu* 'in freedom', *təmohva* 'in darkness'.

ii. NEUTER (Special Forms).

§ 343. Plural:—N.A.V.: YAv. add *aojās-ca* 'powers', GAv. *təmās-cā* 'and darkness'.

§ 344. Transfers to the *a*-declension are very frequent:—

---

¹ See § 33.

Consonant Class: — (12) Stems in original *s*.

Singular. Nom. *arš.vacō* (masc.) 'rightly-speaking'; Acc. (fem. *ā*-decl.) *ravō.vacaṅhǝm* 'whose words go with freedom' Vsp. 7.2; Instr. *harǝna* 'with glory' Yt. 10.141, see § 194; Abl. *tǝmaṅhāda* 'from darkness' (postpositive *a* § 222). — **Dual.** Dat. *aiβyajaṅhaēibya* 'for the two imperishable ones'. — **Plural.** Nom. *amǝṣ̌ǝṅhō* 'undying' (§ 124 Nom. end, stem *aoǰa*- beside *aoǰah*-), *mainyavasō* (nom. pl. masc.) 'following the will *(vasah-)* of the Spirit' Yt. 10.128, beside *mainivasaṅhō*; Instr. *sraṅžiš* 'with words'.

(3) **Stems in -yah. — Comparative Adjectives.**

§ 345. The stems in *-yah* (Skt. *-yas* or *-īyas* § 68) are found in the comparative degree of adjectives. They show an original double form of stem for m a s c u l i n e and n e u t e r: strongest stem *-yāh*, strong stem *-yah*. The superlative *-iš-ta* presents the weak stem. The Skt. has *-yās*, *-yas*, *-iṣ-ṭha*, cf. Brugmann, *Grundriss* ii. § 135 Anm. 5. — The corresponding feminine form has *-ychī-* (i. e. strong stem + *ī*-declension § 257) e. g. Av. *aspō.staoyehīš* (nom. pl. fem.) 'greater than a horse'. — Cf. Whitney, *Skt. Gram.* § 463 seq.

i. MASCULINE.

§ 346. Av. *nāidyah-* 'weaker', *masyah-* 'greater', *kasyah-* 'less', *āsyah-* 'swifter', *frāyah-* 'more', *vaḣyah-* 'better'.

	Av.	Singular:		cf. Skt.
N.	*(nāid-yāu) masyā*			*śrḗ-yān*
A.	*nāid-yāṅhǝm*			*śrḗ-yąsam*
D.	*(nāid-yaṅhe) kasyaṅhe*			*śrḗ-yase*
G.	*nāid-yaṅhō*			*śrḗ-yasas*
		Dual:		
N.A.V.	*(nāid-yaṅha) āsyaṅha*			*śrḗ-yąsāu*
		Plural:		
N.V.	*(nāid-yaṅhō) masyaṅhō*[1]			*śrḗ-yąsas*
I.	*(nāid-yebīš) frāyebīš*			*śrḗ-yobhis*
G.	*(nāid-yaṅhąm) vaṅhaṅhąm*[2]			*śrḗ-yasām*

ii. NEUTER (Separate Forms).

Sg. N.A.V. *mas-yō* . . . . *śrḗ-yas*

---

[1] See Haug, *Zand-Pahlavi Glossary* p. 48, 16. — [2] See § 134.

Forms to be observed in GAv. and YAv.

§ 347. **i. MASCULINE. Singular:** Nom. GAv. observe *vahyå* 'melior' (see § 133 on *h*); Acc. (from strong stem) *vauhaṿhəm* 'meliorem' (see § 134 on *vh* = orig. *sy*), cf. Skt. *kanīyāsam* 'younger', Whitney, *Skt. Gram.* § 405 c. — Observe in paradigm **Dual, Plural** Nom. °*yawha*, °*yaṅhō* (i. e. strong stem) opposed to Skt. °*yā́ṁsau*, °*yā́ṁsas* (i. e. strongest stem). — **ii. NEUTER. Singular:** Nom. YAv. observe *vauhō* 'melius' § 134, GAv. *vahyō* 'melius' § 132. On YAv. *aš̌ō*, GAv. *ašyō* 'worse', see § 162.

(γ) Stems in -*vah*. — Perfect Active Participles.

§ 348. The stems in -*vah* are perfect active participles used adjectively. They show a double form of stem for **masculine** and **neuter**: strongest stem -*vah*, weak stem -*uš*. The Skt. has -*vā́ṁs*, -*uṣ*, cf. Brugmann, *Grundriss* ii. § 136 Anm. 6. — The corresponding feminine form has -*uší*- (i. e. weak stem + *ī*-declension § 257) e. g. Av. *vīpuší* (nom.), *vīpušīm* 'knowing', see § 86 on *p*. — Cf. Whitney, *Skt. Gram.* § 458 seq.

MASCULINE — NEUTER.

§ 349. Av. -*vah*- YAv. *vīdvah*-, GAv. *vīdvah*- 'knowing' = Skt. *vidvás*-.

Av. *dadvah*- 'creator', *iriripwah*- 'having died'.

	Av.	Singular:		cf. Skt.
N.	*vīd-vā̊*			*vid-vā́n*
A.	°*vīd-vā́ṅhəm*[1]			*vid-vā́ṁsam*
I.	*vīp-uša*[2]			*vid-úṣā*
D.	*vīd-ušē* (GAv.)			*vid-úṣe*
Abl.	(*vīp-ušaṯ*) *dapušaṯ*[2]			see gen.
G.	*vīd-ušō* (GAv.)			*vid-úṣas*
		Plural:		
N.	*vīd-vā̊ṅhō*			*vid-vā́ṁsas*
I.	(*vīp-ūžbīš*) *dadūžbīš* (GAv.)			*vid-vádbhis*
G.	(*vīp-ušąm*) *iriripušąm*			*vid-úṣām*

Forms to be observed in GAv. and YAv.

§ 350. **Singular:** Nom. VGAv. also (from weak stem) *mamnuš* 'having thought' Yt. 8.39, *vīpuš* 'knowing' Vd. 4.54; *jaγnuš* 'having striven', Haug,

[1] See Vsp. 19.1; Yt. 10.35. — [2] See § 86.

Consonant Class: — (12) Stems in original *s*. 101

ZPhl. Gloss. p. 16.6; 56.5, *viduš* (GAv.) 'knowing' Ys. 45.8, *vāunuš* 'having won' Ys. 28.5, cf. Whitney, *Skt. Gram.* § 462 c, and Bartholomae, in *K.Z.* xxix. p. 531 = *Flexionslehre* p. 111; — Voc. YAv. (nom. as voc.) *vīspō.vīdvā̊* 'O all-knowing one' Vd. 19.26. — Plural: Uncertain whether acc. pl. or gen. sg. *daduṣō* Ys. 58.6.

Note. On the interchange of *d, ḍ, p* see §§ 82, 83, 86.

§ 351. Transfers to the *a*-decl. may be found: e. g. dat. pl. Av. *vīpuṣaēibyas-ca.*

(b) Radical Stems in -*h* (= orig. -*s*).

(α) Stems in -*āh* (= orig. -*ās*).

§ 352. To this division (masculine, feminine and neuter) belong simple nouns like Av. *māh-* m. 'moon' (Skt. *mā́s-*), *āh-* n. 'mouth' (Skt. *ā́s-*) and the compounds of Av. -*dāh-* 'giving, doing'. The forms have all the long vowel *ā̊ (ā).*— Cf. Horn, *Nominalflexion im Avesta* p. 4 seq., and Lanman, *Noun-Inflection in the Veda* p. 493 seq.

MASCULINE—FEMININE—NEUTER.

§ 353. Av. ⟨script⟩ YGAv. *hudā́h-, hudāh-* 'beneficent' = Skt. *sudā́s-.*

Av. *yās-* n. (metrically dissyllabic) 'decision', *akō.dāh-* 'maleficent'.

	Av.	Singular:			cf. Skt.
N.V.	*hud-ā̊* . . .	. .	. .	*sud-ā́s*
A.	*hud-ā̊ṅhəm* .	. .	. .	*sud-ā́sam*
I.	*hud-ā̊ṅha* . .	. .	. .	*sud-ā́sā*
D.	*hud-ā̊ṅhe*	. .	. .	*sud-ā́se*
Abl.	*hud-ā̊ṅhaṭ* . .	. .		see gen.
G.	*hud-ā̊ṅhō* .	. .	.	*sud-ā́sas*
L.	(*hud-āhi*) *yāhi*	. .	. .	*sud-ā́si*
		Plural:			
N.V.	*hud-ā̊ṅhō* . .	. .	.	*sud-ā́sas*
A.	*hud-ā̊ṅhō* .	. .	.	*sud-ā́sas*
I.	(*hud-ā̊bīš*) *akō.dæbīš*	. . .	.	—
D.	*hud-ā̊byō* .	. .	.	—
G.	*hud-ā̊ṅhąm* .	. .	.	*sud-ā́sām*

Forms to be observed in GAv. and YAv.

§ 354. Plural: Instr. and Dat. often show MS. authority for °*ābīš*, °*ābyō*; the form in -*āb*- above, apparently arises from orig. *ās* being treated as if final, i. e. before °*biš*, °*byō*—pada endings.—Observe Nom. Pl. *za-r*ᵃ*zdå* (GAv.).

§ 355. Transfers to the *a*-declension occur: e. g. Singular: Nom. *måvhō* 'moon' Yt. 10.142 (cf. Skt. *måsas* nom.); Dat. *måṅhōi*; Gen. *måṅhahe* beside *måṅhō*; Voc. *duzda* 'O malevolent one' § 234 b.

Note. The acc. sg. *uṣiḍam* 'giving understanding' nom. propr. is perhaps to be explained as formed after the radical *ā*-decl. § 250, cf. Skt. *vayō-dhām* — cf. Brugmann, *Grundriss* ii. § 134, 1², Lanman, *Noun-Inflection* pp. 555, 443, 446.

(5) Like radical *āh*-Stems.

§ 356. Declension of Av. *mazdåh*- f. 'wisdom, Mazda', Anc. Pers. -*mazdāh*- = Skt. -*mēdhas*-. This word like *uṣåh*-, *uṣah*-, § 357, is after all best considered a contract noun, cf. dat. sg. GAv. (trissyllabic) *mazdāi* (i. e. *mazdā(h)-e*); acc. sg. GAv. (trissyllabic) *mazdam* (i. e. *mazdā(h)-am*); gen. sg. GAv. (trissyllabic) *mazdå* (i. e. *mazdā(h)-as*); nom. pl. GAv. (trissyllabic) *mazdås-cā* (i. e. °*å(h)-as*). The forms are as follows:—

Singular. Nom. *mazdå* (dissyllable GAv.); Acc. *mazdam*; Dat. *mazdāi*; Gen. *mazdō*, *mazdås-ca* (YAv.), *mazdås-cā* (trissyl. GAv.); Voc. (*a*-decl.) *mazda* (YAv.), *mazdā* (GAv.). — Plural. Nom. Voc. *mazdås-cā* (GAv.).

§ 357. Here may be added Av. *uṣåh*-, *uṣah*- f. 'dawn' = Skt. *uṣås*-, *uṣås*-.— Singular: Acc. *uṣōuhem*, *uṣam* (cf. Skt. *uṣāsam*, *usāsam*, *uṣam*).— Plural: Acc. *uṣå* (cf. Skt. *uṣās*); Gen. *uṣaṅham* (cf. Skt. *usāsām*); Loc. *uṣahva*.

Note 1. Parallel, are the sg. nom. acc. Av. *hvāpå*, *hvāpem* 'beneficent' = Skt. *svápās*, *ªsvápām*.

Note 2. An instance of contraction in orig. *as*-stem § 339 similar to the above, seems to be the loc. sg. *zrayāi* (trissyllabic) 'in the sea' Yt. 5.4; 8.31 (= *zraya(h)e* like *vaēyahe*, *arezahe*). But another explanation for *zrayāi* may be suggested: viz. mistake in writing *āi* for *ahi* due to Pahlavi script.— See further, § 341.

Note 3. Transfer to the *a*-declension, sg. nom. *hvāpō* 'beneficent'.

(c) Derivative Stems in -*iš*, -*uš*.

§ 358. The examples are not numerous. The words are chiefly neuter. There is no vowel-gradation.— Cf. Whitney, *Skt. Gram.* § 414.

§ 359. Av. *snaipiš*- n. 'weapon'.—Singular: Nom. Acc. (neut.) *snaipiš*; Acc. (masc. adj.) *nidā.snaipiṣəm* 'having weapons laid down'; Instr. *snaipiša*; Gen. *hadiš̌as-ca* 'of the abode'; Loc. *vipiši* 'at the judgment' (Geldner).— Dual: Instr. *snaipībya*.—Plural: Gen. *snaipišąm*.

Note. Transfers to the *a*-decl. occur: e. g. sg. gen. *hadišahe* 'of the abode'.

§ 360. Similar are the *uš*-nouns: Av. *arəduš*- n. 'assault, battery'. —Singular: Nom. *arəduš*; Instr. *arəduša*; Loc. *tanuši* 'in person'.—Plural: Gen. *arədušąm*.

ADJECTIVES.
Feminine Formation—Comparison.

§ 361. The declension of adjectives, as agreeing exactly with that of nouns, is treated above.

§ 362. **Feminine Formation.** The adjective *a*-stems masc. neut. form their corresponding feminine in -*ā* or -*ī*. The consonant stems and *u*-stems show regularly the fem. in -*ī*, before which the adjective stem usually appears in its weak form.

(1) With -*ā*: Av. *haurva*- (m. n.), *haurvā*- (f.) 'whole'; *sūra*- (m. n.), *sūrā*- (f.) 'mighty'; *ugra*- (m. n.), *ugrā*- (f.) 'strong'; *aspa*- (m.) 'horse', *aspā*- (f.) and *aspī*- (f.) 'mare'.

(2) With -*ī*: Av. *rava*- (m. n.), *ravī*- (f.) 'broad, smooth'; *spitāma*- (m. n.), *spitāmī*- (f.) 'belonging to Spitama'; *daēva*- (m. n.), *daēvī*- (f.) 'devilish'.—*ašavan*- (m. n.), *ašaonī*- (f.) 'righteous'; *barəzaṇt*- (m. n.), *barə-zaitī*- (f.) 'high, great'; *vīdvah*- (m. n.), *vīdušī*- (f.) 'knowing'; *dātar*- (m.), *dāϑrī*- (f.) 'giving, giver'; *ϑrā-tar*- (m.), *ϑrāϑrī*- (f.) 'protector, nurturer'; *vaŋhu* (m. n.), *vaŋuhī*- (f.) 'good'; *driǰu*- (m. n.), *drīvī*- (f.) 'poor'
§ 187

---
[1] For different views on the subject see Horn, *Nominalflexion im Avesta* p. 5; Brugmann, *Grundriss der vergl. Gr.* ii. § 133², but ii. § 134, 1².

§ 363. **Comparison of Adjectives.** In Avesta as also in Sanskrit, there are two ways of forming the comparative and superlative degrees of adjectives: — (1) -tara-, -təma- and (2) -yah-, -išta- added to the stem. The corresponding feminine to these is -tarā-, -təma- and -yehī- (§ 34), -ištā- according to rule, § 362.

(1) -tara- (comparative), -təma- (superlative).

§ 364. Before -tara-, -təma-, adjectives whose stem ends in a appear commonly in the form ō as in noun compounds. The a-stems may, however, retain a unchanged, as in Sanskrit. Other stems commonly remain unchanged, appearing in the weak form if they have one.

baēšazya- 'healing',	baēšazyōtara-,	baēšazyōtəma-
srīra- 'fair',	srīrōtara-,	—
aka- 'bad',	akatara-,	—
huyašta- 'well-sacrificed',	huyaštara-,	—
hubaoidi- 'sweet-scented',	hubaoiditara-,	hubaoiditəma-
ašaojah- 'very strong',	ašaojastara-,[1]	ašaojastəma-
yāskərət- 'energetic',	yāskərəstara-,[2]	yāskərəstəma-
amavaṇt- 'strong',	amavastara-,[2]	amavastəma-
yaētvah- 'having striven',	—	yaētuštəma-

(2) -yah- (comparative), -išta- (superlative).

§ 365. Before -yah-, -išta-, the adjective reverts to its original simple crude stem without formative suffix:

maz- 'great',	mazyah-,	mazišta-
mas- 'great',	masyah-,	—
vaŋhu- } 'good', { vahyah- (GAv.), } vahišta-		
vohu- } { vaŋhah- (YAv.),[3] }		
ās-u- 'swift',	āsyah-,	āsišta-
ak-a- 'bad',	ašyah- (GAv.), ašah- (YAv.),[4]	acišta-

[1] Cf. § 109. — [2] § 151. — [3] §§ 132, 134. — [4] § 162.

Comparison of Adjectives.

Note 1. Some few adjectives, in appearance at least, show both forms of comparison, as above *aka-* 'bad', *akatara-*, and to this also (cf. Note 2) *aṣyah-, aciṣṭa-;* so superlative *aśaojiṣta-* beside *aśaojastara-, aśaoyastəma-* to *aśaojah-* 'very strong'.

Note 2. As seen also above, comparatives and superlatives may be more or less mechanically attached to a positive of similar meaning and containing the same crude stem, see § 365: e. g. to *taḵ-ma-* 'strong', the comparative *tąjyah-*, superl. *tąnciṣṭa-* beside *taḵmōtəma-*, et al.

Note 3. The *an*-stems sometimes follow the analogy of *ant*-stems in their comparison: e. g. *vərəθravan-* 'victorious', comparat. *vərəθravastara-*, superl. *vərəθravastəma-;* *aṣ̌avan-* 'righteous', *aṣ̌avastəma-;* *vərəθrajan-* 'victorious', *vərəθrająstara-, vərəθrająstəma-*.

NUMERALS.

§ 366. The numerals in Avesta correspond generally in form and in usage to the Sanskrit equivalents.—Cf. Whitney, *Skt. Gram.* § 475 seq.

Cardinals.

Av.	cf. Skt.		Av.	cf. Skt.
1. *aēva-*	—		10. *dasa*	*dáśa*
2. *dva-*	*dvi-*		20. *vīsaiti*	*viṃśati-*
3. *ṗri-*	*tri-*		30. *ṗrisat-*	*triṃśát-*
4. *caṗwar-*	*catvár-*		40. *caṗwarǝsat-*	*catvāriṃśát-*
5. *paṇca*	*páñca*		50. *paṇcāsat-*	*pañcāśát-*
6. *ḳšvaš*	*šáš*		60. *ḳšvašti-*	*ṣaṣṭi-*
7. *hapta*	*saptá*		70. *haptāiti-*	*saptati-*
8. *ašta*	*aṣṭá*		80. *aštāiti-*	*aśīti-*
9. *nava*	*náva*		90. *navaiti-*	*navati-*
10. *dasa*	*dáśa*		100. *sata-*	*śatá-*

	Av.		Av.
100.	*sata-*	600.	*ḳšvaš sata*
200.	*duye saite*	700.	*hapta sata*
300.	*tišurō sata*	800.	*ašta sata*
400.	*caṗwārō sata*	900.	*nava sata*
500.	*paṇca sata*	1000.	*hazaṇra-*

10000. *baēvar-*

§ 367. The numbers from 11—19, as far as they occur, are made up as in Skt.: e. g. Av. *dvadasa* '12' = Skt. *dvādaśa*; Av. *paṇcadasa* '15' = Skt. *páñcadaśa* See below under Ordinals, § 374 b.

Note. Observe, the common form+ Av. *ṗrisata-* '30' and *caṗwarǝ-sata-* '40' arise from transfer of *ṗrisat-* etc. to the *a*-decl. The strong form *ṗrisaṇt-* is to be sought in *ṗriṃs* (orig. nom. but crystallized form), etc.

§ 368. In composite numbers the lesser numeral precedes, and *ca—ca* connects the terms: e. g. Av. *pañcāca vīsatica* '25'; *prayasca prisąsca* '33'; *pañcāca capwar³satəmca* '45', etc.

Note. The first member is sometimes put in the sociative instrumental case; e. g. Av. *nava.saiāiš hazaŋrəmca* 'one thousand and nine hundred'.

Declension of Cardinals.

§ 369. (1) Declension of Av. *aēva-* (m. n.), *aēvā-* (f.) 'one, alone' (singular):

i—ii. MASC. NEUT. Sg. Nom. *aēvō*; Acc. *āyum* (§ 63 Note 2), or (abbreviated spelling) *ōim, aoim*; Instr. *aēva*; Gen. *aēvahe*; Loc. *aēvahmi* (§ 443).—iii. FEM. Sg. Nom. *aēva*; Acc. *aēvąm*; Gen. *aēvaŋhå* (§§ 443, 134).

§ 370. (2) Declension of Av. *dva-* 'two' = Skt. *dvá-* (dual)—cf. Whitney, *Skt. Gram.* § 482b.

Du. N.A.V. *dva* (m.), *duye* (f. n.); I.D.Abl. *dvaēibya*; G.L. *dvayå*. Note. Observe *dvaē-ca* Yt. 19.7 beside *duye* § 190.

§ 371. (3) Declension of Av. *þri-* (m. n.), *tišar-* (f.) 'three' = Skt. *trí- tišár-* (plural)—cf. Whitney, *Skt. Gram.* § 482 c.

i—ii. MASC. NEUT. Pl. Nom. *þrāyō*; Acc. *þrāyō*; Dat. Abl. *þribyō*; Gen. *þrayąm.*—iii. FEM. Nom. *þrāyō*; Acc. *tišºrō, tišrō, tišra*; Gen. *tišrąm, tišranąm* (ā-decl.).

Note. Observe *þrāyō* (above) is from strongest stem, cf. § 235.—Also *þrāyə-ca*, on ā cf. § 19 b.—Also neut. (like fem. § 232) *tišºrō*.

§ 372. (4) Declension of Av. *capwar-* (m. n.), *catawhar-* (f.) 'four' = Skt. *catvár-, cátasar-* (plural)—cf. Whitney, *Skt. Gram.* § 482 d.

i. MASC. Pl. Nom. *capwārō, capwðras-ca* (§ 19 b); Acc. *capwārō*. —ii. FEM. Acc. *catanrō* Yt. 14.44.

§ 373. (5) Declension of numerals from 5—10:—The following instances of gen. pl. occur, Av. *pañcanąm, navanąm, dasanąm,* cf. Skt. *pañcānām,* Whitney, *Skt. Gram.* §§ 483, 484.

§ 374. Declension of remaining cardinals:—20 *visaiti* indeclinable; 30 *þrisatəm* (nom. acc. neut.), *þrisatanąm* (gen. pl.); 40 *capwārəsatəm-ca* (§ 19 b); 50 *pañcāsatəm, pañcāsaþbiš-ca* (§ 19 b); 60—70 *hļvastim* (acc. sg.

108   Inflection: Ordinal Numerals and Derivatives.

fem.) etc., also *navaitiš-ca* (acc. pl. fem. beside *navaitīm*).—100—1000 *sata-*, *hazaṇra-* as neut. nouns, *a*-decl. § 237.—10 000 *baēvarə* (acc. sg.), *baēvarāi* (dat. sg. *a*-decl. § 237); *baēvąn* (acc. pl.), *baēvarəbīš* (instr. pl.) cf. 336.

Ordinals.

	Av.	cf. Skt.		Av.	cf. Skt.
1st	{ *fratəma-* / *paoiryaˉ-*	*prathamá- pūrvyá-*	11th	*aēvaṇdasa-*	—
2nd	*bitya-*	*dvitīya-*	12th	*dvadasa-*	*dvādaśá-*
3rd	*þritya-*	*tṛtīya-*	13th	*þridasa-*	*trayodaśá-*
4th	*tūirya-*	*tūrya-*	14th	*caþrudasa-*	*caturdaśá-*
5th	*puχδa-*	*pañcatha-*¹	15th	*paṇcadasa-*	*pañcadaśá-*
6th	*χštva-*	—	16th	*χšvaš.dasa-*	*ṣoḍaśá-*
7th	*haptaþa-*	*saptátha-*	17th	*haptadasa-*	*saptadaśá-*
8th	*aštəma-*	*aṣṭamá-*	18th	*aštadasa-*	*aṣṭádaśá-*
9th	*nāuma-* (§ 64)	*navamá-*	19th	*navadasa-*	*navadaśá-*
10th	*dasəma-*	*daśamá-*	20th	*vīsąstəma-*	—

100th Av. *satōtəma-* = Skt. *śatatamá-*.
1000th Av. *hazaṇrōtəma* = Skt. *sahasratamá-*.

Note 1. The ordinals as adjectives are declined according to the *a*-decl. § 236 seq.
Note 2. Av. *χštva-* 'sixth' has fem. *χštvī-*, cf. § 362.
Note 3. Av. *þrisata-* as 'thirtieth' is found.

Numeral Derivatives.

§ 375. Numeral Adverbs: Av. *hakərət̰* 'once' = Skt. *sakṛ́t;* Av. *biš* 'twice' = Skt. *dvís;* Av. *þriš* 'thrice' = Skt. *tris;* Av. *caþruš* 'four times', cf. Skt. *catúḥ*, Whitney, *Skt. Gram.* § 489.—Also with *ē:* Av. *āβitīm* 'for the second time', *āþritīm* 'for the third time, thrice'; *āχtūirīm* 'for the fourth time'.—Likewise some others.

§ 376. Multiplicative Adverbs: Suffix *-vaṇt*—Av. *bižvat̰* 'two-fold'; *þrižvat̰* 'three-fold'; *vīsaitivå* 'twenty-fold' (nom. masc.); *þrisaþwō* 'thirty-fold'; etc.—Suffix *-þwa:* e. g. *þrisata-þwəm* 'thirty-fold'; etc.

Note. Here also might be added a number of other words *þrižva-* 'a third' et al.; but they belong rather to the dictionary.

¹ Cf. Whitney, *Skt. Gram.* § 487.

PRONOUNS.

§ 377. Pronominal declension in Avesta agrees in its main outlines with the Sanskrit. A synopsis of the Pronouns in Avesta may be given as follows:—

SYNOPSIS OF PRONOMINAL-DECLENSION.

- A. Gender not distinguished.
  1. Personal
     - a. First person *azəm*.
     - b. Second person *tūm*.
     - c. Third person, *hē* and other forms.
- B. Gender distinguished.
  2. Relative — Pronoun *ya-*.
  3. Interrogative — Pronoun *ka-*.
     (Indefinite.)
  4. Demonstrative
     - a. Demonstrative *ta- (hvō)*.
     - b. Demonstrative *aēta-*.
     - c. Demonstrative *aēm (a-, i-, ima-, ana-)*.
     - d. Demonstrative *ava- (hāu)*.
  5. Other pronominal Words and Derivatives.
     (Possessive).
     (Reflexive).
     (Adjectives declined pronominally).

§ 378. **General Remark.** Most of the pronouns in Avesta are closely parallel with those in Sanskrit, and like the latter they show also many marked peculiarities. They are generally made up by combining a number of different stems. The principal points to be observed in regard to their inflection are the following:

i—ii. MASCULINE—NEUTER.

§ 379. **Singular:**—

Nom. Acc. Neut.: Commonly the suffix -*ţ* = Skt. -*t (d)*.— Sometimes in later texts of the V.W. instead of -*ţ*, the ending -*m*, like the neuter ending of the noun-declension, is found: e. g. *yim*, *avm*.

Dat. Abl. Loc.: Show an inserted element -hm- = Skt. -sm-.—The dat. sg. of the two personal pronouns ends in -ōya (-vya), -byō = Skt. -bhya(m), Whitney, *Skt. Gram.* § 492 a.—The loc. sg. in YAv. may take postpositive *a* as in the noun-declension, see § 222.

§ 380. **Plural**:—

Nom. (Acc.): The pronominal *a*-stems make this case end in *e*. This form in *e* often serves also as accusative.

Gen.: Shows -ṣąm = Skt. -sām.—The 'genitives' ahmākəm, yūṣmākəm, yaṛākəm, as in Skt., are really crystallized cases nom. acc. neut. of possessives.

Loc.: In YAv. the loc. pl. may take postpositive *a* as in the noun-declension, see § 224. Similarly also in fem. loc. pl.

iii. FEMININE.

§ 381. **Singular**:—

Dat. Abl. Gen. Loc.: Show an inserted element -hy- (-hy-), -ph- = Skt. -sy-.

§ 382. **Plural**:—

Gen.: Shows -vhąm = Skt. -sām.

§ 383. **Interchange of Neuter with Feminine Forms.** As in the nouns § 232, so also in the pronouns the neuter plural often assumes the form of the feminine or rather interchanges with it.—See also Johannes Schmidt, *Pluralbildungen der indogerm. Neutra* pp. 21, 260, etc.

Note. In formulaic passages, especially in the Yashts (e.g. Yt. 5.13,15), masc. forms *yeŋhe*, *aiŋhe*, *ahmāi* are sometimes used instead of the proper fem. forms. This arises from the mosaic character of such passages.

§ 384. **General Relative Case** is found in YAv. in the instances of *yāiš* as plural, cf. § 229.—For the treatment of *yō*, *yaṭ*, *yim* as stereotyped case (plural and singular) see under Syntax.

A. GENDER NOT DISTINGUISHED.

1. Personal Pronouns.

§ 385. The first and second personal pronouns, as in Skt., show many peculiarities and individulities of inflection. Some cases also use two forms, a fuller and a briefer form, according to the position of the pronoun in the sentence, whether accented, unaccented, or enclitic. Furthermore, on the third personal pronoun, see § 394 seq.

§ 386. (a) **First Person**, Av. ͱᴵꞩ azəm 'I' = Skt. ahám.

Av.	Singular:	cf. Skt.
N.	azəm	ahám
A.	mąm; mā (encl.)	mā́m; mā
D.	māvᵒya¹; mē (encl.)	máhyam; mē
Abl.	mat̰	mā́t
G.	mana; mē (encl.)	máma; mē
	Plural:	
N.	vaēm²	vayám
A.	ahma³; nō (encl.)	asmā́n; nas
D.	ahmaibyā (GAv.); nō (encl.)	asmábhyam; nas
Abl.	ahmat̰	asmā́t
G.	ahmākəm; nō (encl.)	asmā́kam; nas

Forms to be observed in GAv. and YAv.

§ 387. GAv. has in general the same forms as YAv., but shows also a number of peculiarities to be marked; these are likewise occasionally found in YAv., perhaps borrowed.

§ 388. Singular:—
Nom.: GAv. azə̄m. § 32.—Also once (unaccented or proclitic) os-cit̰ Ys. 46.18.
Dat.: YAv. the form māvᵃya before -ca, -cit̰, § 386 Note 1.—GAv. maibyā, maibyō, and (encl.) moi.
Gen.: Observe gen. Av. mana (note -n-) contrasted with Skt. máma (-m-).

§ 389. Plural:—
Nom.: GAv. (sporadic) nom. pl. unaccented (second place in sentence) vā Ys. 40.4, cf. Skt. va-yám, cf. § 393.
Acc.: GAv. regularly nā̊, cf. also at Vsp. 15.2 = Ys. 15.3 nā̊, Gāthā reminiscence, see § 387.
Dat.: GAv. ahmaibyā (above), ahmāi, and (encl.) nə̄, cf. also at Vsp. 12.4 nə̄, see § 387.
Gen.: GAv. also (unaccented) ahmāi, ə̄hmā, and (encl.) nə̄.

---

¹ Also before -ca, -cit̰ written māvᵃya. See also § 388.
² i. e. vayəm, § 64.
³ Yt. 1.24 variant; i. e. Av. ahma = Skt. asmā́n; Av. aspa = Skt. áśvān

Inflection: Declension of Pronouns.

§ 390. (b) Second Person, Av. tūm 'thou' = Skt. tvám.

	Av. Singular:	cf. Skt.
N.	tūm¹; tū	tvám
A.	θwąm; θwā (encl.)	t-vām; tvā
I.	θwā²	tvā (Ved.)
D.	taibyā (GAv.); tē (encl.) . .	tubhyam; te
Abl.	θwat	tvát
G.	tava; tē (encl.) . .	táva; te

Dual:
G. yavākəm³ . . . —

Plural:
N.	yūžəm	yūyám
A.	vō (encl.)	vas
D.	yūšmaoyō, ẋšmāvōya; vō (encl.) .	yuṣmábhyam; vas
Abl.	yūšmat	yuṣmát
G.	yūšnąkəm; vō (encl.) . .	yuṣmākam; vas

Forms to be observed in GAv. and YAv.

§ 391. GAv. has in general the same forms as YAv., but shows also a number of peculiarities to be marked; these are likewise sometimes found in YAv., perhaps borrowed.

§ 392. Singular:—
Nom.: GAv. tvəm (cf. §§ 32, 93 Note 1), tū.
Dat.: GAv. taibyā (above), also taibyō, and (encl.) toi.
Gen.: GAv. tavā; toi (encl.) see § 56.

§ 393. Plural:—
Nom.: GAv. also yūš i. e. Av. yūš; Skt. yū-yám :: Av. vō (§ 389); Skt. va-yám.
Acc.: GAv. regularly vā.
Dat.: GAv. yūšmaibyā, ẋšmaibyā; vō (encl.), cf. also YAv. (Gāthā reminiscence) vō Ys. 14.1, etc.
Abl.: GAv. also ẋšmat.
Gen.: GAv. ẋšmākəm and (encl.) vō.—Also ẋšmā Ys. 43.11.

---
¹ i. e. tvəm, see § 63.
² Ys. 43.10.
³ Yr. 6.1 and Haug, ZPhl. Glossary pp. 3, 46, see § 68 Note 3, cf. Skt. yuvākú, see § 380.

§ 394. (c) **Third Person**, Av. ⸱⸱⸱ ⸱⸱⸱ *hē* (*šē*) and other forms.

The proper third personal pronoun *hīm*, *hē* etc. (enclitic) is defective; its deficiencies are partly supplied by the demonstrative pronoun, and partly by enclitic forms of *di-*, *i-* used with personal force. These latter show distinction of gender, but they may best be included here.

§ 395. The following forms of the proper third personal (often used anaphorically, sometimes used reflexively, see also § 416) occur in GYAv.; they are all enclitic:

  Singular. Acc. *hīm* (GYAv.); Dat. Gen. *hē* or *šē* § 155 (YAv.), *hōi* (GAv.). — Dual. N.A.V. *hī* (GAv.). — Plural. Acc. *hīš* (GYAv.).

  Note 1. The form *hē* dat. gen. sg. seems in some passages in YAv. to serve as plural. See under Syntax.

  Note 2. With the above Avesta forms compare Skt. acc. sg. *sīm*; Prakrit dat. gen. *se* — all enclitic. See Wackernagel in K.Z. xxiv. p. 605 seq.

§ 396. Similar to *hē* in usage are the forms from stem YAv. *di-* — likewise enclitic: —

  Sg. Acc. *dim* m. f.; *dit* n. — Pl. Acc. *dīš* m. f.; *dī* n. Ys. 65.8.

§ 397. Of like usage (cf. also § 422), is stem G(Y)Av. *i-* enclitic — sometimes employed almost pleonastically: —

  Sg. Acc. *īm* m.; *īt* n. (GAv.), *ī* (YAv., particle). — Du. N.A.V. *ī*. — Pl. Nom. *ī* n.; Acc. *īš* m.; *ī* n.

§ 398. On *hvō*, *hvāviya* used as personal (and reflexive) see §§ 416, 436 Note 3.

B. GENDER DISTINGUISHED.

2. Relative Pronoun.

§ 399. **Relative** Av. ⸱⸱⸱ *ya-* 'who, which' = Skt. *yá-*.

The relative stem *ya-*, *yā-* = Skt. *yá-*, *yā́-*, shows the following forms. — Cf. Whitney, *Skt. Gram.* § 508.

8

i. MASCULINE — NEUTER.

	Av.	Singular:	cf. Skt.
N.	*y-ō*		*y-ás*
A.	*y-im*[1]		*y-am*
I.	*y-ā*		*y-éna*
D.	*y-ahmāi*		*y-ásmāi*
Abl.	*y-ahmāt*		*y-ásmāt*
G.	*y-ehe, y-eŋhe*[2]		*y-ásya*
L.	*y-ahmi*		*y-ásmin*

Dual:

N.	*y-ā*		*y-ā́* (Ved.)
G.	*y-ayau*		*y-áyōs*

Plural:

N.	*y-ōi*		*y-é*
A.	*y-ą*		*y-án*
I.	*y-āiš*		*y-áis*
D.Abl.	*y-aēibyō*		*y-ébhyas*
G.	*y-aēšąm*		*y-ēšā́m*
L.	*y-aēšū* (GAv.)		*y-éšu*

ii. NEUTER.

Sg. N.A.V.	*y-at*		*y-át*
Pl. N.A.V.	*y-ā*		*y-ā́* (Ved.)

iii. FEMININE.

Singular:

N.	*y-ā*		*y-ā́*
A.	*y-ąm*		*y-ā́m*
Abl.	*y-eŋhāt, -āda*		see gen.
G.	*y-eŋhā̊*		*y-ásyās*
L.	*y-eŋhe*[3]		*y-ásyām*

Plural:

N.A.	*y-ā̊*		*y-ā́s*
D.Abl.	*y-ābyō*		*y-ā́bhyas*
G.	*y-āŋhąm*		*y-ā́sām*
L.	*y-āhu, y-āhva*		*y-ā́su*

[1] cf. § 30. — [2] cf. §§ 137, 136, 34. — [3] i. e. *yasyā(m)*, uncertain Vs. 9.32, cf. *oŋhe* § 422.

Forms to be observed in GAv. and YAv.

§ 400. GAv. has generally the same forms as YAv., but shows also some peculiarities to be marked; these are occasionally found likewise in YAv., perhaps borrowed.

i. MASCULINE—NEUTER.

§ 401. Singular:—

Nom.: YAv. *yas-ca, yasə̆ ē.*—In VAv. (commonly in late passages, but cf. Yt. 10.119) the form *yə̄* is sometimes found as general relative case, cf. § 384, and under Syntax.—GAv. *yə̄, yas-cā* (also YAv. borrowed *yə̄,* cf. § 400).

Acc.: GAv. *yə̆m, yim,* see §§ 32, 30.

Abl.: YAv. also *yahmāṭ,* on *ā* see § 19 (b).—GAv. once adverbial *yāṭ* Ys. 36.6 = Ys. 58.8, like Skt. *yát,* cf. Whitney § 509 a.

Gen.: GAv. *yehyā,* see § 132.

Loc.: YAv. also (with postpos. *a* § 380) *yahmya.*—GAv. only *yahmī.*

§ 402. Plural:—

Nom.: VGAv. *yae-ca, yaē-cā.*—In YAv. (late) a form *yə̄* as nom. acc. pl. (cf. *tā,* § 413) occurs, cf. noun-inflection *a*-stems § 236.

Acc.: GAv. *yə̄ṇg, yə̄ṇgs-tū, yus-cā.*

Instr.: YAv., *yāiš* commonly occurs as general plural case, cf. § 384.

Dat. Abl.: GAv. *yaēibyas-cā.*

ii. NEUTER.

§ 403. Singular:—

Nom. Acc.: YAv. also *yim* like neut. noun-declension, but generally in late passages.—On *yas-ca = yiṭ-ca* see § 151 Note.—GAv. *hyaṭ* (variants *yaṭ, yiaṭ,* e. g. Ys. 28.9, 30.6 etc.).

§ 404. Plural:—

Nom. Acc.: YAv. also neut. (like fem. § 383) *yā̊.*

iii. FEMININE.

§ 405. Plural:—

Nom. Acc.: YAv. *yā̊s-ca.*—Also rare (like neut.) *yə̄,* cf. Ys. 10.78.—GAv. *yā̊s-cā.*

3. Interrogative Pronoun.

§ 406. Interrogative Av. *ka-* 'who, which, what?' = Skt. *ká-.*

The interrogative *ka-*, *kā-* = Skt. *ká-*, *kā́-*, is identical in inflection with the relative and requires no full paradigm to be given.—Cf. Whitney, *Skt. Gram.* § 504.

i. MASCULINE—NEUTER.

	Av.	Singular:	cf. Skt.
N.	*k-ō* . . .	. .	. *k-as*
A.	*k-əm* etc. .	. .	*k-ám*

ii. NEUTER.

Sg.	N.A.V. *k-at* etc.	*k-át*

iii. FEMININE.

Sg.	N.	*k-ā* etc.	*k-ā́*

Note. YAv. also an instr. sg. *kana* = Skt. *kéna* beside Av. *ka*.— YAv. also dat. *cahmāi* (indef.) beside *kahmāi*; GAv. *cahyā* beside *kahyā*. —YAv. as gen. pl. (or perhaps fem. sg. form = neut.) *k̄qm* m. f.

§ 407. Some special forms of interrogative are worthy of note.

1) Stem *ki-*, *ci-* 'quis':—**Sg. Nom.** (m. f.) *ciš*, cf. Skt. *ná-kis*, Acc. (m. n.) *cim*, *cim*, cf. Skt. *kím*.—**Pl. Nom.** (m. n.) *kaya*, *cayō*.—Neut. also **Sg. Nom. Acc.** *cit*, *cīt*.

2) Stem *kuti-*, *cati-* 'what, how much':—**Sg. Acc.** (neut.) *caiti* = Skt. *káti*.

Note. Here also Av. *cina-* 'what'.—Likewise some forms of the interrogative used adverbially:—e. g. *kat* 'how, nonne?'.—*cā* 'how'. Perhaps *kəm* Vd. 17.1 (?).—Uncertain *cyawhat* 'how' Ys. 44.12 abl. (?) or *ci-avhat* doubtful.

Indefinite.

§ 408. The indefinite force is usually given in Av., as in Skt., by combining a particle *-cit*, *-cīt* = Skt. *-cit*, *-ca*, *-cat* etc., with the interrogative or relative. Sometimes it is added by the particle *-cina* (*-cana* Afr. 3.7 = Skt. *-cana*), which is likewise attached to nouns and adjectives; sometimes, again, reduplication of the pronoun (rel. interrog.) gives an indefinite or a distributive force.

Av. *kahmāicit* 'to whomsoever' = Skt. *kásmāicit*; Av. *kapacina* 'howsoever, in any way'; *cayascā* 'quicunque' Ys. 45.5, *cīcā* 'quaecunque' Ys. 47.5 (fr. *ci + ca*); *yaþa kaþaca* 'even as', *kahmi kahmicit̰* 'in any case whatever', et al.

Note. Indefinite negatives are Av. *naē-cit̰* 'no one' = Skt. *ná-kis*; Av. *mā-cit̰* (imperative) 'no one' = Skt. *mó-kis*.

4. Demonstrative Pronouns.

§ 409. (a) Demonstrative Av. ta- 'this' = Skt. *tá-*. The demonstrative stem *ha-, hā-, ta-* 'ὁ, ἡ, τό' = Skt. *sá-, sā-, tá-*, serves also as personal of the third person.— Cf. Whitney, *Skt. Gram.* § 495.

i. MASCULINE—NEUTER.

	Av.	Singular:	cf. Skt.
N.	*h-ō*		*s-ás*
A.	*t-əm*		*t-ám*
I.	*t-ā*		*t-éna*
G.	*t-ahe*[1]		*t-ásya*

Dual:

| N.A.V. | *t-ā*[2], *t-āv*[2] | | *t-ā́, t-āú* |

Plural:

N.	*t-ē*		*t-é*
A.	*t-ə̄*		*t-ā́n*
I.	*t-āiš*		*t-āís*
D.Abl.	*t-aēibyō*		*t-ébhyas*

ii. NEUTER.

| Sg. N.A.V. | *t-at̰* | | *t-át* |
| Pl. N.A.V. | *t-ā* | | *t-ā́* (Ved.) |

iii. FEMININE.

Singular:

| N. | *h-ā* | | *s-ā́* |
| A. | *t-ąm* | | *t-ā́m* |

Plural:

| N.A. | *t-ā̊* | | *t-ā́s* |

---

[1] See Vd. 6.29 with v. l. *ca hē*. — [2] Yt. 8.22

Forms to be observed in GAv. and YAv.

§ 410. GAv. has in general the same forms as YAv., but shows also some peculiarities; these are occasionally found likewise in YAv., perhaps borrowed.

i. MASCULINE — NEUTER.

§ 411. Singular:—

Nom.: YAv. *has-cit*.—Observe *hā* Vsp. 12.1 = Skt. *sá*, Whitney, *Skt. Gram.* §§ 498, 176a, also Av. *aēša* § 418.—GAv. *hē* Ys. 58.4, *hə̄-cā* Ys. 46.1; cf. also at Vsp. 12.1, Ys. 27.6; YAv. (Gatha reminiscence?) *hə̄-ca*.

Acc.: GAv. *tə̄m*, see § 32 for *ə*.

§ 412. Dual:—

Nom.: GAv. *tōi* Ys. 34.11 is probably used as fem. du.

§ 413. Plural:—

Nom.: YAv. *taē-ca*.—Also rare (like neut. or *a*-decl.) *tā*, cf. § 236.—GAv. *tōi, taē-cit*.

Acc.: YAv. also (see nom.) *tā*, cf. § 380.— Late *tā*.—GAv. *təng, təs-cā*, and later dialect *tą* Ys. 63.1 = Ys. 15.2.

ii. NEUTER.

§ 414. Plural:—

Acc.: YAv. also (like fem., see § 383) *tå, tås-ca*.

iii. FEMININE.

§ 415. Plural:—

Acc.: YAv. rarely (like neut., cf. § 383) *tā* Yt. 10.79, cf. similarly *yā* § 405. —GAv. *tås-cā*.

§ 416. Here is to be added also G(Y)Av. **nominative singular** *hvō* 'ille, ipse', **dative** *hvāvōya* (like *māvōya*) properly originally reflexive, see §§ 398, 436 N. 1, 3.

Note. In oldest GAv., *hvō* takes the place of demonstr. *hō*, which form does not occur in the metrical Gāthās.

§ 417. (b) **Demonstrative** Av. *aēta-* 'this' = Skt. *etá-*.

The demonstrative *aēša-*, *aēšā-*, *aēta-* 'this, here' = Skt. *eṣá-, eṣā-, etá-*, is identical in declension with *ha-, hā-, ta-* from which it is derived by prefixing *aē-* which makes it the nearer demonstrative. The only GAv. form noted is

Demonstrative Pronouns.

nom. sg. fem. *aēṣā* 12.9 (later GAv.).—Cf. Whitney, *Skt. Gram.* § 499b.

i. MASCULINE—NEUTER.

Av.	Singular:	cf. Skt.
N. *aēṣ-ō*		*ēṣ-ás*
A. *aēt-əm*		*ēt-ám*
I. *aēt-a*		*ēt-éna*
D. *aēt-ahmāi*		*ēt-ásmāi*
Abl. *aēt-ahmāṯ*		*ēt-ásmāt*
G. *aēt-ahe*		*ēt-ásya*
L. *aēt-ahmi*		*ēt-ásmin*

Dual:

| G. *aēt-ayā̊* | | *ēt-áyōs* |

Plural:

N.(A.) *aēt-e*		*ēt-é*
G. *aēt-aēṣąm*		*ēt-éṣām*
L. *aēt-aēṣva*		*ēt-éṣu*

ii. NEUTER.

| Sg. N.A.V. *aēt-aṯ* | | *ēt-át* |
| Pl. N.A.V. *aēt-a* | | *ēt-á* |

iii. FEMININE.

N. *aēṣ-a*		*ēṣ-ā́*
A. *aēt-ąm*		*ēt-ā́m*
I. *aēt-aya*		*ēt-áyā*
G. *aēt-aṅhā̊* [1], *aēt-ayā̊*		*ēt-ásyās*

Forms to be observed in GAv. and YAv.

i. MASCULINE—NEUTER.

§ 418. Singular:—

Nom.: YAv. also *aēṣa* = Skt. *ēṣá*, Whitney, *Skt. Gram.* § 176a, cf. *hā* above § 411.

§ 419. Plural:—

Nom. Acc.: YAv. notice that *aēte* like *tē* above §§ 413, 380 serves as both nom. and acc. masc. and also neut.

---

[1] See § 134.

ii. NEUTER.

§ 420 **Plural:**—
Nom. Acc.: YAv. also (like fem., § 383) *aētā*.—On *aē'e* see § 380.
Gen.: YAv. also (contaminated with fem.) *aētavhąm*.

iii. FEMININE.

§ 421 **Singular:**—
Nom.: GAv. (only occurrence) *aēā* Ys. 12.9.
Gen.: YAv. the form *aētayā̊*, *aētayā̊-cit* follows the noun-inflection, *ā*-decl.

§ 422. (c) **Demonstrative** Av. *aēm* 'this' = Skt. *ayám*

The demonstrative *aēm*, as in Skt., is made up from defective stems *a*-, *i*-, *ima*-, *ana*- = Skt. *a*-, *i*-, *ima*-, *ana*- combined to fill out a complete declension.

It is to be observed (in GAv. it is evident) that beside the accented forms, there occur likewise unaccented forms (not found at beginning of a pada). These forms generally come from the brief stem.

i. MASCULINE—NEUTER.

	Av.	Singular:	cf. Skt.
N.	*aēm*[1]		*ayám*
A.	*iməm*		*imám*
I.	*ana*		*anéna*
D.	*ahmāi*		*asmāi*
Abl.	*ahmāt*		*asmāt*
G.	*ahe, aŋhe*[2]		*asyá*
L.	*ahmi*		*asmin*

Dual:

N.A.V.	*ima*		*imā́* (Ved.)
G.	{ *ayā̊*		*ayṓs* (Ved.)
	{ *anayā̊*[3]		*anáyōs*

Plural:

N.	*ime*		*imé*
A.	*imą*		*imā́n*
I.	*aēibiš* (YAv.), *anāiš* (GAv.)		*ebhis*
D.Abl.	*aēibyō*		*ebhyás*
G.	*aēšąm*		*eṣā́m*
L.	*aēšu, aēšva*		*eṣú*

[1] i. e. *ayam*, § 64. — [2] See §§ 136, 137. — [3] Uncertain, see Vd. 4.48.

Demonstrative Pronouns.

	Av.	ii. NEUTER.	cf. Skt.
Sg.	N.A.V. *imaṱ*	. . .	*idám*
Pl.	N.A.V. *ima*		*imá* (Ved.)

iii. FEMININE.
Singular:

	Av.		cf. Skt.
N.	*īm*[1]	.	*iyám*
A.	*imąm* .	. .	*imā́m*
I.	*āya, aya* .		*ayā́* (Ved.)
D.	*aiŋhāi* .		*asyāí*
Abl.	*aiŋhāṱ* . .		see gen.
G.	*aiŋhā̊* .		*asyā́s*
L.	*aiŋhe*[2] .		*asyā́m*

Dual:

I.D.Abl. *ābyā* (GAv.) . . . . . . *ābhyā́m*

Plural:

N.A.	*imā̊*	.	.	*imā́s*
I.	*ābīš*	. . .	.	*ābhís*
D.Abl.	*ābyō*		. .	*ābhyás*
G.	*āŋhąm*	. . . . .	.	*āsā́m*
L.	*āhū* (GAv.), *āhva* . . .			*āsú*

Forms to be observed in GAv. and YAv.

§ 423. GAv. has in general the same forms as YAv., with lengthened final wherever possible. There are also some peculiarities worthy of note.

i. MASCULINE—NEUTER.

§ 424. Singular:—
Nom.: GAv. also *ayə̄m* beside *aēm*, see § 32.
Abl.: YAv. also *aṅmāṱ*, on *ā* see § 19(b).
Gen.: GAv. *ahyā, ahyā-ca*, cf. §§ 132, 133.
Loc.: YAv. also (with postpos. *a*, § 379) *ahmya*.

---

[1] i. e. *iyəm*, see §§ 63, 51. — [2] i. e. orig. **asyā(m)*.

§ 425. Dual:—
Gen.: GAv. also (from stem *a*-, § 431) *aš-cā*.

§ 426. Plural:—
Nom. (Acc.): YAv. *imē* serves also as acc. pl., see § 380.
Instr: GAv. observe the form *anāiš* above from stem *ana-*, and *āiš* below
  § 431 from stem *a-*.
Dat. Abl.: YAv. *aēibyas-ciṭ*.

ii. NEUTER.

§ 427. Singular:—
Nom. Acc.: YAv. observe *imaṭ* above as opposed to Skt. *idam*.

§ 428. Plural:—
N.A.V.: YAv. also (like fem., § 383) *imå*.—GAv. regularly *imā* which is the only GAv. instance noted of this stem *ima-*.
Loc.: YAv. also (see fem. § 383) *āŋhąm*.

iii. FEMININE.

§ 429. Singular:—
Instr.: GAv. *ayā* cf. YAv. *avā* above in paradigm.
Dat.: GAv. *aḥyāi*, cf. § 133.
Abl.: YAv. also *aiŋhāṭ*, on *ṯ* see § 19(b).
Gen.: YAv. *aiŋhās̆-ca*, see § 124 Note.
Loc.: YAv. also, identical with instrumental, *aya*.

§ 430. Plural:—
Nom. Acc.: YAv., also a form *imåsca* before *ṯ*, see § 124 Note.
Dat. Abl.: YAv., also *āibyas-ciṭ, āiwyas-ca*, on *ā* see § 19 Note.

§ 431. Directly from stem *a-* come:— Singular. Acc. Neut. (as particle) *aṭ* (GYAv.); Dat. (uncertain?) *āi* Vd. 3.23 (neut. fem.); Abl. (as particle) *āṭ* (GAv.), *āaṭ* (YAv.).— Dual. Gen. *aṣ-cā* (GAv.).—Plural. Instr. (also used adv.bl.) *āiš* (GAv.).

§ 432. (d) Demonstrative *hau, ava-* 'that' = Skt. *asáu*, —.

The remote demonstrative in Av. *ava-* 'that, yonder' (cf. Old Pers. *ava-*), combined with *hāu*, is to be contrasted with Skt. *amú-, asáu-*. The Av. shows *ava-* throughout where the Skt. has *amú-*.—Cf. Whitney, *Skt. Gram.* § 501.

i. MASCULINE — NEUTER.

	Av.	Singular:	cf. Skt.
N.	hāu		asāú
A.	ao-m [1]		—
I.	av-a		—
G.	av-aiŋhe		—

Plural:

N.(A.)	av-e		—
I.	av-āiš		—
G.	av-aēšąm		—

ii. NEUTER.

Sg. N.A.V.	av-aṱ, ao-m		—
Pl. N.A.V.	av-a		—

iii. FEMININE.
Singular:

N.	hāu		—
A.	av-ąm		—
Abl.	av-aiŋhāṱ		—
G.	av-aiŋhā̊, av-aŋhā̊		—

Plural:

N.A.	av-ā̊		—
D.Abl.	av-abyō		—

Forms to be observed in GAv. and YAv.

§ 433. Plural. Acc. Neut.: YAv. also (neut. like fem. § 383) avā̊.
Note. For the derivatives avaṇt-, avavaṇt- (avaṇt-) from ava- see § 441.

---

5. Other Pronominal Words and Derivatives.
Possessive — Reflexive,
Pronominal Derivatives and Adverbs.

§ 434. Under the above head belong the possessives and a number of words which have chiefly the nature of

---

[1] i. e. ᵉavǝm, § 63.

adjectives and are inflected partly according to the pronominal declension, partly according to the nominal. They answer in general to corresponding forms in Sanskrit.—Cf. Whitney, *Skt. Gram.* § 515 seq.

Possessive - Reflexive.

§ 435. Here may be enumerated as connected with the personal pronoun, the following p o s s e s s i v e (and reflexive) forms:— Av. *ma-* 'meus', *þwa-* 'tuus', *hva-*, *h^va-*, *hava-* (reflexive) 'suus', *ahmāka-* 'our', *yūšmāka-*, *h̨šmāka-* 'your'.—*mavaṇt-* 'like me', *þwāvaṇt-* 'like thee', *yušmāvaṇt-*, *h̨šmāvaṇt-* 'like you'.—*h^vaēpaiþya-* 'own'.

Other Pronominal Derivatives and Adverbs.

§ 436. The following d e r i v a t i v e s may further be noted:—Relative, *yavaṇt-* 'how much', *yatāra-* 'which of two'.—Interrogative, *cvaṇt-* 'how much?', *katāra-* 'which of two?'.—Demonstrative, *aētavaṇt-* 'so much', *avaṇt-* 'that, such', *avavaṇt- (avaṇt-* § 194) 'so much'.—Likewise here, numerous pronominal a d v e r b s *ya-þa* 'how, as', *ka-da* 'how, when?', *cū* 'how?', *i-da* 'here', etc.

Note 1. Here observe Av. *hatō* 'reciprocally, each other' = Skt. *svātas*.

Note 2. On *hvō* 'ipse, ille' as personal pronoun, see §§ 398, 416.

Note 3. From same stem as *hvō* (in Note 2) comes the interesting reflex. dat. *hvavōya* 'self' (like *māyōya* § 388), cf. Lat. *s(v)ibi*.

Note 4. From an assumed demonstrative stem *tva-* comes the neut. adverb *þwat* 'then again' Ys. 44.3 = Skt. *tvat*.

Note 5. Instances of GAv. *ahyā* gen. of demonstr. (= pers.), from *aēm* § 422, instead of the reflex. possessive, occur.

Declension of Pronominal Derivatives.

§ 437. In regard to inflection, the pronominal derivatives follow partly the pronominal declension and partly the nominal. The following forms of the p o s s e s s i v e s (reflexive), and of the d e m o n s t r a t i v e d e r i v a t i v e s declined according to the pronominal declension are worthy of note.

§ 438. i. Declension of the possessive pronoun GAv. *ma-* 'meus'.

i—ii. MASC.—NEUT. Sg. Nom. *mə̄*; Dat. *mahmāi*; Gen. *mahyā*.— Pl. Acc. (Neut.) *mā*.—iii. FEM. Sg. Gen. *mahyā* (§ 133).

§ 439. ii. Declension of the possessive pronoun GAv. *þwa-* 'tuus'.

i—ii. MASC.—NEUT. Sg. Nom. *þwə̄*; Instr. *þwā*; Dat. *þwahmāi*; Abl. *þwahmāṭ*; Gen. *þwahyā*; Loc. *þwahmi*.— Pl. Nom. *þwōi* (masc.); Acc. *þwā* (neut.).—iii. FEM. Sg. Nom. *þwōi*; Gen. *þwahyā̊*.—Pl. Loc. *þwāhu*.

§ 440. iii. Declension of GYAv. *hva-, hva- (hava-)* 'suus' = Skt. *svá*.—GAv. has only ⸺, YAv. ⸺ (from GAv.), ⸺ and ⸺.

i—ii. MASC.—NEUT. Sg. Nom. *hə̄* (GAv.), *hvō* (YAv.); Instr. *hā*; Gen. *hahe*; Loc. *hvahmi*.—'Du. Acc. *hva*.— Pl. Instr. *hāiš*; Loc. *hvaešu* (? emended Fn. 4.2).—iii. FEM. Nom. *hvaē-rā* (GAv.), *hva* (YAv.); Dat. *hahyāi*.

Note 1. From the by-form *hava-* come: Masc. Neut. Sg. Nom. *havō*; Acc. *haem* (§ 64); Instr. *hava*; etc. regularly according to nominal declension (§ 236 *a*-decl.).— Fem. Sg. Nom. *hava*; Acc. *havąm*; Dat. *havajāi* with variant *hacyāi* (§ 62, 2); Gen. *havayā̊* beside *haoyā̊* (§ 62, 2).

Note 2. The possessives *ahmāka-* 'our', *þwāvaṇt-* 'like thee' etc. follow the noun-inflection.

Note 3. Observe that *ahmākəm, yūšmąm, yušmākəm* employed as 'genitives' of the personal pronoun §§ 386, 390, are really stereotyped cases of possessive adjectives, as similarly in Skt. *asmākam, yuvākú, yuṣmākam*.

§ 441. iv. Declension of the demonstrative derivative *avaṇt-* 'that, such', from stem *ava-* § 430. This is to be distinguished from *avavaṇt- (avaṇt-* § 194) in § 442.

MASC. Sg. Nom. *avā̊*.—Pl. Dat. Abl. *avaṭbyo*.—NEUT. Sg. Nom. Acc. *avaṭ* above in paradigm.

§ 442. v. Declension of the demonstrative derivative *avavaṇt- (avaṇt-* § 194, cf. variants) 'so great'—to be distinguished from *avaṇt-* § 441.

Sg. Nom. (neut.) *avavaṭ*; Acc. (masc.) *avāṇtəm* (§§ 194, 44) and *avavaṇtəm* (neut. adv. *a*-decl.); Instr. *avavata*; Gen. *avavatō*.— Pl. Gen. *avavatąm*.

Adjectives declined pronominally.

§ 443. A few adjectives in Av., like their corresponding Skt. equivalents, also follow the pronominal declension wholly or in part. Cf. Whitney, *Skt. Gram.* § 522 seq.— Instances are: Av. *aēva-* 'one, alone'; Av. *anya-* 'other' = Skt. *anyá-*; Av. *vīspa-* 'all' = Skt. *víśva-*.

For example: Pl. Nom. Acc. m. *vīspe, vīspə* (pronominal) beside Nom. m. *vīspåvhō;* Acc. *vīspīs-ca* (YAv.), *vīspąs-cā, vīspə̄ņg* (GAv.) i. e. nominal declension; — Gen. *vīspaēšąm* (pronominal) beside *vīspanąm* (nominal); et al.

CONJUGATION,
VERBS.

§ 444. The Avesta verb corresponds closely to the Sanskrit in form, character, and in usage. The Av. texts, however, are not so extensive as to give the verb complete in all its parts; some few gaps in the conjugation-system therefore occur.

Modelled after the Sanskrit, the Avesta verbal system may be presented as on the next page.

§ 445. **Voice, Mode, Tense.** The Av. agrees with the Skt. — especially with the language of the Vedas — in v o i c e s active. middle (passive), in t e n s e s present (and preterite), perfect (and pluperfect), aorist, future, and in m o d e s indicative, imperative, subjunctive, optative. In usage likewise these generally correspond with the Sanskrit.

Note 1. The middle voice. as in Skt., is often used with a passive force. A formative passive, as in Skt., however also occurs (cf. V. a).

Note 2. Under tenses, observe that 'injunctive' or 'improper subjunctive' is a convenient designation for certain forms of augmentless preterites used with imperative force. These are enumerated under the simple preterite. Cf. Whitney, *Skt. Gram.* § 563.

§ 446. **Infinitive, Participle.** Like the Skt., the Av. conjugation-system possesses also infinitive forms (abstract verbal nouns) and participial forms (active and middle in each tense-system) and gerundives. See VI below.

§ 447. **Person, Number.** The Av. like the Skt. distinguishes t h r e e p e r s o n s, and t h r e e n u m b e r s.

Note. It is to be observed that the first persons imperat. are supplied by subjunctive forms.

128 Inflection: Conjugation of Verbs.

SYNOPSIS OF VERB-SYSTEM

I. **Present-System** (10 Classes) — i. ACTIVE — ii. MIDDLE
  1. Indicative
     a. Present.
     b. Preterite (Injunctive).
  2. Imperative.
  3. Subjunctive (Pres. and Pret. Forms).
  4. Optative.
  5. Participle.

II. **Perfect-System** — i. ACTIVE — ii. MIDDLE
  1. Indicative
     a. Perfect (Present).
     b. Pluperfect (Preterite).
  2. Imperative.
  3. Subjunctive (Pres. and Pret. Forms).
  4. Optative.
  5. Participle.

III. **Aorist-System** (non -s-, and s-Class) — i. ACTIVE — ii. MIDDLE
  1. Indicative (Preterite = Aor.).
  2. Imperative.
  3. Subjunctive (Pres. and Pret. Forms).
  4. Optative.
  5. Participle.

IV. **Future-System**
  1. Indicative (Act. and Mid.).
  2. Participle.

V. **Secondary Conjugations.**
  a. Passive.   d. Inchoative.
  b. Causative.   e. Desiderative.
  c. Denominative.   f. Intensive.

VI. **Verbal Abstract Forms.**
  a. Participles. b. Gerunds. c. Infinitives.

VII. **Periphrastic Verbal Phrases.**

Personal Endings of Verbs. 129

§ 448. **Personal Endings.** These are either (a) primary (pres. and fut. indic., and partly subjunct.) or they are (b) secondary (pret. indic., opt., aor., and partly subjunct.). Some individual peculiarities of form occur in (c) the imperative and in (d) the perfect; the endings, therefore, of the latter two also are separately enumerated.

The scheme of normal endings in comparison with the Skt.,—cf. Whitney, *Skt. Gram.* § 553—is as follows:

(Observe the Av. 3 du. forms often identical with Skt. 2 du.)

a. Primary Endings.

	i. ACTIVE			ii. MIDDLE	
Av.	Singular:	cf. Skt.	Av.	Singular:	cf. Skt.
1. -mi	. . .	-mi	-e	. . .	-ě
2. -hi (-ši)	.	-si (-ṣi)	-(ṅ)he (-še)	.	-sě (-ṣě)
3. -ti	. . .	-ti	-te	. . .	-tě
	Dual:			Dual:	
1. -vahī (GAv.)		-vas	—	. .	-vahě
2. —	.	-thas	—	.	-āthě
3. -tō, -pō	. .	-tas	-āpe	. .	-ātě
	Plural:			Plural:	
1. -mahi	. .	-masi (Ved.)	-maide	. . .	-mahě
2. -pa	.	-tha	-pwe	. .	-dhwě
3. -ṇti	.	-nti	-ṇte	.	-ṇtě

b. Secondary Endings.

	i. ACTIVE			ii. MIDDLE	
Av.	Singular:	cf. Skt.	Av.	Singular:	cf. Skt.
1. -m	. .	-m	-i, -a	. .	-i, -a
2. -s (-š)	.	-s (-ṣ)	-ṅha (-ša)	.	[-thās]
3. -ṭ	. .	-t	-ta	. .	-ta
	Dual:			Dual:	
1. -va	. . .	-va	—	. . .	-vahi
2. —	. .	-tam	—	. .	-āthām
3. -təm	.	-tām	-ātəm	. .	-ātām

9

130 Inflection: Conjugation of Verbs.

	Plural:		Plural:	
1. -*ma*		-*ma*	-*maⁱdī* (GAv.) -*maⁱde* (YAv.)	-*mahi*
2. -*ta*		-*ta*	-*dwəm*	-*dhvam*
3. -*n*		-*n*	-*ŋta*	-*nta*

c. Imperative Endings.

i. ACTIVE.			ii. MIDDLE.		
Av.	Singular:	cf. Skt.	Av.	Singular:	cf. Skt.
2. -*di*, —		-*dhi*, —	-*ŋuha* (-*ṣvā*)		-*sva* (-*sva*)
3. -*tu*		-*tu*	-*tąm*		-*tām*
	Plural:			Plural:	
2. -*ta*, -*nā* (GAv.)[1]		-*ta*	-*dwəm*		-*dhvam*
3. -*ŋtu*		-*ntu*	-*ŋtąm*		-*ntām*

d. Perfect Endings.

i. ACTIVE.			ii. MIDDLE.		
Av.	Singular:	cf. Skt.	Av.	Singular:	cf. Skt.
1. -*a*		-*a*	-*e*		-*ē*
2. -*ṯa*		-*tha*	—		-*sē*
3. -*a*		-*a*	-*e*		-*e*
	Dual:			Dual:	
1. —		-*va*	—		-*vahe*
2. —		-*athur*	—		-*āthē*
3. -*atarə*		-*atur*	-*aⁱtē* (GAv.)		-*ātē*
	Plural:			Plural:	
1. -*ma*		-*ma*	—		-*mahē*
2. -*a*		-*a*	—		-*dhvē*
3. -*arə*, -*arəš*		-*ur*	—		-*rē*

General Remarks on the Endings.

§ 449. In general, GAv. has the same forms as YAv. above, with the long final vowel wherever possible, cf. § 26; but there are also a number of peculiarities to be remarked upon in connection with GAv. as well as with reference to YAv.

---

[1] Sporadic, cf. § 457.

Remarks on the Endings. 131

Note. Observe that Av. 3 du. is in form often like Skt. 2 du.: e. g. Av. -*pō* (beside -*tō*) 3 du. pres. act. = Skt. -*tas* 3 du. (but -*thas* 2 du.); —again Av. -*təm* 3 du. pret. act. = Skt. -*tām* 3 du. (but -*tam* 2 du.), et al.—Compare the Homeric interchange of -τον, -την in secondary tenses.

a. Primary Endings (Observations).

§ 450. **Singular**:—

First Person: i. ACTIVE. Indicative. GYAv. also -*ā*, -*a*—i. e. GAv. has -*ā* regularly in the thematic or *a*-conjugation pres. indic., and -*mī* in the unthematic or non-*a*-conj. pres. indic.; but in YAv. this distinction is not sharply drawn.—Subjunctive. YAv. -*ni*, -*a*, GAv. -*ni*, -*ā*.—ii. MIDDLE. Indicative. GAv. also -*ōi* (§ 56, beside -*ē*).—Subjunctive. GYAv. -*nē*, -*ne*, -*āi* (i. c. *ā* + *e*).

Second Person: i. ACTIVE. Subjunctive. In later texts of YAv. -*ā(h)i* sometimes drops its *h* and becomes -*āi*. e. g. YAv. *yazāi* 'mayest thou worship' Yt. 10.140.—ii. MIDDLE. Indicative. YAv., observe -*se* (after -*a* [-*t*] §§ 151, 186) *vaose* 'thou growest' Ys. 10.4.—GAv. also indic. subjunct. -*ŋhōi* § 56.

Third Person: ii. MIDDLE. GYAv. also (but not common; cf. also perf. below) like 1 sg. -*e* = Skt. -*ē* beside *tē*.

§ 451. **Dual**:—

Third Person: i. ACTIVE. YAv., observe -*pō* in *yūidyapō* 'they both fight' Yt. 8.22, a 3 du.-form (like Skt. -*thas* 2 du.-form) beside -*tō* above, see § 449 Note.—ii. MIDDLE. YGAv. occasionally -*te* or -*aite* e. g. *baraite* 'they two bring' ZPhl. Gloss. pp. 54. 8 = 107. 13, *varəntaitē* 'both believe' (indic.) Ys. 31.17.—Again -*ītē*, GAv. *jamaētē* 'they both may come' (aor. subjunct.) Ys. 44.15.

§ 452. **Plural**:—

First Person: ii. MIDDLE. YAv. only occasionally is the MS. variant -*maide* (observe *d*) is noted.

Second Person: ii. MIDDLE. GAv. regularly -*duyē* = Skt. -*dhvē* § 190.

Third Person: i. ACTIVE—ii. MIDDLE. Indicative. YGAv. occasionally have in the 3 pl. of the non-*a*-conjugation (unthematic) the form -*aiti* (i. e. -*ṇti*) or even -*āiti* = Skt. -*ati* in the active, and -*aitē* (i. e. -*ṇtē*) = Skt. -*atē* in the mid.; but more commonly in the non-*a*-conj. (unthematic) the ending (-*aṇti*) -*ṇti*, (-*aṇtē*) -*ṇte* of the *a*-conj. (thematic) is assumed instead.—Uncommon in the pres. is -*re*, cf. indicative *sōire* 'they lie down' Yt. 10.80 = Skt. *śēre* Whitney, Skt. Gram. § 629, and subjunctive *mravāire* 'they may say' Yt. 13.64, *niẓrāire* 'they may throw' Yt. 10.40, cf. §§ 486, 521.

b. Secondary Endings (Observations).

§ 453. Singular:—

First Person: ii. MIDDLE. Observe that the normal ending *i* coalesces with the final of an *a*-stem into -*ē* e. g. *a̯ṣ̌aē* 'I laid myself' opp. to *aojī* 'I spake'.—The ending -*a* is found in the optative.

Second Person: i. ACTIVE. The normal ending -*s* unites with *a* in the *a*-conj. and gives -*ō* (-*ō̄* subjunct.); the *š*-form occurs according to rule § 156.—ii. MIDDLE. YGAv. notice the suffix is -*ṣ̌a* (cf. Gk. -σο) contrasted with Skt. -*thās*.

Third Person: i. ACTIVE. YGAv., orig. *t* is retained (unchanged to -*t*) after *s* (*š*), e. g. *mōist* 'he turned', *cōiṣ̌t* 'he promised', §§ 81, 192. — Notice *ās* (i. e. *ās-t*) 'he was' and *cinas* 'he promised' § 192 Note.

§ 454. Dual:—

Third Person: i. ACTIVE. YAv., observe that the 3 du. Av. -*təm* is in form like the 2 du. Skt. -*tam*—on this interchange in form between 3 du. and 2 du. see § 449 Note.—ii. MIDDLE. YGAv., note Av. -*ātəm* opp. to Skt. -*ātām*, see again § 449 Note.—Again (like primary 2 du., but) with secondary meaning YAv. -*āiδe* = Skt. -*āthē* and some other forms—see Bartholomae, *K.Z.* xxix. p. 286 seq. = *Flexions-lehre* p. 17 seq.

§ 455. Plural:—

First Person: ii. MIDDLE. Observe that GAv. has a proper secondary ending -*maidī* (cf. opt. *vairīmaidī*) = Skt. -*mahi*, but YAv. substitutes for this -*maide* drawn from the present.

Second Person: ii. MIDDLE. GAv. shows -*dūm* = Skt. -*dhvam*, § 63.

Third Person: i. ACTIVE. In redupl. formations GAv. has occasionally an unthematic 3 pl. pret. in -*at* (i. e. -*n̥t*) corresponding to the occasional -*ati* = -*n̥ti* of the pres., e. g. *ca.at* 'they drove away', et al. —GYAv., remark also opt. -*ārəš*, -*ārš*, thus *buyārəš* 'they would be', *hyārə* beside *hyąn*. Also -*arə* aor. pret. GAv. *ādarə* 'they made Ys. 43.15 = Skt. *ādhur*; YAv. *aš.arə* 'they elapsed' Vd. 1.4, cf. Whitney, *Skt. Gram.* §§ 829, 550 — cf. also under perfect endings (Pf. ii, below).—ii. MIDDLE. YAv. also sporadic traces of secondary 3 pl. mid. -*rəm* = Skt. -*ram* in Av. *vaociram* Yt. 19.69, cf. Whitney, *Skt. Gram.* § 834 b (perhaps best as pluperf.).

c. Imperative Endings (Observations).

§ 456. Singular:—

Second Person: i. ACTIVE. YGAv.. the *a*-verbs (thematic) have no ending, the simple stem form in -*a*, -*ā* is used. - The non-*a*-verbs (unthematic) show -*dī* (-*dī* § 83. 1), GAv. -*dī*.— ii. MIDDLE. YAv. regularly *-uuha* = Skt. *-sva* — GAv. *-svā* (in *daivā* 'give' = **dad-sva* § 186), *-ṣvā*, *-hvā* § 130, 2 a.

Third Person: ii. MIDDLE. A suffix *-qm* = Skt. *-ām*, 3 sg. mid. is found in GAv. *ərəžūcqm* 'let him speak aright' Ys. 48.9, *vīdqm* 'shall decide' *vi + dā* Ys. 32.6, Geldner, in *B.B.* xv. p. 261, cf. Whitney, *Skt. Gram.* § 618.

§ 457. Plural:—

Second Person: i. ACTIVE — ii. MIDDLE. The forms are undistinguishable from an augmentless imperfect § 445 Note 2.—A genuine instance of *-na* cf. Skt. *-tana* 2 pl. active imperat. is GAv. *baranā* Ys. 30.9, cf. Skt. *bhajatana*, Whitney, *Skt. Gram.* § 740.

Third Person: i. ACTIVE—ii. MIDDLE. The endings *-aṇtu, -əṇtu, -əṇtqm* occur in both *a*-verbs and in non-*a*-verbs — (in the latter case by transfer § 471 to *a*-conj.).

d. Perfect Endings.

§ 458. For observations on the perfect endings see Pf. ii below.

Mode-Formation.

1. Indicative Mode.

§ 459. The indicative has no special mode-sign other than the use of the present stem itself. The endings are the primary in the present, the secondary in the preterite.

Note. For special remarks on the strong and weak stem-forms in the indicative, see below §§ 467, 476 and observe under the different conjugation classes.

2. Imperative Mode.
(Cf. Whitney, *Skt. Gram.* § 569.)

§ 460. The imperative has no characteristic mode-sign, the stem is identical with that of the indicative, the special endings are simply added.

Note 1. For special remarks on the strong and weak stem-forms see below under the imperatives of the various conjugation-classes.

Note 2. For remarks on the endings see § 456.

3. Subjunctive Mode.
(Cf. Whitney, *Skt. Gram.* § 557 seq.)

§ 461. In Av., as in Skt., the subjunctive has as its characteristic mark an *a* added to the stem to form the special mode-stem. In the *a*-conjugation (thematic) this *a* unites of course with the stem-final and forms *ā*:—e. g. (1) thematic *a*-stem, Av. *bar-a-hi* 'mayest thou bear' (i. e. *bara-a-hi*) = Skt. *bhár-ā-si;*—(2) unthematic, Av. *jan-a-iti* 'may he smite' (cf. pres. indicat. *ja'n-ti*) = Skt. *hán-a-ti*.

§ 462. The endings of the subjunctive are partly primary (i. e. pres. subjunct.), partly secondary (i. e. pret. subjunct.),—the former predominating. Observe in 1 sg. active YGAv. *-ni*, *-nī* (i. e. *-āni*) or also YGAv. *-a*, *-ō;*—and in 1 sg. middle it is *-ne* (i. e. *-āne*) beside *-āi*. Cf. Whitney, *Skt. Gram.* § 562.

Subjunctive Endings combined with Mode-Sign.

	i. ACTIVE.				ii. MIDDLE.	
	Av. Singular:		cf. Skt.	Av.	Singular:	cf. Skt.
1.	*-āni*, *-a*	. . . .	*-āni*, *-ā*	*-āne*, *-āi*	. . . .	*-āi*
2.	*-ahi*, (*-ā[h]i*)	. .	*-asi*	*-avhe*		*-ase*
	-ō, *-ā* . .	. .	*-as*			
3.	*-āti*	. . . .	*-āti*	*-ātē* . .	. . .	*-ātē*
	-at . .	. .	*-āt*	*-āta* .	. .	. .
	Dual:				Dual:	
1.	*-āva*	. .	*-āva*	— .	. . . .	*-āvahē*
2.	— .	. .	*-athas*	— .	. . . .	*-āithē*
3.	*-ātō* .	. .	*-atas*	— .		*-āitē*
	-atəm	. . .	—			
	Plural:				Plural:	
1.	*-āma*	. . .	*-āma*	*-āmaide*	. . . .	*-āmahe*
2.	*-ataa* .	. .	*-atha*	— .		*-adhve*
3.	*-əṇti* .	. . .	—	*-ṇte*, *-aire*	. .	*-antē*
	-ən .	. . . .	*-an*			

Note 1. Observe (late) YAv. 2 sg. *-āi* = *-āhi* § 450.
Note 2. On improper subjunctive or imperative see § 445 Note 2.

4. Optative Mode.
(Cf. Whitney, *Skt. Gram.* § 564 seq.)

§ 463. The characteristic mode-sign of the optative in Av., as in Skt., is *-yā-*, *-ī-* added to the weak-stem for the non-*a*-conjugation (unthematic), or it is *-ī-* added to the regular tense-stem of the class for the *a*-conjugation (thematic).

In the *a*-stems (thematic) the mode-sign -$\bar{\imath}$- unites with the stem-final *a* into -*aē*- (-*ōi*-) §§ 55, 56. In the non-*a*-conj. the distinction between -*yā*-, -$\bar{\imath}$- is that -*yā*- was employed in the active and -*i*- in the middle.

Note. Instead of -*i*-, instances of -$\bar{\imath}$- (§ 21 Note) occur, e. g. *daiḍiža* beside *daiḍiža* 'mayest thou give'. — Similarly occur instances of -*yā*- for -*yā*- (§ 18 Note 1), cf. *buyata*, *buyamа* 'may ye, we be'. — Probably also GAv. *daidyaṭ* Ys. 44.10.

§ 464. The endings of the optative are the secondary ones throughout. In YAv., however, the 1 pl. mid. -*maide* (primary, e. g. Ys. 9.21) instead of GAv. -*maidi* (secondary) is found. Observe in the *a*-conj. (thematic) the 3 pl. act. mid. Av. -*ən*, -*ənta* (cf. Gk. λέγ-οι-εν, λέγ-οι-ντο) is to be contrasted with Av. non-*a*-verbs which show -*arə*, -*arəš* = Skt. -*ur*, -*ran* (act. mid. in both *a*- and non-*a*-stems).

Optative Endings combined with Mode-Sign.
a. *a*-conjugation (thematic).

	i. ACTIVE.			ii. MIDDLE.	
Av.	Singular:	cf. Skt.	Av.	Singular:	cf. Skt.
1. —		-*ēyam*	-*aya*[1]		-*ēya*
2. -*ōiš*		-*ēs*	-*aēša*		-*ēthās*
3. -*ōiṭ*		-*ēt*	-*aēta*		-*ēta*
	Plural:			Plural:	
1. -*aēma*		-*ēma*	-*ōimaidi* (GAv.) / -*ōimaide* (YAv.)		-*ēmahi*
2. -*aēta*		-*ēta*	-*ōidwəm*		-*ēdhvam*
3. -*ayən*		-*ēyur*	-*ayanta*		-*ēran*

b. Non-*a*-conjugation (unthematic).

	i. ACTIVE.			ii. MIDDLE.	
Av.	Singular:	cf. Skt.	Av.	Singular:	cf. Skt.
1. -*yąm*		-*yām*	-*ya*		-*īya*
2. -*yā̊*		-*yās*	-*īša*		-*īthās*
3. -*yāṭ*		-*yāt*	-*īta*		-*īta*
	Plural:			Plural:	
1. -*yāma*[2]		-*yāma*	-*īmaidi*		-*īmahi*
2. -*yāta*		-*yāta*	—		-*īdhvam*
3. { -*yqn* / -*yārə* / -*yārəš* }		— / -*yur* / —	—		-*īran*

[1] Cf. Ys. 8.7. — [2] See Yt. 24.58.

Reduplication and Augment.

a. Reduplication.
(Cf. Whitney, *Skt. Gram.* § 588 seq.)

§ 465. (a) Reduplication in Av., as in Skt., is found in certain parts of the verb-conjugation (pres. of 3rd. class, and in the desiderative, and intensive), in the perfect, and sometimes in the aorist. The reduplication consists in the repetition of a part of the root.—The rules of reduplication should be noted:—

(b) A long internal or final vowel of the root is commonly shortened in the reduplicated syllable; sometimes —see desiderative, intensive—it is lengthened or strengthened. Radical *ar* (*r*-vowel) is reduplicated by *i*. An initial vowel, by repetition of itself, of course merely becomes long in reduplicating.

(c) Roots beginning with a consonant repeat that consonant, but a guttural is reduplicated by the corresponding palatal; an original *s* (including *st, sp, sm*) is reduplicated by *h,* an orig. palatal *ś* by *s,* an initial spirant by the corresponding smooth:—e. g. Av. *ja-jm-aṭ* (√*gam-* 'go'), *hi-šta-iti* (√*stā-* 'stand'), *hi-spōs-əmna* (√*spas-* 'see'), *hi-šmar-əntō* (√*mar-*, **smar-* 'remember'), *tu-þru-ye* (√*þru-* 'nourish').

Note 1. The original guttural instead of palatal is retained in reduplication before *u,* cf. Av. *ku-hšnv-qna* (√*hšnu-* 'rejoice, please').

Note 2. Observe the redupl. form (desiderative participle) *ci-hšnauh-əmnå* Yt. 13.49, cf. Skt. *ji-jñās-amānas.*

b. Augment.
(Cf. Whitney, *Skt. Gram.* § 585.)

§ 466. In Av. the augment is comparatively rare, the instances of its omission far exceed in proportion those of the Vedic Sanskrit.

The augment, as in Skt., consists of short *a* prefixed to the preterite tense—imperfect, aorist, pluperfect. This *a*, as likewise in Skt., combines with an initial vowel into the corresponding *vṛddhi*.

It is often difficult to decide whether an *a* is the augment *a* or the verbalprefix $a = \bar{a}$.

<small>Note 1. For metrical purposes it seems sometimes that augment must be restored in reading where the texts omit it. — See Geldner, *Metrik* p. 38.</small>

<small>Note 2. Instead of *a*, GAv. shows once a form *ĵ* in augment before *v*, cf. GAv. *ĵvaocaṯ* (but written *ĵ. voacaṯ*) § 32.</small>

<small>Note 3. On augmentless preterites ('injunctive') with imperat.-subjunct. force, see § 445 Note.</small>

§ 467. **Vowel-Variation (Strong and Weak).** In Av., quite as in Skt., verb-stems commonly show vowel-variation —strongest, middle or strong, and weak forms, cf. § 235. This phenomenon must of course go hand in hand with an original shift of accent.

I. PRESENT-SYSTEM.

§ 468. The present-system is the most important of the systems, its forms are by far the most frequent in occurrence, and upon the basis of present-formation may be founded in Av., as in Skt., the conjugation-groups and classification of verbs. See the following § 469.

Classes of Verbs.

§ 469. Taking the Sanskrit Grammar as model, we may in the Av. present-system likewise distinguish ten classes of verbs according to the method of forming the present-stem. In Av., however, the phenomenon of accent (§ 2 end) is not always so clearly discernible.

The ten classes fall into two great groups of conjugation according as the endings are attached to the root with or without the (thematic) stem-vowel *a*. The (I) first group, the thematic or *a*-conjugation (Cl. **1, 6, 4, 10**), assumes *a* in the formation of its present-stem; the

(II) second group, the unthematic or non-*a*-conjugation (Cl. 2, 3, 7, 5, 8, 9), attaches the endings directly to the root (the latter as stem, however, subject to modification) without this *a* as formative element of the stem.—Cf. Whitney, *Skt. Gram.* § 602 seq.

§ 470. The classification of Av. verbs on the basis of the Sanskrit Grammar is the following:—

I. *a*-Conjugation (thematic).

First Formation—Class 1—see § 478 seq.

(1) *a*-class with strengthened root-form = Skt. first (*bhū-*) class.

 Av. √*bū-*, *bav-a-iti* 'he becomes'.

Second Formation—Class 6—see § 479 seq.

(6) *a*-class with unstrengthened root-form = Skt. sixth (*tud-*) class.

 Av. √*druj-*, *druž-a-iti* 'he deceives'.

Third Formation—Class 4—see § 480 seq.

(4) *ya*-class (unstrengthened root-form) = Skt. fourth (*div-*) class.

 Av. √*nas-*, *nas-ye-iti* 'he vanishes'.

Fourth Formation—Class 10—see § 481 seq.

(10) *aya*-class (strengthened root-form), causal = Skt. tenth (*cur-*) class.

 Av. √*ruc-*, *raoc-aye-iti* 'he lights up'.

II. Non-*a*-Conjugation (unthematic).

First Formation—Class 2—see § 516 seq.

(2) Root-class—root itself is present stem = Skt. second (*ad-*) class.

 Av. √*jan-*, *jaṇ-ti* 'he smites'.

Second Formation—Class 3—see § 540 seq.

(3) Reduplicating class—root redupl. is pres. stem = Skt. third (*hu-*) class.

 Av. √*dā-*, *da-dā-iti* 'he gives'.

Third Formation—Class 7—see § 554 seq.

(7) **Nasal-class**—inserted -*na*- (str.), -*n*- (wk.) = Skt. seventh (*rudh*-) class.

　　　Av. √*ric*-, *iri-na-ḫti* 'lets go'.

Fourth Formation—Class 5—see § 566 seq.

(5) *nu*-class—root adds *nao*- (str.), *nu*- (wk.) = Skt. fifth (*su*-) class.

　　　Av. √*kar*-, *karə-nuo-iti* 'he makes'.

Fifth Formation—Class 8—see § 577 seq.

(8) *u*-class—root adds *u*- alone = Skt. eigth (*tan*-) class.

　　　Av. √*āp*-, *āfənte* (i. e. *āp-v-ante* § 95) 'are overtaken'.

Sixth Formation—Class 9—see § 584 seq.

(9) *nā*-class—root adds *nā*- (str.), *n*-, *na*- (wk.) = Skt. ninth (*krī*-) class.

　　　Av. √*garw*-, *gərəw-nā-iti* 'he seizes'.

§ 471. **Transfer of Conjugation.** A verb is not always inflected according to one and the same conjugation and class throughout. The majority of the forms of a verb may be made up after one conjugation and class of the present system, while a few forms of the same verb may be made up after another; the same part of the verb being thus occasionally formed according to two classes. Instances of such transition in forms from one class to another are not rare; in general, examples of the tendency for verbs of the non-*a*-conjugation (unthematic) to pass over to the inflection of the *a*-conjugation, are not difficult to find.—See §§ 529, 553 etc.

---

i. The *a*-Conjugation (thematic).

§ 472. **General Remark.** The thematic or *a*-conjugation in the present-system comprises four classes (Cl. 1, 6, 4, 10), in all which the endings are attached to the root by means of a thematic vowel *a* (in 1 person ā, a). The root-vowel may, or may not be strengthened according to the class of the verb; it remains then as in the indicative throughout the other modes of the present-system.—The verbs of the *a*-conj. are numerous.—Cf. Whitney, *Skt. Gram.* § 733 seq.

Note. The 1 plur. thematic shows *ā* more often than *ă* (Skt. *ā*): e. g. Av. *yazāmaide* commoner than *barāmaide*.

Mode Formation—Special Remark.

1. Indicative.

§ 473. The various endings are simply attached by means of the thematic *a* (in 1 person *ā*) directly to the stem formed according to the rules of its particular class.

2. Imperative.

§ 474. The normal endings are attached by means of the thematic *a* directly to the present-stem of the class.

3. Subjunctive.

§ 475. The characteristic *a* of the subjunctive unites with the thematic *a* into *ā* in attaching the subjunctive endings given above, § 462.

4. Optative.

§ 476. In the *a*-verbs the optative sign is -*ī*- (instead of -*yā*-) and it unites with the thematic *a* into -*aē*- (-*ōi* § 56) in attaching the endings.

5. Participle.

§ 477. The participial forms (verbal adjectives) are made in each class by attaching to the present-stem the formative element -*nt* (§ 291, -*ntī* fem.) for the active, and -*mna* (§ 237, -*mnā* fem.)—also -*āna* (-*ana*), see Note —for the middle.

Note. On middle ptcpl. in -*āna* (-*ana*) see § 507.

Classes of the *a*-Conjugation (thematic).
Cl. 1, 6, 4, 10.

§ 478. **Class 1**—*a*-class with strengthened root-form = Skt. first (*bhū-*) class.—To form the present-stem, the thematic *a* is attached to the root which has the strong (middle) form. Cf. Whitney, *Skt. Gram.* § 734.—Examples are numerous.

Av. √*bar-* 'to bear', *bar-a-iti* = Skt. *bhár-a-ti*; Av. √*hši-* 'to rule', *hšay-e-iti* = Skt. *kšáy-a-ti*; Av. √*bū-* 'to be', *bav-a-iti* = Skt. *bháv-a-ti*.

Note 1. Here for convenience, as in Skt., may be included the roots Av. *stā-*, *had-* (orig. redupl.) = Skt. *sthā-*, *sad-*, e. g. Av. *hištaiti* 'he stands' = Skt. *tišṭhati*; Av. *hidaiti* 'he sits' = Skt. *sídati*, cf. Whitney, *Skt. Gram.* §§ 748, 749 a.

Note 2. Some roots in *a* + cons. show a fluctuation between *ā* and *ă*, cf. Whitney, *Skt. Gram.* § 745 d, e: Av. √*nam-* 'to bow' has *nəm-a-* beside *nām-a-* = Skt. *nám-a-*; Av. √*dvar-* 'to run' has *dvar-a-* beside *dvār-a-*, cf. also § 18 Note 1, and Whitney, *Skt. Gram.* § 545 c.

§ 479. **Class 6**—*a*-class with unstrengthened rootform = Skt. sixth *(tud-)* class.—The thematic *a* is simply attached to the root in its weak form to make up the present-stem.—Cf. Whitney, *Skt. Gram.* § 751.

Av. √*iš-* 'to seek, desire', *iš-a-ite* = Skt. *iš-á-tē*; Av. √*vīs-* 'to become', *vīs-a-iti* (cf. § 20 on *ī*) = Skt. *viš-á-ti*; et al.

Note. With nasal strengthening Av. *hiṇc-a-iti* 'he sprinkles' (√*hic-*) = Skt. *siñc-á-ti*.

§ 480. **Class 4**—*ya*-class (unstrengthened root-form) = Skt. fourth *(div-)* class.—Also here the Passive, cf. V. a below.—The present-stem is formed by adding *ya-* (*ye-* § 34) to the simple unstrengthened root.—Cf. Whitney, *Skt. Gram.* § 759.

Av. √*nas-* 'to vanish', *nas-ye-iti* = Skt. *náś-ya-ti*; Av. √*prā-* 'to protect', *prā-ye-iṇtē* = Skt. *trá-ya-ntē*.

Note 1. For the Passive formation see V. a below.

Note 2. The strong form of the stem (*-ae-* instead of *-i-*) is to be noted in the verb Av. *sraēš-ye-iti* 'it clings' = Skt. *śliš-ya-ti*.

§ 481. **Class 10**—*aya*-class (strengthened root-form) = Skt. tenth *(cur-)* class.—This class includes in part the secondary formation causative, denominative, see V. b, c, below. The formative element *aya* is added to the strengthened root.—The roots in internal *a* generally, but not always, receive the *vṛddhi* strengthening; the roots in *i, u* commonly receive the *guṇa* increase.

Av. √*tap-* 'to warm', *tāp-aye-iti* = Skt. *tāp-áya-ti;*
Av. √*pat-* 'to fly', *apat-ayə-n* = Skt. *ápāt-aya-n;* Av.
√*riš-* 'to wound', *raēš-aya-ṭ* = Skt. *rḗṣ-áya-t;* Av.
√*ruc-* 'to light up', *raoc-aye-iti* = Skt. *rōc-áya-ti.*

Note 1. Observe that the roots with *a* do not always show the *vṛddhi* stage.
Note 2. Some exceptions to the rule for *guṇa* of *i-* and *u-*roots occur.
Note 3. In Av., as in Skt., a heavy syllable ending in consonant does not take *vṛddhi* or *guṇa*.

Paradigms of the *a*-Conjugation (thematic).
Cl. 1, 6, 4, 10.
(Cf. Whitney, *Skt. Gram.* § 734 seq.)

§ 482. Av. ᭞ *bar-* 'bear, carry' = Skt. *bhár-*.

Cl. 1. Av. *xši-* 'rule, possess', *zū-* 'call, bless, curse', *vaēn-* 'see', *yaz-* 'worship', *jas-* 'come', *jiv-* 'live', *čiš-* 'teach, point out', *car-* 'move, go', *hvar-* 'eat', *az-* 'drive, win', *yās-* 'desire, seek', *pac-* 'cook', *van-* 'win', *pwars-* 'cut, make', *ram-* 'delight', *miz-* 'make urine'.—Cl. 6. *vaš-* 'speak', *vīs-* 'become'.—Cl. 4. *yud-* 'fight', *zan-, zā-* 'give birth, be born', *varz-* 'work', *bud-* 'mark, know'.—Cl. 10. *vid-* 'know', *taurv-* 'overcome', *var-* 'to cover', *ŗar-* 'go, make go', *dar-* 'hold fast', *haxš-* 'incite'.

§ 483. 1. Indicative.—a. Present.

i. ACTIVE.

	Av.	Singular:	cf. Skt.
1.	*bar-ā-mi* .	. .	*bhár-ā-mi*
2.	*bar-a-hi* .	. .	*bhár-a-si*
3.	*bar-a-iti* .	. .	*bhár-a-ti*
		Dual:	
1.	—	.	. *bhár-ā-vas*
2.	—	.	. *bhár-a-thas*
3.	{ *bar-a-tō* . . . { -*a-pō yuidyapō*[1] . . .	. . . . .	} *bhar-a-tas*

---
[1] Cf. § 449 Note.

a-Conjugation (thematic):—Cl. 1, 6, 4, 10.

Av.	Plural:	cf. Skt.
1. { *bar-ā-mahi* . . . . { -*ā-mahi vaēdoyamahi*	.	*bhár-ā-masi* (Ved.)
2. (*bar-a-þa*) *hōyaþa* (GAv.)	. . .	*bhár-a-tha*
3. { *bar-ə-ṇti* . . . . { -*a-iṇti zavaiṇti* .	.	*bhár-a-nti*

ii. MIDDLE.

Av.	Singular:	cf. Skt.
1. *bair-e*	. . .	*bhár-ē*
2. { *bar-a-he*¹ . . { -*a-ṇhe vajaṇhe* .	.	*bhár-a-sē*
3. *bar-a-ite* .	.	*bhár-a-tē*

Dual:

1.	—	. . .	*bhár-ā-vahē*
2.	—	. . .	*bhár-ē-thē*
3. (*bar-ōi-þe*) *vaēnōiþe*²		*bhár-ē-tē*

Plural:

1. { (*bar-ā-maide*) *yazamaide* . { -*ā-maide* . .	.	*bhár-ā-mahē*
2. (*bar-a-þwe*) *coraþwe*³ .	.	*bhár-a-dhvē*
3. *bar-ə-ṇte* .	.	*bhár-a-ntē*

§ 484. b. **Preterite** (and Injunctive).⁴

i. ACTIVE.

Av.	Singular:	cf. Skt.
1. *bar-ə-m* .	. .	*á-bhar-a-m*
2. (*bar-ō*) *jasō* .	.	*á-bhar-a-s*
3. *bar-a-ṭ* .	.	*á-bhar-a-t*

Dual:

1. (*bar-ā-va*) *jvāva*⁴	. . .	*á-bhar-ā-va*
2.	—	. . .	*á-bhar-a-tam*
3. (*bar-a-təm*) *taurvayatəm*⁵ . . .		*á-bhar-a-tām*

---

¹ Cf. § 116. — ² Cf. § 449 Note. — ³ See Yt. 13.34. — ⁴ On augmentless Pret.—Subjunct. Imperat. (Injunctive) see § 445. — ⁵ Cf. § 449 Note.

Av.	Plural:	cf. Skt.
1. *bar-ā-ma*		*á-bhar-ā-ma*
-ā-ma bārayama		
2. (*bar-a-ta*) *taⁿrvayata*		*á-bhar-a-ta*
3. *bar-ə-n*		*á-bhar-a-n*

ii. MIDDLE.
Singular:

1. *bair-e*[1]		*á-bhar-e*
2. (*bar-a-ŋha*) *zayaŋha*		*á-bhar-a-thās*
3. *bar-a-ta*		*á-bhar-a-ta*

Dual:

1. —		*á-bhar-ā-vahi*
2. —		*á-bhar-e-tham*
3. (*bar-aē-təm*) *caēşaētəm*		*á-bhar-e-tām*
(*bar-ōi-þe*) *caroipe*[2]		—

Plural:

1. —		*á-bhar-ā-mahi*
2. (*bar-a-dwəm*) *vārayadwəm*[3]		*á-bhar-a-dhvam*
3. (*bar-ə-ŋta*) *carəŋta*		*á-bhar-a-nta*

§ 485. 2. Imperative.
i. ACTIVE.

Av.	Singular:	cf. Skt.
2. *bar-a*		*bhár-a*
3. *bar-a-tu*		*bhár-a-tu*

Plural:

2. (*bar-a-ta*) *barata*		*bhár-a-ta*
3. *bar-ə-ŋtu*		*bhár-a-ntu*
-a-ŋtu pārayaŋtu		

ii. MIDDLE.
Singular:

2. *bar-a-ŋuha*		*bhár-a-sva*
3. (*bar-a-tąm*) *vərəzyatąm*[4]		*bhár-a-tām*

---

[1] Yt. 5.6, cf. *apərəsē, uzuzē*. — [2] Vs. 9.5, cf. § 449 Note, cf. Delbrück, *Altind. Vb.* § 106, Bartholomae, *Altiran. Vb.* p. 52, 53. — [3] Cf. § 484 Foot-Note 4. — [4] See Vsp. 15.1, best reading.

a-Conjugation (thematic):—Cl. 1, 6, 4. 10.   145

	Av.	Plural:	cf. Skt.
2.	(*bar-a-dwəm*)	*dārayadwəm*	*bhár-a-dhvam*
3.	(*bar-ə-ṇtąm*)	*jasəṇtąm* .	*bhár-a-ntām*

§ 486. 3. Subjunctive.
i. ACTIVE.

	Av.	Singular:	cf. Skt.
1.	*bar-ā-ni*		*bhár-ā-ni*
2.	*bar-ā-hi*		*bhár-ā-si*
3.	{(*bar-ā-ⁱti*) *carāⁱti* . .		*bhár-ā-ti*
	bar-ā-ṭ		*bhár-ā-t*

Dual:

1.	— . . .	*bhár-ā-va*
2.	—	*bhár-ā-thas*
3.	(*bar-ā-tō*) *jasātō*	*bhár-ā-tas*

Plural:

1.	*bar-ā-ma*[1]	*bhár-ā-ma*
2.	(*bar-ā-þa*) *azāþā* (GAv.) . . .	*bhár-ā-tha*
3.	*bar-ą-n*	*bhár-ā-n*

ii. MIDDLE.

	Av.	Singular:	cf. Skt.
1.	{(*bar-ā-ne*) *vīsāne*		—
	(*bar-āi*) *vīsāi*		*bhár-āi*
2.	(*bar-ā̊-ṅhe*) *yāsą̊ṅhe* .		*bhár-ā-sē*
3.	(*bar-ā-ⁱte*) *pacāⁱte* . . .		*bhár-ā-tē*

Plural:

3.	{(*bar-ā̊-ṅte*) *yazą̊ṅte*	—
	-ā-ⁱre *mravāⁱre*[2]	—

§ 487. 4. Optative.
i. ACTIVE.

	Av.	Singular:	cf. Skt.
1.	—		*bhár-ē-yam*
2.	*bar-ōi-š*		*bhár-ē-s*
3.	*bar-ōi-ṭ*		*bhár-ē-t*

---
[1] Cf. § 484 Note 1. — [2] By transfer to *a*-conj. from 1t. cl. 2, √*mru* §§ 521, 452.

146   Inflection: Conjugation of Verbs.

	Av.	Plural:	cf. Skt.
1.	(bar-aē-ma) vanaēma		bhár-ē-ma
2.	(bar-aē-ta) pwərəsaēta .		bhár-ē-ta
3.	bar-ay-ən	. . .	bhár-ē-yus

ii. MIDDLE.
Singular:

1.	(bar-ay-a) haŋžaya¹ .	. . .	bhár-ē-ya
2.	(bar-aē-ša) haŋžaēšu	.	bhár-ē-thās
3.	bar-aē-ta . .	. . .	bhár-ē-ta

Plural:

1.	(bar-ōi-maide) bṇidyoimaide		bhōr-ē-mahi
2.	(bar-ōi-dwəm) rāmōidwəm		bhár-ē-dhvam
3.	(bar-ay-aṇta) maēzayaṇta²		bhár-ē-ran

§ 488.   5. Participle.

    Av.   i. ACTIVE.   cf. Skt.
bar-a-ṇt- (fem. -əṇtī-) . . . . . bhár-a-nt- (fem. -antī-)

ii. MIDDLE.
bar-ə-mna- (fem. -ə-mnā-) . . . bhár-a-māna- (fem. -a-mānā-)

Forms to be observed in GAv. and YAv.

§ 489. GAv. shows in general the same forms as above, but with the long final vowel, cf. § 26. It has, however, a certain number of individual differences; these as well as other variations in YAv. also may here be noted.

§ 490. (1) The original unmodified forms of 3 pl. act. mid. -aṇti, -aṇte, cf. zavaiṇte above, occasionally stand instead of being changed to -əṇti, -əṇte, e. g.:—

    GAv. vanaiṇti, YAv. vanəṇti 'they win' Yt. 13.154, GAv. hacaiṇte beside YAv. haciṇte 'they follow' (§§ 30, 491).

§ 491. (2) According to § 30, the forms -iṇti, -iṇte, -in are often found after palatals, instead of -əṇti, -aiṇti etc., e. g.:—

    Av. frataciṇti 'they run forth' (variants ətacaiṇti, ətacəṇti Ys. 65.3, √tac-), frataciṇ 'they ran forth'; haciṇte (YAv.) beside hacaiṇte

---

¹ Ys. 8.7. — ² i. e. *maēz-aē-aṇta for *maēz-a-i-aṇta.

(GAv.) 'they follow'; *yaziṇti* 'they worship' Yt. 8.11 beside *yazaṇtu* Yt. 8.24, cf. Yt. 10.54 *yazaṇte, yaziṇti; snaēžiṇtaē-ca* 'and they drop as snow' (cf. § 55).

§ 492. (3) GYAv., when *y* precedes the thematic -*a*- (-*ā*-), especially in Cl. 4, 10, the combination -*ya*- (-*yā*-) generally becomes -*ye*- according to § 34, e. g.:—

Av. *sādayemi, sādayehi, sādayeiti* 'I, thou, he appear' (√*sad*- Cl. 10); *jaidyemi, jaidyehi, jaidyeiṇti* 'I, thou, they beseech' (√*jad*- Cl. 4); *h͜šayehī* (GAv.), *h͜šayeiti, h͜šayeite, h͜šayeiṇti, h͜šayeni* (subjunct. -*āni*) 'thou, he etc. rule, possess' (√*h͜ši*- Cl. 1); *zbayemi, zbayehi, zbayeiti* 'I invoke', etc.; *baṇdayeni* 'I may bind' (subjunct.).

§ 493. (4) Some reductions of -*ya*-, -*va*- before *m, n* (§ 63) occur, e. g.:—

Av. *varəziṇti* 'they work' (i. e. *varəzyaṇti,* √*varz*- Cl. 4); *irišiṇti* 'they wound' (i. e. *irišyaṇti,* √*iriš*- Cl. 4); *urvaēsiṇti* 'they turn'; *uh͜šin* 'they grew' (i. e. *uh͜šyan,* √*vah͜š* Cl. 4); *fyavhuṇte* 'they shower sleet' (i. e. *fyavhvaṇte*).—So imperat. 2 sg. *naṣe* 'perish' (i. e. *nasya*).

§ 494. (5) Some reductions of -*aya*-, -*ava*- (-*āya*-, -*āva*-) before final *m, n* (§ 64) occur, e. g.:—

Av. *daēsaem* 'I showed' (i. e. *daēsayam,* √*dis*- Cl. 10); *abaom* 'I became' (i. e. *abavam,* √*bū*- Cl. 1) Yt. 19.57,61,63, *baon* 'they became' Yt. 5.98 etc.

§ 495. Certain other peculiarities likewise require detailed notice.

1. Indicative.

a. Present.

§ 496. **Singular:**—

First Person: i. ACT. GAv. shows only the ending -*ā* (Gk. -ω), instead of -*āmi* in the thematic verbs and only -*mī* in the non-*a*-verbs (unthematic), e. g. GAv. *ufyā* 'I praise', *kayā* 'I discern'.—YAv. similar but rare (perhaps borrowed) *zbaya* 'I invoke' at Vsp. 6.1 by the side of *frayeze* which likewise is an indicative.

§ 497. **Dual:**—

Third Person: i. ACT. GAv. add *caratas-cā* 'both come' Ys. 51.12.— ii. MID. *APhl. Gloss.* p. 54.8 has *baraite* 'they two bring' cf. *A. O. S. Proceedings* Oct. 1889 p. 165.

§ 498. **Plural:**—

First Person: i. ACT. YAv., similarly with short *ā* (as above) *zbayāmahi* 'we invoke'.

Second Person: i. ACT. YAv. also isolated (-*t*- like pret. form) *ŋarata* 'ye eat' Vd. 7.57.—ii. MID. GAv. -*dʰve* (cf. § 190) *dīdraẓōiduyē* 'ye keep holding' (desiderative)—on -*ō*- for -*a*- of stem, see § 39.

Third Person: See general details above § 490 seq.

b. Preterite.

§ 499. Plural:—

Third Person: ii. MID. GAv., observe *vīsəṇta* 'they entered' (on -*ə*-, cf. § 32).

2. Imperative.

§ 500. Singular:—

Second Person: i. ACT. YAv., note (by reduction §§ 34, 493) *nase* 'perish thou' (i. e. *nasya*, √*nas*- Cl. 4).—ii. MID. GAv., only -*hvā*: *gūšahvā* 'hear thou', *baxšōhvā* 'share thou' (on -*ō*- for -*a*-, see § 39).

Third Person: i. ACT. GAv., observe -*ō*- (cf. § 39) in *varəzyōtū* 'let him work' (√*varz*- Cl. 4), *vātayōtū* 'let him announce' (√*vat*- Cl. 10).

§ 501. Plural:—

Second Person: i. ACT. GAv. with ending -*na* (cf. Skt. -*tana*) *baratā* 'bear ye' Ys. 30.9, cf. § 457 above, and Whitney, *Skt. Gram.* § 740. —ii. MID. GAv. *gūšōdūm* 'hear ye' = Skt. *ghóṣadhvam*.

3. Subjunctive.

§ 502. Singular:—

Second Person: i. ACT. YAv. occasionally -*āi* for -*ā(h)i* § 450: *apa.yasāi* 'thou wilt destroy' (i. e. *yasāhi*); *vazāi*, *vazāhi* (as variants) 'mayest thou bring' Vd. 5.16.—YAv., a form with secondary ending (but syntax bad) is *bavaō* Yt. 24.8.

§ 503. Plural:—

Third Person: i. ACT. GAv. shows also -*ən* (for -*ąn*) in *rapən* 'they may hold'.—ii. MID. YAv. like *mravāire* above § 452, also *nijrāire* 'they may strike' Yt. 10.40, so again *ā̆vhāire* Yt. 10.45.

4. Optative.

§ 504. Singular:—

First Person: ii. MID. YAv., observe *mainya* 'I would think' Yt. 10.106 (for *mainyaya* § 194).

§ 505. Plural:—

First Person: i. ACT. GAv. (with regular secondary ending -*maidī*, cf. Skt. -*mahi*) *rourāimaidī* 'we would cause to believe'.

Third Person: YAv. like *maēzayanta* in paradigm is *yazayanta* 'they would sacrifice'.

5. Participle.

§ 506. On the relation of Av. -*mna* (metrically often -*mana*) to Skt. -*māna*, see § 18 Note 2.

§ 507. In Av. more often than in Skt. (cf. Whitney, *Skt. Gram.* § 741 a) there appear instances of middle (passive) participles of *a*-verbs formed with the participial suffix -*ana*, -*āna* (= Skt. -*āna*, § 18) instead of -*mna*, e. g. *barana*- 'bearing', °*azana* 'driving';—*yasāna*- 'worshipping'; *starāna*- 'strewing'.

ii. The non-*a*-Conjugation (unthematic).

§ 508. **General Remark.** In Av., as in Skt., the verbs of the non-*a*-conjugation (unthematic) are not so numerous as those of the thematic conjugation. They may be grouped in six classes (Cl. 2, 3, 7, 5, 8, 9), in each of which the endings are attached directly (without an interposed *a*) to the stem which is subject to modification.

The striking characteristic of the entire group is the variation of the root in different forms. The modified root or the suffix assumes now a stronger form, again a weaker form.

§ 509. **Strong and Weak Stem-Forms.** The strong (*guṇa*) forms, as a rule, are:—(1) the Sing. Indic. Act. (Pres. Pret.),—(2) the 3rd. Sing. Imperat. Act.,—(3) the entire Subjunct.—The remaining forms are weak. Many fluctuations and transfers, however, occur; especially often is the strong stem employed in forms (see 3rd. plurals) modelled after the *a*-conjugation.

Mode Formation.—Special Remark.
1. Indicative.

§ 510. The endings of the non-thematic indicative require some remark. GAv. generally shows the older use of -*mī* (§ 450) and -*aiti̯*, -*aitē*, -*aṭ* (for thematic -*anti*, -*aṇte* -*an* § 452). In YAv. this old distinction is not sharply preserved. The stem in general to which the endings are directly attached shows a variation of str. and wk. forms according to the preceding rule, § 509.

2. Imperative.

§ 511. The ending of the Imperat. 2 sing. is -*dī, -di*. The endings in general are attached directly to the prepared class-stem. This shows the strong form in the 3 sg. act.; in the other forms it has the weak grade, but fluctuations occur.

3. Subjunctive.

§ 512. The endings are attached by means of the mode-sign *a* to the prepared class-stem which shows the strong form throughout.

4. Optative.

§ 513. The regular optative endings are attached by the mode-sign -*yā-, -ī- (ī)* in accordance with the rules given above at § 463. The stem regularly shows its weak form throughout, but variations from this sometimes occur.

5. Participle.

§ 514. The participial forms (verbal adjectives) are made by attaching to the present stem in its weak grade the formative element -*ant, -at* (i. e. -*ņt*) for the active, and -*āna, -ana* beside -*mna*, for the middle.

Classes of the non-*a*-Conjugation (unthematic).
Cl. 2, 3, 7, 5, 8, 9.

§ 515. The six classes of unthematic verbs have certain characteristics in common but they have also certain individual peculiarities, these classes will now each be taken up in detail.

Class 2—Root-Class.

§ 516. Class 2—Root-Class—root itself is present stem = Skt. second *(ad-)* class.—The stem may have the strong or the weak form according to § 509, the endings are then attached directly to the stem. Examples are quite numerous:

Av. √pā- 'to keep, protect', pā-iti (3 sg. pres.) = Skt. pā-ti; Av. √i- 'to go', aē-iti (3 sg.), y-einti (3 pl. pres. § 34) = Skt. ė-ti, y-ánti; Av. √stu- 'to praise', stao-iti = Skt. stáu-ti (§ 60 Note c); Av. √jan- 'to slay', jain-ti (3 sg. pres. indic.) = Skt. hán-ti; Av. √vas- 'to wish', vaš-tī (3 sg.), us-mahi (1 pl. pres. indic.) = Skt. váṣ-ti, uś-mási (Ved.).

Paradigm of Class 2.
(Cf. Whitney, *Skt. Gram.* § 612 seq.)

§ 517. Av. √mrū- 'to say' = Skt. √brū-.

Av. *hap-* 'promote', *vas-*, *us-* 'wish', *āh-* 'sit', *rūd-* 'grow', *stu-* 'praise', *i-* 'go', *is-* 'be able'.

§ 518. 1. Indicative. — a. Present:

i. ACTIVE.

Av. Singular:	cf. Skt.
1. *mrao-mi*	*bráv-ī-mi*
2. (*mrao-ši*) *hafši* (GAv.) . .	*bráv-ī-ši*
3. *mrao-iti*	*bráv-ī-ti*

Dual:

| 1. (*mrvahi*¹) *usvahī* (GAv.) . . | *brū-vasi* |

Plural:

| 1. (*mrū-mahi*) *usmahi* . . . | *brū-masi* |
| 3. (*mrv-ainti*) *ævhənti*² . . . | *brúv-anti* |

ii. MIDDLE.

Singular:

1. *mruy-ē*³	*bruv-ė́*
2. (*mrū-še*) cf. *raose*⁴	*brū-sḗ*
3. { *mrū-ite* . . .	*brū-tḗ*
{ *mruy-ē*⁵	*bruv-ḗ*

Plural:

| 1. *mrū-maide* . . . . . | *brū-máhē* |
| 3. (*mrv-ante*) *ævhənte*⁶ . . . | *bruv-átē* |

---

¹ i. e. *mrv-vahi* § 68.1. — ² Yt. 17.10. — ³ § 190. — ⁴ Strong form § 509. — ⁵ Ys. 19.10, cf. § 450 end. — ⁶ Yt. 17.11; Vs. 9.22.

§ 519.   b. Preterite Indicative (and Injunctive).

i. ACTIVE.

Av.	Singular:	cf. Skt.
1. *mrao-m*		*á-brav-am*
2. *mrao-š*		*á-brav-i-s*
3. *mrao-t̰*		*á-brav-i-t*
	Plural:	
3. (*mrav-n?*[1]) *usən*		*á-bruv-an*

ii. MIDDLE.

	Singular:	
1. *mrav-i*[2]		*á-mruv-i*
3. { *mrū-ta*		*á-brū-ta*
{ *mrao-ta* (GAv.)		—
	Plural:	
3. *mrav-aṇta*[3]		*á-bruv-ata*

§ 520.   2. Imperative.

i. ACTIVE.

Av.	Singular:	cf. Skt.
2. *mrū-idi*		*brū-hi*
3. *mrav-tū* (GAv.)		*brav-i-tu*
	Plural:	
2. (*mrao-ta*) *staota*[4]		*brū-ta*
3. (*mrav-aṇtu*) *yaṇtu*		*bruv-aṇtu*

§ 521.   3. Subjunctive.

i. ACTIVE.

Av.	Singular:	cf. Skt.
1. *mrav-ā-ni*[5]		*bráv-ā-ni*
3. { *mrav-a-iti* (GAv.)		*bráv-a-ti*
{ *mrav-a-t̰*[6]		*brav-a-t*
	Plural:	
1. (*mrav-ā-ma*) *janāma*		*bráv-ā-ma*
3. (*mrav-ə-n*) *vasən*		*bráv-a-n*

[1] § 64. — [2] Observe str. stem; or is it *mrāvī* § 68 Note 3? — [3] Cf. § 509 end. — [4] Strong form (I), cf. § 509. — [5] Yt. 15.50; 12.2. — [6] See ZPGl. Gloss. p. 111.

ii. MIDDLE.

	Av.	Singular:	cf. Skt.
1.	(*mrav-āi*) *isōi*		*bráv-āi*
	*mrav-āne*¹ .	. . . . .	—
		Plural:	
3.	*mrav-ā-ire*²	. .	—

§ 522.   **4. Optative.**

i. ACTIVE.

	Av.	Singular:	cf. Skt.
2.	*mru-yā̊* .	. . .	*brū-yā́-s*
3.	*mru-yā-ṭ* .	. . .	*brū-yā́-t*

ii. MIDDLE.
Singular:

			cf. Skt.
2.	*mrv-i-ša*³ . .	. . . .	*bruv-ī-thās*
3.	*mrv-ī-tā* (GAv.)	.	*bruv-ī-tá*

§ 523.   **5. Participle.**

Av.	i. ACTIVE.	cf. Skt.
mrv-at-	. . . . .	*bruv-ánt-*

ii. MIDDLE.

		cf. Skt.
*mrav-āna-*⁴		*bruv-āná-*
*mrao-mna-*⁵		—

Forms to be observed in GAv. and YAv.

§ 524. Beside the above paradigm, a certain number of forms in GAv. and YAv. are worthy of note.

1. Indicative.

a. Present.

§ 525. Singular:—

First Person: i. ACTIVE. GAv., notice (from strongest stem) *stāumī* 'I praise' (but v. l. *staomi*) Ys. 43.8, cf. Skt. *stāúti* (Ved. 3 sg.).

Second Person: i. ACTIVE. YAv., observe likewise as regular form (§ 122) *pāhi* 'thou protectest'.

Third Person: ii. MIDDLE. YAv. also (like 1st.—3rd. sg. pres., above) *ni-ɀne* 'he smites'.

---

¹ Yt. 5.82. — ² *a*-conj. cf. §§ 486, 452 end. — ³ Cf. § 21 Note. — ⁴ Cf. Skt. *stávāna-*, Whitney § 619d. — ⁵ i. e. like *a*-conj. ptcpl.

§ 526. **Plural:—**
First Person: ii. MID. YAv., note (from str. stem) *staomaide* 'we praise'. —GAv., observe (-*aē-ca* § 55) *aoj̄madaō-cā* 'and we name'.
Third Person: ii. MID. YAv., seldom the plur. ending -*atē* (= *ptē*): Av. *aojaite* 'they say' Yt. 8.51, etc. — Observe also Av. *sōire* 'they lie' Yt. 10.80 = Skt. *śére*.

b. Preterite.

§ 527. **Singular:—**
Second Person: ii. MID. GAv., note as a regular 2 sing. *aojsā* 'thou saidst' Ys. 43.12.
Third Person: i. ACT. GAv., observe (with inserted -*i*- like Skt. *ábravīt*) the form *sāhīṭ* 'he taught' Ys. 50.6. — ii. MID. YAv. also (from str. stem, like *mravāta* above) *staota* 'he praised'.

5. Participle.

§ 528. ii. MID. Observe also -*āna* (for -*āna*) and (like *a*-conj. §§ 514, 477) -*əmna*: Av. *aojāna*-, *aojəmna*- 'speaking'.

Transfers to the *a*-Conjugation (thematic).

§ 529. A number of transfers from the Root-Class to the *a*-conjugation are to be found.

1. Indicative. i. ACT. b. Pret. GAv. *mrav-o-ṭ* 'he said' Ys. 45.2.
2. Imperative. i. ACT. YAv. *mrav-a*, *mrv-a* 'say thou'. — ii. MID. YAv. *stav-a-ṇha* 'praise thou'.
3. Subjunctive. i. ACT. YAv. *mrav-āi* (for -*āhi* § 502) 'if thou say' Ys. 71.15. — ii. MID. YAv. (above in paradigm) *mrav-āire* 'if they say' § 452 end.
4. Optative. i. ACT. YAv. *stav-ōi-ṭ* 'he might praise' beside *stuyāṭ*.

§ 530. Inflection of Av. √*ah*-, *h*- 'to be'—only act. — = Skt. √*as*-, *s*-, cf. Whitney, *Skt. Gram.* § 636.

§ 531. 1. **Indicative.—a. Present.**

Av.	Singular:	cf. Skt.
1. *ah-mi*	. . . .	*ás-mi*
2. *ahi*[1]	. . . .	*ási*
3. *as-ti* .	. . . .	*ás-ti*
	Dual:	
3. *s-tō*	. . . .	*s-tás*

[1] i. e. for *ah-hi*: Skt. *ási* for *ás-si*.

The non-*a*-Conjugation (unthematic):—Cl. 2 (√*ah*-).

Av.	Plural:	cf. Skt.
1. *mahi*[1]	. . . .	*s-mási* (Ved.)
2. *s-tā*[2]	. . . .	*s-thá*
3. *h-ənti*	. . . .	*s-ánti*

§ 532.   b. Preterite.
Singular:

3.	*āṣ*[3]	. .	*ās* (Ved.)
	as	. .	*ās-ī-t*

Dual:
1. *ahvā* (GAv.)	. . . .	*ās-va*

Plural:
3. *h-ən*	. . . .	*ās-an*

§ 533.   2. Imperative.
Av.	Singular:	cf. Skt.
2. *z-dī* (GAv.)	. . . . . .	*ē-dhí*
3. *as-tu*	. . . .	*ás-tu*

Plural:
3. *h-əntū* (GAv.)	. . . .	*s-ántu*

§ 534.   3. Subjunctive.
Av.	Singular:	cf. Skt.
2. *avh-ō*	. . . .	*ás-a-s*
3. *avh-a-itī* (GAv.)	. . . . . .	*ás-a-ti*
avh-a-ṭ	. . . .	*ás-a-t*

Plural:
3. *avh-ə-n*	. . . .	*ás-a-n*

§ 535.   4. Optative.
Av.	Singular:	cf. Skt.
1. *h-yā-m* (GAv.)[4]	. . . . . .	*s-yā-m*
2. *h-yā* (GAv.)	. . . .	*s-yā-s*
3. *h-yā-ṭ* (GAv.), *n̄-yā-ṭ* (YAv.)[5]	. . .	*s-yā-t*

Plural:
1. *h-yā-mā* (GAv.)	. . . .	*s-yā-ma*
2. *h-yā-tā* (GAv.)	. . . .	*s-yā-ta*
3. *h-yə-n* (GAv.), *h-yā-n* (YAv.), *h-yārə* (YAv.)	. . .	*s-yúr*

§ 536.   5. Participle.
Av. *h-aṇt-* . . . . cf. Skt. *s-ánt-*

---
[1] Cf. § 140. — [2] For *s-ṭa*, cf. § 78 a. — [3] See § 192 Note. — [4] Cf. § 32. — [5] Cf. §§ 132, 133.

Forms to be observed.

§ 537. YAv., notice in a late passage Yt. 24.12 (2 pl. opt. with primary ending!) *h-yā-pa* 'might ye be'.

§ 538. Transfers to the *a*-conjugation: — 1. Indic. Pret. 3 sg. *avh-a-ṭ.*— 3. Subjunct. 3 sg. *avh-ā-ᵢti*.

§ 539. Beside all the above paradigm of the present-system, there is made from this root *ah* 'to be', as in Skt., a regular perfect *āvha* etc. § 606 = Skt. *āsa* etc.

Class 3.—Reduplicating Class.

§ 540. **Class 3.**—Reduplicating Class. The root is reduplicated to form the present stem. The stem then shows a variation of strong and weak forms (§ 509); the endings are attached to it directly.

The general rules for reduplication have been given above § 465. As examples of formation, the following may be taken:—

Av. √*dā-* 'to give, to place' (Stems *dadā-*, *dadā-*; *dad-*, *dap-*, *dad-*, §§ 82, 83, 86), *da-dā-ⁱti* (YAv.), *da-dā-ⁱti* (GAv.), *da-da-m*, *da-pa-m* = Skt. *dá-d(h)ā-ti*, *á-da-d(h)ā-m*;—Av. √*ci-* 'to atone' (Stems *ci-kay-*, *ci-ki-*), *ci-kay-aṭ* 3 sg. subjunct. = Skt. *cikayat;* —Av. √*hac-* 'to follow', *hi-šhaḵ-ti*, *hi-šc-a-maidē* (Ys. 40.4) = Skt. *si-ṣak-ti;*—Av. √*jan-* 'to slay', *ni-ja-ɣn-aṇti* = Skt. *ji-ghn-anti*.

Paradigm of Class 3.
(Cf. Whitney, *Skt. Gram.* § 647 seq.)

§ 541. Av. ⸺ √*dā-* 'to give, to place' (str. stem YAv. *dadā*, GAv. *dadā-*; wk. stem YAv. *dad-*, *dap-*, GAv. *dad-*) = Skt. √*dā-*, √*dhā-*—stems *dad(h)a-*, *dad(h)-*, cf. Whitney, *Skt. Gram.* § 667 seq.

Note. Observe that orig. *dā-*, *dhā-* are practically fallen together in Av. as *da-*, §§ 82, 83.—On the interchange of *d*, *ḍ*, *p*, see §§ 82, 83, 86.

The non-a-Conjugation (unthematic):—Cl. 3 (redupl.).

§ 542. 1. Indicative.—a. Present.

i. ACTIVE.

Av.	Singular:	cf. Skt.
1. *dadā-mi* .	. . . . . .	*dád(h)ā-mi*
2. *dadā-hi* .	. . . . .	*dád(h)ā-si*
3. { *dadā-ⁱti* .	. . . .	*dád(h)ā-ti*
{ *das-ti* (YAv.)[1]	. . . .	—[2]

Plural:

1. *dadᵊ-mahi*	. . . . . .	*dad(h)-mási* (Ved.)
2. —	. . . . . .	*d(h)at-tá*
3. { *dada-ⁱtī* (GAv.)[3]	. . .	} *dád(h)-ati*
{ *dadā-ⁱti* (YAv.)[4]	. . .	

ii. MIDDLE.

Av.	Singular:	cf. Skt.
1. { *daⁱd-e* (YAv.), *dad-ē* (GAv.) .		*dad(h)-ē*
{ *daⁱp-e*[5]	. . . .	—
2. —	. . . . .	*d(h)at-sē*
3. { *das-te* (GYAv.)[6] . .		*d(h)at-tē*
{ *daz-dē* (GAv.)[5]		—

Plural:

| 1. *dadᵊ-maⁱde* . | . . . . | *dád(h)-mahē* |

§ 543. b. Preterite Indicative (and Injunctive).

i. ACTIVE.

Av.	Singular:	cf. Skt.
1. *dadą-m, dapą-m* .		*á-dad(h)ā-m*
2. *dadā̊* (GAv.) .	. . . . .	*á-dad(h)ā-s*
3. *dadā-ṯ* (YAv.), *dadā-ṯ* (GAv.)	.	*á-dad(h)ā-t*

Dual:

| 3. *daⁱd-i-təm*[7] . | . . . . | *á-d(h)at-tām* |

Plural:

| 2. *das-ta*[8] | . . . . | *á-d(h)at-ta* |
| 3. *dad-aṯ* (GAv.)[9] | . . . . | *á-dad(h)-ur* |

---

[1] From weak stem *dad-*. On *s*, cf. §§ 151, 170. — [2] Cf. Epic.Skt. *dadmi*. — [3] Ys. 46.1, i. e. -*g/i*. — [4] i. e. -*g̑ti*, uncertain, Yt. 10.3. — [5] § 541 Note. — [6] § 542 Foot-Note 1. — [7] Cf. §§ 550. 449 Note. — [8] §§ 151, 445 Note 2. — [9] Ys. 32.14, i. e. **dad-ṇṯ*.

	ii. MIDDLE.	
Av.	Singular:	cf. Skt.
3. *das-ta*	. . . .	*á-d(h)at-ta*

§ 544.   2. Imperative.
i. ACTIVE.

Av.	Singular:	cf. Skt.
2. *daz-di*[1] . .	. .	*d(h)ĕ-hí*
3. *dadā-tū* (GAv.)	. . .	*dád(h)ā-tu*
	Plural:	
3. *das-ta*[2] .	. . . .	*d(h)at-tá*
	ii. MIDDLE.	
2. *dasva*[3]	. . . .	*d(h)at-sva*

§ 545.   3. Subjunctive.
i. ACTIVE.

Av.	Singular:	cf. Skt.
1. *dapā-ni* .	. .	*dád(h)ā-ni*
3. *dadā-ṭ*[1] .	. . .	*dád(h)ā-t*
	Plural:	
1. *dapā-ma*	. . . . .	*dád(h)ā-ma*
	ii. MIDDLE.	
1. *dapā-ne*[5]	. . . .	—

§ 546.   4. Optative.
i. ACTIVE.

Av.	Singular:	cf. Skt.
1. *daid-yą-m*	. .	*dad(h)-yā́-m*
2. *daip-yā̊* .	. .	*dád(h)-yā́-s*
3. *daip-yā-ṭ*	. . .	*dád(h)-yā́-t*
	Plural:	
3. { *daip-yą-n*	. . .	—
{ *daip-yā-rəš* .	. . . .	*dad(h)-y-úr*
	ii. MIDDLE.	
	Singular:	
2. *daip-ī-ša*[6]	. . . . . .	*dad(h)-ī-thā́s*
3. *daip-ī-ta* (YAv.), *daid-ī-tā* (GAv.)	. .	*dad(h)-ī-tá*

---

[1] § 151. — [2] Cf. Injunctive §§ 543, 445 Note 2. — [3] § 186. — [4] Not distinguishable from augmentless imperfect above. — [5] Ny. 4.8. — [6] Yt. 3.1 with variants *daidiša*, *dapiš*.

§ 547. 5. Participle.

i. ACTIVE.   cf. Skt.

Av. °daþ-ə̣nt-[1] . . . . dád(h)-at-

ii. MIDDLE.

Av. daþ-āna-   . . . .   . dád(h)-āna-

Forms to be observed in GAv. and YAv.

§ 548. There are both in GAv. and in YAv. a number of forms beside the above, that deserve special notice.

1. Indicative.

§ 549. a. Present. i. ACT.—ii. MID. GAv., observe that the forms dāitī, dāitē, dā̊ṇtē resembling pres. indic. forms after Class 2, are best regarded as radical aor. subjunct., cf. § 633 below.—Note GAv. hišcamaidē (with v. l. hišcimaidē) 'we follow' 1 pl. pres. indic. mid. Ys. 40.4—(observe a, Bartholomae, K.Z. xxix. p. 273 = Flexionslehre p. 4).—Add also 3 sg. pres. indic. act. zazaṇti 'he produces' Vd. 3.5 = Skt. jajánti.

§ 550. b. Preterite. i. ACT. YGAv., observe with interposed i (like Skt. ábravīt etc.) and from weak stem: daidīš (YAv. 2 sg. pret. indic.), daidīṭ (YAv. Yt. 13.12), daidīṭ (GAv. 3 sg. pret.), daidītəm (3 du. cf. above paradigm).—Remark 3 pl. in -aṭ (= -ṇṭ) GAv. jīgərəzaṭ 'let them lament' (injunctive).—ii. MID. YAv., observe from strong stem, 2 sg. pret. mid. ji-gaē-ša 'thou didst live, mayest live' ($\sqrt{gi}$-, ji-).

3. Subjunctive.

§ 551. Sg. Pl. i. ACT. YAv., add (regularly) from $\sqrt{ci}$- 'to atone', ci-kay-aṭ (3 sg. subjunct.), ci-kay-a-tō (3 du. subjunct. ZPhl. Gloss. p. 92, 34), ci-kaēn (3 pl. subjunct.) i. e. *ci-kay-ṇṭ § 64.

4. Optative.

§ 552. Beside the mid. forms with long i (-īša, -īta) are found also the variants -iša, -ita, cf. § 21 Note.

Transfers to the a-Conjugation (thematic).

§ 553. A number of transitions from the Third Class to the a-conjugation occur. The reduplicated wk. stem daþ- (YAv.), dad- (GAv.) of $\sqrt{dā}$- in Av. as in Skt.—cf. Whitney, Skt. Gram. § 672—thus not infrequently assumes the inflection of an a-stem, § 483.

---

[1] Ys. 9.1.

1. Indicative. i. ACT a. Pres. YAv. *daþ-a-iti, daþ-ɔ-ŋti*. — b. Pret. YGAv. *daþ-ɔ-ni, daþ-ō, daþ-a-ţ. dad-a-ţ; daþ-ɔ-n, dad-ɔ-n* (beside *dadaţ* § 563 Foot-Note). — ii. MID. YAv. *daþ-a-ite*. - GAv. *dad-ɔ-ŋtē* 'they are placed'.

Note. Similarly transferred Av. *zīzanɔŋti, zīzanɔn, zīzanaţ* from √*zan-* 'beget, bear'. The Skt. shows *jījanat* as redupl. aor. Whitney, *Skt. Gram.* § 864.

Class 7.—Nasal Class.

§ 554. The roots of the nasal class all end in a consonant; the class has for its characteristic feature the assumption of an internal nasal to form the stem. That is, the root has a *-na-* (in strong forms), an *-n-* (in weak forms) inserted immediately before its final consonant to form the present stem. The root itself retains its weak grade; the endings are attached directly to the stem.— Cf. Skt. seventh Class, Whitney, *Skt. Gram.* § 683 seq.

Here belong for example: Av. √*ciš-* 'to announce, promise' *ci-na-sti*; Av. √*iric-* 'to let go' *iri-na-hti* = Skt. *ri-ṇa-kti*, and some others—see following paradigm § 555.

Paradigm of Class 7.
(Cf. Whitney, *Skt. Gram.* § 684.)

§ 555. Av. √*ciš-* 'to announce, promise', *ciþ-* 'to proclaim, think', *mark-* (*marɔŋc-*) 'kill', *kart-* 'to cut', *mis-* 'mingle', *vid-* 'find, receive'. Cf. Skt. √*chid-* 'to cut'.

§ 556. 1. Indicative.—a. Present.
i. ACTIVE.

Av.	Singular:	cf. Skt.
1. *ci-na-hmī* (GAv.)[1]	. . . .	*chi-ná-dmi*
2. *ci-na-sti*	. . . .	*chi-ná-tti*

ii. MIDDLE.
Singular:

3. *karɔ-ŋ-te*[2] . .	. . . .	*chi-n-té*

Plural:

2. *marɔ-ŋ-gɔ-duyē* (GAv.)	. . . .	*chi-n-ddhvé*
3. *marɔ-ŋ-caitē* (GAv.)[3]	. . . .	*chi-n-dátē*

---
[1] Cf. § 141. — [2] Vd. 7.38, cf. imperat. *kɔrɔŋtu*, but *kɔrɔŋtaiti* a-conj. as Skt. *kṛntáti*. — [3] Ys. 31.1, *-atē = -ŋtē*.

The non-*a*-Conjugation (unthematic):—Cl. 7 (nasal class). 161

§ 557.
b. Preterite.
i. ACTIVE.

Av.	Singular:	cf. Skt.
2. *mi-na-ṣ̌*[1]		*á-chi-na-t*
3. *ci-na-s*[2]		*á-chi-na-t*

§ 558.
2. Imperative.
i. ACTIVE.

Av.	Singular:	cf. Skt.
3. *kərə-n-tu*[3]	. . .	*chi-ná-ttu*

§ 559.
3. Subjunctive.
ii. MIDDLE.

Av.	Plural:	cf. Skt.
1. *ci-na-pāmaide*[4]	. .	*chi-ná-dāmahāi*

§ 560.
4. Optative.

i. ACTIVE.			ii. MIDDLE.		
Av.	Singular:	cf. Skt.	Av.	Singular:	cf. Skt.
3. *mərəǰ-yā-ṭ*[5] .		*chi-n-d-yā-t*	3. *vi-n-dīta*[6] .		*chi-n-dītá*

§ 561.
5. Participle.

Av.	i. ACTIVE.	cf. Skt.	Av.	ii. MIDDLE.	cf. Skt.
vi-n-da(n)t-[7]		*chi-n-dánt-*	*vi-n-dəmna-* .		*chi-n-dāná-*

Forms to be observed in GAv. and YAv.

§ 562. The form Av. *mərəǰəṇte* stands perhaps for **mərə-n-gte* (3 sg. mid.). If so, the formation would be regularly after this (7) class. But the form is quite uncertain.

Transfers to the *a*-Conjugation.

§ 563. The stem *mərənc-* 'kill' has practically become stereotyped as a root according to the *a*-conj. by transfer; hence the thematic forms:—Pres. Act. 3 sg. *mərəncaiti*; 3 pl. *mərənciṇti*;—Mid. 3 sg. *mərəncaite*, 3 pl. *mərəncaṇte* (above).—Imperat. Mid. 2 sg. *mərəncavuha*.

§ 564. The root GAv. *mard-* (as *mərəṇd-* § 39) 'to destroy' has likewise become practically crystallized according to *a*-conj.: Pret. Act. 3 sg. *mərəṇtat*, 3 pl. *mərəṇdən* (on -ō-, cf. § 39 end).

---

[1] i. e. *mi-na-s-s*, § 158. — [2] i. e. *ci-na-s-t*, § 192. — [3] Vd. 7.38, weak form! — [4] *a*-conj. by transfer as in Skt. — [5] On -*rq*- = *r + n*, see § 49. On *ǰ*, cf. § 162. — [6] Yt. 17.54, with variant *viṇdīta (i)*. — [7] In compounds.

§ 565. Similar instances of stereotyped forms and transfer to *a*-conjugation as also in Skt., are: Av. 2 *vid-* 'find, obtain' *(viṇd-,* like Skt. *vi-n-d-a-ti)* *vi-ŋ-d-ə-ŋ-ti* (3 pl. indic.), *vi-n-d-ā-iti* (3 sg. subjunct. Vd. 13.36) beside unthematic *vi-na-sti* (GAv.), *vi-ŋ-d-tu* (YAv. opt. above).—Likewise Av. *kart-* 'to cut' *(kərəṇt-,* like Skt. *kṛ-n-t-a-ti) kərə-ŋ-t-aiti* (3 sg. indicative), *kərə-ŋ-t-a-ṭ* (pret.).—Also some others.

Note. Peculiar is 2 sing. pret. act. *mərəŋ uiniš* 'thou didst destroy' —weak nasalized root with added *an* (= *ṇu*). On *-iš* - *iš* cf. § 527 end.

Class 5.—*nu*-Class.

§ 566. The verbs of this class are not numerous. The root adds *nao-* (in the strong forms), *nu- nv-* (in the weak forms) to make the present stem. The root itself retains its weak grade.

Here belong for example: Av. √*kar-* 'to make' *kərə-nao-iti* = Skt. *kṛ-nó-ti*; Av. √*sru-* 'to hear' *surunao-iti* = Skt. *śr-ṇó-ti*; Av. √*as-* 'to attain' *aš-nao-iti* = Skt. *aś-nó-ti*, and a few others.

Paradigm of Class 5.
(Cf. Whitney, *Skt. Gram.* § 698.)

§ 567. Av. √*kar-* 'to make', *var-* 'cover choose', *dub-* 'deceive', *nu-* 'press', *sri-* 'give over', *sru-* 'hear'.—Cf. Skt. √*kṛ-*.

§ 568. 1. Indicative.—a. Present.

i. ACTIVE.

Av.	Singular:	cf. Skt.
1. *kərə-nao-mi*		*kṛ-ṇó-mi*
2. *kərə-nū-ši*[1]		*kṛ-ṇó-ṣi*
3. *kərə-nao-iti*		*kṛ-ṇó-ti*
	Plural:	
3. *kərə-nəv-aṇti*[2]		*kṛ-ṇv-ánti*

ii. MIDDLE.

	Singular:	
3. *vərə-nū-ite*		*kṛ-ṇu-té*
	Dual:	
3. *vərə-nv-aite* (GAv.)[3]		*kṛ-ṇv-áite*

---
[1] On *ā*, cf. § 60 Note b. — [2] Yt. 13.26, so metrically. Cf. § 68 Note 3. — [3] Ys. 31.17.

The non-*a*-Conjugation (unthematic):—Cl. 5 (*nu*-class). 163

Av.	Plural:	cf. Skt.
3. *vərə-nv-a^{i}ṇte*¹	. . . . .	*kṛ-ṇv-áte*

§ 569. **b. Preterite.**
i. ACTIVE.

Av.	Singular:	cf. Skt.
3. *kərə-nao-ṭ*	. . .	*á-kṛ-ṇō-t*
	Plural:	
2. *də b-ənao-tā* (GAv.)²	. . . . .	*á-kṛ-ṇō-ta*

ii. MIDDLE.

| 3. *hu-nū-ta* . | . . . . | *á-kṛ-ṇu-ta* |

§ 570. **2. Imperative.**
i. ACTIVE.

Av.	Singular:	cf. Skt.
3. *kərə-nū-idi* .	. . . .	*kṛ-ṇu-hi*
	Plural:	
2. *s^{u}ri-nao-ta*³ .	. . .	*kṛ-ṇō-ta*

§ 571. **3. Subjunctive.**
i. ACTIVE.

Av.	Singular:	cf. Skt.
1. *kərə-nav-āni*	. . . .	*kṛ-ṇáv-āni*
	Plural:	
3. *kərə-nāu-n*⁴ .	. . .	*kṛ-ṇáv-an*

ii. MIDDLE.
Singular:

| 1. *kərə-nav-āne* | . . . . | *kṛ-ṇáv-āi* |

§ 572. **4. Optative.**
i. ACTIVE.

Av.	Singular:	cf. Skt.
2. *s^{u}ru-nu-yå* .	. .	*kṛ-ṇu-yās*
3. *kərə-nu-yāṭ* .	. .	*kṛ-ṇu-yāt*

§ 573. **5. Participle.**

| i. ACTIVE. Av. *hu-nv-a(n)t-* | . . . | *kṛ-ṇv-á(n)t-* |
| ii. MIDDLE. *hu-nv-ana-* | . . . . . | *kṛ-ṇv-āná-* |

---

¹ After *a*-conj. — ² Ys. 32.5, from str. st. form, cf. Whitney, *Skt. Gram.* § 707. — ³ Str. stem form, as Skt. *kṛṇóta*, Whitney, *Skt. Gram.* § 704. — ⁴ On -*āun*, cf. § 64.

Forms to be observed in GAv. and YAv.

§ 574. Instances of transfer to the *a*-conj. (beside the 3 pl. above) are not infrequent:

1. Indicative. i. ACT. a. Pres. YAv. *kərə-nav-a-iti* 'he covers'. – b. Pret. *kərə nav-o* 'thou didst make'.

2. Imperative. i. ACT. YAv. *kərə-nava* 'make thou'.—ii. MID. YAv. *hu-nv-avuha* 'press thou'.

3. Subjunctive. i. ACT. YAv. *kərə-nav-ā-hi*, *kərə-nav-āt*, *kərə-nav-ąn* 'if thou, he, they make'.

§ 575. On instances of *kar-* made up after class 9, see below § 591.

Class 8.—*u*-Class.

§ 576. The eigth class (Skt. *tan*-class, Whitney, *Skt. Gram.* § 697 seq.) is hardly more than a variety of the preceding (5) class. It comprises, however, enough roots to be distinguishable. The present stem is made by adding to the root *ao-*, *av-* (in the str. forms), *u-*, *v-* (in the wk. forms).

Included under this class are the roots: Av. √*tan-* 'to stretch' = Skt. √*tan-*; Av. √*in-* 'drive' = Skt. √*in-*. Likewise here, parts of Av. √*ap-* 'to reach' = Skt. √*ap-*; Av. √*žar-* 'flow' (pres. participle), cf. Skt. √*kṣar-*; Av. √*har-* 'protect'.

Paradigm of Class 8.
(Cf. Whitney, *Skt. Gram.* § 698 b.)

§ 577. Av. √*in-* 'to drive', *tan-* 'stretch', *van-* 'strike', *žar-* 'flow', *žan-* 'destroy'. Cf. Skt. √*tan-* 'to stretch'.

§ 578.   1. Indicative.– a. Present.
              i. ACTIVE.

Av.	Singular:	cf. Skt.
3. *in-av-iti*	. . . .	*tan-ṓ-ti*
	Plural:	
2. *spaž-u-pā* [1] (?)	. . .	*tan-u-thá*
	ii. MIDDLE.	
	Plural:	
3. *uf-yąte* [2]		*tan-v-áte*

---

[1] Uncertain: Vs. 53.6. — [2] i. e. *up-v-ante after *a*-conj. On *f*, see § 95.

§ 579.   3. Subjunctive.
                 i. ACTIVE.
    Av.   Singular: cf. Skt.
1. tan-av-a   . . . .   tan-áv-ā (Ved.)

§ 580.   4. Optative.
    i. ACTIVE.   ii. MIDDLE.
Av.   Singular: cf. Skt.   Av.   Singular: cf. Skt.
3. van-u-yāt . . . . tan-u-yāt 1. tan-u-ya¹ . . . . tan-v-īyá

§ 581.   5. Participle.
Av.   i. ACTIVE.   cf. Skt.   Av.   ii. MIDDLE. cf. Skt.
žiar-v-a(n)t- . . . tan-v-á(n)t- žān-v-amna² . . . tan-v-āná

Forms to be observed.

§ 582. 1. Indic. Pres. Act. 3 sg. *haur-v-aiti* (after *a*-conjugation).—Mid. 3 pl. *fyavuntaē-ca* 'and they rain' (i. e. *fyavh-v-ante* § 63).

Class 9.—*nā*-Class.

§ 583. In the ninth class *nā*- is added to the root to form the strong present-stem; *n*-, *na*- (i. e. *n* + *a*-conj.) is added to make the weak pres. stem. The form *na*- (i. e. *a*-conj.) is commoner than *n*-. The endings are attached directly; the root itself retains its weak grade.

The Skt. ninth class likewise adds *nā*- in the strong forms, but *n*-, *nī*- (i. e. *nī* before cons.) in the weak. — Cf. Whitney, *Skt. Gram.* § 717 seq., esp. § 731.

Here belong: Av. √*frī*- 'to love' *frī-nā-mi* = Skt. *prī-nā́-mi*; Av. √*garw*- 'to seize' *garw-nā-iti* = Skt. *grbh-nā́-ti*; Av. √*var*- 'to choose' *var²-n-tē* = Skt. *vr-nī-té*; Av. √*gar*- 'to sing' *gar²-n-te* = Skt. *gr-nī-té*. Likewise some others—see following paradigm § 584.

Paradigm of Class 9.
(Cf. Whitney, *Skt. Gram.* § 718).

§ 584. Av. √*frī*- 'to love', *garw*- 'seize', *var*- 'choose', *hu*- 'to press', *par*- 'fight'.—Cf. Skt. √*prī*- 'to please', √*var*- 'to choose'.

---

¹ cf. Skt. *tan-v-ī-ya* § 62. — ² Like *a*-conj., -*amna*. On *ā*, cf. § 39.

§ 585.   1. **Indicative.**—a. Present.
i. ACTIVE.

Av.	Singular:	cf. Skt.
1. frī-nā-mi		prī ṇā-mi
3. gərəw-nā-iti		prī-ṇā-ti
	Plural:	
1. fry-q-mahi (GAv.)[1]		prī-ṇī-masi
3. frī-n-əṇti		prī-ṇ-ánti

ii. MIDDLE.
Singular:

| 1. vərə-n-e | | vṛ-ṇ-é |
| 3. vərə-ṇ-tē | | vṛ-ṇī-tē |

§ 586.   b. Preterite.
i. ACTIVE.

Av.	Singular:	cf. Skt.
3. miþ-nā-ṭ		á-prī-ṇā-t

ii. MIDDLE.
Singular:

| 3. fraorə-ṇ-ta[2] | | á-vṛ-ṇī-ta |

Plural:

| 3. vərə-n-ātā (GAv.)[3] | | á-vṛ-ṇ-ata |

§ 587.   2. **Imperative.**
i. ACTIVE.

Av.	Plural:	cf. Skt.
3. frī-n-əṇtu		prī-ṇ-ántu

§ 588.   3. **Subjunctive.**
i. ACTIVE.

Av.	Singular:	cf. Skt.
1. frī-nā-ni		prī ṇā-ni
3. { hu-nā-iti (GAv.)		prī-ṇā-ti
{ frī-nā-ṭ		prī-ṇā-t

Plural:

| 3. gərəw-nq-n | | prī-ṇā-n |

---

[1] i. e. frī-n̄-mahi or frv-ṇn-mahi. — [2] Vs. 57.24, Yt. 10.92, i. e. fra-vərə-ṇ-ta, cf. § 62.2. — [3] i. e. ⁕vərə-n-ā̆ta.

ii. MIDDLE.

Av.	Singular:	cf. Skt.
1. { pərə-nā́-ne	. . . . .	—
{ frī-nāi	. . . . .	prī-ṇái
3. pərə-nā́-ite	. . . . .	prī-ṇá-tāi
	Plural:	
3. vərə-nā̀-ṇte [1]	. . . .	vṛ-ṇá-ntāi

§ 589.   5. Participle.

ii. MIDDLE. Av. frī-n-əmna-[2] .   prī-ṇ-āná-

Forms to be observed.

§ 590. The **weak forms** in *na-* (i. e. *a*-conjugation by transfer) are frequent; the instances of 3 pl. thus formed are noted above. Other examples of this transfer (*-n·a*) are given in the next section § 591.

§ 591. The transfers to the *a*-conjugation with weak stem (*na*) are:

1. Indicative. i. ACT. a. Pres. *hu-n-a-hi* 'thou pressest', *frī-n-a-iti*, *frī-n-ā-mahi*, *frī-n-əṇti* (above).—ii. MID. *kərə-n-əṇte* 'they make, cut'.—b. Pret. i. ACT *kərə-n-əm* 'I made, cut', *sa-n-a-ṭ* 'it appeared' (i. e. *sad-n-aṭ* § 185) Yt. 14.7.— ii. MID. *stərə-n·a-ta* 'he strewed'.

2. Imperative. i. ACT. GAv. *pərə-n·ā* 'fulfil thou' Yt. 28.10, YAv. *miṇ-n-a-tu* 'let him turn', *frī-n-əṇtu* (above).—ii. MID. *brī-n-a-nuha* 'cut thou'.

4. Optative. i. ACT. *kərə-n-ōi-ṭ*, *zᵃra-n-aē-mā* (GAv.) 'we might anger' Ys. 28.9, *stərə-n-ay-ən* 'let them strew'.—ii. MID. *stərə-n-aē-ta* 'let him strew'.

II. PERFECT-SYSTEM.
Perfect.
(Cf. Whitney, *Skt. Gram.* § 780 seq.)

§ 592. **General Remark.** The chief characteristic of the perfect is the reduplication; the endings also differ in some respects from those of the present-system; the perfect shows likewise a distinction of strong and weak forms. As to signification, the perfect (and pluperfect) as

---
[1] Vd. 5.59. — [2] *-əmna* like *a*-conj.

168 Inflection: Conjugation of Verbs.

in Skt. commonly denotes simple past time; sometimes present time is expressed.

Note 1. An assumed periphrastic form of the perfect sporadically occurs, see § 623.

Note 2. On the absence of reduplication, see § 620.

Reduplicated Syllable.

§ 593. The principal points to be observed in regard to reduplication of the vowels (cf. Whitney, *Skt. Gram.* § 783) are:

1. Internal or final *a* or *ā* is regularly reduplicated by *a* (sometimes by *ā*—cf. Whitney. *Skt. Gram.* § 786a), occasionally by *i*. For example—

Av. *ta-taṣ-a* 'he has formed' (√*taš-*) = Skt. *ta-tākṣ-a*; Av. *da-dā-ba* 'thou hast created' (√*dā-*) = Skt. *da-dhā-tha*; Av. *dā-darəs-a* 'I have seen' (√*darəs-*) = Skt. *da-dárś-a*; Av. *ā-ḥr-arə* 'they have made' (√*kar-*) = Skt. *ca-kr-úr*; GAv. *vā-vərəz-ōi* 'he has worked' (mid.) √*varəz-*; Av. *ji-gaurv-a* (observe palatal *j* § 465 c) 'I have perceived' (√*garw-*) = Skt. *pī-gŕbh-a*.

2. Internal or final *i*, *u* or *ī*, *ū* are reduplicated by *i*, *u* (sometimes *ī*, *ū*). For example—

Av. *di-dvaēṣ-a* 'I have hated' (√*dviš-*) = Skt. *di-dvéṣ-a*; Av. *di-day-a* 'he has seen' (√*dī-*) = Skt. *dī-dhay-a*; Av. *tū-tav-a* 'he has been able' (√*tū-*) = Skt. *tū-táv-a*.

Note. Worthy of remark is Av. *bā-bv-arə* (with *ā* from √*bū-* 'to be') Yt. 13.150 = Skt. *ba-bhūv-úr*, but Av. *bvāva* (i. e. *bu-vāv-a*, Yt. 13.2, cf. § 68 b = Skt. *ba-bhūv-a*.

3. Initial *a* by reduplication with itself becomes *ā*. For example—

Av. *ā-vh-a* 'he has been' (√*ah-*) = Skt. *ā-s-a*.

4. Initial *i* (or *u* if found) is reduplicated by " *y* i. e. *i-y* (or *u* i. e. *u-v*), cf. § 68 a.

Av. ⲭⲟⲩⲟⲩ *yeyą* (i. e. *iv-ay-qn*) 'they may have come' Ys. 42.6 (√*i-* subjunct. *a*-inflect. if not redupl. pres.). So also ⲙⲟⲩⲟⲩ *yaēṣa* i. e. *iyaēṣa* Yt. 13.99.

§ 594. The laws for the reduplication of consonants have been sufficiently treated above, § 465 c.

Radical Syllable.
Strong and weak Stem-Forms.

§ 595. The **strong** stem or guṇa-form of the radical syllable, as in the non-*a*-conjugation (unthematic), is found in the perfect-system 1) in the **Indicative** Act. 1, 2, 3 sg. Pres. Pret.; 2) in the **Imperative** Act. 3 sg.; 3) in the **Subjunctive** entire. The remaining forms are **weak**. But numerous fluctuations in this rule occur.

Note. In GAv., as in Vedic Skt., medial short *a* before a single consonant is lengthened to *ā* in the radical syllable of the 3 sg. pf. act. For YAv. no rule is laid down.—Cf. Whitney, *Skt. Gram.* § 793 c. Thus, GAv. *nš-nās-a* 'it is lost' ($\sqrt{nas}$-) = Skt. *na-nāś-a*.

§ 596. With reference to the weak forms, some observations as regards the radical syllable may be made. An internal or final *i, u* remains unchanged e. g. *irī-rip-arə* 'they lie' ($\sqrt{rip}$-), *su-sru-yē* 'I have heard' ($\sqrt{sru}$-) Yt. 17.17, yet *sū-srū-ma* 'we have heard' Yt. 13.198; but a number of roots having medial *a* between **single** consonants (cf. Whitney, *Skt. Gram.* § 794 e) and certain others, by loss of the vowel in weak forms may undergo some change:

1. Roots in -*ar* show weak forms in -*r*- before vowels: Av. *ba-wr-arə* 'they bore' ($\sqrt{bar}$-), beside GAv. *vā-vər̄z-ōi* 'he worked' 3 sg. pf. mid. ($\sqrt{varz}$- i. e. two cons.).

2. Roots in -*am*, -*an* show weak forms in -*m*-, -*n*-: Av. *ja-ǵm-yąm* 'I would have come' ($\sqrt{gam}$-); GAv. *cā-ḵn-arə* 'they have desired' ($\sqrt{kan}$-).

3. Roots with initial *ya*-, *va*- by contraction with the reduplicated syllable show in the weak forms *yaē*- (*yōi*-), *vao*- (*vāu*-) i. e. *ya-i*-, *va-u*-: Av. $\sqrt{yat}$- 'to strive' makes 1 pl. act. YAv. *yaēpma*, GAv. *yōipmā* (i. e. *ya-yi-ma*, *va-it-ma*); Av. $\sqrt{van}$- 'win' makes 3 pl. act. *vaonarə* (i. e. *va-vn-ar*, *va-un-ar*). Cf. § 63 seq.

4. Roots with radical final *ā* **lose** this *ā* before endings beginning with a vowel, so also before endings where Skt. shows the union-vowel *i*, Whitney, *Skt. Gram.* § 794 end: Av. $\sqrt{stā}$- 'to stand', *hi-št-a* 1, 3 sg. pf. act.; $\sqrt{dā}$- 'give, place', *da-d-a* 3 sg. act., *da-id-e* 3 sg. mid.; *da-d-vā̊* ptcpl. (Skt. *da-d-i-vą́s* or *da-d-vą́s*).

Personal Endings
and their connection with the Stem.

§ 597. The endings of the perfect, especially in the middle voice, are mostly primary. They are attached directly to the tense-stem as in the unthematic conjugation; sporadic traces of a 'union-vowel' *i, ə* (cf. Whitney, *Skt. Gram.* § 797 seq.) perhaps however exist. See Bartholomae, *A.F.* ii. p. 97.

§ 598. The endings agree with those of the Skt.; some forms however are to be specially observed, see below § 599 seq.

Perfect Endings.

	i. ACTIVE.			ii. MIDDLE.	
Av.	Singular:	cf. Skt.	Av.	Singular:	cf. Skt.
1.	-a	-a	-e		-ē
2.	-ßa	-tha	—		-sē
3.	-a	-a	-e		-ē
	Dual:			Dual:	
1.	—	-va	—		-vahē
2.	—	-athur	—		-āthē
3.	-atarə	-atur	-aitē (GAv.), -tē		-ātē
	Plural:			Plural:	
1.	-ma	-ma	—		-mahē
2.	-a	-a	—		-dhvē
3.	-arə, -ərəš	-ur	—		-rē

Perfect Endings (Observations).

§ 599. Singular:—

First Person: **ii. MIDDLE**. A 1st. sg. mid. form in -*ō* (i. e. -*āu* § 54 = Skt. -*āu*) from a root ending in long *ā* is perhaps to be found in *dadō* 'I have made' Ys. 10.9 = Skt. *dadhāu*, Whitney, *Skt. Gram.* § 800 c.

Second Person: **i. ACTIVE**. Note the form -*ta* (for -*ßa* § 78 end) after *s* in GAv. *vōistā* 'thou knowest'.

§ 600. Dual:—

Third Person: **ii. MIDDLE**. Observe the suffix -*tē* 3 du. mid. in GAv. *dazdē* 'they both created' Ys. 30.4 (i. e. **dhazdhai, dha-dh-tai*), cf. Bartholomae, *K.Z.* xxix. p. 285 = *Flexionslehre* p. 16.

§ 601. **Plural:**—
Third Person: i. ACTIVE. The ending *-ərəš* (above) beside *-arə* is found in GAv. *ci-kōit-ərəš* 'they have thought, taught' Ys. 32.11.

Pluperfect (Preterite).
(Cf. Whitney, *Skt. Gram.* § 817 seq.)

§ 602. The existence of a preterite (pluperfect) indicative corresponding to the present perfect, seems to be shown by a few forms. There is, however, some uncertainty, see Note. The forms here recognized as pluperfect are made by adding the **secondary endings directly to the perfect stem**. The strong stem appears in the singular active; the weak stem elsewhere. The thematic *a* (transferring to the *a*-inflection) is sometimes found.—Cf. Whitney, *Skt. Gram.* § 817 seq.

Note. There is much difficulty in distinguishing a pluperfect from some other reduplic. forms. Some of the examples may equally well be referred to other forms (impf., aor.) of the redupl. preterite.

Mode-Formation of the Perfect.

§ 603. The perfect like the other tense-systems shows an **indicative** (pres perf.; pret. pluperf.), **imperative, subjunctive** (prim. and sec.), **optative and participle** (cf. Whitney, *Skt. Gram.* § 808 seq.). These are formed as in the non-*a*-conjugation (unthematic); the subjunctive has the strong stem + mode-sign *a;* the optative has the weak stem + *-yā-, -ī-*.

§ 604. A number of transfers to the *a*-inflection instead of the thematic are found in pluperfect, imperat., subjunct., optative, and participle. See § 619.

Paradigm of the Perfect-System.
(Cf. Whitney, *Skt. Gram.* § 800 seq.)

§ 605. Examples of the inflection of the perfect may be taken from the following roots:—

Av. √*garw-* 'to seize' = Skt. √*grabh-*; Av. √*dviš-* 'hate' = Skt. √*dviš-*; Av. √*i rud-* 'grow' = Skt. √*i rudh-*; Av. √*dars-* 'see'

Inflection: Conjugation of Verbs.

= Skt. √ānrs-; Av. √dā- 'give, make' = Skt. √dā-, dhā-; Av. √kan- 'love' = Skt. √kan-; Av. √tu- 'be able' = Skt. √tu-; Av. √dar- 'hold' = Skt. √dhur-; Av. √sru- 'hear' = Skt. √śru-; Av. √yat- 'strain, strive' = Skt. √yat-; Av. √han- 'earn' = Skt. √san-; Av. √bar- 'bear' = Skt. √bhar-; Av. √kar- 'make' = Skt. √kar-; Av. √pru- 'support, nourish'; Av. √man- 'think' = Skt. √man-; Av. √āi- 'consider, see' = Skt. √dhī-; Av. √2 rud- 'obstruct' = Skt. √2 rudh; Av. √sac- 'learn, can' = Skt. śac-; Av. √aś-, aś- 'attain' = Skt. aś-, aś-; Av. √vaz- 'carry' = Skt. √vah-; Av. √ar- 'go, rise' = Skt. √ar-; Av. √har- 'protect'; Av. √ah- 'be' = Skt. √as-; Av. √vraz- 'proceed'; Av. √gam- 'go, come' = Skt. √gam-; Av. √van- 'strive, contend, win' = Skt. √van-.

§ 606. 1. **Indicative.**—a. Perfect (Present).

i. ACTIVE.

Av.	Singular:	cf. Skt.
1. { *ji-gaurv-a, di-dvaēṣ-a* .		*ja-grāhh-a, di-dvēṣ-a*
{ *urū-raod-a, dā-darəs-a* .		*ru-rōdh-a, da-darś-a*
2. *da-dā-ṭa*¹		*da-d(h)ī-tha*
3. { *ca-kan-a, tū-tav-a*		*cā-kan-a, tū-tāv-a*
{ *da-dar-a* .	. . .	*da-dhār-a, dā-dhār-a*

Dual:

3. *yaēt-atarə*² . . . (*yēt-atur*)

Plural:

1. { *di-dvīṣ-ma*¹, *sū-srū-ma* . .		*di-dvis-i-má, vi-viṣ-ma*
{ *yaēṭ-ma*¹		(*yet-i-má*)
2. *ha-vhān-a* .		
3. *ba-var-arə, cā-hr-arə* .		*ja-bhr-úr, cā-kr-úr*

ii. MIDDLE.

Singular:

1. *su-sruy-e* . . . *su-śruv-é*
3. *tu-ṭruy-e* . . . *su-śruv-é*

Dual:

3. { *ma-man-āitē*³ . . . *ma-mn-ātē*
  { *da-z-dē*⁶ . . . —

---

¹ Ys. 71.10. — ² ZPhl. Gloss. p. 56.11. — ³ On *i* after *v* cf. § 20. — ⁴ cf. § 590.3. — ⁵ Ys. 13.4, Bartholomae, K.Z. xxix, p. 288 = *Flexionslehre* p. 17, 19. — ⁶ GAv. Ys. 30.4, cf. § 600.

§ 607.   b. Pluperfect (Preterite).
i. ACTIVE.

Av.	Singular:	cf. Skt.
1. di-daē-m [1]		a-ja-grabh-am [2]
3. urū-raos-t [3]	. .	a-ci-kē-t
	Plural:	
3. sa-šk-ən [4]	. . .	—

ii. MIDDLE.
Singular:

3. ən-āḣš-ta (GAv.) [5]	. . .	—
	Plural:	
3. vaoz-i-rəm [6]	. . .	—

§ 608.   2. Imperative.
i. ACTIVE.

Av.	Singular:	cf. Skt.
3. ni-ša-vhar-a-tū [7]	. .	—

ii. MIDDLE.

| 2. ārə-ṣvā (GAv.) | . . . | — [8] |

§ 609.   3. Subjunctive.
i. ACTIVE.
Plural:

| 1. awh-āma [9] | . . . | ās-āma |
| 2. vavrāz-a pā (GAv.) | . . | va-vraj-a-tha |

ii. MIDDLE.
Plural:

| 3. ā̊wh-a-ire [10] | . . . | — |

§ 610.   4. Optative.
i. ACTIVE.

Av.	Singular:	cf. Skt.
1. ja-jm-yąm		ju-gam-yām
2. tū-tu-yā̊ [11]		tū-tu-yās
3. vaon-yāṯ	. . . .	ma-mun-yāt

[1] Can as well be redupl. pret. Cl. 3. — [2] cf. Whitney, *Skt. Gram.* § 818 a. — [3] Skt. *V̍2 rudh-*, cf. § 151. — [4] Ys. 53.1 i. e. *saškən-cā*. — [5] cf. Bartholomae, *B.B.* xiii. p. 65. — [6] cf. §§ 455, 616. — [7] Ys. 58.4, *u*-inflect. by transfer, Whitney, *Skt. Gram.* § 814. — [8] cf. Whitney, *Skt. Gram.* § 813 end. — [9] cf. *u*-inflect. — [10] Ys. 9.23 cf. § 452, v. l. *ā̊whāirə*. — [11] Ys. 9.29, used as 3 sg.

§ 611.   5. Participle.   cf. Skt.
i. ACTIVE. Av. *ha-vhan-vah-* .   *sa-can-vás-*
ii. MIDDLE.   *ha-vhan-ana-* .   . . . .   *sa-san-āná-*

Forms to be observed in GAv. and YAv.
1. Indicative. a. Perfect.

§ 612. Singular:—
First Person: ii. MID. GAv., add *āroi* 'I have earned' (√*ar-*) Ys. 33.9, on *-ōi-* cf. § 56.—On a possible 1st. sg. mid. in *-ē* (i. e. *-āṅ*) = Skt. *-au*, from √*dā-*, see § 599 above.
Third Person. i. ACT. Observe radical *ā* in (root with medial *a* before one consonant) GAv. *nanāsā* 'it is lost', YAv. *dadāra* 'he fixed'—see § 595 Note, but likewise *ā*, YAv. *cakāna* 'he loved' (√*kan-*), *yayāta* 'he strove' (√*yat-*), *bavāra* 'he bore' (√*bar-*).—Again from weak stem (final radical *ā* lost before vowels, § 596.4) *da-d a* 'he made' (√*dā-*).—ii. MID. GAv. also (with strengthened reduplication) *vā-varə-ōi* 'he has worked', cf. § 56.—Add GAv. *āraē-cā* 'has been earned' (√*ar-*) Ys. 56.3.

§ 613. Dual:—
Third Person: i. ACT. GAv. (note *-ā-*) *vaocātarə* 'they both have spoken', *dāvərəzātarə* 'they both have done' Vs. 13.4.

§ 614. Plural:—
First Person: i. ACT. GAv., note *yōiṣəmā* 'we strive' (*-ōi-* § 56) beside YAv. *yaēpma* above.
Second Person: i. ACT. YAv., note the long *ā* strongest stem in *havhāna* above in paradigm.
Third Person: i. ACT. YAv. from weak stem (final radical *ā* lost before vowels § 596.4) and str. redupl. *dā-d-arə* 'they made' (√*dā-*) = Skt. *dadhúr*.—Likewise note (§ 62.2) YAv. *vaonarə*, GAv. *vaonarə* 'they strove' (i. e. *va-vn-ar* § 596.3).—Long redupl. syl. *cā-hr-arə* 'they have made' Vd. 4.46.—GAv. also (suffix *-arəš*) *ci-kōit-arəš* 'they thought'.

b. Pluperfect.
§ 615. Singular:—
Third Person: ii. MID. GAv. *ənāhṣtā* (in paradigm, see Foot-Note) presents 'Attic reduplication'.

§ 616. Plural:—
Third Person: ii. MID. YAv. *vaozirəm* (i. e. *va-vz-i-rəm* √*vaz-*) above in paradigm shows 3 pl. ending in *-rəm* = Skt. *-ram* (cf. Whitney, *Skt. Gram.* §§ 834 b, 867) with connecting vowel. See above § 455 end.

4. Optative.

§ 617. **Plural**:—
First Person: i. ACT. YAv., perhaps here *daídyāma* Yt. 24.58.

5. Participle.

§ 618. **i. ACT.** On inflectional forms of the pf. act. ptcpl. see §§ 349, 350.—**ii. MID.** Also suffix -*āna* (beside -*āna*) *vavr̥tāna-* 'driven', *dadrāṇa-*, *dadrāna-* 'held'.

Transitions to the thematic (a) inflection.

§ 619. A number of transfers to the *a*-inflection occur cf. § 604.

1. Indicative. **i. ACT.** b. Pluperf. **Sg. 3.** YAv. *ta-taš-a-ṭ* 'he formed'; *ja-ym-a-ṭ*.
2. Imperative. **i. ACT. Sg. 3.** GAv. *ni-šauhar-a-tū* (in paradigm).
3. Subjunctive. **i. ACT. Sg. 3.** YAv. *aōhāṭ* 'may be'; Du. 3. *aōhātəm* Yt. 13.12; Pl. 3. *iyəyą ŕiieṇq* = *iy-av-a-an) 'they may go' (√*i*-) Ys. 42.6 (if not desiderative).—**ii. MID. Pl. 3.** YAv. *aōhāire* Yt. 10.45, cf. §§ 452, 486.

Absence of Reduplication.

§ 620. In Av., as in Skt., the absence of a reduplicated syllable is met with in a number of cases. This is familiar in *vaēda* 'oἶδα' == Skt. *véda*, and in some other forms.—Cf. Whitney, *Skt. Gram.* § 790.

§ 621. As example of perf. lacking reduplication may be given G(Y)Av. √*vid*- 'to know' = Skt. √*vid*-.

1. Indic. a. Perf. **Sg.** 1. *vaēdā*, 2. *vōistā*, 3. *vaēdā*, *vaēda* (YAv.).
2. Imperat. **Pl. 2.** *voizdūm* Ys. 33.8.
3. Subjunct. **Sg.** 1. *vaēdā* Ys. 48.9; **Pl. 2.** *vaēdāṭhm* (§ 39).
4. Optat. **Sg. 3.** *vidyāṭ*.
5. Partic. **i. ACT.** *vīdvah-* (GAv.), *vidvah-* (YAv.).—**ii. MID.** *vaēdəna-* Ys. 34.7, *vaēdəmna-* (themat.).

§ 622. Other examples of pf. wanting redupl. are: GAv. √*cag-* 'grant', *cagəmā* (1 pl. pf. act.), *cagədō* (3 du. plpf.), *cagvā̊* (ptcpl.).—Also GAv. *apānō* 'attained' (ptcpl. √*ap-*).

Periphrastic Perfect.

§ 623. In YAv. traces of a periphrasis which may be construed as forming a perfect are found.—Cf. also Whitney, *Skt. Gram.* §§ 1070, 1072. In Av. the acc. sg. fem. of the pres. participle is united with the perfect of the auxiliary *ah-* to be.—

    YAv. *sraoṣyeṇtīm āvhāṭ* 'it may have clung' (subjunct.), *āčarayeiṇtīm āvhāṭ* 'should have corrupted'.—Perhaps also here *bixvīṇvha* 'he had frightened' Yt. 19.48,50 (? nom. sg. ptcp. √*bī-* + *āvha*, cf. variants).

III. AORIST-SYSTEM.
Aorist.
(Chiefly found in Gāthā Avesta.)

§ 624. **General Remark.** In regard to form the aorist in Av. may perhaps best be defined as a preterite, whose exact corresponding present is missing and which consequently attaches itself to an analogous present and preterite, and forms a new system subordinate to these.

In regard to meaning the aorist in Avesta commonly denotes a simple past action, usually but not always momentary. It may often, as in Skt., be rendered by our 'have'.

The instances of aorist formation are found chiefly in the Gāthā portions of the literature, but occurences in the later parts are by no means uncommon.

    Note. The resemblance in form which the aorist bears to the preterite (imperfect) sometimes gives rise to question whether certain given forms are to be classed as preterite (imperfect) or as aorist; the decision depends chiefly upon whether or not we assume a present to the form— e. g. cf. Bartholomae, *Verbum* p. 63 seq.

§ 625. Two groups of aorists may conveniently be distinguished; they are 1. non-sigmatic, 2. sigmatic. These comprise several sub-varieties of formation (7 as in Skt.), as follows. Cf. Whitney, *Skt. Gram.* § 824.

		1. Root-aorist.
	i. Non-Sigmatic	2. Simple *a*-aorist (thematic).
		3. Reduplicated aorist.
Aorist-System		
		4. *h*- (*s*-) aorist.
	ii. Sigmatic	5. *ha*- (*sa*-) aorist (or *h*-thematic).
		6. *iš*-aorist.
		7. *hiš*-aorist.

§ 626. **Augment and Endings.** The augment in aorist forms as elsewhere in Av. is commonly missing; the augmentless forms, moreover, often have a subjunctive (imperative) signification (cf. § 445 Note 2 injunctive). The endings in the indicative are the secondary.

§ 627. **Modes of the Aorist.** The modes—imperative, subjunctive (prim., sec.), optative—of the aorist are formed according to the regular laws of the other systems.

Note. Observe the existence of a form 3 sg. imperat. mid. in -*qm* = Skt. -*ām*: GAv. *srəžūcqm* 'speak', *vīdqm* 'it shall decide' Ys. 32.6, cf. Skt. *duhām*, Whitney, *Skt. Gram.* § 618.

i. Non-Sigmatic Group.

§ 628. The aorists of the non-sigmatic group—1. root-aorist, 2. simple *a*-aorist (thematic), 3. reduplicated aorist—resemble preterites (imperfects) which correspond respectively to the root-class, the *a*-conjugation (thematic), and to the reduplicated class.

1. Root-Aorist.
(Cf. Whitney, *Skt. Gram.* § 829.)

§ 629. The root-aorist is like an imperfect of the root-class without a corresponding present indicative. The endings are attached directly to the root in its strong or its weak form. The distribution of strong and weak stem-forms is in general the same as in the present and perfect systems. The modes show their characteristic mode-signs.

§ 630. Example of root-aorist inflection (almost exclusively GAv.).

Av. —) √dā- 'to give, do, make' (str. stem dā-, da-, wk. stem d-)
= Skt. √dā-, dhā-, Whitney, Skt. Gram. § 829.

§ 631. 1. **Indicative.**—Aorist (Preterite).

i. ACTIVE.

(G)Av.	Singular:	cf. Skt.
1. —	. . . . . .	á-d(h)ā-m
2. dāv, dass-cā	. . , . .	á-d(h)ā-s
3. dā ṭ	. . . . .	á-d(h)ā-t
	Plural:	
1. dā-mā	. . .	á-d(h)ā-ma
2. dā-tā	. . . .	á-d(h)ā-ta
3. d-arə	. . . .	á-d(h)-ur

ii. MIDDLE.
Plural:

| 3. d-ātā [1] | . . . . . | — |

§ 632. 2. **Imperative.**

i. ACTIVE.

(G)Av.	Singular:	cf. Skt.
2. dā-di	. . .	—
3. dā-tū	. . . .	d(h)á-tu

§ 633. 3. **Subjunctive.**

i. ACTIVE.
Singular:

| 2. dā-hi | . . . . | — |
| 3. dā-iti | . . , . | d(h)á-ti |

Plural:

| 2. da-mahi [2] | . . . | — |
| 3. d'a-n | . . . | — |

ii. MIDDLE.
Singular:

1. dā-nē [3]	. . .	—
2. { dā-nhē		—
dā-nhā	. .	—
3. dā-itē	. . . .	—

Plural:

| 3. dā-ṇtē | . . . . . . | — |

---

[1] i. e. d'ita. — [2] Vs. 68.1. — [3] Vs. 44.9.

§ 634.   4. Optative.
i. ACTIVE.

(G)Av.	Singular:	cf. Skt.
1. *d-yąm*	. . . . . .	*d(h)ɜ-yām*
2. *da-yā̊*[1], *dā-yā̊*[2]	. . . . .	---
3. *d-yāṯ, da-yāṯ*[3]	. . . . . .	---

Plural:

| 2. *dā-yata*[4] | . . . . . | --- |

ii. MIDDLE.

1. *d-yā̊*[5]	. . . . . .	---
2. *d-īṣ̌ā*	. . . . .	---
3. *d-yātąm*	. . . . .	---

§ 635.   5. Participle.
i. ACTIVE. Av. *daṇt-* . . . . ---

Forms to be observed in GAv. and YAv.

§ 636. Some further examples of inflection in GAv. and some forms also in YAv. may be observed.

1. Indicative.—Aorist.

§ 637. Singular:—

First Person: i. ACT. GAv. *darəsəm* 'I saw'; note *srəv-ī-m* 'I heard' (observe *-ī-*, like §§ 527, 550).

Second Person: i. ACT. GAv. *varəš* 'thou hast done' (*varz + s* § 165).

Third Person: i. ACT. GAv. *mōist* 'he turned' (√*mip-*), *cōrəṯ* 'he made' (√*kar-*, *-ō- = -a-* § 39). — Here probably also *yaogəṯ* Ys. 44.4. — Observe GAv. *sōh-ī-ṯ* 'he taught' (*sāh-*), YAv. *vaiṇ-i-ṯ* 'let conquer' Ys. 60.5 (if not opt. with wk. ending).

§ 638. Dual:—

Third Person: ii. MID. GAv. *asrvātəm* 'they called'.

§ 639. Plural:—

First Person: ii. MID. YAv. *yaoẖmaide* 'we joined' GAv. *varəmaidī* 'we have chosen'.

Third Person: i. ACT. YAv. *u-šk-arə* 'they elapsed' (√*sac-*) Vd. 1.4; also *bun* 'they become'. — GAv. *ǰn̥*, *gəmən* 'they came'. — ii. MID. *fracarəṇta* 'they provided' (√*kar-*) Vd. 2.11.

---

[1] From strong stem. So metrically Yt. 10.114; Ys. 57.26. — [2] From strongest stem. — [3] From str. stem. So metrically Yt. 13.50 cf. Vd. 3.32. — [4] From strongest stem. — [5] i. e. *dīya*.

2. Imperative.

§ 640. Singular:—
Second Person: ii. MID. GAv. *kərəi̯uuā* 'make thou'.
Third Person: ii. MID. GAv. (ending *-qm* above §§ 456, 627 Note) *srāuuacąm* 'speak right', *vīdąm* 'shall decide'.

§ 641. Plural:—
Third Person: i. ACT. GAv. *sčaṇtū* 'let them follow' (√*sac-*).

3. Subjunctive.

§ 642. Singular:—
First Person: i. ACT. YAv. *hištā* 'I will stand'.—GAv. *yaoǰā* 'I will yoke', *varānī* 'I will choose'.—ii. MID. *gərane͂*, *gərəzōi* 'I will complain', *sruy̆e* 'I may be heard'. YAv. *búye* 'I may be' (√*bū-*) Afr. 1.10,11.
Third Person: i. ACT. YAv. *braṭ* 'will become'.—GAv. *jimaṭ* 'he may come'.

§ 643. Dual:—
Third Person: ii. MID. GAv. *jamaētē* 'they may come'.

§ 644. Plural:—
First Person: i. ACT. YAv. *jimama* 'we shall come'.
Second Person: i. ACT. GAv. *vī-carapā* 'ye distinguish'.
Third Person: i. ACT. GAv. *hvaṇti-cā* 'and they will be', *jimən* 'may they come'.

4. Optative.

§ 645. Singular:—
Second Person: i. ACT. YAv., similarly *hšnuuō* 'thou mightest rejoice'.
Third Person: i. ACT. YAv. also (from str. stem) *jam-yāṭ* 'he might come'; again (from wk. stem as above) *dis-yāṭ* 'let him show' Afr. 3.7 etc., likewise GAv. *mīṇ́yāṭ* 'he might deprive'.—ii. MID. GAv. *ārītā* 'he might hold' (√*dar-*).

§ 646. Plural:—
First Person: i. ACT. YAv. *jamyāma* beside *jamyāma* 'we might come'. —GAv. *buyāma* 'we might be'.—ii. MID. GAv. *vairimaidī* 'we might choose'.
Second Person: i. ACT. YAv. *buyātā* 'might ye be'.
Third Person: i. ACT. YAv. *buyąn*, *buyārəš* 'they might be'.

Note. For fuller GAv. lists in regard to the root-aorist see Bartholomae, *K.Z.* xxiv. p. 313 seq. = *Flexionslehre* p. 44 seq.

§ 647. Transfers to the thematic *a*-inflection are found, e.g. GAv. *vahš-a-ṭ* 'he increased', GAv. *frā-jm-a-ṭ* 'he came' (√*gam-*).

2. Simple *a*-Aorist (thematic).
(Cf. Whitney, *Skt. Gram.* § 846 seq.)

§ 648. The instances of the simple *a*-aorist are not very numerous; in Av. this aorist plays a part similar to that in the Skt. of the Rig Veda. In formation and inflection it is identical with a preterite (imperfect) of the 6th class. The root in its weak form simply assumes the thematic vowel *a*; the secondary endings are then added for the indicative.—Cf. Whitney, *Skt. Gram.* § 846.

§ 649. Examples of the *a*-aorist (chiefly GAv.) are the following:

> 1. Indicative. i. ACT. Aor. (pret.) Sg. 3. *vīdaṯ* 'he found' (beside 3 sg. pres. pret. *viṇḍ-aṯ*), *būjaṯ* 'he absolved' (beside pres. *bunj-aiṇti*).—ii. MID. Pl. 3. *ẋ́šayta* 'they ruled' ($\sqrt{}$ *ẋ́šā*-).
> 2. Imperative. i. ACT. Sg. 2. *vīdā* 'find thou'.—ii. MID. Pl. 3. *ẋ́šṇtąm* 'let them rule'.
> 3. Subjunctive. i. ACT. Sg. 1. *hanāni*, 3. *hanāṯ* 'let me, him earn'.
> 4. Optative. ii. MID. Sg. 3. *ẋ́šaēta* 'might be rule'.
> 5. Participle. i. ACT. *vīdat*° (in compounds).

Likewise some other forms might be added.

3. Reduplicated Aorist.
(Cf. Whitney, *Skt. Gram.* § 856 seq.)

§ 650. The reduplicated aorist is comparatively rare. The stem is made by reduplicating the root which then appears in its weak form and assumes the thematic *a*. The secondary endings are added for the indicative.—Cf. Whitney, *Skt. Gram.* § 856.

§ 651. Example of inflection, Av. ₋₊₋ $\sqrt{}$ *vac-* 'to speak' (stem *vaoc-a-* i. e. *va-uc-*, *va-vc-*) = Skt. $\sqrt{}$ *vac-* (*vóca-*):

> 1. Indicative. i. ACT. Sg. 1. *vaocǝm*, *vaocim* (§ 30), 2. *vaocō*, *vaocas-cā*, 3. *vaocaṯ*, *vaocaṯ* (§§ 32, 466).—Pl. 1. *vaocāma*, *vaocǝmā*.
> 2. Imperative. i. ACT. Sg. 2. *vaocā*.
> 3. Subjunctive. i. ACT. Sg. 1. *vaoca* (Ys. 45.3), 3. *vaocāṯ*.
> 4. Optative. i. ACT. Sg. 3. *vaocōiṯ*.—Pl. 1. *vaocōimā*.

Note 1. Similarly GAv. *ṇsaṯ* 'he disappeared' (i. e. *na-ns-aṯ*, $\sqrt{}$ *nas-* = Skt. $\sqrt{}$ *naś-*).

Note 2. To the redupl. aor. possibly belong the obscure forms YAv. *uru rūd-n-ja* 'thou didst grow' 2 sg. mid. Ys. 10.3, GAv. *at-aš-u-tā* 'it has been accomplished'. The *u* may be anaptyctic, or is it from a pres. formation?

§ 652. Instances of the true **causative aorist** with strengthened reduplication (cf. Whitney, *Skt. Gram.* §§ 1046. 856) are: √*var-* 'to believe, cause to believe', GAv. *vāurāitē* (3 sg. subjunct. mid.); *vāuraya* (1 sg. opt. mid.), *vāuröimaidi* (1 pl. opt. mid.). On *vaurāite* etc. for *va-vr-āite* see § 62. 2 above.

Note 1. The forms *zīzanəm*, *zīzanāt* (cf. Skt. *ajījanat*, Whitney, *Skt. Gram.* §§ 864, 866) are best reckoned under Cl. 3 in Av. on account of pres. indic. *zīzanəṇti* Yt. 13.15.

Note 2. The form *vavzirarə* Yt. 19.69 is reckoned under pluperf. above § 616.

ii. Sigmatic Group.
4. *h- (s-)* Aorist.
(Cf. Whitney, *Skt. Gram.* § 878 seq.)

§ 653. The characteristic mark of this aorist is an orig. sibilant *s* (= Av. *h, s, š*) which is added in forming the stem. The inflection is unthematic, the endings being attached directly to the root which shows different degrees of strengthening, see next section § 654.

§ 654. The indicative sg. act. has the vṛddhi-strengthening, the indic. plur. act. and generally both numbers of the indic. mid. have the guṇa form. The imperative mid. and the entire subjunctive act. show likewise guṇa. The optative and some instances of indic. plur. mid. generally have the weak form.

§ 655. Examples of inflection of this aorist are taken from the following roots:

Av. √*dī-* 'regard, think' = Skt. √*dhī-*; Av. √*dar-* 'hold, hold back' = Skt. √*dhar-*; Av. √*sand-* 'show, present, appear' = Skt. √*chand-* § 142; Av. √*man-* 'think' = Skt. √*man-*; Av. √*hwars-* 'shape, create'; Av. √*fras-* 'ask' = Skt. √*praś-*; Av. √*prā-* 'protect' = Skt. √*trā-*; Av. √*van-* 'win' = Skt √*van-*; Av. √*naṣ-, nas-* 'cause to vanish' = Skt. √*naś-, naś-*; Av. √*varz-* 'work'

= Skt. √varj-; Av. √′fā- 'protect' = Skt. √′fā-; Av. √vac- 'speak'
= Skt. √vac-; Av. √dā- 'give, do, make' = Skt. √dā-, dhā-; Av.
√anqs-, nas- 'attain' = Skt. √anqs-, nas-.

§ 656.   1. Indicative.—Aorist (Preterite).

i. ACTIVE.

(G)Av.	Singular:	cf. Skt.
2. dāi-š, sqs[1]		bhāi-s[2], achān
3. dārəšt, dōrəšt[3], sqs[4]		á-bhār[5], achān

ii. MIDDLE.
Singular:

1. mōvh-ī[6], frašī		mqs-i
2. mōnghā		—
3. mąs-tā		mqs-ta

Plural:

1. a-mōh-maidī[7], mōh-maidī[7]		á-gas-mahi
2. pwarəž-dum[8]		á-vṛ-dhvam

§ 657.   2. Imperative.

ii. MIDDLE.
Singular:

2. fərašvā . . . . ⸺

Plural:

2. prāz-dūm[9] . . . . trá-dhvam

§ 658.   3. Subjunctive.

i. ACTIVE.

(G)Av.	Singular:	cf. Skt.
3. { vənvh-aitī		vás-ati
{ vəngh-aṭ		vás-at

Plural:

1. nāš-āmā[10]		vás-āma
3. { varəš-əṇtī[11]		
{ vəngh-ən		vqs-an

---

[1] Ys. 46.19. — [2] Wh., Skt. Gram. § 891. — [3] § 39. — [4] Ys. 43.11. —
[5] Wh., Skt. Gram. § 890. — [6] Also mōṅhī. — [7] i. e. wk. form, *masmadī from
mṇ-s-madī. — [8] §§ 71, 179. — [9] § 171. — [10] § 158 -i- + s. — [11] § 165 -ṇ + s.

ii. MIDDLE.

Av	Singular:	cf. Skt.
1. paṁh-e, mḯngh-ai¹	. .	mḁs-āi
2. paṁh-ahe²	. . . .	mḁs-ase
3. varǰ-aitē³	. . .	mḁs-ate
	Plural:	
2. ·dáṁh-ōdūm¹	. . .	dās-adhvam
3. vaḱṣ-ontē⁵	. .	vakṣ-ante

§ 659.   4. Optative.
i. ACTIVE.

Av.	Plural:	cf. Skt.
1. nāṣ̌-īma (YAv.)⁶	. . . . .	—

§ 660.   5. Participle.

ii. MIDDLE.	(V)Av. maṁh-āna-⁷	. . .	—⁸
	(G)Av. diš-əmna-⁹	. . .	dhiṣ-amā́na- (RV.)

Forms to be observed.

§ 661. GAv. rā́-phaṁh-āi 'thou wilt give 2 sg. subjunctive mid. Vra-, cf. YAv. paṁhahe (in paradigm).

Note. GAv. mḯngāi (above) is by transfer thematic like Skt. mḁsāi cf. § 663.

5. ha- (sa-) Aorist.
(Cf. Whitney, Skt. Gram. § 916 seq.)

§ 662. The orig. sa-aorist (= Av. ha, ṡha) in Av. is really only a variety of the preceding s-aorist. It arises by transfer of the s-aorist to the a-inflection.

§ 663. Examples of the ha- (sa-) aorist inflection are the following:

   1. Indicative. i. ACT. Sg. 3. YAv. asʲṣ-a-ṭ 'he fulfilled, offered' (Vanh- above § 656) Vd. 19.15 = Skt. á-chant-s-at.

   2. Imperative. i. ACT. Pl. 3. YAv. jaṽhəṇtu 'they will smite' (Vjan-) Vd. 2.22.

---

¹ themat. § 661. — ² Yt. 8.1. — ³ § 165. — ⁴ Ys. 45.7, cf. § 30, ā = a.
— ⁵ Vat- Say. coll. — ⁶ Ys. 70.4, vra- = orig. -s + s. — ⁷ Yt. 8.47.
— ⁸ Cf. Whitney, Skt. Gram. § 897. — ⁹ themat. Ys. 51.1.

3. **Subjunctive. i. ACT. Sg.** 3. YAv. *nāṣ-ā-iti* 'will disappear' Yt. 2.11 (√*i naś-* = Skt. √*i naś-* § 158); *jahāṭ* Ny. 1.1.—**ii. MID.** YAv. *nāṣ-ā-ite*. Likewise here 1 sg. subj. mid. *maṅghāi* above § 661.

5. **Participle. ii. MID.** GAv. *hinaoṣ-əmna-* (√*hinu-* 'to gratify'), *diṣəmna* above in paradigm § 660.

6. *iṣ*-Aorist.
(Cf. Whitney, *Skt. Gram.* § 898 seq.)

§ 664. One or two instances (GAv.) of the *iṣ*-aorist —see Whitney, *Skt. Gram.* § 898—are quotable. They are from √*kū-*, *ciū-* 'look for, hope', √*hṣnu-* 'gratify, delight':—

1. **Indic. ii. MID. Aor. (pret.). Sg.** 1. *cīv-īṣ-ī* (on long -*ī*- after *v* see § 20). 3. *cīv-īṣ-tā*.
3. **Subjunct. i. ACT. Sg.** 1. *hṣnəv-īṣ-ā*.

7. *hiṣ*-Aorist.
(Cf. Whitney, *Skt. Gram.* § 911.)

§ 665. An instance (YAv.) of the *hiṣ-* (*siṣ-*) aorist is apparently the following:

1. **Indic. i. ACT. Sg.** 2. *°dā-hiṣ* 'thou hast made' (√*dā-*) Yt. 3.2 cf. Skt. *g'āsīs*, Whitney, *Skt. Gram.* §§ 912, 913.

§ 666. No certain instance of a **precative** seems to be found in Avesta.

Aorist Passive, third Singular.
(Cf. Whitney, *Skt. Gram.* § 842.)

§ 667. In Av. as in Skt. an aor. 3rd. singular in -*i* with passive meaning occurs, though it is not of common use. The form is made by adding *i* to the verbal root which has either the vṛddhi or guṇa strengthening. The form may take the augment as in Skt.

§ 668. Examples of 3rd. sg. Aor. Pass. are the following:—

(a) With vṛddhi.—From Av. √*vac-* 'speak, call' *vācī*, *avācī* (GAv.) = Skt. *vācī*, *avācī*; Av. √*sru-* 'hear, call' *srāvī* (GAv.) = Skt. *srāvi*; so Av. *āidi* 'is said, spoken of' √*ad-* (so Geldner) = Skt.

ah- — (b) With guṇa (or middle) form. — From Av. √*mrū-* 'say' *mraoi* (GAv. i. e. *mravī-*), Av. √*vaē-* 'understand' *vaēdī* (GAv.), Av. √*jan-* 'slay' *jaini* (YAv.).

Note. The form YAv. *us̆ạ̄vi* 'it was granted, obtained' (√*ar-*) is made, not directly from the root, but from the prepared stem *ərə-nu-, ərə-nāu-*.

IV. FUTURE-SYSTEM.
Future.
(Cf. Whitney, *Skt. Gram.* § 932 seq.)

§ 669. The characteristic mark of the future in Avesta as in Sanskrit is *-hy-* (*-šy-* § 133) = Skt. *-sy- (-ṣy-)* added to the root. The root assumes the guṇa-form; the inflection is thematic (*-hya, -šya*). — Cf. Whitney, *Skt. Gram.* § 932 seq.

Modes of the Future.

§ 670. The instances of the future are in general not very numerous; they are confined to the indicative mode and to the participle. The place of the other modes is often taken by a subjunctive of other parts of the verb used in a future sense. Cf. Whitney, *Skt. Gram.* § 938.

Future Formation and Inflection.

§ 671. Examples of future formation and inflection are taken from the following roots. Cf. Whitney, *Skt. Gram.* § 953.

Av. √*vac-* 'to speak' = Skt. √*vac-*; Av. √*harz-* 'let go, drop' Skt. √*sṛj-*; Av. √*sū-* 'further, save' = Skt. √*sā-*.

§ 672. 1. **Indicative.** — Future.

i. ACTIVE

	Av. Singular:	cf. Skt.
1.	*vaχ-šy-ā* (GAv.)	*vakṣy-āmi*

ii. MIDDLE.

	Singular:	
3.	*vaχ šy-eite*[1]	*vakṣy-áte*

	Plural:	
3.	*harə-šy-eṇte*[2]	*sarkṣy-aṇte*[3]

---

[1] Ys. 19.10; Vsp. 15.3. — [2] Vsp. 12.1. On *z + s* see § 165. — [3] Cf. Skt. *varkṣyanti* from √*vṛj-*.

§ 673.   **2. Participle.**
i. ACTIVE. Av. *sao-šy-ant-* . . . . cf. Skt. *kṣa-sy-ánt-*
ii. MIDDLE. *harᵊ-šy-amna-* . . . . . *yak-sy-amāna-*

Forms to be observed.

§ 674. Notice the long vowel instead of strengthening in the Av. participles *bū-šy-ant-* from √*bū-*, opp. to Skt. *bhav-i-syánt-* (§ 61 Note 2), cf. Skt. RV. *sū-sy-ant-*. Observe also *hrvī-šy-ant-* beside *hrvī-šy-ant-* from √*hrvī-* 'be raw, bloody'.

V. SECONDARY CONJUGATIONS.

§ 675. The secondary conjugations consist of the following formations (thematic), a. Passive, b. Causative, c. Denominative, d. Inchoative, e. Desiderative, and f. Intensive (unthematic).

A. Passive.
(Cf. Whitney, *Skt. Gram.* § 768 seq.)

§ 676. **General Remark.** The passive force may be given in any tense-system simply by employing the middle voice in a passive sense. In the present-system, however, there is also a formative passive made by means of the passive sign *-ya-* (cf. Cl. 4) attached to the prepared root.

Note. The connection between this formative passive in *ya* and Cl. 4 of the present-system is generally acknowledged. In Skt. the difference of accent distinguishes the two, the passive having accented *yá*, but Cl. 4 an unaccented *ya*. As no written accent is found in Av., such a distinction cannot always be sharply drawn; it is therefore sometimes doubtful whether a given form is really a passive or merely a middle used with passive sense, e. g. *manyete* (pass.) Ys. 44.12 identical in form with *manyete* (mid.) Yt. 10.139 = Skt. *manyáte, mányate*.

§ 677 **Formation of the Passive.** The passive sign is *-ya-* (= Skt. accented *-yá-*) attached to the root which then assumes the weak form.

Note. The *ar*-roots require some remark as they frequently show MS. variations as to the way in which the radical *r*-vowel is expressed: e. g. Av. √*mar-* 'to die', *mir-ye-iti*, *mir-ye-ite*, *maṛᵊ-ye-iti*, *maĩr-ye-ite* Vd. 3.33 = Skt. *mriyáte;* again Av. √*kar-* 'to make', *kir-ye-iti* Yt. 10.109, *kir-ye-iṇte* v. l. *kair-ye-iṇte* Vd. 3.9, cf. § 48 above. The development in such cases evidently is

$$*mṛ-ya-te$$

| Av. *mar-va-te* (or -*aīr*- § 48) | Skt. *mr-i-yá-tē* |
| or *mir-ya-te* (-*ir*- § 70) | *mr-i-yá-te* |

§ 678. Endings. In Skt. the passive form assumes the middle endings, but some exceptions with active endings occur, cf. Whitney, *Skt. Gram.* § 774. In Av. also, the middle endings are used but the active ones likewise are not very uncommon. Observe especially the MS. variants in final *e, i* (§ 35 Note 2) *kiryeiti, kiryeite*. The intransitive passive force seems therefore to lie in the *ya*-element.

Note. An undoubted example of act. ending but passive force is *frā-yez-yāṭ* in Yt. 13.50 *kahe vā urvā* (nom. masc.) *frāvezyāṭ* 'of which one of you will the soul be worshipped?' Apparently also with active ending (from √*dā*-) *dayāṭ* (subjunct.) Vd. 3.32, *ni-dayaṭ* (impf.) Yt. 12.17.

Modes of the Passive.

§ 679. The modes of the passive are the usual ones of the present-system; a complete list of forms, however, cannot be gathered from the texts.

Passive Inflection.

§ 680. Examples of passive voice with middle and active endings are the following:

1. **Indicative. a. Pres. Sg. 3.** *bairyeite* v. l. *bairyeiti* 'he is borne', *kiryeiti* v. l. *kiryeite* 'it is made'; **Pl. 3.** *kiryeiṇte* v. l. *kairyeiṇte* 'they are made' (§ 48).— **Pret. Sg. 2.** *maiṛyauha* 'didst die' v. l. *marəyauha*, **3.** *vī-sruyata* 'was heard', *ni-dayaṭ* 'was placed'.

3. **Subjunctive. Sg. 3.** *mairyāite* v. l. *miryaite, miryāiti* 'is destroyed, dies'; *yezyāṭ* 'is worshipped'; **Pl. 3.** *bairyāṇte* 'they will be borne', *janyāṇte* 'they will be slain' Yt. 14.43.

5. **Participle.** Av. *suyamna*- 'being advanced, saved'.

Note. From √*var*- 'to cover' is found a form *ni-vōir-ye-ite* (v. l. •*ti*), —on *ō*, cf. § 39.

§ 681. A Perf. Pass. Participle in -*ta* or -*na* also belongs to the passive conjugation. See § 710 below.

§ 682. A Fut. Pass. Participle (Gerundive) in *ya-* is formed according to § 716 below.

§ 683. The Aorist Passive 3rd. Singular likewise falls under this formation. It is treated above, § 668.

B. Causative.

§ 684. **General Remark.** In Av. as in Skt. the causative *(-aya-)*, like the Denominative is identical in form with Cl. 10, the latter being originally a causative formation. The causal is found in the Present-System.

Note. In Skt. many of the so-called causatives do not have a strict causative value and are therefore reckoned as belonging to the Skt. *cur*-Class (10); similarly in Av., a number of causative forms have been treated above under Class 10, cf. § 482 seq.

§ 685. **Formation.** The present-stem of the causative is formed by adding the causal formative element *-aya-* to the root which is usually strengthened. The strengthening of the root is subject to certain variations.

a. Internal or initial *a* before a single consonant is generally lengthened (vṛddhi), but sometimes it remains unchanged, thus: Lengthened *ā*, Av. √*vat-* 'to comprehend', caus. 'make known' *vātaya-* = Skt. *vātáya-*; Av. √*tap-* 'to warm, be warm', caus. 'make warm' *tāpaya-* = Skt. *tāpáya-*; Av. √*gam-, jam-* 'go, come' *jāmaya-* = Skt. *gāmáya-* (Whitney, *Skt. Gram.* § 1042 g).—Unchanged *a*. Av. √*pat-* 'to fall, fly' *pataya-* = Skt. *patáya-*; Av. √*sad-* 'appear' *sadaya-* = Skt. *chadáya-*; Av. √*ap-* 'obtain', *apaya-*, opp. to Skt. *āpáya-*.

b. Internal and initial *a* before two consonants (i. e. long by position) remains unchanged: Av. √*dakš-* 'to know, cause to know' *dakšaya-* = Skt. *dakšáya-*; Av. √*vakš-* 'grow, cause to grow' *vakšaya-* = Skt. *vakšáya-*; Av. √*band-* 'bind' *bandaya-* = Skt. *bandháya-*; Av. √*zamb-* 'crush' *zambaya-* = Skt. *jambháya-*.

c. Final long *ā* disappears: Av. √*stā-* 'to stand, cause to stand' *staya-* opp. to Skt. *sthāpáya-*, cf. Whitney, *Skt. Gram.* § 1042 i.

d. Internal or initial *i, u* before single consonants (i. e. in light syllables) have the guṇa-strengthening: Av. √*vid-* 'to know', caus. 'inform' *vaēdaya-* = Skt. *vedáya-*; Av. √*ruc-* 'light up' *raocaya-* = Skt. *rocáya-*.

c. Final *n* (or *i*) receives the vṛddhi-strengthening: Av. √*sru*- to hear' *srāvaya*- = Skt. *śrāvaya*-.

Note 1. The nasal of the present-stem (Cl. 9) appears in Av. *kərəntaya*- from √*kart*- 'to cut' as in Skt. *kṛntáya*-, cf. Whitney, *Skt. Gram.* § 1042 h. So also Av. *bunjaya*- from √*buj*- 'to release'.

Note 2. The root *zā*- 'to let go' makes *zayaya*-, cf. Whitney, *Skt. Gram.* § 1042.

Note 3. Observe with lengthening instead of strengthening of root (§ 61 Note) GAv. *ūrūpayeiṇtī* 'they cause pain' (√*rup*-) = Skt. *ropáyantī*; GAv. *ūrūdōyatā* 'he caused to lament' = Skt. *rudháyata*.

Modes of the Causative.

§ 686. The Causative shows the same modes, 1 Indicative, 2 Imperative, 3. Subjunctive, 4. Optative, including also 5. Participle, as the present-system naturally does.

Inflection of the Causative: Present-System.

§ 687. The causal in the present-system is inflected after the *a*-conjugation (thematic), see Cl. 10 above, §§ 481, 482 seq.

Other Causative Formations.

§ 688. To the causal formation belongs not only the causative of the present-system, but also a causal aorist (see § 652); possibly likewise a causative perfect (pluperfect), and some other parts.

§ 689. On the reduplicated Causative Aorist, see § 652 above.

§ 690. Possibly here belongs as Periphrastic Perfect (Plupf.), Av. *viwirāwha* 'he had frightened', see § 623

§ 691. A causal derivative from √*hwap*- 'to sleep' is made by attaching the root *dā*- 'to make, do' in its causal form directly to the radical element; thus, Av. *ẋwabdayeiti* 'puts to sleep'.

§ 692. Other causative derivatives made with root *dā*- (cf. § 691) but without causal form, are *ava-whab-ḍaitā* 'he would cause to sleep' (√*hwap*-), *hraoidat* 'caused to howl' (√*hrus*-), *yaoždāiti* 'makes pure' (√*yaož*-).

§ 693. Some forms with causal signification but without the *aya*-formation occur: Av. *vaxṣat* 'he caused to grow' Ys. 48.6 opp. to *vaxš-ayu-tā* 'they both cause to grow' Ys. 10.3.

§ 694. An occasional verbal noun (infinitive) or adjective (participle) is likewise to be noted under the causal formation: Av. *frasruta*- 'made famous, renowned', *urvaēšta*- 'turned' Ys. 11.2. Cf. Whitney, *Skt. Gram.* § 1051 seq.

C. Denominative.
(Cf. Whitney, *Skt. Gram.* § 1053 seq.)

§ 695. Denominative verbs are formed from a noun-stem (substantive or adjective) by adding -*ya* or -*a* = Skt. -*yá* or -*a* to the stem. In Skt. the -*yá* is accented, but as there is no written accent in Av., it is sometimes hard to decide whether a certain given verb-form in -*aya* be really a denominative from an *a*-stem or not rather simply a causative. As to meaning, the denominative usually signifies 'to make, use, cause, be, or practise' that which the noun-stem itself denotes.

§ 696. Formation and Inflection. The denominative is found in the Present-System and is made 1. by adding -*ya* (= Skt. -*yá*), or more rarely 2. -*a* (= Skt. -*a*) directly to a noun-stem. The inflection is therefore that of the present-system *a*-conjugation (thematic).—Cf. Whitney, *Skt. Gram.* §§ 1054, 1068.

1. *ya* added: Av. *aša*- n. 'holiness' (*a*-stem) denom. *aša-ya*- 'to gain by holiness', *ašayeiti* = Skt. *ṛtáyá-*; Av. *vāra*- m. 'rain' denom. *vāra-ye-mi* 'I rain down';—Av. *ahu*- m. 'lord' (*u*-stem) denom. *ahu-ya*- 'to become lord of', *ahuyāite*;—Av. *namah*- n. 'homage' (cons. stem) denom. *namah-ya*- 'do homage' *namohyāmahī* = Skt. *namasyá-*;—Av. *ižud*- f. 'debt' (cons. stem) denom. *ižud-ya*- 'incur a debt', *ižudyāmahī* = Skt. *iṣudhyá-*.

2. Simple *a* added: Av. *paiti*- 'lord' (*i*-stem) denom. *paipy-a*- 'to possess as lord', *paipyeiti* = Skt. *pátya-*;—Av. *hratu*- m. 'wisdom' (*u*-stem) denom. *hrapw-a*- 'be wise', ptcpl. mid. *hrapwəmnahe* 'of him that is wise';—Av. *fyanhu*- m. 'mist' (*u*-stem) denom. *fyanhv-a*- 'to fall as mist', *fyanhuṇtaē-ca* (§§ 63, 493, 582);—Av. *aēnah*- n. 'sin' (cons. stem) denom. *aēnavh-a*- 'to commit sin', *aēnavhaiti* Ys. 9.29 opp. Skt. *ēnas-yá-*.

Note. Final *a* of a noun-stem seems occasionally to disappear (cf. in Skt. after *n* or *r*, Whitney, *Skt. Gram.* § 1059 e). Thus, Av. *baēšaz-ya-ti* etc. 'he practises healing' Yt. 8.43 (*baēšaza*- n.), *vāstryaē-ta* 'let him pasture' (*vāstra*- n.), *parəsan-ye-iti* 'he asks' Yt. 8.15. So probably also

Av. *paçvaiti* 'he lights' (*pajana-* n., *pajnā-* f.), cf. Skt. *pŗtanyati*, Whitney, *Skt. Gram.* § 1060.

D. Inchoative.
(Cf. Whitney, *Skt. Gram.* §§ 608, 747.)

§ 697. The existence of the inchoative in Av., as in Skt., is shown by a few verbs. The inchoative sign is *s* = Skt. *ch* (§ 142) added directly to the root in its weak stage. The thematic *a*-inflection is then assumed. The instances of inchoative are comparatively so few that these inchoative *s*-forms have sometimes been reckoned as independent roots.

§ 698. **Examples of Inchoatives.** The formation and inflection is shown by the following instances.

Av. √*gam-*, *jas-* (i. e. *gm̥-s-*) 'to go, come' *ja-s-a-iti*, cf. βάσκω = Skt. *gá-ch-a-ti*; Av. √*yam-*, *yas-* (i. e. *ym̥-s-*) 'come, reach' *yu-s-a-ite* = Skt. *yá-ch-a-te*; Av. √*fras-*, *parəs-* (i. e. *pr̥s-s-*) 'ask' *parə-s-aite*, cf. Lat. *po(r)scit* = Skt. *pŗ-ch-a-ti*; Av. √*vah-*, *us-* (i. e. *us-s-*) 'to light up' *us-a-iti* = Skt. *ucháti*; Av. √*tap-*, *tafs-* 'to warm, grow warm' *taf-s-a-t*, cf. Lat. *tepesco*. Also a few others.

Note. Observe the assimilation and loss of consonants before *s* in the following examples: Av. *tarəsaiti* 'he trembles' (i. e. *tarəs-s-aiti), cf. Skt. √*tras-*; Av. *usaiti* just above § 698. So Av. *hisņt* 'he began to sweat' √*ivid-* = Skt. √*svid-*. See §§ 184, 185 above.

E. Desiderative.
(Cf. Whitney, *Skt. Gram.* § 1026 seq.)

§ 699. The desiderative in Av. resembles the Skt. in formation and signification. The root is reduplicated and the formative element -*ha* (-*wha*, -*ja*, -*za*) = Skt. -*sa* as desiderative sign is added. The vowel of the reduplicated syllable is always -*i*- (-*i*- § 21 Note); the initial consonant of the root in reduplicating follows the usual rules above § 465.

The root of the desiderative appears ordinarily in its weak grade, sometimes, however, in its strong (middle) form. The desiderative is confined to the present-system; the inflection (-ḥa, -sa) is thematic.

§ 700. **Examples of Desiderative Formation.** The instances of the desiderative are not very numerous; the following may be noted.

Av. √ji- 'to conquer, win', desid. jī-ji-ṣa- 'seek to win over' = Skt. ji-jī-ṣa-; Av. √hṣnu- 'gratify, rejoice', desid. ci-hṣnu-ṣa-, Av. √zna- 'know', desid. zi-hṣnā̊-vha- (§§ 164, 465 Note 2) = Skt. ji-jñā-sa-; Av. √dab- 'deceive', desid. GAv. di-w-ža- (i. e. di-dbh-ža § 89) 'seek to deceive' = Skt. dipsa-; Av. √sac- 'teach, learn, can', desid. sīṣa- (i. e. *si-šk-sa-) = Skt. śi-k-ṣa-. Likewise a few other forms, e. g. dīdərəṣa- from √darz- 'make firm', mimaxṣa- from √manj- 'magnify', vīvarəṣa- from √varz- 'do'.

§ 701. **Examples of Inflection.** These are confined to the present-system thematic.

1. Indicative. a. Pres. i. ACT. Pl. 3. GAv. jī-ji-ṣəṇtī Ys. 39.1.—ii. MID. Pl. 2. di-draẓ-židuyē Ys. 48.7.—b. Pret i. ACT. Sg. 2. ci-hṣnu-šō Ys. 45.9.—ii. MID. Sg. 3. di darə-ṣatā 'he held back' (√dar-).
2. Imperative. i. ACT. Sg. 3. GAv. vī-vəŋgha-tū 'let him seek to surpass' (√van-).—ii. MID. Sg. 2. YAv. mi-marəẏ-ṣanuha.
3. Subjunctive. i. ACT. Sg. 1. GAv. ci-hṣnu-ṣa Ys. 49.1; 3. YAv. jī-ji-ṣā-iti.—ii. MID. Sg. 3. mi-marəẏ-ṣā-ite.
5. Participle. i. ACT. GAv. ci-hṣnu-ṣaṇt- Ys. 43.15.—ii. MID. YAv. zi-hṣnā̊-vhəmna- § 465 Note 2.

Note. A Perf. Participle of the desid. Act. is jaḫṣavā̊ 'having the desire to slay' (√jan-) ZPhl. Glossary p. 92.

F. Intensive.

(Cf. Whitney, Skt. Gram. § 1000 seq.)

§ 702. The characteristic features of the Intensive are reduplication and the unthematic inflection. In formation, the Intensive in Av., as in Skt., closely resembles the reduplicating class (Cl. 3) of the present-system; it is distinguished from Cl. 3 by having a strengthened reduplicated syllable.

§ 703. As regards the reduplication, the formation of the Intensive in Av. is twofold.

1. The reduplicated syllable is made by repeating the initial consonant followed by the radical vowel in a strengthened form (*a* being strengthened to *ā*, —*i* to *aē*, *ōi*; —*u* to *ao*). — Cf. Whitney, *Skt. Gram.* § 1002.

2. The reduplicated syllable is made by repeating the entire root. — Cf. Whitney, *Skt. Gram.* § 1002 ii.

§ 704. As regards the radical syllable itself, this assumes sometimes the strong form, sometimes the weak grade, according to the person or the mode in which it is found. The inflection as stated above is unthematic.

§ 705. Examples of Formation. As instances to illustrate the Intensive formation the following may be taken:

1. Strengthened Reduplication: Av. √*part*- 'to fight', intens. *pā-parət-*; — Av. √*dis*- 'show, teach' *daē-dōis-*, *daē-dis-* = Skt. *dē-dēś-*, *dē-diś-*; Av. √*vid*- 'find' *vōi-vid-* = Skt. *vē-vid-*; — Av. √*zū*- 'call' *zao-zao-* = Skt. *jō-hav-*.

2. Repeated Root: Av. √*dar*- 'to tear' *dar-dar-* = Skt. *dar-dar-*. Av. √*kar*- 'make' *car-kərə-* = Skt. *cár-kr-*; Av. √*žar*- 'stream, flow' *žar-žarə-* (in participle) opp. Skt. *cá-kṣar-*.

Note. An intensive with the *ya*-inflection (Cl. 4 thematic) is to be found in the following instance: Av. √*raē*- 'to wound', GAv. *rā-rəš-yeiṇtī* (indic.) Ys. 47.4; *rā-rəš-yąn* (subjunct.) Ys. 32.11; YAv. *rā-rəš-ya-ṇtō* (nom. pl. ptcpl.) Yt. 11.6; but un-thematic GAv. *ra-rəš-ō* (ptcpl.) Ys. 49.2 cf. Skt. *rā-rakṣ-*; see also Whitney, *Skt. Gram.* § 1016. Similarly, Av. √*yah*- 'be heated, boil' *vaēyu*- (i. e. *ya-uš-ya-*) in the ptcpl. *vaēyaṇt-* = Skt. *yā-yas-*.

§ 706. Examples of Inflection. These are confined to the present-system unthematic, and they are mostly from GAv. Thus:

1. Indicative. a. Pres. i. ACT. Sg. 1. GAv. *zao-zao-mī*; Pl. 1. GAv. *carə-karə-mahī* Ys. 58.4. — ii. MID. Sg. 1. GAv. *vōi-vid-ē*. —
b. Pret. Sg. 3. *daē-dōiš-t*.

4. Optative. i. ACT. Sg. 3. YAv. *darə-dair-yāṭ* (with str. rad. stem -*dar*- instead of expected wk. -*dərə*-).

5. Participle. i. ACT. YAv. *žarə-žar-aṇt-* (*a*-inflect.).

§ 707. Transfers to the *a*-inflection are found, e. g. Indic. Pres. 3 sg. act. YAv. *naē-niž-aiti* 'it removes', et al.

VI. VERBAL ABSTRACT FORMS.
Participle, Gerund, Infinitive.

§ 708. To the verbal system there also belong the Participle or verbal adjective, the Gerund, with Gerundive, and the Infinitive or verbal noun.

A. Participle.
1. Participle in -*aṇt*, -*at* (Act.); -*mna*, -*āna* (Mid.).
(Cf. Whitney, *Skt. Gram.* §§ 583, 584 etc.)

§ 709. Participial forms in -*aṇt*, -*at* (i. e. -*ṇt*), fem. -*aiṇtī*, -*aitī* in the Active, and forms in -*mna*, -*āna* (-*āna*) in the Middle, are found in each tense-system. As these attach themselves directly rather to the tense-systems, they have been discussed above under the respective systems, cf. §§ 488, 533 etc.

2. Passive Participle in -*ta*.
(Cf. Whitney, *Skt. Gram.* § 952 seq.)

§ 710. A passive participle or past passive participle, is made in Av., as in Skt., by adding the suffix -*ta* = Skt. -*tá* (accented) directly to the verbal root, which is subject however to certain euphonic changes. This verbal adjective in -*ta* (m. n.), -*tā* (f) is regularly declined according to the *a*-declension §§ 236, 243. Examples of the formation are Av. *pāta-* 'protected' (√*pā-*) = Skt. *pātá-*; Av. *gərəpta-* 'grasped' (√*garə-* § 74) = Skt. *gṛbhītá*; Av. *druhta-* 'deceived' (√*druj-* § 90) = Skt. *drugdhá-*.

§ 711. Treatment of the Root before -*ta*. The form of the root is subject to modification and is liable to vary before the added suffix. The following points may be noted:—

> 1. The root very commonly (but not always) shows the weak form, if it has one, before -*ta*; a penultimate nasal is accordingly dropped. Thus, with weak form, from Av. √*vac-* 'to speak' ptcpl. *uḫta-* = Skt. *uktá-*; Av. √*hu-* 'press out' *huta-* = Skt. *sutá-*; —Av. √*panj-* 'draw, drive' *paḫta-*; Av. √*vanj-* 'encircle' *vaḫta-* =

Skt. *srakt³-*; Av. |/*kay.t-* 'to bind' *ba-ta-* (§ 151) = Skt. *baddha-*. Strong form or unchanged, Av. |/*dā-* 'to place' *dāta-* opp. Skt. *hita-*; Av. |/*taš-* 'cut, form' *tašta-* = Skt. *taṣṭá-*.

2. Roots in final *-a* retain this. Thus, Av. |/*stā-* 'to stand' *stāta-* opp. Skt. *sthitá-*; Av. |/*dā-* 'place' opp. Skt. *hitá-*; Av. |/*snā-* 'bathe' = Skt. *snātá-*; Av. |/*pā-* 'protect' = Skt. *pātá-*.

3. Roots in *-ar* often show MS. variations between *-ərəta* and *-arəta*, cf. § 47 Note. Thus, Av. |/*bar-* 'to bear' *bərəta-*, *barəta-* (e. g. Ys. 62.9) = Skt. *bhṛtá-*; Av. |/*star-* 'stretch, strew' *frastərəta-*, *frastarəta-*.

4. Roots in *-an*, *-am* in Av., as in Skt., often form *-ata* (i. e. *-ṇta̱*, *-ṇtá*); sometimes they show *-āta*. Thus, Av. |/*jan-* 'to slay' *jata-* = Skt. *hatá-*; Av. |/*man-* 'think' *mata-* = Skt. *matá-*; Av. |/*gam-* 'go' *gata-* = Skt. *gatá-*; Av. *zan-* 'beget, bear' *zāta-* = Skt. *jātá-*.

5. But roots in *-an*, *-am* often retain the nasal (*m* being assimilated to *n* before *t*). Thus, Av. |/*kan-* 'to dig' *•kanta-* (cf. also *kata-*) opp. Skt. *khātá-*; Av. |/*zan-* 'know' *•zanta-*; Av. |/*gram-* 'be angry' *granta-*.

6. Sometimes a radical short *u* appears as long *ū* before *-ta*, cf. § 20. Thus, Av. |/*sru-* 'to hear' *srūta-* = Skt. *śrutá-*; Av. |/*dru-* 'run' *drūta-* = Skt. *drutá-*.

§ 712. The past participle in *-ita*, although common in Skt., hardly appears in Av.; the instances Av. *darśita-* Ys. 57.11 = Skt. *dhṛṣitá-*, Av. *raodita-*, *zairita-* are best treated under Suffixes below, § 786 Note 1.

3. Passive Participle in *-na*.
(Cf. Whitney, Skt. Gram. § 952.)

§ 713. The *na*-formation of the passive participle is very rare in Avesta. The instances are hardly distinguishable from adjectives. As examples may be given, Av. | *tan-* 'to stretch' *us-tāna-* 'upstretched' = Skt. *uttāná-*; Av. |/*ū-* 'be wanting' *ūna-* = Skt. *ūná-*; Av. |/*par-* 'fill' *pərəna-* = Skt. *pūrṇá-*.

4. Perfect Active Participle in *-vah*.
(Cf. Whitney, Skt. Gram. § 802.)

§ 714. The formation of the Perf. Act. Participle has been treated above under the Perfect system, see §§ 611, 618, 399.

5. Perfect Middle Participle in -āna, -āna.
(Cf. Whitney, *Skt. Gram.* § 806.)

§ 715. On the formation of the Perf. Mid. Participle, see above under Perfect-System, §§ 611, 618.

B. Gerundive and Gerund.

1. Gerundive: (a) Fut. Pass. Participle in -ya (declined).
(Cf. Whitney, *Skt. Gram.* § 961.)

§ 716. A declined derivative adjective with verbal force is made from some verbs by attaching the formative element -*ya* to the root. Such an adjective is regularly inflected according to the *a*-declension. In meaning, it often corresponds to the Latin form in -*ndus*; it is therefore commonly called a gerundive or future passive participle.

>Examples are from Av. √iš- 'to wish', a gerundive (vbl. adj.) išya- = Skt. *išya-;* Av. √karš- 'draw furrows, plow' karšya- = Skt. *kṛṣya-;* Av. √var- 'choose, believe' vairya- = Skt. *várya-.* Other instances occur.

2. Gerundive: (b) Fut. Pass. Participle in -tva, -ƥwa (declined).
(Cf. Whitney, *Skt. Gram.* § 966 a.)

§ 717. A declined derivative adjective of like signification (-*ndus*) with the preceding (§ 716) is made by adding -*tva, -ƥwa, -ðwa* (§§ 94. 96; see also under Suffixes) directly to the root in its strong form. Such a verbal adjective is regularly inflected after the *a*-declension.

>Examples are: Av. *jaƥwa-* 'worthy to be killed' (√*jan-*) = Skt. *hántva-;* Av. *ḣšnaoƥwa-* 'worthy to be satisfied' (√*kšnu-*); Av. *varštva-* 'to be done' (√*varz-*), *maƥwa-* 'to be thought', *vaḣƥwa-* 'to be spoken'.

3. Gerund (Absolutive) in -ya (indeclinable).
(Cf. Whitney, *Skt. Gram.* § 989 seq.)

§ 718. A species of Gerund or Absolute (indeclinable) in -*ya* seems to occur in the following instances with *daíƥe:* Av. *aibigaírya* 'seizing' = Skt. °*gīrya;* Av. *paítiricya* 'throwing away'. But cf. Bartholomae in *B.B.* xv. 237.

C. Infinitive.

(Cf. Whitney, *Skt. Gram.* §§ 538, 968.)

§ 719. The Infinitive is a verbal noun, an abstract derived from a verb. It is formed either directly from the root, or sometimes from a tense-stem. Such a derivative noun is used with an infinitival or a semi-infinitival force. The noun form is found most often in the dative case; sometimes, however, in other cases. The abstracts used as infinitives are most commonly cases of a substantive stem made by means of the suffix *-di, -ti, -ah*; less often they are formed from stems in *-man, -van, -a*; or they are from suffixless stems.

§ 720. Examples of Infinitives or Verbal Nouns so used, are the following. Cf. also Whitney, *Skt. Gram.* § 970.

1. **Ending Av.** *-dyāi, -dyāi* **dative = Skt.** *-dhyāi.*
(Chiefly GAv.; rare YAv.)

From root: GAv. *dərədyāi* 'for holding' ($\sqrt{dar}$-). — From pres. stem: GAv. *vərəzyeidyāi* 'to work', YAv. *vazaidyāi* 'for driving' ($\sqrt{vaz}$-) Yt. 15.28, *srāvayeitȳāi* 'to proclaim' Yt. 24.46.

2. **Ending Av.** *-tēe, -tayaē-ca* **dative = Skt.** *-taye.*
(Only YAv., but frequent.)

From root: YAv. *anu-matēe, anu-matayaē-ca* (§ 254) 'to think, according to' ($\sqrt{man}$-) = Skt. *ánu-mataye*; Av. *kərətēe* 'for making' ($\sqrt{kar}$-) = Skt. *kŕ̥taye*; Av. *bərətēe* 'for bearing', etc.

3. **Ending Av.** *-avhe* **dative = Skt.** *-ase.*
(Chiefly GAv.)

From pres. stem: GAv. *vaēnavhē* 'to see' ($\sqrt{vaēn}$-), *srāvayeŋhē* 'to repeat' ($\sqrt{sru}$-, causal), GAv. *avaŋhē*, GAv. *avaiŋhe, avuŋhaē-ca* 'to aid' ($\sqrt{av}$-). — From aor. stem redupl., GAv. *vaocaŋhē* 'to speak' ($\sqrt{vac}$-).

4. **Ending Av.** *-maine, -vaine* **dative = Skt.** *-mane, -vane.*
(GAv. and YAv.)

From pres. stem: YAv. *staomaine* 'for praising' ($\sqrt{stu}$-), GAv. *vidvanōi* 'to know' ($\sqrt{vid}$-) § 56. Also a couple of others.

5. **Ending Av. -āi dative** (*a*-decl.) = Skt. *āi*.
(GAv. and YAv.)

From root: YAv. *jayāi* 'to win' (√*ji*-). — From stem: GYAv. *fradapāi* 'to promote' (√*dā*-).

6. **Ending Av. -ē dative** (radical) = Skt. -*ē*.
(Chiefly GAv.)

From root: GAv. *darᵊsōi* 'to see' (√*dars*-), *suyē*, *savōi* 'to profit, save' (√*su*-), *pōi* 'to protect'.

7. **Ending -*te* locative.**
(GAv. and YAv.)

From root: GAv. *āitē* 'to go to' (√*i*-) Ys. 31.9. — From stem: YAv. *daste* 'to put, make' Vsp. 15.1.

§ 721. A number of other formations in the acc., gen., loc., cases of abstract nouns may be regarded as infinitives. For examples, see Geldner, in *K.Z.* xxvii. p. 226; Bartholomae, in *K.Z.* xxviii. p. 17, *B.B.* xv. p. 215 seq.

VII. PERIPHRASTIC VERBAL PHRASES.

§ 722. In the Av., there is an inclination occasionally to use periphrastic phrases made up by means of an adj., a participle or a noun, with a copula verb or auxiliary, instead of a regularly formed tense-stem. The auxiliary may sometimes even be omitted. The periphrastic phrase is chiefly found in YAv.; its presence, however, is recognized in GAv. — Cf. Whitney, *Skt. Gram.* § 1069 seq.

§ 723. The possible existence of a Periphrastic Perfect has been noted above, § 623.

§ 724. A number of Periphrastic Expressions made by means of an adjective, a participle, or a noun combined with a verb, deserve special mention.

1. Periphrastic with Av. √*i*- 'to go' = Skt. √*i*-, cf. Whitney, *Skt. Gram.* § 1075 a. GAv. *stavas ayenī* 'I shall praise' Ys. 50.9.

2. With Av. √*āh*- 'sit' = Skt. √*ās*-, and Av. √*stā*- 'stand' = Skt. √*sthā*-, cf. Whitney, *Skt. Gram.* § 1075 c. YAv. *upa.ma'tīm āste* 'remains', *tē hištenti jẑarᵊjẑarᵊṇtiš* 'they keep flowing'.

3. With Av. √ah- 'be' = Skt. √as-, and Av. √bu- 'be' = Skt. √bhu-, cf. Whitney, Skt. Gram. § 1075 d. GAv. ahiā frīnamāi 'let us both pray to', 1 du injunct. Ys. 29.5; GAv. hyāt cikhnušō 'let one be gratifying' Ys. 43.15; GAv. isvā has 'being able, possessed of'; YAv. pairikərəntiš aŋhən 'may be looking about'; YAv. yaoždayən aŋhən. Cf. also fraoirisiā· Yt. 13.25. — YAv. yot bavāni aiwi.vanyā 'that I may be conquering'; YAv. yaoždā!n būn 'they become cleansed', vazana buye 'become victorious'.

4. With √dā- 'give, make, do'. So apparently YAv. ạiβigairyā daiþē 'I do accept', paitiricyō daiþē 'he does throw away' cf. § 718.

INDECLINABLES.

§ 725. **General Remark.** The indeclinable words in Avesta, correspond in general to those in Sanskrit and in the other Indo-Germanic languages. Under Indeclinables are comprised Adverbs, Prepositions, Conjunctions, and Interjections. These may be taken up in detail.

A. Adverbs.

§ 726. The adverbs in Av., as in Skt., may be made either from a pronominal stem or from a noun-stem by means of a suffix, or their forms are merely crystallized cases of old or abandoned nouns.

1. Adverbs made by Suffix.
(Cf. Whitney, *Skt. Gram.* § 1097.)

§ 727. A number of adverbs are made by adding suffixes to a noun or an adjective stem, or especially to a pronominal stem. Their meaning is various.

a. Adverbs of Place.
(Cf. Whitney, *Skt. Gram.* §§ 1099, 1100.)

§ 728. The principal adverbs of place made by means of a suffix are:

Suffix Av. *-tō* = Skt. *-tas*, Av. *aiwitō* 'around' = Skt. *abhitas*. — Suffix *-pra* = Skt. *-tra*, Av. *kupra* 'where' = Skt. *kútra;* Av. *hapra* 'along, with' = Skt. *satrā*. — Suffix *-da* = Skt. *-ha*, Av. *iδa* 'here, now' = Skt. *ihá*. Likewise a number of others.

b. Adverbs of Time.
(Cf. Whitney, *Skt. Gram.* § 1103.)

§ 729. The number of temporal adverbs that are made by means of a suffix is not extensive but corresponds in proportion to the Sanskrit. Examples are:

Suffix GYAv. -*dā*, -*da* = Skt. -*dā*, -*dhā*, -*dha*, Av. *yadā*, *yada* 'when' = Skt. *yadā*; Av. *kada*, *kadā* 'when?' = Skt. *kadā*. So Av. *aδa* 'then' = Skt. *ádha, ádhā*.

c. Adverbs of Manner and Degree
(Cf. Whitney, *Skt. Gram.* §§ 1101, 1104 seq.)

§ 730. The adverbs of manner and degree made by means of a suffix are numerous.

Suffix Av. -*pa* = Skt. -*thā*, GYAv. *yapa*, *yapa* 'as' = Skt. *yáthā*; Av. *apa*, *apu* 'so' = Skt. *átha (áthā)*.—Suffix -*š* = Skt. -*s* (Whitney, § 1105), Av. *priš* 'thrice' = Skt. *tris*.—Suffix -*ti* = Skt. -*ti* (Wh., § 1102), Av. *uiti* 'thus'.—Suffix -*vaṯ* (acc. sg. advbl.) = Skt. -*vat* (Wh., § 1106), Av. *vacastaštivaṯ* 'after the manner of the text'. Similarly Av. *hakərəṯ* 'once' = Skt. *sakŕt*.

2. Case-forms as Adverbs.
(Cf. Whitney, *Skt. Gram.* § 1110 seq.)

§ 731. Many adverbs in Av., as in Skt., are really only stereotyped cases of nouns, adjectives, or pronouns, used with an adverbial force.

1. **Accusative as Adverb** — frequent (cf. Whitney, § 1111): (a) From pron. stem, Av. *iṯ* 'even' = Skt. *it*; Av. *kaṯ* 'how' = Skt. *kát*; Av. *°cit* particle = Skt. *°cit*; Av. *cōit* (cpd. w. *iṯ*) particle = Skt. *cét*; Av. *noiṯ*, *naēδa* 'not' = Skt. *nét*.—(b) From adj. stem, Av. *nūrąm* (acc. sg. f.), *nūrəm* (acc. sg. n.) 'now, quick', cf. Skt. *nūnám*; Av. *aparəm* 'hereafter' = Skt. *áparam*.—(c) From noun-stem, Av. *nąma* 'by name' = Skt. *nāma*.

2. **Instrumental as Adverb** (cf. Wh., § 1112): (a) From pron. stem, Av. *yavata* 'as long' = Skt. *yāvatā*; Av. *tā* 'by this, therefore', *yā* 'by which, whereby', *aiš* 'thereby' (§ 431).—(b) From adj., Av. *dašina* 'to the right' = Skt. *dákṣiṇena*; Av. *yesnyata* 'praiseworthy' (cf. Wh, § 1112 d); Av. *tarasca* 'across' (§ 287 above) = Skt. *tirascā*; Av. *fraca* 'forth' Ys. 9.8 (cf. § 287), cf. Skt. *prácā*.

3. **Dative as Adverb** (cf. Wh., § 1113): Av. *bityāi*, *þrityāi* 'for second, third time', Vd. 16.15, v. l.

4. **Ablative as Adverb** (cf. Wh., § 1114): (a) From pron. stem, *āṯ* (GAv.), *aaṯ* (YAv.) 'then' cf. § 431 above = Skt. *āt*.— (b) From noun-stem, *aŋtarə.naēmāṯ* 'within'. (c) From adj. stem, Av. *dūrāṯ* 'from afar' = Skt. *dūrāt*; Av. *paskāṯ* 'behind' = Skt. *paścát*.

5. **Genitive as Advero** — in temporal sense (cf. Wh., § 1115): Av. *xšapō* 'at night'.

6. Locative as Adverb (cf. Wh., § 1116): From noun and adj. stems, Av. *dūire, dūraē-ca* 'afar' = Skt. *dūrḗ;* Av. *asne, asnaē-ca* 'near'.

3. Miscellaneous Adverbs and Particles.
(Cf. Whitney, *Skt. Gram.* § 1122.)

§ 732. A number of adverbial words, chiefly monosyllabic forms, deserve mention here. Examples are:

a. Place. Av. *kva (k^ava)* 'where' = Skt. *kvà;* Av. *haca* 'with, forth' = Skt. *sáca;* Av. *parąitarǝ* 'outside'. Likewise some others; see § 728 above.

b. Time. Av. *nū* 'now' = Skt. *nú, nū́;* Av. *mošu* 'soon, quickly' (§ 38) = Skt. *makṣú;* Av. *pascaēta* 'after'.

c. Manner. Av. *aēva* 'so' = Skt. *ēvá;* GAv. *nanā* 'differently, specially' (§ 17) = Skt. *nā́nā;* Av. *cū* 'how'.

d. Negative. Av. *mā* 'not' (prohibitive) = Skt. *mā́*.

e. Asseverative. Av. *bā* 'indeed, truly', *bāδā* 'even, indeed, always'.

4. Adverbial Prefixes.
(Cf. Whitney, *Skt. Gram.* § 1118 seq.)

§ 733. Here belong the verbal prefixes treated below (§ 749), some of which however show at times more or less distinctly their original adverbial value. Examples are:

Av. *aipi, aipī* (GAv.) 'even, for, afterward' = Skt. *ápi;* GAv. *aibī,* YAv. *aiwi* 'to, unto' (occasionally advbl.) = Skt. *abhí;* Av. *ava, avā* (GAv.), *avō* (Ys. 30.10 extra metrum) 'down' = Skt. *áva, avás;* Av. *parō* 'forth, before, beyond' = Skt. *parás;* Av. *haca* 'with, forth' = Skt. *sácā;* Av. *upairi* 'above' = Skt. *upári.*

B. Prepositions.
(Cf. Whitney, *Skt. Gram.* § 1123 seq.)

§ 734. Prepositions in the sense of words that 'govern' oblique cases do not strictly exist in Avesta, any more than in Sanskrit. There are, however, a number of adverbial words which are used with the oblique cases and which define such cases more precisely. Their office is thus directive. These are termed Prepositions, and sometimes they seem really to govern the cases with which they stand.

§ 735. A fuller discussion of the Prepositions and of the cases with which they are used, belongs rather to Syntax. A mere enumeration of these forms in comparison with the Skt. is here given. Some of the words are case-forms used adverbially with a prepositional value; see under Syntax.

Principal Avesta Prepositions.

aipi (with acc., loc.) 'upon, after, for', cf. Gk. ἐπί = Skt. *ápi*
aiwi, GAv. *aibî* (w. acc., dat., loc.) 'to, unto, upon', cf. ἀμφί = Skt. *abhí*
aḍairi (w. acc.) 'under, beneath', cf. Skt. *adhár* (adv.)
ana (w. acc.) 'along, upon', cf. Gk. ἀνά
anu (w. acc.) 'along, after, according to' = Skt. *ánu*
antarə (w. acc., instr., loc.) 'between, among', cf. Lat. *inter* = Skt. *antir*
upa (w. dat.) 'away, off', cf. Gk. ἀπό = Skt. *ápa*
arəm (w. abl., Ys. 51.14) 'without', opp. Skt. *áram*
avi, aoi (w. acc., dat., gen.) 'to, upon'; (w. abl.) 'from'; (loc.) 'in'
ā (w. acc., dat., abl., gen., loc.) 'hither, from, to, until' = Skt. *ā*
upa (w. acc., loc.) 'unto, in', cf. Gk. ὑπό = Skt. *úpa*
upairi (w. acc., instr.) 'above, over', cf. Gk. ὑπέρ = Skt. *upári*
tarō, tarasca (w. acc.) 'through, across', cf. Lat. *trans* = Skt. *tirás, tirascá*
paiti (w. acc., instr., dat., abl., gen., loc.) 'to, at, for, with', cf. ποτί = Skt. *práti*
pairi (w. acc., abl.) 'around, from around', cf. περί = Skt. *pári*
para (w. acc., instr., abl., gen.) 'before, from', cf. πέρα = Skt. *párā*
parō, GAv. *parə* (w. abl., gen., loc.) 'before, beside', cf. πάρος = Skt. *parás*
pasca (w. acc., instr., abl., gen.) 'after, behind' = Skt. *pascā*
pascaeta (w. acc.) 'after, following'
pasne (w. acc., gen.) 'behind, on the other side of', cf. Lat. *pōne*
mat̃ (w. instr., abl., gen.) 'with' = Skt. *smát* (§ 140 above)
haca (w. acc., instr., abl., gen.) 'with, in consequence of' = Skt. *sácā*
hapra (w. acc., instr., dat.) 'with, along with' = Skt. *satrá*
hada (w. instr., dat., abl.) 'with, along with' = Skt. *sahá*.

§ 736. The Prepositions, as in other languages, are not infrequently placed **after** the case which they determine, instead of before it; they thus become 'Postpositions'. Examples are numerous:

Av. *apəm ā* 'to the water', *raocanəm paiti* 'at the window', *aṱāt̃ haca* 'in accordance with righteousness', etc. Similarly in the loc. case -*hva*, -*va* = *su* + *a*; so *ahmya* 'therein' = *ahmi* + *a*. Others likewise.

§ 737. The abl. phrase YAv. *aṇtarāṭ naēmāṭ* 'within' is employed, in addition to its adverbial use, also with a force that is practically equivalent to a preposition: Av. *aṇtarāṭ naēmāṭ yārədrajō* 'within a year's time'; *aṇtarāṭ naēmāṭ barəþrišva* 'within the wombs'.

C. Conjunctions.
(Cf. Whitney, *Skt. Gram.* § 1231 seq.)

§ 738. The conjunctions and particles of adverbial value have in part been treated above under Adverbs. It remains only to emphasize the conjunctive force of some of the most important Co-ordinates and Subordinates. They are mostly postpositive in position.

1. Co-ordinate Conjunctions.

§ 739. The chief co-ordinate conjunctions, copulative, adversative, etc. are here noted.

a. Copulative. Av. *ca* 'and, que' = Skt. *ca*; Av. *ca ... ca* 'both ... and' = Skt. *ca ... ca*; Av. *uta* 'also' = Skt. *utá*; Av. *uta ... uta* 'both ... and' = Skt. *uta ... uta*. Negative, Av. *noiṭ* 'not' = Skt. *néd*; Av. *noiṭ ... noiṭ*, *noiṭ ... naēda, nava ... noiṭ* 'neither ... nor'.

b. Adversative. The only one in use seems to be Av. *tū* 'but, however' = Skt. *tú*.

c. Disjunctive. Av. *vā* 'or, else', e. g. Vd. 12.1 = Skt. *vā*; Av. *vā ... vā* 'either ... or' = Skt. *vā ... vā*.

d. Causal. Av. *zī* 'for' (orig. asseverative, and often so used in Av. as in Skt.) = Skt. *hí*.

e. Illative. Here may be noticed Av. *aþa* 'so, therefore' = Skt. *átha*. Perhaps also some others.

2. Subordinate Conjunctions.

§ 740. The subordinate conjunctions, temporal, modal, final, etc., with adverbial force, have been noted above under Adverbs (§ 728 seq.), e. g. Av. *yada* 'when', *yaþa* 'as, that', etc. To these may be added the conditional conjunction Av. *yezi, yedi* 'if' = Skt. *yádi*.

D. Interjections.

§ 741. A few exclamations are worthy of notice; they are, in part, remnants of cases of unused words crystallized as Interjections. Examples are not numerous.

§ 742. The most important Interjections are: Av. *āi* 'O' (w. voc.) = Skt. *āi*; Av. *uš̌ta* 'hail' (an old loc.). Likewise a few others, probably originally case-forms of nouns or adjectives, e. g. Av. *āvōya* 'alas' (old instr.), cf. *āvōya mē bavōya* 'woe, woe indeed to me' Yt. 3.14; Av. *inja* 'ha, here', *tinja* 'ho, there'.

WORD-FORMATION.

FORMATION OF DECLINABLE STEMS.

§ 743. **General Remark.** Words are made from roots either directly without an affix, or they are more commonly formed by means of added suffixes, or again by composition.

(1) Only a small proportion of declinable stems, however, are made directly from verbal or pronominal radicals in their bare root-form without any affix. The simple root does sometimes serve as a declinable stem (see discussion below, § 744), but this happens chiefly in compounds.

(2) The great majority of words, in Av. as in other tongues, is derived from radicals by assuming an affix (suffix or prefix). The root-part of the word contains the fundamental idea; the prefix or suffix modifies its meaning.

(3) A third method of making new words is by combining words already formed so as to build up a compound.

The formation of verbs and pronouns has been sufficiently treated above; attention is here given to the formation of noun-words.

1. Suffixless Formation.
Root-Words.
(Cf. Whitney, *Skt. Gram.* § 1147.)

§ 744. A limited number of declinable stems, nouns and adjectives, in Av. as in Skt., are made directly from a simple root without assuming any suffix. The suffixless stems have been discussed above, under Declension §§ 248, 261 etc. They occur oftenest as finals of compounds; they are therefore frequently made up with verbal prefixes.

As to signification, the root-words, as in Skt. (cf. Whitney, *Skt. Grqm.* § 1147 a), are action-words, especially infinitives; or they may be nouns of agency. Sometimes they are adjectives.

§ 745. As examples of Root-Words without Suffix may be given:

Av. *vac-* 'voice, word' — Skt. *vāc-*; Av. *druj-* 'deceit, Fiend' — Skt. *drúh-*; Av. *adruh-* 'undeceiving' — Skt. *adrúh-*; Av. *aiwi-šac-* 'following' = Skt. *abhi-sác-*.

Note 1. In Av., as in Skt., root-words at the end of a compound are subject to some variation. (a) Internal *ā* is often lengthened, *anuš-hāc-* 'attending'. — (b) Radical *i, u* remain unchanged. — (c) Roots ending in a short vowel including *ar* usually assume a *t*, as in Skt. (cf. Whitney, *Skt. Gram.* § 1147 d). Av. *āθarvī-* title of a priest (√*tar-*), cf. Skt. *ṛhyt-*, Whitney, *Skt. Gram.* § 383 h. Similarly in the prior member of a compound Av. *sruṭ.gaoša-* 'of listening ears' (√*sru-*), cf. Skt *śrut-karṇa-*, Av. *jitasta-* (√*ji-*), cf. Whitney, *Skt. Gram.* §§ 1147 e, 383 h.

Note 2. Reduplication is perhaps to be sought in Av. *tu-tue-*, cf. loc. pl. *tutuḳšva* Vd. 6.51, cf. Skt. *tvac-*.

2. Derivation by Prefix and Suffix.
(Cf. Whitney, *Skt. Gram.* §§ 1118, 1136.)

§ 746. Words are derived from radicals chiefly by the addition of prefixes and suffixes. The Prefixes and Suffixes may now be taken up in detail.

PREFIXES.
a. Nominal Prefixes, Substantive and Adjective.
(Cf. Whitney, *Skt. Gram.* § 1121.)

§ 747. A number of prefixes are used in making new words of substantival or adjectival value out of words already formed; these may be called nominal or noun-prefixes. The most important Nominal Prefixes (subst. and adj.) in Av. are: *a-* negative, *hu-* 'well', *duš-* 'ill'.

§ 748. Examples of nouns and adjectives formed with modifying nominal prefixes are:

Av. *a-* negative (*an-* before vowels, *ǝ-* before *v;* rare *ana-*) = Skt. *a-*, *an-* e. g. Av. *a-srušti-* 'disobedience'; Av. *an-arǝpa-* 'wrong' = Skt. *anartha-;* Av. *ǝ-visti-* 'ignorance' = Skt. *ávitti-;* Av. *ana-marždika* 'unmerciful'.

Av. *hu-* (occasionally *hao-*) 'well' = Skt. *su-;* e. g. Av. *hu-žiti-* 'prosperity' = Skt. *sukṣiti-;* Av. *hao-ząθwa-* 'friendship'.

Av. *duš-* (sporadic *dǝuš-*) 'ill' = Skt. *dus-;* e. g. Av. *dužiti-* (i. e. *duš-žiti-* § 186) 'distress'; sporadic Av. *dǝuš-sravah-* 'inglorious'. Likewise a few others.

b. Verbal Prefixes.

(Cf. Whitney, *Skt. Gram.* § 1076 seq.)

§ 749. A number of verbal prefixes or so-called 'prepositions' occur in combination with verbs; they modify or define the meaning of these more clearly. Some of these prefixes were originally stereotyped cases of nouns that have assumed an adverbial character.

§ 750. The most important verbal prefixes in Av. are the following. The meanings given are of course only general and approximate. See Whitney, *Skt. Gram.* § 1077.

Av. *aiti* 'past, over, beyond', $\sqrt{bar}$- + *aiti* 'bring over to' = Skt. *áti*
aipi 'upon, on', $\sqrt{jan}$- + *aipi* 'smite upon' = Skt. *api*
aiwi, GAv. *aibī* 'to, upon, against', $\sqrt{gam}$- + *aiwi, aibi* 'come upon' = Skt. *abhi*
anu 'after, along', $\sqrt{i}$- + *anu* 'go after' = Skt. *ánu*
antarǝ 'between, among', $\sqrt{mrū}$- + *antarǝ* 'interdict' = Skt. *antár*
apa 'away, forth, off', $\sqrt{bar}$- + *apa* 'bear away' = Skt. *ápa*
ava 'down, upon', $\sqrt{jan}$- + *ava* 'strike down' = Skt. *áva*
avi, aoi 'to, upon', $\sqrt{bar}$- + *avi* 'bring to'
ā 'to, unto', $\sqrt{bar}$- + *ā* 'bring to' = Skt. *ā́*
upa 'to, unto, toward', $\sqrt{bar}$- + *upa* 'bring up' = Skt. *úpa*
us, uz 'up, forth, out', $\sqrt{bar}$- + *us, uz* 'bring forth' = Skt. *úd*
nī 'down, in into', $\sqrt{jan}$- + *nī* 'smite down' = Skt. *ní*
niš, niž 'out, forth, away', $\sqrt{bar}$- + *niš, niž* 'bring away' = Skt. *nis*
para 'away, forth', $\sqrt{bar}$- + *para* 'bear away' = Skt. *párā*
pairi 'round about, around', $\sqrt{bar}$- + *pairi* 'bear around' = Skt. *pári*

frā 'forth, fore, forward', √*bar-* + *frā* 'bring forth' = Skt. *pra*
paiti 'towards, against, back', √*bar-* + *paiti* 'bring towards' = Skt. *práti*
vī 'apart, away, out', √*bar-* + *vī* 'bear asunder' = Skt. *ví*
ham, hṃ-, GAv. *hām, hǝṃ-* 'together'. √*bar-* + *hąm* 'bear together' = Skt. *sám*.

Note. Instances of stereotyped case forms of a noun entering into verbal combination as prefix, are to be found: e. g. Av. *yaoš* + √*dā-*, *yaoš-dāiti* 'makes pure', cf. Av. *yaoš* Ys. 44.9 = Skt. *yóḥ*.

§ 751. The connection between the prefix and the verb, in Av. as in Vedic Skt. (Whitney, *Skt. Gram.* § 1081) is very loose; several words, therefore, often intervene between the prefix and the predicate, so that sometimes it is difficult to tell whether the prefix is to be connected directly with the verb or is to be regarded merely as an adverb: e. g. *apa ḵaca ązahibyō | miθra barōiš* 'mayest thou, O Mithra, bring us away from distresses' Yt. 10.23, beside *apa-baraiti* 'he brings away' Vd. 5.38.

§ 752. A repetition of the prefix is not uncommon, that is, the prefix may stand at some distance before the predicate and then be repeated in combination with the verb:

As an example of such repetition compare, Av. *hąm ida ǰaētǝm hąm.bārayǝn* 'let them c o l l e c t possessions t o g e t h e r there' Vd. 4.44.

Note 1. In GAv., the metre shows that the second prefix is regularly to be expunged: e. g. GAv. *hyaṯ hǝ̄m vohū* || *mazdā* [*hǝ̄m*]-*frāštā manaŋhā* 'when he conferred with Vohu Manah' Ys. 47.3. Again *hyaṯ ṯwā hǝm cašmainī* [*hǝ̄m*]-*grǝbǝm* 'when I conceived thee in mine eye' Ys. 31.8. Similarly *us* ... [*us*]-*jǝn* Ys. 46.12; et al.

Note 2. In the case of a long predicate, when several subjects or objects belong to the same verb, the verb itself is sometimes expressed but once, the prefix being then repeated each time with the subject or object as the case may be: e. g. *aya daēnaya fravārǝṇta | ahuro mazdā ašava | fra vohu mano, frā ... frā ... frā ...* 'Ahura Mazda professed his faith according to this law, Vohu Manah professed it, so did' etc. Ys. 57.24.

§ 753. When the prefix immediately precedes the verb to which it belongs, the form of the prefix is sometimes made subject to the rules of sandhi (see Sandhi, below); sometimes, however, it undergoes no change but is allowed to remain unaltered, cf. §§ 51, 52 above. Thus:

(a) With Sandhi. Av. $\sqrt{}$ az- 'to drive' + $av\bar{a}$, *upa*, *para* may give $av\bar{a}z\bar{o}it$ $(ava + az\cdot)$, $up\bar{a}za^iti$ $(upa + az\cdot)$, $par\bar{a}z\partial nti$ $(para + az\cdot)$;—Av. $\sqrt{}$ i- 'to go' + *upa*, *para* gives $upa\bar{e}ta\text{-}$ $(upa + ita)$, $par\bar{a}^iti$ $(para + a\bar{e}iti)$;—Av. $\sqrt{}$ vac- 'to speak' shows $paityaohta$ 'he spoke' Ys. 9.2, and $a^ipy\bar{u}hda\text{-}$ $(a^ipi + uhda)$, cf. § 52 Note 1;—Av. $\sqrt{}$ hac- 'follow', $upavhaca^iti$ $(upa + hac\text{-})$; —Av. $\sqrt{}$ harz- 'let go', $upavhar\partial za^iti$, $fravhar\partial za^iti$.

(b) Without Sandhi. Av. $\sqrt{}$ as- 'to reach, obtain', $ava.a\check{s}nao^iti$, $paiti.a\check{s}nao^iti$ (beside $fr\bar{a}\check{s}nao^iti$ with sandhi). Also many other examples.

Note 1. The metre sometimes determines whether sandhi is to take place, or whether the hiatus is to be allowed to remain; compare instances like $paiti.apaya\underline{t}$ Yt. 8.38, $pairi.apaya$ Yt. 10.105, et al.

Note 2. The forms *us*, *ni$\check{s}$* (with voiceless *s*) are used chiefly before voiceless consonants, the forms *uz*, *niž* are used before voiced; but this rule is likewise by no means without exception. Thus Av. *uzburonti*, *uzuhšyąn*, *nižharəta*, so *arəzuhda-* (*z* before voiced sounds); but *usaja-*, *nišąsya* Ys. 50.12, *aršuhda-* (*s* before voiced).

Note 3. The preposition Av. $h\rho m$ 'σύν' = Skt. *sám* appears in various forms, the form being assimilated to the sound following: thus, *ham-* (before vowels), *hąm* (before labials and some other consonants), *haŋ* (before gutturals, palatals, dentals), also *hõm*, *hõŋ-* occur in GAv.—Examples are Av. *hamarəna-*, *hąmbārayən*, *haŋkārayemi*, *hanjasəŋte*, *haŋtacaiti*. Some exceptions to the law of assimilation occur, e. g. *mainyu.hąm.taštā-* 'constructed by the spirit'; et al.

§ 754. Specially to be observed in compounds is the treatment of an original *s* after a prefix ending in *i*, *u*.

1. The original *s*, as expected, becomes *š* after *i*, *u*, cf. Whitney, *Skt. Gram.* § 185. Thus, YAv. *ništāiti* ($\sqrt{}$ *stā-*) Yt. 14.42; YAv. *ništayeiti* ($\sqrt{}$ *stā-*) Yt. 10.109 (but GAv. *paitistavas* with *s* Ys. 50.9); Av. *aiwišāc-* 'accompanying' Ys. 52.1 = Skt. *abhiṣāc-*; Av. *paitišmarəmna-* (v. l. *paiti.šmarəmna-*, *paiti.marəmna-*) 'thinking upon' (Av. $\sqrt{}$ *mar-* = Skt. $\sqrt{}$ *smar-* § 140) Vt. 10.86.—Similarly in internal

reduplication, unless followed by *p* §§ 155, 109. Thus, Av. *hišmarəṇt-* 'remembering'. But (with *sp*) Av. *hispōsəṇtəm*, *hispōsəmna* 'spying' Yt. 8.36, Yt. 10.45.

2. Frequently the peculiar writing *šh*, *žh* is found after *i*, *u*. It seems to be an attempt at etymological restoration. Thus, Av. *ānuš.hac-* 'attending' Ys. 31.12 = Skt. *ānuṣāc-*; Av. *aiwišhuta-* (v. l. *viwišhuta-*) 'pressed haoma-juice' (Av. √*hu-* = Skt. √*su-*) Ys. 11.3; Av. *pairišhuḥta-* 'encircled' Ys. 11.8 = Skt. *parisvakta-*; Av. *hušhafa* 'soundly sleeping' (§ 95) Ys. 57.17 — Similarly in internal reduplication, Av. *hišhaḥti* 'it clings' (√*hac-*).

3. Complicated are the following formations: GAv. *niš-a-wharatū* 'let him protect' Ys. 58.4 (beside Av. *nī* ... *haraitē* Ys. 19.10); YAv. *niš-a-ṇhasti* 'he settles down' Ys. 57.30 (beside *nišādayaṭ* Ys. 9.24); Av. *pairiṇharšta-* 'imbrued' (beside v. l. *pairiṇharšta-*).

SUFFIXES.

§ 755. Most derivatives, in Av. as in other languages, are made by means of suffixes. These resemble the corresponding suffixes in Skt., and they may likewise be divided into two general classes:

a. **Primary Suffixes**, or those added directly to original roots or to words resembling such.

b. **Secondary Suffixes**, or those added to derivative stems which have already been formed with a suffix.

These two classes may now be taken up in detail.

A. Primary Derivatives.
(Cf. Whitney, *Skt. Gram.* § 1143.)

§ 756. A Primary Derivative is a word that is formed by adding one of the so-called Primary Suffixes directly to an original root.

§ 757. **Form of the Root**. The root to which the primary suffix is added may undergo more or less change in its form. Most generally the root is strengthened either to the *guṇa* or the *vṛddhi* stage. Such variations for the most part answer to corresponding changes in Skt.; they will not be taken up in detail here; reference may be made to Justi, *Handbuch der Zendsprache* pp. 366—383.

§ 758. Some general remarks, subject to exceptions, however, may be made with regard to the strengthening of the root.

   (a) In Av., as in Skt., internal radical *a* is commonly vṛddhied before the suffix *a;* but it commonly remains unchanged before the suffix *i*.
   (b) Internal and initial *i, u* are gunated before the suffix *a* and *i*.
   (c) Internal and final *i, u* are gunated before the suffixes *-ana, -ah, -pra, -pwu, -man*.
   (d) The root generally remains unstrengthened before the suffixes *-ta, -ti, -u, -pu, -ra, -van,* and in some other cases.

The Principal Primary Suffixes.
(Cf. Whitney, *Skt. Gram.* § 1146 a.)

§ 759. A list of the principal primary suffixes may here be given in connection with the Sanskrit, see Whitney, *Skt. Gram.* § 1146 a. One or two of these here given might perhaps be further resolved and regarded as secondary, but it is found convenient to include them here.

1 -*a*	17 -*uš*	33 -*ma*
2 -*an*	18 -*ū*	34 -*man*
3 -*ana*	19 -*ka* (-*ika*)	35 -*mi*
4 -*aini*	20 -*ta* (-*da*)	36 -*mna, -mona*
5 -*ant* (-*ayt*)	-*ita, -ata*	37 -*ya*
6 -*ar*	21 -*tar* (-*dar*)	38 -*yah, -išta*
7 -*ah*	22 -*ti*	39 -*yu*
8 -*ā*	23 -*tu*	40 -*ra*
9 -*āna* (-*ăna*)	24 -*tra* (-*pra, -dra*)	41 -*ri*
10 -*i*	25 -*tva* (-*pwa*)	42 -*ru*
11 -*in*	26 -*pa* (-*da*)	43 -*va*
12 -*ina*	27 -*pi*	44 -*van* (-*pvan*)
13 -*iš*	28 -*pu*	45 -*vayt* (-*pwayt*)
14 -*išī*	29 -*na* (-*ana*)	46 -*vah*
15 -*ī*	30 -*nah*	47 -*vur* (-*vura*)
16 -*u*	31 -*ni*	
-*una*	32 -*nu*	

A few other Primary Suffixes.

§ 760. A few other suffixes occur sporadically and may also for convenience be classed under the primary division, though their secondary origin may be possibly traced. As examples may be taken:

Suffix, Av. *-aya* in *zaraḍaya-*; Av. *-āra* in *daḵṣ̌āra-*; Av. *-ura* in *vazura-*; Av. *-taš* in *parštāh-* (Whitney, § 1152 a). Likewise some others.

Discussion of the Primary Suffixes.

1. Av. *-a* = Skt. *-a* (Whitney, § 1148).

§ 761. With this suffix a great number of derivatives are formed. Their signification is various; they are adjectives, action-nouns, agent-nouns. The root is generally strengthened by *guṇa* or *vr̥ddhi*. Examples are very numerous:

Noun (masc., neut.). Av. *vāza-* 'strength' = Skt. *vája-*; Av. *maēǵa-* 'cloud' = Skt. *méghá-*; Av. *gaoša-* 'ear' = Skt. *ghóṣa-*; Av. *caḵra-* 'wheel' (neut.) = Skt. *cakrá-*. — Adjective. Av. *ama-* 'strong' = Skt. *áma-*; Av. *asāra-* 'headless'; Av. *amaṣ̌a-* 'immortal' = Skt. *amŕ̥ta-*; Av. *draoja-* 'deceitful' = Skt. *drógha-*. Also many others.

2. Av. *-an* = Skt. *-an* (Whitney, § 1160).

§ 762. This suffix forms a limited number of neuter and masculine nouns of action and agency, including also a few adjectives. Examples are:

Noun. Av. *uḵšan-* m. 'ox' = Skt. *ukṣán-*; Av. *tašan-* m. 'shaper' = Skt. *tákṣan-*; Av. *urvan-* m. 'soul'; Av. *masan-* n. 'greatness' = Skt. *mahán-*. — Adjective. Av. *avinḍan-* 'not receiving'; Av. *ǰasrvan-* 'conquering'.

3. Av. *-ana* (*-ana*) = Skt. *-ana* (Whitney, § 1150).

§ 763. This suffix, as in Skt., forms many derivatives, nouns and adjectives of varied value. Roots in *i, u* commonly receive the *guṇa*-strengthening before this suffix.

Some of the adjectival derivatives made with this element can hardly be distinguished from participles. Examples are:

Noun. Av. *vaŋhana-* n. 'clothing' = Skt. *vásana-*; Av. *hąjamana-* n. 'assembly' = Skt. *saŋgámana-*; Av. *bajina-* n. 'dish' = Skt. *bhājana-*, § 17. 30; Av. *maēθana-* n. 'dwelling'; Av. *raocana-* n. 'light, window' = Skt. *rócana-*. — Adj. Av. *zayana-* 'wintry'.

§ 764. After an *r*, the Av. form *-ana* answers in some instances to orig. *-ana*, while in others it corresponds to *-na* (i. e. *-ə̄na*, see § 802). These must be distinguished. As examples after *r*:

(a) Av. *-ana* = Skt. *-ana* (i. e. *-ᵃna*), Av. *varəna-* m. 'choice, belief' = Skt. *varaṇá-*; Av. *hamərəna-* n. 'battle, conflict' = Skt. *samáraṇa-*. Likewise some others. But observe Av. *karana- (-ana)* 'side, shore' Yt. 5.38 etc. opp. to Av. *karəna- (-na)* 'car' Yt. 11.2 = Skt. *káraṇa-*; yet consult the variants.

(b) Examples of Av. *-ana* (i. e. *-ə̄na*) = Skt. *-na*, after *r*, are given below under *-na* § 802.

4. Av. *-aini* = Skt. *-ani* (Whitney, § 1159).

§ 765. Sporadic traces of the suffix *-ani* in Av., as in Skt., are to be found. As example may be quoted:

Av. *duž-aini-* adj. 'evil' Vd. 14.5.

5. Av. *-aṇt (-əṇt, -iṇt)* = Skt. *-ant* (Whitney, § 1172).

§ 766. This is the suffix which forms the pres. and fut. participles. It has been sufficiently treated above, §§ 477, 514.

6. Av. *-ar (-ara)* = Skt. *-ar* (Whitney, §§ 169 a, 1151 l).

§ 767. This suffix forms a limited number of nouns; they are almost all of the neuter gender. It occurs likewise in adverbs and prepositions, probably there representing old case-endings. In some nouns the form becomes *-ara* by the *a*-transfer. The prefix *-ar* must be connected with *-an*, cf. § 337. Examples:

Av. *vadar-* n. 'weapon' = Skt. *vádhar-*; Av. *zafar-* n. 'jaw'; Av. *baēvar-, baēvara-* (*a*-inflection) 'thousand'; Av. *nar-, nara-* m. 'man' = Skt. *nár-, nara-*. Observe the adverbs Av. *aṇtarə* 'between, inter' = Skt. *antár*; Av. *iθarə* 'immediately'.

7. Av. *-ah* = Skt. *-as* (Whitney, § 1151).

§ 768. From this very common suffix, in Av. as in Skt., a great number of derivatives are made. They are chiefly abstract neuter nouns and some adjectives (probably originally distinguished from the latter by a difference of accent, cf. Whitney, *Skt. Gram.* § 1151 e). The roots in *i, u* show *guṇa*-strengthening before this suffix. Examples are:

Noun. Av. *avah* n. 'aid' = Skt. *ávas*-; Av. *aēnah*- n. 'sin' = Skt. *énas*-; Av. *taṃah*- n. 'darkness' = Skt. *tamas*-; Av. *raocah*- n. 'light'. — Noun, Adjective GAv. *dvaēṣah*- n. 'hate'. *dvaēṣah*- adj. 'hateful' Ys. 43.8 = Skt. *dvéṣas*-; Av. *vasah*- n. 'will', *vasah*- adj. 'willing' Ys 31.11, cf. Whitney, *Skt. Gram.* § 1151 e. A feminine noun in Av., as in Skt., is Av. *uṣah*- f. 'dawn' = Skt. *uṣás*-, cf. § 357 above.

8. Av. -*ā* = Skt. *ā* (Whitney, § 1149).

§ 769. This suffix makes feminine adjectives answering to masculine and neuter *a*-stems. It also makes a considerable number of feminine action-nouns. Its form is often obscured, as it frequently appears as *ā* §§ 25, 17, 18. Examples have been given under declension of fem. nouns and adjectives §§ 362, 243.

9. Av. -*āna* (-*āna*) = Skt. -*āna* (Whitney, § 1175).

§ 770. This suffix is used in forming middle and passive participles; it has therefore been treated under the different tense-systems, §§ 477, 507 etc. Examples of participles mid. and pass. are:

Av. *isāna*- 'ruling' = Skt. *iśāna*-; Av. *maṇhāna*- 'thinking' (aorist ptcpl.); Av. *yazāna*- 'worshipping'. *pāpərətāna*- 'fighting'. Also others.

Note. A few noun-stems in -*an* also show -*āna* as a sporadic heavy form with *a*-transfer, e. g. *arṣāna*- 'male' § 310.

10. Av. -*i* = Skt. -*i* (Whitney, § 1155).

§ 771. With this suffix a considerable number of derivatives are formed. They are adjectives and substantives.

The masculines are chiefly agent-nouns, the feminines are abstracts; there is an occasional neuter. The root generally shows the *guṇa* stage. Examples are:

Nouns. Av. *aži-* m. 'dragon' = Skt. *áhi-*; Av. *kavi* m. 'Kavi, king' = Skt. *kaví-*.—Av. *karši-* f. 'circle, circuit' = Skt. *kr̥ṣi-*; Av. *dāhi-* f. 'creation' = Skt. *dhāsi-*; Av. *maēni-* f. 'wrath, punishment' Ys. 31.15, 44.19 = Skt. *mēni-*.—Av. *aši-* n. 'eye' = Skt. *ákṣi-*. —Adjective. Av. *zairi-* 'yellow, golden' = Skt. *hári-*; Av. *darši-* 'bold', etc.

§ 772. On Av. *-ita* = Skt. *-ita*, see § 786 below.
§ 773. On Av. *-iti* = Skt. *-iti*, see § 789 below.

11. Av. *-in* = Skt. *-in* (Whitney, § 1183).

§ 774. Only a few undoubted instances of this suffix as a primary derivative are noted; its use in secondary formation of possessives is more familiar (§ 835), though not so common as in Sanskrit. Quotable examples of the primary usage of this suffix are:

Noun. Av. *kainīn-* f. 'maiden'.—Adjective. Av. *stacin* (in *afstucino*) 'flowing, running'.

12. Av. *-ina* = Skt. *-ina* (Whitney, § 1177 c).

§ 775. There are a few quotable derivatives that show this suffix. Examples are:

Adjective. Av. *dakšina-* 'right' = Skt. *dákṣiṇa-*; Av. *zairina-* 'golden' = Skt. *hariṇá-*.

13. Av. *-iš* = Skt. *-is* (Whitney, § 1153).

§ 776. A small number of neuter nouns are made by means of this suffix. Instances are:

Noun. Av. *barəziš-* n. 'cover, mat', cf. Skt. *barhis-*; Av. *hadiš-* n. 'abode'; Av. *vipiš-* n. 'judgment', *snaipiš-* n. 'weapon', cf. § 359 above.

14. Av. *-iši* = Skt. *-iṣī* (cf. Whitney, §§ 1153, 1156 a).

§ 777. This suffix belongs perhaps rather under secondary derivation than under primary endings. It occurs in only one or two words and may best be mentioned here. It seems to answer as a corresponding feminine formation

(-*išī*) to the preceding -*iš*. The root is strengthened before it. Examples are:

Noun. Av. *tәvišī-* f. 'power, might' = Skt. *távišī-*; Av. *hāirišī-* f. 'mother'.

§ 778. On -*išta* in superlatives see § 813 below.

15. Av. -*ī* = Skt. -*ī* (Whitney, § 1156).

§ 779. This suffix is to be sought in feminine nouns and adjectives, cf. also Whitney, *Skt. Gram.* § 1156 b. Such feminines correspond for the most part to masc. and neut. stems in -*a*, -*i* or a consonant. Sometimes it is doubtful whether it would not be better to regard some of the nouns and adjectives as secondary in origin.

Noun. Av. *maxšī-* f. 'fly', *vaidi-* f. 'stream, river'. — Adjective. Av. *daēvī-* 'fiendish' = Skt. *devī-*; Av. *drīvī-* f. 'poor' (§ 187, fem. to *driju-* m. n.). Likewise certain others, cf. § 362.

16. Av. -*u* = Skt. -*u* (Whitney, § 1178).

§ 780. This suffix which closely resembles the corresponding one in Skt., forms derivative nouns and adjectives. The nouns are chiefly masculine. Examples are:

Noun. Av. *asu-* m. 'branch, twig' = Skt. *asú-*; Av. *išu-* m. 'arrow' = Skt. *išu-*; Av. *pasu-* m. 'small cattle' = Skt. *paśú-*; Av. *tanu-*, *tanū-* f. 'body' = Skt. *tanū́*, *tanū́-*; Av. *madu-* n. 'honey' = Skt. *mádhu-*. — Adjective. Av. *pouru-* 'full' = Skt. *purú-*; Av. *vauhu-*, *vohu-* 'good' = Skt. *vasu-*; Av. *driju-* 'poor'. Likewise others.

§ 781. On Av. -*uwa* = Skt. -*uva*, see § 802 below.

§ 782. On Av. -*ura* = Skt. -*ura*, see § 816 be'ow.

17. Av. -*uš* = Skt. -*us* (Whitney, § 1154).

§ 783. This suffix forms a few derivatives; they are chiefly neuter nouns. As examples may be quoted:

Av. *arәduš-* n. 'assault, battery', *garәuš-* n. 'milk', *tanuš-* n. 'person' Ys. 43.7, cf. § 360. Add also *manuš-* masc. nom. propr.

18. Av. -*ā* = Skt. -*ā* (Whitney, § 1179).

§ 784. With this suffix only an occasional feminine noun is made. As an example may be quoted Av. *tanū-* (*tanu-*) f. 'body' = Skt. *tanū-* (*tanu-*).

19. Av. -*ka* = Skt. -*ka* (Whitney, § 1186).

§ 785. This suffix forms a few primary derivatives; they are nouns and adjectives. Its use in secondary derivation, as in Skt., is more common. Examples of -*ka* as primary suffix are:

Noun. Av. *aδka-* m. 'garment, robe' Yt. 5.126 = Skt. *átka-*; Av. *mahrka-* m. 'death' = Skt. *markā-*.—Adjective. Av. *huška-* 'dry' = Skt. *šúṣka-*.

20. Av. -*ta* (-*ita*, -*ata*) = Skt. -*ta* (-*ita*, -*ata*), Whitney, § 1176.

§ 786. The suffix -*ta* is used chiefly (1) in forming past-passive participles directly from the conjugation-stem as explained above under Participles, § 710 seq. It appears also (2) in a few general nouns and adjectives which show more or less of a participial character. The feminine form shows -*tā*. Examples are:

(1) Past-Passive Participles in -*ta*, see § 711 above.—(2) Nouns and Adjectives: Av. *dūta-* m. 'messenger' = Skt. *dūta-*; Av. *anguštā-* m. 'toe' = Skt. *anguṣṭha-*; Av. *zasta-* m. 'hand' = Skt. *hásta-*; Av. *aša-* n. 'right' (-*ša* = -*rta*, § 163) = Skt. *ṛtá-*; Av. *anāhitā-* fem. 'Anahita' nom. propr.

Note 1. The suffix Av. -*ita* = Skt. -*ita* (Whitney, § 1176 d) appears in a few adjectives: e. g. Av. *zairita-* 'yellow, green' = Skt. *hárita-*; Av. *masita-* 'great'; perhaps in Av. *ruxšita-* 'red'. Likewise in the ptcpl. adj. Av. *darṣita-* 'emboldened, daring' (√*darš-*) Ys. 57.11 = Skt. *dhṛṣitá-*, cf. § 712 above.

Note 2. A suffix -*ata* (stem *a* + *ta*) = Skt. -*ata* (Whitney, § 1176 c) may be assumed in a few nouns and adjectives which show partly a gerundive force. Av. *ərəzata-* n. 'silver' = Skt. *rajatá-*; Av. *vazata-* m. 'adorable, divinity'.

Note 3. The suffix -*ta* is sometimes disguised as -*da* in accordance with certain phonetic changes, cf. § 89 etc. Av. *vərəzda-* 'grown great, mighty' (i. e *varδh* + *ta*) = Skt. *vṛddha-*. So Av. *drəvda-* Yt. 13.11. Likewise -*r-ta* is often disguised as -*ša*, cf. § 163.

21. Av. -tar (dar) = Skt. -tar (Whitney, § 1182).

§ 787. This suffix is used in forming masculine, and a few feminine, nouns of agency and relationship, cf. § 321 seq. The suffix is attached directly to the root; and radical *i, u* are generally strengthened before it. There is a corresponding feminine *-trī* besides. Examples of *-tar* are: (1) Nouns of Agency. Av. *dātar-* m. 'giver, creator' = Skt. *d(h)ātar-*; Av. *zaotar-* m. name of priest = Skt. *hótar-* et al. — (2) Nouns of Relationship. Av. *patar-* m. 'father' = Skt. *pitár-*; Av. *mātar-* f. 'mother' = Skt. *mātár-*.

Note 1. The suffix *-tar* is sometimes disguised (cf. § 163). Av. *kāṣ̌ar-* m. 'eater'; Av. *bāṣ̌ar-* m. 'rider' = Skt. *bhártar-*.

Note 2. Observe the form of the suffix in YAv. *duγdar-*, GAv. *dugǝdar-* f. 'daughter' Yt. 17.2, Ys. 45.4 = Skt. *duhitár-*.

Note 3. Observe *-tar* as neuter in infin. YAv. *vidōiγre* Yt. 10.82 (perhaps here *harǝpre* v. l. Ys. 62.2).

22. Av. -ti = Skt. -ti (Whitney, § 1157).

§ 788. This suffix is used in forming a large number of feminine nouns, chiefly abstracts, and also an occasional masculine noun or adjective. The suffix is added directly to the root in its weak form. Examples are numerous: Noun. Av. *anumaiti-* f. 'thought, agreement' = Skt. *ánumati-*; Av. *cisti-* f. 'wisdom' = Skt. *citti-*; Av. *stūiti-* f. 'praise' = Skt. *stuti-*; Av. *supti-* f. 'shoulder' = Skt. *śupti-*; Av. *paiti-* masc. 'lord' = Skt. *pati-*. — Disguised form, Av. *aṣ̌i-* f. 'Rectitude' = *ar-ti* § 163.

§ 789. A form Av. *-iti* = Skt. *-iti* (Whitney, § 1157 g) is found in a few words: Av. *spusiti-* Yt. 19.6, *āskaiti-* (cf. § 32) Ys. 44.17.

23. Av. -tu = Skt. -tu (Whitney, § 1161).

§ 790. With this suffix, in Av. as in Skt., are formed a number of abstract and concrete derivatives. They are prevailingly masculine. The root is commonly strengthened before the *-tu*. Examples are:

Av. *yātu-* m. 'sorcerer' = Skt. *yātú-*; Av. *haétu-* m. 'bridge' = Skt. *sétu-*; Av. *ḥratu-* m. 'wisdom' = Skt. *krátu-*; Av. *pitu-* m. 'food' = Skt. *pitú-*; Av. *vaṇtu-* m a s c. 'spouse'; Av. *jyātu-* (fem.?) 'life' = Skt. *jīvátu-*.

24. Av. *-tra (-þra, -dra)* = Skt. *-tra* (Whitney, § 1185).

§ 791. The suffix *-tra (-þra, -dra, -dra)* forms numerous nouns, which are chiefly neuter, and a few adjectives. The root usually has the *guṇa*-strengthening, but sometimes it remains unaltered. The original form (1) *-tra* of the suffix is preserved only after sibilants or a written nasal (§ 78); otherwise it becomes regularly (2) *-þra* (§ 77, 2). The forms (3) *-dra* (in *-fdr-*, *-ḥdr-*) and *-dra* (in *-zdr-*, *-ždr-*) appear only under special circumstances, see §§ 79, 89, 90. The corresponding feminine is *-trā*. Examples are:

Noun. Av. *uštra-* m. 'camel' = Skt. *úṣṭra-*; Av. *vastra-* n. 'garment' = Skt. *vástra-*.— Av. *puþra-* m. 'son' = Skt. *putrá-*; Av. *ḥšaþra-* n. 'rule, kingdom' = Skt. *kṣatrá-*.— Av. *yaohᵊdra-* n. 'girdle' Yt. 15.54 (cf. § 79) = Skt. *yóktra-*; Av. *vahᵊdra-* n. 'word', cf. Skt. *vaktrá-*; Av. *važdra-* m. 'bearer'.—Adjective. Av. *fraoᵘrvaēštra-* 'productive'.— Av. *bróiþra-* 'cutting' Yt. 10.130 etc. (√*brī-*).— Av. *mązdra-* 'learned, wise' (§ 90), *siždra-* Yt. 8.36; Vd. 13.2.

Note. A few feminines with suffix Av. *-trā* = Skt. *-trā* (Whitney, § 1185 d) may here be noted: Av. *aštrā-* f. 'goad' = Skt. *aṣṭrā-*; Av. *zaoþrā-* f. 'libation' = Skt. *hótrā-*.

25. Av. *-tva (-þwa, -dwa)* = Skt. *-tva* (Whitney, § 966 a).

§ 792. The suffix *-tva, (-þwa, -dwa* §§ 94, 96) is used (1) chiefly in forming the Gerundive, or declinable future-passive participle of adjectival value (Latin *-ndus*) as described above § 717. But it is found also (2) in a few abstract nouns. The feminine form is *-tvā, -þwā*.

1. Gerundive. Examples of the suffix so used have been given above.—2. Noun. Av. *staoþwa-* n. 'praise'; *dąstvā-* f. 'skill', *vafᵘšī-* f. 'herd'.

26. Av. -pa (-da, -da) = Skt. -tha (Whitney, § 1163).

§ 793. With the suffix -pa (-da, -da §§ 89, 90, 77 Note 3) are made, in Av. as in Skt., a number of action-nouns of different genders, and a few verbal adjectives with passive signification. The root usually appears in its weak form. The feminine is regularly -pā. Examples are:

Noun. Av. *rapa-* m. 'chariot' = Skt. *rátha-*; Av. *hamərəpa-* m. 'foe'; Av. *vīcipa-* m. 'decision'; Av. *zapa-* m. 'birth'.—Av. *arəpa-* n. 'subject, thing' = Skt. *ártha-*.—Av. *gāpā-* f. 'song, hymn' = Skt. *gáthā-*; Av. *gaēpā-* f. 'being, creature'; Av. *cipā-* f. 'penalty'.— Adjective. Av. *uḫḍa-* 'spoken, word' (§ 77 Note 3) = Skt. *ukthá-*; Av. *xšnūta-* 'gratified'; Av. *yūḫḍa-* 'girt, compact' Yt. 10.127.

Note 1. On Av. -*da* : orig. -*ta*, see § 786 above.

Note 2. The form -*apa* (probably thematic *a* + *pa*) = Skt. -*atha* (Whitney, § 1163 c) occurs in some words: Av. *vaxšapa-* n. 'growth' = Skt. *vakṣátha-*.

27, 28. Av. -pi, -pu = Skt. -thi, -thu (Whitney, § 1164).

§ 794. The suffix Av. -*pi* = Skt. -*thi* occurs in one or two words; it is also disguised as -*ti*. The suffix Av. -*pu* = Skt. -*thu* is likewise quotable. Both of these elements are used in making nouns, the suffix being attached to the weak form of the root. Examples are:

Suffix -*pi*: Av. *cipi-* f. 'punishment'; Av. *aipi-* f. dread, terror'. So Av. *asti-* m. 'minister', cf. Skt. *átithi-*; Av. *haḫti-* n. 'thigh' = Skt. *sákthi-*.—Suffix -*pu*: Av. *hipu-* m. 'dweller, socius'.

§ 795. On the form -*pra*, see -*tra* § 791 above.
§ 796. On the form -*pwa*, see -*tva* § 792 above.
§ 797. On -*pwan*, see -*van* § 820 below.
§ 798. On the form -*pwaṇt*, see below, § 821.
§ 799. On the form -*da*, see -*ta* § 786, and -*pa* § 793 above.
§ 800. On -*da* see above, -*pa* § 793.
§ 801. On the form -*dra* see -*tra*, -*pra* § 791 above.

29. Av. -na, (-una) = Skt. -na, (-una), Whitney, § 1177.

§ 802. The suffix -*na* is used (1) in making a few past-passive participles equivalent to those in -*ta*. It is

Prim. Deriv.:—Suffix *-pa, -pi, -pu, -na, -una, -nah, -ni, -nu, -inu.* 223

also employed (2) in forming some abstract nouns and likewise adjectives whose verbal character is easily recognized. The root is generally not strengthened.

(1) Passive Participle in *-na*. Examples of this formation have been given at § 713 above.— (2) Noun. Av. *frašna-* m. 'question' = Skt. *praśná-*: Av. *yasna-* m. 'sacrifice' = Skt. *yajñá-*; Av. *hafna-* m. 'sleep' = Skt. *svápna-*.—Av. *parəna-* n. m. 'wing' = Skt. *parṇá-*.—Av. *haēnā-* f. 'army' = Skt. *sḗnā-*.— Adjective. Av. *majna-* 'naked' = Skt. *nagná-*; Av. *kamna-* 'few'. See also § 713.

§ 803. The suffix form Av. *-una* = Skt. *-una* (Whitney, § 1177 e), doubtless of secondary origin, is distinguishable in a few words: Av. *tauruna-* 'young' = Skt. *táruṇa-*; Av. *auruna-* 'fiery' = Skt. *aruṇá-*.

30. Av. *-nah* = Skt. *-nas* (Whitney, § 1152).

§ 804. The suffix *-nah* is perhaps somewhat more common in Av. than in Sanskrit. It forms neuter abstracts. Radical *i, u* are strengthened before it; *a* remains unchanged. Examples are:

Av. *raēḵnah-* n. 'possession' = Skt. *rékṇas-*; Av. *harənah-* n. 'splendor'; Av. *draonah-* 'offering' = Skt. *dráviṇas-*; Av. *parənah-* n. (in *parənaṇhuṇtəm*) 'fulness' = Skt. *páriṇas-*; Av. *rafnah-* n. 'help, comfort'.

31. Av. *-ni* = Skt. *-ni* (Whitney, § 1158).

§ 805. With this suffix, as in Skt., are made a small number of nouns and adjectives. Strengthening of the root occurs. Examples are:

Av. *varšni-* m. and adj. 'virile, male' = Skt. *vŕ̥ṣṇi-*; Av. *sraoni-* f. 'hip' = Skt. *śróṇi-*; Av. *fšaoni-* f. 'fatness'.

32. Av. *-nu, (-inu)* = Skt. *-nu, (-snu)*, Whitney, §§ 1162, 1194.

§ 806. With the suffix *-nu*, as in Skt., a small number of nouns or adjectives are made. Examples are:

Av. *bānu-* m. 'light, ray' = Skt. *bhānú-*; Av. *garənu-* m. 'itch' = Skt. *gr̥dhnú-*; Av. *tafnu-* m. 'fever' = Skt. *tapnú-*.—Av. *daēnu-* f. 'female, cow' = Skt. *dhenú-*.

§ 807. The suffix Av. *-inu* = Skt. *-snu* (Whitney, § 1194) is likewise quotable: e. g. Av. *raočinu-* m. 'light, brightness' = Skt. *róčiṣṇu-*; Av. *pąsnu-* f. 'dust', cf. Skt. *pąsu.*

224   Word-Formation: Primary Suffixes.

33. Av. -ma = Skt. -ma (Whitney § 1166).

§ 808. With this suffix a considerable number of derivatives are made; they are adjectives and nouns. The nouns are chiefly masculine. The root is often strengthened. Examples are

Noun. Av. *haoma-* m. 'haoma' = Skt. *sóma-*, Av *aẑma-* n. 'fury'; Av. *urupma-* m. 'growth'. — Av. *garəma-* n. 'heat' = Skt. *gharmá-*. — Adjective. Av. *bāma* 'shining' = Skt. *bhāma-*. Av. *tahma-* 'strong, swift'; Av. *garəma-* 'hot' = Skt. *gharmá-*.

34. Av. -*man* = Skt. -*man* (Whitney, § 1168).

§ 809. The suffix -*man* in Av., as in Skt., forms a number of derivative action-nouns; most of these are neuter; a few are masculine. The root generally shows the guṇa-strengthening. Examples are:

Noun. Av. *asman-* m. 'stone, heaven' = Skt. *áśman-*; Av. *rasman-* m. 'column, rank'. —Av. *nāman-*, *nman-* n. 'name' = Skt. *nāman-*; Av. *vaesman-* 'dwelling' (in *vaēsmən-da* Vt. 10.86) = Skt. *vēśman-*; Av. *taohman-* n. 'seed' = Skt. *tókman-*; Av. *barəsman-* n. 'barsom'.

35. Av. -*mi* = Skt. -*mi* (Whitney, § 1167).

§ 810. This suffix, as in Skt., is found in a very few masculine and feminine nouns. Examples are:

Av. *varəmi-* m. 'wave, billow' = Skt. *ūrmi-*; Av. *dami-* m. 'creator' Ys. 31.8; Av. *zāmi-* m. 'birth' = Skt. *jāmi*. — Av. *būmi-* f. 'earth' = Skt. *bhūmi-*, *bhūmi-*.

36. Av. -*mna*, -*mana* = Skt. -*māna* (Whitney, § 1174).

§ 811. This suffix is used in forming the middle (passive) participles of the different systems. It has been discussed above, § 709 etc. Furthermore on Av. *mna*, -*mana* (Gk. -μενος) opp. to Skt. -*mana*, see § 18 Note 2

37. Av. -*ya* = Skt. -*ya* (Whitney, § 1213)

§ 812. This suffix is used in making the Gerundive (fut. pass. ptcpl. § 716) and also verbal adjectives; likewise a few nouns. It is sometimes difficult, in Av. as in Skt., to distinguish the primary from the secondary deri-

vatives made with this suffix. The root is usually weak. The corresponding feminine form is *-yā*. Examples are:
Gerundive and Adjective (cf. also § 716): Av. *iǰya-* 'desirable' = Skt. *ęsya-*; Av. *āyya-* 'living, fresh' = Skt. *jīvya-*; Av. *maińya-* 'deadly'; Av. *haiþya-* 'true' = Skt. *satyá-*; Av. *maiδya-* 'middle' = Skt. *mádhya-*. — Noun. Av. *hahya-* n. 'grain' = Skt. *sasyá-*; Av. *qiþyā-* fem. 'beam', cf. Lat. *antae*.

38. Av. *-yah, (-išta)* = Skt. *-īyas, (-iṣṭha),* Whitney, § 1184.

§ 813. These suffixes are used respectively to form the comparative and superlative degree of a number of old adjectives. The form *-išta* is perhaps more strictly secondary, but as both forms are practically added directly to the crude stem (§ 365) it is more convenient to keep both together under the head of primary derivation. For examples, see § 365.

39. Av. *-yu* = Skt. *-yu* (Whitney, § 1165).

§ 814. This suffix is attached in forming a very few nouns. The root remains unstrengthened before it. Examples are:
Noun. Av. *mainyu-* m. 'spirit', cf. Skt. *manyá-*; Av. *mərəθyu-* m. 'death' ($\sqrt{mar-}$ + *t* as in Skt.) = Skt. *mr̥tyú-*; Av. *dahyu- dai'hhu-* fem. 'country', cf. Skt. *dásyu-*.

40. Av. *-ra* = Skt. *-ra* (Whitney, § 1188).

§ 815. This suffix is common, in Av. as in Skt.; numerous adjectives are formed by it; these adjectives may also be used as nouns of all three genders. The root is usually weak. Examples are:
Noun. Av. *vazra-* m. 'club' = Skt. *vájra-*; Av. *caxra-* n. 'wheel' = Skt. *cakrá-*; Av. *hurā-* f. 'a drink' = Skt. *súrā-*. — Adjective. Av. *ugra-* 'mighty' = Skt. *ugrá-*; Av. *cipra-* 'bright' = Skt. *citrá-*; Av. *suxra-* 'red' = Skt. *śukrá-*; Av. *gufra-* 'deep'.

§ 816. The form Av. *-ura* = Skt. *-ura* (Whitney, § 1188 f) used apparently as a primary suffix has sporadic traces: Av. *vazura-* m. f. 'forest'. Perhaps also *arəzura-* n. nomen propr. Mt. Demāvand (*-ura*).

41. Av. *-ri* = Skt. *-ri* (Whitney, § 1191).

§ 817. This suffix is found in a very few derivatives. Examples are: Av. *būri-* f. 'abundance', cf. Skt. *bhūri-*; Av. *tiǰri-* m. nomen propr.

42. Av. -ru = Skt. -ru (Whitney, § 1192).

§ 818. This suffix occurs in a very few words. Noun and adjective examples are quotable:

Noun. Av. *asru-* n. 'tear' = Skt. *áśru-*. — Adjective. Av. *vaŋdru-* 'desiring'. Uncertain *amru-*, *camru-*.

43. Av. -va (-dva, -spa) = Skt. -va (Whitney, § 1190).

§ 819. With this suffix are formed a few derivative adjectives and nouns. The root generally appears in its weak form. The suffix is sometimes disguised in -*spa*, -*dva* §§ 96, 97. The corresponding feminine form is -*vā*.

Noun. Av. *saᵘrva-* m. nomen propr., cf. Skt. *śarvá-*; Av. *aspa-* m. 'horse' (§ 97) = Skt. *áśva-*; Av. *aŋhvā-* f. 'soul'; Av. *gadwā-* f. 'bitch'. — Adjective. Av. *haᵘrva-* 'whole' = Skt. *sárva-*; Av. *hraoždva-* 'hard'; Av. *ərədva-* 'high, arduus' = Skt. *ūrdhvá-*; Av. *aᵘrva-* 'speedy'.

44. Av. -van (-ƥwan) = Skt. -van (Whitney, § 1169).

§ 820. The suffix -*van* is comparatively rare in Avesta. It forms derivative nouns and adjectives. The root remains unstrengthened. A *t* is added, as in Skt., to roots ending in a short vowel, including -*ar*; this gives rise to the form -*ƥwan* § 94. Examples are:

Noun. GYAv. *advan-*, *aδwan-* m. 'way' = Skt. *ádhvan-*; Av. *karəƥwan-* m. 'doer' (√*kar-* + *t*, see just above) = Skt. *kŕ́tvan-*; Av. *karšvan-* f. n. 'clime, zone'. — Adjective. Av. *isvan-* 'able, potent' (√*is-*). With reduplication Av. *yōiƥwan-* 'active' (i. e. *ya-it-van* fr. √*yut-*).

45. Av. -vaŋt (-ƥwaŋt) = Skt. -vant (Whitney, § 1233 g).

§ 821. The ending -*vaŋt* as primary suffix occurs in a few words, chiefly verbal adjectives. Some of these derivatives bear resemblance to an *aŋt*-participle of Cl. 8. As above (§ 820), a *t* is added after a root ending in a short vowel, including -*ar*; this gives rise to the form -*ƥwaŋt* § 94. The weak form of the root is the rule. The suffix -*vaŋt* sometimes seems to add the force of possession as it does when secondary. Examples are:

Av. *aᵘrvaŋt-* adj. and noun 'swift, courser' = Skt. *árvant-*; Av. *srunvaŋt-* 'audible'; Av. *bəzvaŋt-* 'advantageous' (§ 31); Av. *vivaŋhvaŋt-* m. nomen propr. = Skt. *vivásvant-*; Av. *starəƥwaŋt-* 'levelling' (√*star-* + *t*, see above); Av. *vibarəƥwaŋt-* 'divided, having pauses' (√*bar-* + *t* added).

46. Av. *-vah (-vāṅh-, -uš)* = Skt. *-vas (-vā̇s, -us)*, Whitney, § 1173.

§ 822. With the suffix *-vah (-vāṅh* str. *-uš* wk.) is made the perfect active participle. The root is reduplicated except in a few words which make the perfect without reduplication. For examples, see § 348 seq.

47. Av. *-var (-vara)* = Skt. *-vara* (Whitney, § 1171).

§ 823. With the suffix *-van (-vara)* are made a considerable number of neuter nouns. They commonly show a parallel stem with suffix *-van* (§ 820). The form *-vara* arises by transfer to the *a*-declension. Examples are:

Av. *karšvar-* n. f. beside *karšvan-* 'clime, zone'; Av. *zafar-* (i. e. *zap-var* § 95) n. beside *zafan-* 'jaw'; Av. *baēvar-* n. beside *baēvan-* 'myriad'. So *mišwara-* n. *(-vara)* beside *mišwan-* 'pair'. Observe Av. *srvara-* (for *sruvara-* § 68) 'horned, Sravara'.

B. Secondary Derivatives.
(Cf. Whitney, *Skt. Gram.* § 1202 seq.)

§ 824. The so-called Secondary Suffixes are those which are added to make new derivatives from primary derivatives or words which already show a suffix. The forms thus arising are termed Secondary Derivatives. The great majority of them are adjectives, but often they are nouns.

§ 825. **Form of the Stem.** In assuming the secondary suffix the stem, though it is already prepared, may still undergo other changes in form.

(a) Final *-a* of a stem disappears before suffixes beginning with a vowel or *y*.

(b) Final *-i*, *-u* of a stem are generally strengthened before suffixes beginning with a vowel, though *u*, as in Skt., sometimes remains unchanged, cf. Whitney, *Skt. Gram.* § 1203 a, b.

(c) Final *-an* of the stem appears as *-an*, *-n*, depending chiefly upon the difficulty of pronunciation (cf. Whitney, § 1203 c): Av. *barəsmanya-* 'relating to the barsom', *vyāḫa*'*nya-* 'ruling in the council'; Av. *vārəθrajni-* 'victorious' (from *an*-stem), cf. Skt. *vṛtraghna-*.

228   Word-Formation: Secondary Suffixes.

(d) The initial syllable of the stem receives the vṛddhi-strengthening in secondary derivation less often in Av. than in Skt., cf. Whitney, § 1204. Examples of vṛddhi (cf. § 60) are: Av. āhūiri- 'of the Ahurian', cf. Skt. āsuri-; Av. māzdayacni- 'belonging to the worship of Mazda'; Av. gāoya- beside gaoya 'belonging to the cow', opp. Skt. gāvya- (§ 60 Note d); Av. hāvani- 'relating to Havana'; Av. ārštya- 'belonging to a spear'. For guṇa-forms, see above § 60 Note c.

The Principal Secondary Suffixes.
(Cf. Whitney, *Skt. Gram.* § 1207.)

§ 826. A list of the principal secondary suffixes may here be given in connection with the Sanskrit, see Whitney, *Skt. Gram.* § 1207.

1 -a	11 -u	21 -ya
2 -aena (-aeni, -aini)	12 -ka (-ako, -ika)	22 -ma
3 -aona	13 -ta	23 -man (-mana, -mna)
4 -an	14 -tara, -tema	24 -maṇt
5 -ana (-āna, -āni)	15 -tāt	25 -ya
6 -aṇc	16 -ti	26 -ra
7 -i	17 -tha (-ti)	27 -va
8 -in	18 -tya	28 -van
9 -ina	19 -thwa	29 -vaṇt
10 -ī	20 -thwana	30 -vaṇt

A few other Secondary Suffixes.

§ 827. A few other secondary suffixes occur sporadically and may for convenience be mentioned here.

Suffix. Av. -*ϑra* in numerals, *ϑrišva-* 'a third', *cuϑrušva-* 'a fourth', *paṇtaṇhva-* 'a fifth' Ys. 19.7. Also Av. -*sa* = Skt. -*sa* (Whitney, § 1229), Av. *navasa-*, *iδasa-*, *aϑasa-*.

1. Av. -*a* = Skt. -*a* (Whitney, § 1208).

§ 828. This suffix, in Av. as in Skt., is very common. It forms secondary derivatives from nouns or from adjectives. The derivatives thus made are chiefly adjectives denoting 'relating to', 'of', 'with'; but there are also numerous nouns, including patronymics.

The secondary *a* is especially common in compound words, transferring the whole compound to the *a*-declension; the treatment of that, however, does not really belong here. Examples of *a* as secondary suffix are:

Noun. Av. *haoząpwa-* n. 'the goodly company'; Av. *ayaŋha-* m. n. 'iron' Ys. 11.7 = Skt. *ayasá-*; Av. *narava-* m. 'descendant of Naru' (patronym.). — Adjective. Av. *tәmaŋha-* 'dark' = Skt *tāmasa-* (w. vṛddhi); Av. *upa-sm-a-* 'upon the earth' (°m-) § 836.

Note. Final -*i*, -*u* of the primitive generally, but not always, appear as -*ay-*, -*av-* before this suffix. Thus, Av. *kāvaya-* 'kingly' (*kavi-*) = Skt. *kāvyá-*; Av. *darәγa.arštaya-* 'long-speared'; Av. *mainyava-* 'spiritual' (*mainyu-*). But simple *y*, *v* in *staomya-* (fr. *staomi-*), *haoząpwa-* (fr. *huząntu-*) above § 828.

2. Av. -*aēna* (-*aēni*, -*aini*) = Skt. -*ēna* (Whitney, § 1223 e).

§ 829. This suffix in Av. makes adjectives of material, cf. Skt. *sāmidhēnā-*, Whitney, § 1223 e. The form -*aēni* is found beside it in the same adjectives; the sporadic -*aini* appears to be a mere variation of the latter, cf. § 193 Note 2. Examples are:

Av. *ayaŋhaēna-*, *ayaŋhaēni-* 'made of iron'; Av. *әrәzataēna-*, °*aēni-* 'of silver'; Av. *zaranaēna-*, °*aēni-* 'golden'; Av. *bawraini-* 'of beaver-skin'.

3. Av. -*aona*, cf. Skt. -*ana*.

§ 830. This suffix (perhaps primitive *u*-stem -|- *ana* § 832) occurs in Av. *fraētaona-* m. 'Thraetaona' = Skt. *trāitana-*; Av. *arәjaona-* m. nomen propr. Yt. 13.117 (? cf. Skt. *arhaya-* n.); Av. *pitaona-* m. nomen propr. Perhaps also in Av. *marfaona-* adj. 'deadly'.

4. Av. -*an* (cf. Skt. -*in*).

§ 831. This derivative suffix forming secondary nouns and adjectives occurs in a few words. It corresponds in part to the Skt. suffix -*in*. A final stem vowel disappears before it. Examples are:

Noun. Av. *mąθran-* m. 'prophet', cf. Skt. *mantrín-*; Av. *hāvanan-* m. nomen propr.—Adjective. Av. *puθran-* 'having a son', cf. Skt. *putrín-*; Av. *vīsan-* 'possessing a house'.

5. Av. -*ana* (-*āna*, -*ānī*) = Skt. -*ana* (-*āna*, -*ānī*). Whitney, §§ 1175 a, 1223 a, b.

§ 832. This suffix is a patronymic and is found chiefly in proper nouns and adjectives. Before -*ana* a final stem vowel *a* may be dropped, or it may coalesce with the ending, thus giving -āna. A final i is strengthened before -ana. The form -ānī (-ānī) seems to be a corresponding feminine. The initial syllable is not always strengthened. Examples are:

Noun. Av. jāmāspāna- m. 'son of Jamaspa'; Av. gaoraȳāna-m. 'son of Gaori' Yt. 13.118;--Av. vəhrkāna- m. 'Hyrcania'; Av. ahurānī- f. 'daughter of Ahura'.— Adjective. Av. haēcaṭ.aspāna- 'descended from Haecataspa'; Av. āθrayāna-, āθravānī- 'belonging to the Athwyas' (Skt. āptyá-).

6. Av. -aṇc, -ac = Skt. -añc, -ac (Whitney, § 407 seq.).

§ 833. The ending Av. -aṇc, -ac (of verbal origin) is combined with prepositions and some other words to make a few derivative adjectives. It may practically be regarded as a secondary suffix. See § 287 above.

Av. paurvaṇc- 'advancing' (§ 287 above); Av. fraṇc-, frac- 'forward' = Skt. prāñc-, prāc-; Av. nyaṇc- 'downward' = Skt. nyàñc-; Av. vīśvaṇc- 'on all sides' = Skt. viṣvañc-.

7. Av. -i = Skt. -i (Whitney, § 1221).

§ 834. With this suffix are made some derivative adjectives and substantives chiefly patronymic. They are formed from noun-stems in -a; and most of the examples show the vṛddhi-strengthening.

Noun. Av. hāvani- m. nomen propr. (cf. Av. havana- = Skt. sávana-); Av. nidaēzi- m. beside nidaēza- 'heap'; Av. hvavhavi- m. 'blessedness' Ys. 53.1. — Adjective. Av. āhuiri- 'of the Ahurian' (§ 60), cf. Skt. āsuri-; Av. māzdayasni- 'Mazdayasnian' (fr. māzda-yasna-); Av. vārəθrajni- 'victorious', cf. Skt. vārtraghna-; Av. zāra-θuštri- 'of Zarathushtra'; Av. raji- 'belonging to Ragha' (raja-).

8. Av. -in = Skt. -in (Whitney, § 1230).

§ 835. The suffix -in is used as a secondary ending in Av., as in Skt., in forming possessive adjectives. They are not numerous. A final vowel disappears before the suffix. Examples are:

Av. parənin- adj. 'having a feather' (parəna-) Yt. 14.38 = Skt. parvin-; Av. myezdin- 'having offering' Yt. 13.64; Av. drujin- 'possessed of a devil' (druj-) Yt. 4.7.

9. Av. -ina = Skt. -ina (Whitney, § 1209 c).

§ 836. A secondary suffix -ina (apparently an a-inflection of -in) may be assumed for a few nouns and adjectives. As examples:

Noun. Av. *rapiþwina-* m. nomen propr.; Av. *ušahina-* m. nomen propr. — Adjective. Av. *vacahina-* 'consisting of a word, verbal' Vd. 4.2. Similarly the ending *-ini* in Av. *maēšini-* 'belonging to sheep' (fr. *maēši-*).

10. Av. *-ī* = Skt. *-ī* (cf. Whitney, § 1156 a).

§ 837 The primary derivatives in *-ī* have been treated above; one or two words however seem to show a more distinctive secondary origin, e. g. Av. *nāirī-* f. 'woman' (observe vrddhi) = Skt. *nārī-*.

11. Av. *n*.

§ 838. The suffix *n*, used in forming secondary derivatives, is to be recognized in one or two instances: Noun. Av. *hajdavhu-* m. 'satisfaction, fill' Ys. 62.9.

12. Av. *-ka (-aka, -ika)* = Skt. *-ka (-aka, -ika)*, Whitney, § 1222 seq.

§ 839. With the suffix *-ka* are made a number of nouns and adjectives. The forms in *-aka, -āka, -ika* may conveniently grouped with it, cf. Whitney, §§ 1186 c, 1181 d. The corresponding feminine is *-kā*. As examples:

Noun. Av. *araska-* m. 'disorder'; Av. *pasuka-* m. 'cattle, beast'; Av. *drafšaka-* m. 'banner' (in *drafšakavant-*); Av. *duždka-* m. nomen propr.; Av. *mašyāka-* m. 'man'; — Av. *marždika-* n. 'mercy' (cf. Whitney, § 1186 c) = Skt. *mrdīkā-*; Av. *ainika-* m. n. 'face' = Skt. *ánīka-*; — Av. *nāirikā-* f. 'woman'; Av. *pairikā-* f. 'fairy, Peri'. — Adjective. Av. *kasvika-* 'trifling'; Av. *kutaka-* 'small'. Pronominal adj. Av. *ahmāka-* 'ours' = Skt. *asmāka-*; Av. *yžmāka-* 'your' = Skt. *yuṣmāka-*, cf. Whitney, § 1222 c.

13. Av. *-ta* = Skt. *-ta* (Whitney, § 1245 e).

§ 840. This ending as secondary suffix occurs in a few words, adjectival and substantival. Examples are:

Noun. Av. *frita-* m. 'Thrita', cf. Skt. *tritá-*; Av. *būšyąstā-* f. 'Bushyansta'. — Adjective. Av. *ošavasta-* adj. 'righteous', m. 'righteousness'; Av. *fᵃlarəta-* 'winged'.

14. Av. *-tara, -təma* = Skt. *-tara, -tama* (Whitney, § 1242).

§ 841. These suffixes are used respectively in forming the comparative and superlative degree of adjectives, the latter also in the ordinals *vīsąstəma-, satōtəma-, ha-*

saprōtəma-. The treatment of the stem-final before these endings has already been given. Examples, see §§ 364, 374.

15. Av. -tāt = Skt. -tāt (Whitney, §§ 1238, 383 k).

§ 842. This suffix makes feminine abstracts. Its independent origin is shown, for example, in Av. yavaēca.tāite beside yavaētāitaēca Ys. 62.6, Yt. 13.50, cf § 893. Examples:

Av. uparatāt- f. 'supremacy' = Skt. uparātāt-; Av. haurvatāt- f. 'completeness, Salvation' = Skt. sarvātāt-. Likewise others.

16. Av. -ti = Skt. -ti (Whitney, § 1157 b).

§ 843. The suffix -ti appears as secondary ending in a few words; the most important of these are the numerals. Examples are:

Av. paŋtaŋhti- f. 'bow' (cf. pancar-); Av. χšvašti- 'sixty' = Skt. ṣaṣṭi-; Av. haptāiti- 'seventy' = Skt. saptati-; Av. navaiti- 'ninety' = Skt. navati-, see § 366 above.

17. Av. -θa (-ta) = Skt. -tha (Whitney, § 1242 d).

§ 844. The secondary suffix -θa is to be sought in one or two numeral and pronominal words. As examples: Av. haptaθa- 'seventh' = Skt. saptatha-; Av. puxδa- 'fifth', cf. Skt. pañc-a-tha-; — Av. avaθa- 'thus, so'.

18. Av. -hya = Skt. -tya (Whitney, § 1245 b).

§ 845. This suffix in Av., as in Skt., makes one or two derivative adjectives from prepositions and adverbs. As instances: Av. aiwihya- 'away, distant'; Av. pascaihya- 'behind'.

19. Av. -hwa = Skt. -tva (Whitney, § 1239).

§ 846. With this suffix, as in Skt., a few neuter nouns denoting 'condition', 'state' are formed from adjectives and nouns. Examples:

Av. awhuhwa- n. 'lordship'; Av. ratuhwa- n. 'mastership'; Av. vanhuhwa- n. 'good deed' = Skt. vasutva-.

20. Av. -hwana = Skt. -tvana (Whitney, § 1240).

§ 847. This suffix is hardly more than an extension of the preceding, which it resembles in meaning. A quotable example is the abstract noun, Av. nāirihwana- n. 'marriage', cf. Skt. patitvana-, Whitney, § 1240.

21. Av. -na = Skt. -na (Whitney, § 1223 a).

§ 848. With this suffix a very few secondary derivatives are formed. Examples are:

Noun. Av. *ahuna-* m. 'the Ahuna formula'. — Adjective Av. *ḣayana-* 'belonging to a well' Yt. 6.2; Av. *zrayana-* 'of the sea'; Av. *vahmana-* 'praiseworthy'; Av. *airyana-* 'Aryan'.

22. Av. *-ma* = Skt. *-ma* (Whitney, § 1224 b).

§ 849. With *-ma* as secondary suffix are made a few superlatives from prepositions, a few ordinal numerals, a small number of adjectives from nouns, and one or two derivative substantives likewise. Examples are:

Noun. Av. *spitāma-, spitama-* m. 'Spitama'. — Adjective. Av. *apama-* 'last' = Skt. *apamá-*; Av. *upama-* 'highest' = Skt. *upamá-*; — Av. *fratəma-* 'first' = Skt. *prathamá-* (Whitney, § 487 b); Av. *nāuma-* 'ninth' (§§ 64, 374) = Skt. *navamá-*; — Av. *daḣyuma-* 'belonging to the country' *(daḣyu-)*; Av. *zaṇtuma-* 'belonging to the tribe'.

23. Av. *-man (-mana, -mna)* = Skt. *-man (-mna)*, Whitney, §§ 1168 i, 1234 c.

§ 850. A very few words show the suffix *-man*, or its variations *-mana, -mna*. The examples are:

Noun. Av. *airyaman-* m. 'connection, family, Airyaman', cf. Skt. *aryamán-*. — Adjective. Av. *yātumana-* 'relating to a sorcerer'; Av. *zaranimna-* 'angered' Yt. 10.47.

24. Av. *-maṇt* = Skt. *-mant* (Whitney, § 1235).

§ 851. The secondary suffix *-maṇt*, like *-vaṇt* below, is used in making a number of possessive adjectives from noun-stems. The noun-stems with which it is used, as in Skt., are chiefly *a*-stems. Examples are:

Av. *ḣratumaṇt-* 'having wisdom' = Skt. *krátumant-*;
Av. *gaomaṇt-* 'having milk, flesh' = Skt. *gómant-*;
Av. *madumaṇt-* 'rich in sweets' = Skt. *mádhumant-*;
— Av. *arᵊṣ̌amaṇt-* 'right, true to fact' (from *a*-stem);
— Av. *afraṣ̌īmaṇt-* 'not progressing' (fr. *i*-stem).

25. Av. *-ya (-aya)* = Skt. *-ya (-iya, -īya)*, Whitney, §§ 1210, 1214, 1215.

§ 852. The suffix *-ya* corresponds to Skt. *-ya, -iya* (§ 68, 1), and forms a large number of secondary derivatives. These are chiefly adjectives; less often they are nouns. The vṛddhi-strengthening which is often found in Skt. (Whitney, § 1211) is almost wanting in Avesta. The feminine form is -yā.

Before this suffix, the stems in -a, -ā, drop their final vowel; the stems ending in -u retain the u unchanged, unless it unites with a preceding t into p̄c, § 94.

A few forms in -aya occur, either by retention of stem-a, or by extension (§ 68 Note 3), compare Skt. -iya, Whitney, § 1214. Examples of -ya are:

Noun. Av. aɵrya- m. 'pupil'; Av. nɒuhalpya- n. nomen propr., cf. Skt. nāsatya-; Av. vāstrya- adj. 'farming', m. 'farmer': — Av. avhuyā- f. 'lordship'. — Adjective. From a-stem: Av. āhūirya- 'lordly' (observe vṛddhi fr. ahura-) Yt. 13.82, 14.39; Av. agrya- 'topmost' = Skt. ágrya-, agriyá-; Av. haomya- 'relating to haoma' = Skt. sōmya-; Av. ḥṣaprya- 'kingly' = Skt. kṣatriya-; Av. yesnya- 'revered' = Skt. yajñiya-. — From ā-stem: Av. haēnya- 'belonging to an army' = Skt. sēnya-; Av. gaēɵya- 'material, earthly'. — From u-stem: Av. rapiɵya- 'reasonable', cf. Skt. ṛtviya-; Av. pouruya- 'first' = Skt. purvyá-; so Av. gaoya-, gāvya- 'belonging to the cow' = Skt. gávya-. — From consonant stem: Av. visya- 'of the clan' = Skt. viśya-.

Note. Observe the few forms that show -aya as remarked upon just above § 852 c. Examples are: Noun. Av. zarədaya- n. 'heart' = Skt. hṛ́daya-; Av. zarəmaya- adj. 'green', n. 'verdure', cf. Skt. harmyá-. — Adjective. Av. aspaya- (acc. aspaēm) 'belonging to a horse' = Skt. áśvya-; Av. nāvaya- 'flowing, navigable' = Skt. nāvyá-, cf. § 68 Note 3.

26. Av. -ra = Skt. -ra (Whitney, §§ 1226, 474).

§ 853. This suffix occurs in a very few words, chiefly pronominal derivatives. Examples are:

Av. adara- adj. 'under, lower' = Skt. ádhara-; Av. apara- adj. 'later, behind' = Skt. ápara-; Av. upara- adj. 'further, above' = Skt. úpara-. Probably Av. hazaura- adj. and n. 'thousand' = Skt. sahásra-. Observe Av. ahura- m. 'lord, Ahura' = Skt. ásura-.

27. Av. -va, (-vya) = Skt. -va, (-vya), Whitney, § 1228.

§ 854. The ending -va as secondary suffix occurs in a very few adjectives. These must be distinguished from orig. u-adjectives transferred to the a-inflection. Examples of -va as secondary suffix are:

Av. *aĵrava-* 'belonging to the head' *(aĵra-)*; Av. *būnava-* 'belonging to the tail' *(buna-* § 185).

Note. The suffix Av. *-vya* = Skt. *-vya* (Whitney, § 1228 c) is disguised in one or two words, names of kindred: Av. *brātūirya-* m. 'uncle' § 191, cf. Skt. *bhrātṛvya-*.

28. Av. *-van*, (f. *-vairī*) = Skt. *-van*, (f. *-varī*), Whitney, § 1234.

§ 855. A few secondary derivatives are made with the suffix *-van*. They show also a corresponding feminine *-vairī*. Examples are:

Av. *aĵavan-* adj. m., *aĵavairī-* (beside *aśaonī-*) adj. f. 'righteous' = Skt. *ṛtāvan-* (f. *-varī*); Av. *āpravan-* m. 'priest' = Skt. *átharvan-*; Av. *haptō.karšvan-* n. 'seven karshvars', Av. *haptō.karšvairī-* 'belonging to the seven karshvars'.

29. Av. *-vana* = Skt. *-vana* (Whitney, § 1245 l).

§ 856. This suffix arises apparently by transfer of the preceding *-van* to the *a*-inflection. It bears also a relation to *-var* § 337. It is to be recognized in a couple of instances: Av. *āfrivana-* n. 'blessing'; Av. *panvana-* m. 'bow'; Av. *hūpravana-* adj. 'splendid'.

30. Av. *-vaṇt* = Skt. *-vant* (Whitney, § 1233).

§ 857. The suffix *-vant* is closely akin to the suffix *-mant*, and like the latter it is used in making a large number of possessive adjectives from nouns. The suffix *-vaṇt* is used with *a-, i-* and consonant stems, *-mant* being employed chiefly with *u*-stems as noted above § 251. Examples are numerous:

From *a*-stem. Av. *amavaṇt-* adj. 'strong' = Skt. *ámavant-*; Av. *puþravaṇt-* 'having a son' = Skt. *putravánt-*; Av. *haomavaṇt-* 'having haoma' = Skt. *sómavant-*.—From *i*-stem: Av. *frazaintivaṇt-* 'having offspring'; Av. *nāirivaṇt-* 'having a wife'; Av. *raēvaṇt-* 'radiant' = Skt. *revánt-*.—From consonant stem: Av. *aojaṅhvaṇt-, aojōṅhvaṇt-* 'mighty' Ys. 57.11, Ys. 31.4 = Skt. *ójasvant-*; Av. *təmaṅhvaṇt-* 'dark' = Skt. *támasvant-*; Av. *paēmavaṇt-* 'with milk' *(paēman-)*; Av. *arṣnavaṇt-* 'possessing a stallion' *(arṣan-)*.

Note 1. A trace of the lengthening of the final vowel before -vant (cf. Whitney, § 1233 d) is to be found in Av. zairimyā̊vaṇt- 'producing verdure' Yt. 7.5, cf. Skt. vṛṣṇyāvant-. So Av. vṛjmā̊vaṇt-, ḫ̌nāvaṇt-.

Note 2. A few words, chiefly pronominal derivatives in -vaṇt, have the meaning 'like to', 'resembling', cf. Whitney, Skt. Gram. § 1233 f. Examples are: Av. māvaṇt- 'like me' = Skt. māvant-; Av. ṭ̌wāvaṇt- 'like thee, your Grace' = Skt. tvāvant-. So also Av. vīsaitivaṇt- 'twenty-fold'; Av. satavaṇt- 'hundred-fold', § 376.

FORMATION OF COMPOUND STEMS.

§ 858. **General Remark.** Compounds, Verbal and Nominal, occur in Avesta as in Sanskrit, but in Av. since most words are written separately in the MSS. and each is followed by a point, the compounds are not always so easily recognized as in Skt., nor are the rules of Sandhi so rigorously carried out.

Verbal Composition has been sufficiently treated above, § 749 seq.; it is necessary here to take up only the Noun-Compounds.

Note. In printed texts the compounds are differently marked in different editions; Geldner's Avesta has the compound united in printing and retains the separating point (.); Westergaard likewise but a small dash (-) is used; Spiegel's edition does not designate the compounds.

NOUN-COMPOSITION.

§ 859. Noun-compounds have either a substantival or an adjectival force. They consist usually of two members, more rarely of three (§ 894), e. g. *drva-aṣ̌a-ciþra* 'the sound offspring of righteousness'. The members which enter into composition may be nouns, adjectives, or indeclinables; or they may be parts of a verb, either radical or participial. The final member of the compound receives the inflection. The first member is subject to some modification in form, generally assuming the weak grade.

§ 860. Examples of different combinations, nouns, adjectives, etc., entering into composition are:

Av. *vīspaiti* (subst. + subst.) m. 'lord of the clan' = Skt. *viśpáti-*; Av. *darəɣō.bāzu-* (adj. + subst.) adj. 'longimanus' = Skt. *dīrghabāhu-*; Av. *vīspō.hāmya-* (adj. + adj.) adj. 'all-shining'; Av. *hvaspa-* (indecl. + subst.) adj. 'well-horsed' = Skt. *sváśva-*; Av. *raθaēštā-*, *raθaēštar-* (subst. + rad.) m. 'warrior standing in chariot' = Skt. *rathēṣṭhā́-*; Av. *nidāsnaipiš-* (rad. + subst.) adj. 'having weapons laid down'; Av. *starətō.barəsman-* (ptcpl. + subst.) adj. 'with outspread barsom'. Likewise some other combinations.

Union of the Members of Compounds.

a. Contraction and Hiatus.

§ 861. The rules of Sandhi for concurrent vowels and consonants are in great measure carried out, though sometimes they are disregarded. Hiatus, for example, is at times allowed to remain between concurrent vowels.

§ 862. Examples of the different methods of treatment of vowels are:

With Contraction or Resolution. Av. *auruṣāspa-* 'having white horses' (*auruṣa* + *aspa*); Av. *aiwyāma-* 'over-mighty' (*aiwi* + *ama*); Av. *paityāsti-*, *paityasti-* (v. l. *paipi.asti-*), *paipyesti-* 'repetition' (*paiti* + *as°*) Vs. 53.3, Afr. 1.8, Vd. 22.13; so Av. *aityaojana-* beside *aiti aojana-* 'thus speaking', Av. *paityauhta* beside *paiti aohta* 'he answered'; Av. *mazdaohta-* 'spoken by Mazda' (*-a* + *uhta*) Ys. 19.16. — With Hiatus. Av. *āsu.aspa-* 'swift-horsed' = Skt. *āśuáśva-*; GAv. *ciprā.avah-* beside YAv. *cipravah-* 'manifestly aiding' Ys. 34.4, Ny. 3.10; Av. *iṣviwi.išu-* 'having darting arrows'. See §§ 51, 52 above.

Note. In the Gāthās, as is shown by the metre, all contractions in compounds are to be resolved. See § 51 Note 2.

§ 863. Examples of consonant Sandhi in compounds are common. The following examples illustrate the interchange of voiced and voiceless § 74. Observe orig. *s*.

Av. *duškərəta-* 'ill-done' = Skt. *duṣkṛtá-*; Av. *duścipra-* 'of evil seed'; Av. *dušuhta-* 'ill-spoken' = Skt. *duruktá-*; Av. *dušdaēna-* 'of evil conscience'; Av. *vavhazdāh-* 'giving what is best'.

b. Treatment of the prior Member.

§ 864. Owing to the tendency in Av. to write all words separately the connection between the parts of the noun-compound is much looser than in Skt.; hence the frequent variations in the form of the prior member. Observe particularly that the first member often assumes the form identical with its nominative singular. The principal points may be presented in detail.

§ 865. Final -a of the stem may remain unchanged before consonants, but more often it appears as -ō like the nominative. Occasionally, though more rarely, it is lengthened. Examples are:

Av. *hazavra.gaoša-*, *hazavrō.gaoša-*, *hazavrā.gaoša-* 'thousand-eared' Yt. 17.16, Yt. 10.91, Yt. 10.141 etc. So *hvā-*, *hvā-* 'self' in composition, *hvōdāta-* 'self-governed', *hvāvastra-* 'self-clothed'.

Note. Observe that *a* when preceded by *y* may give *ya*, *yō*, *yā*, but sporadic traces of reduction (§ 67) are found, e. g. Av. *naire.manah-* (*naĭrya + m°*) 'manly-minded' Ys. 9.11, beside *haipyā.dāta-* Yt. 11.3, *haipyā.varəz-*. Similarly traces of *u* for *va*, *vā* are found in Av. *varədusma-* 'soft-earth' (*varədva-*).

§ 866. Original *ā* of feminine stems may remain unchanged, but sometimes, like *a*, it becomes -*ō*. Examples are:

Av. *daēnā.vazah-* nomen propr., *daēnō.disa-* m. 'teacher of the law' (*daēnā-*), *urvarō.bazuza-* adj. 'having the balm of plants' (*urvarā-*).

Note. Original *mā* (prohibitive) appears as *mā-* in composition in YAv. *makasərə mastri* 'no dwarf, no woman' et al. Yt. 5.92; GAv. *mavacpa-* 'not failing' Ys. 41.1.

§ 867. Final *i, ī, u, (ū)* of a stem remain as a rule unchanged in the prior member of a compound, though *ī* usually appears for *i*. Examples are:

Av. *zairi.gaona-* 'yellow-colored' (*zairi-*), *mušti.masah-* 'large as the fist' (*mušti-*), *nāiri.cinah-* 'seeking a wife' (*nāiri-*). — Av. *āsu.kairya-* 'quickly working', *vouru.gaoyaoiti-* 'having wide pastures'.

Note 1. The *u*-stems occasionally show -*uš*, like the nominative singular: e. g. Av. *bāzuš.aojah-* 'strong-armed' (observe -*š*), *nasuš.ava.bərəta-* 'corpse-defiled'. Somewhat different is the -*š* in Av. *ānuš.hac-* 'accompanying' (Skt. *ānuṣác-*), Av. *pasuš.haurva-* 'cattle-protecting', see above § 754, 2. Observe also YAv. *nasuspacya-* 'corpse-burning' (with *s* before *p*, § 754).

Note 2. Av. *gāu-, gao-* 'cow' appears in composition as *gao-, gavā-, gavō-* (cf. Whitney, *Skt. Gram.* § 361 f): e. g. Av. *gaoyaoiti-* 'cow-pasture' = Skt. *gávyūti-;* Av. *gavašiti-* 'abode of cows', Av. *gavō.stāna-* 'cow-stall' = Skt. *gōsthāna-*.

§ 868. Simple stems ending in *p* show forms identical with the nominative singular. Examples are:

Av. *afścipra-* 'containing the seed of waters' (*ap-*), *awždāta-* 'contained in the waters', *kərəfxvar-* 'corpse-eating' (*kəhrp-*).

§ 869. The *ant-*stems as a rule show the weak form *-aṭ* as final of a prior member. Sometimes, however, they show *-ō*, *-as*, like nominative, § 295. Examples are:

Av. *raēvaṭ.aspa-* 'having splendid horses', *varə.daṭ.gaēþa-* 'increasing the world'. — Av. *barō.zaoþra-* (observe *-ō*), beside *baraṭ.zaoþra-* (observe *-aṭ*) 'bearing the libation' Yt. 10.30, Yt. 10.126; *raēvas.cipra-* 'of splendid family' (but cf. also § 151).

Note. Observe the form *th* instead of *ṭ* in Av. *zarathuštra-* 'Zoroaster', *hamaspaþmaēdaya-* name of a season.

§ 870. The *an-*stems show *a* in composition as in Sanskrit (cf. Whitney, *Skt. Gram.* § 1315 a), or they appear as *-ō*. Examples are:

Av. *aṣavajan-* 'slaying the righteous' (*aṣavan-*), *nąma.azbāiti-* 'invocation by name', *rāma.šayana-* 'having an abode of repose' (*rāman-*). — Beside Av. *rāmō.šiti-* 'abode of repose' (*rāman-*), *zrvō.dāta-* 'created in eternity' (*zrvan-*).

§ 871. The *ar-*stems naturally have anaptyctic (*ə*) § 72, and form respectively *arə*, *ərə*. As examples may be noted:

Av. *ayarə.bara-* 'day's journey', *hvarə.barəzah-* 'height of the sun'; — *narə.barəzah-* 'height of a man'. Observe commonly *ātərə.-ṭāta-*, *ātərə.savah-*, *ātərə-* etc. Yt. 13.102, but *ātravaxša-* name of priest Vsp. 3.6 etc.

§ 872. The *ah-*stems may appear in their original form *-as* under certain circumstances (§ 110), but otherwise they become *-ō* as usual (§ 120). Examples are:

Av. *təmascipra-* 'containing the seed of darkness', *manaspaoirya-* 'having the mind pre-eminent', — Av. *ayō.xaoδa-* 'having a helmet of iron' (*ayah-*), *sanō.gaēþa-* 'useful to the world', *harənō.δāh-* 'glory-giving'.

Note 1. Observe *z* (§ 170) in Av. *vauhazdāh-* 'giving what is better' Ys. 65.12. Remark also the weak form of *-vah* in Av. *yaētuš.gao-* nomen propr. Yt. 13.123, *viduš.yasna-* 'knowing the Yasna'.

Note 2. Observe the peculiarity (*-ah* retained) in *miþahvacā* 'false-speaking' (*miþah-* + *v°*) Ys. 31.12.

c. Treatment of the final Member.

§ 873. The final member of a compound in Av. as in Skt. (cf. Whitney, *Skt. Gram.* § 1315) often undergoes changes in its original inflection; these will be noticed in the following in detail.

§ 874. There is a special tendency for the final member of a compound to assume the *a*-inflection; a compound is often thus transferred from the consonant to the vowel declension (cf. Whitney, *Skt. Gram.* § 1316 c). Examples are:

Av. *hvarə.darəsa-* (Skt. *svardṛś-*) 'sunlike' beside *parō.darəs-parō.darəsa-*; Av. *ātarə.vaxša-* title of a priest, beside *ātarə.vaxš-* (cons.).

§ 875. An *an*-stem in the final member often undergoes transformation, as in Skt. (cf. Whitney, *Skt. Gram.* § 1315). As examples may be taken:

Av. *caθru.cašma-* (observe *-a*) 'four-eyed', beside *bacvarə.cašmana-* (observe *-ana*) 'thousand-eyed', from *cašman-*.

§ 876. The final member sometimes undergoes abbreviation, owing to an original change of accent in assuming the weak form, or to other causes (cf. Whitney, *Skt. Gram.* § 1315). As examples:

Av. *upasma-* 'upon earth' (*zəm-*), *frabda-* 'fore part of the foot' (*pāda-*), *frafšu-* 'abundance of cattle' (*pasu-*). Likewise others.

d. Case-form appears in prior Member.

§ 877. In Av., as in Skt. (cf. Whitney, *Skt. Gram.* § 1250), a case-form is sometimes found in the prior member of a compound. Examples are:

a. Accusative (especially before radical finals). Av. *ahūm-marəy-* 'destroying the soul', *ašəm-aoja-* 'confounding righteousness' (*ašəm maojū, m ∴ m ∴ n*, § 189), *ahūmbiš-* 'healing the soul', *daēvō.jan-* 'daeva-smiting'. – b. Dative. Av. *yavaē-jī-* 'living forever'. – c. Genitive. Av. *zəmascipra-* 'having the seed of earth'. – d. Locative. Av. *duraēdarə-* 'seeing at a distance', *raθaēšti-, raθaēštar-* 'warrior standing in a chariot' (*raθe-*), *maiδyōi.paitištāna-* 'to the middle of the breast'.

Classes of Compounds.

(Cf. Whitney, *Skt. Gram.* § 1246 seq.)

§ 878. Modelled after the Sanskrit Grammar the compounds in Avesta may conveniently be divided into the following classes:—

Classes of Compounds.

SYNOPSIS OF COMPOUNDS
- i. Copulative.
- ii. Determinative
  - a. Dependent.
  - b. Descriptive.
- iii. Secondary Adjective Compounds
  - a. Possessive.
  - b. With governed Final.
- iv. Other Compound Forms.

These different classes may be taken up in detail in comparison with the corresponding Sanskrit divisions.

i. Copulative Compounds.
(Cf. Whitney, *Skt. Gram.* §§ 1252, 1255.)

§ 879. Copulative Compounds (Skt. Dvandva). Two co-ordinate terms which would form a pair connected by 'both—and' may dispense with the conjunction and unite into a compound. The Av. Dvandva-Compounds differ from the Skt. in this that in Av. each member assumes the dual form and is separately declined. Examples of Copulative or Dvandva-Compounds are:

> Av. *pasu vīra* 'cattle and men' Ys. 9.4 etc.; *pasubya vīraēibya* 'by cattle and men' Vd. 6.32 etc.; *pasvā̊ vīrayā̊* 'of both cattle and men' Vsp. 7.3 etc.; *āpa urvaire, āpe urvaire* 'water and trees' Ys. 9.4, Gāh 4.5; *pāyū θwōrəštāra* 'the keeper and the judge' Ys. 57.2.

Note. A rather late instance may be cited in which several successive members, though ordinarily found only in the singular, unite as a series each in the plural and form an aggregative compound: Vsp. 10.1 *āyese yešti arəzahibyō savahibyō fradaδafšubyō vīdaδafšubyō vouru.barəštibyō vouru.jarəštibyō aheca karšvanō yaṭ hvanirabahe.*

ii. Determinative Compounds.
(Cf. Whitney, *Skt. Gram.* § 1262 seq.)

§ 880. Determinative Compounds are divided into two classes, (a) Dependent Compounds, (b) Descriptive Compounds. In regard to signification, the Determinative may have either a substantival or an adjectival value.

a. Dependent Compounds.
(Cf. Whitney, *Skt. Gram.* § 1264 seq.)

§ 881. Dependent Compounds (Skt. Tatpuruṣa) are those in which the former member stands in relation to

16

the latter member as though it were governed by the latter. The force of the prior member is that of an oblique case (acc., instr. gen. etc.) depending upon the latter; and actual case-forms in such instances do sometimes occur, see § 877 above. The compound has noun or adjectival value according to its final member.

1. Noun value (Whitney, § 1264): Accusative relation. Av. *miprōdruj-* m. 'one that breaks his pledge'. — Gen. relation. Av. *vispaiti-* m. 'lord of the clan'. — Loc. relation. Av. *raθaēštā-* m. 'warrior standing in a chariot' (*raθe* = actual loc. cf. § 877).

2. Adjective value (Whitney, § 1265). Acc. relation. Av. *kamərəḏa-jan-* 'smiting the head'. — Dat. relation. Av. *dāmidāto-* 'created for all creatures'. — Instr. relation. Av. *ahuradāta-* 'made by Ahura'. — Abl. relation. Av. *qaoβuj-* 'freeing from distress'. — Loc. relation. Av. *zəmarəguz-* 'hiding in the earth'.

b. Descriptive Compounds.
(Cf. Whitney, *Skt. Gram.* § 1279 seq.)

§ 882. Descriptive Compounds (Skt. Karmadharya) are those in which the former member stands not in a case-relation but in attributive relation to the second and adds some qualification to it. The value of the compound itself is substantival or adjectival according to its final member.

1. Noun value (Whitney, § 1280 b, d): Av. *darəγōjiti-* f. 'a long residence', *pərənōmāoha-* n. 'full-moon'; — Av. *uštraδaēnu-* f. 'she-camel', cf. Whitney, *Skt. Gram.* § 1280 d.

2. Adjective value (Whitney, § 1282): Av. *vīspō.bāmya-* 'all-brilliant', *upərō.kairya-* 'making higher, raising up'. With adverbial prefixes (*a-*, *an-*, *hu-*, *dus-*, *arš-* etc.), Av. *hukərəta-* 'well-made', Av. *aršuxδa-* 'right-spoken'. Likewise some others.

iii. Secondary Adjective Compounds.
(Cf. Whitney, *Skt. Gram.* § 1292 seq.)

§ 883. The secondary adjective compounds are of two kinds, (a) Possessive, (b) those with governed final member.

Noun-Composition:—Determinative, Adjective Compounds. 243

a. Possessive Compounds.
(Cf. Whitney, *Skt. Gram.* § 1293 seq.)

§ 884. Possessive Compounds (Skt. Bahuvrīhi) are composite adjectives formed from a corresponding Determinative compound (§ 880) merely by adding to the latter the idea of 'having' or 'possessing' that which the determinative itself denotes.

§ 885. The Skt. shows a difference of accent between a Determinative and its corresponding Possessive; in Av., as there is no written accent, the distinction cannot be drawn in that manner.

§ 886. The second member of the Possessive is generally a substantive; the first member may be a substantive, adjective, pronoun, numeral, participle or indeclinable. The force of the compound always remains adjectival.

Possessive Adjectives.— Noun initial. Av. *apčipra-* 'having the seed of waters'. — Adj. initial. Av. *darəɣō.bāzu-* 'having long arms, longimanus'. — Pron. initial. Av. *hvavastra-* 'having own clothing', *yā.šyaopna-* 'having what actions' Vs. 31.16. - Num. initial. Av *hazaṇra.gaoša-* 'having a thousand ears' (cf. Whitney, § 1300). — Ptcpl. initial. Av. *uzgərəptō.drafša-* 'with uplifted banners'. — Indecl. initial (Whitney, § 1304). Av. *aɣvafna-* 'not-sleeping', *aiwyāma-* 'having excessive might' (Whitney, § 1305).

b. Adjective Compounds with governed final Member.
(Cf. Whitney, *Skt. Gram.* § 1309 seq.)

§ 887. These adjectives are exactly the reverse of Dependent compounds; they are attributives in which the first member practically governs the second member. The second member is always a noun and stands in case-relation to the first. The compound itself has an adjectival value.

This group shows two subdivisions, (1) Participial, (2) Prepositional, according as the prior member is a participle or a preposition. Details follow.

1. Participial Adjective Compounds.
(Cf. Whitney, *Skt. Gram.* § 1309.)

§ 888. These compounds are old in Av, as they are in Sanskrit. The prior member is a present participle which in meaning governs the second part. The whole is an adjective. Examples are:

Av. *vanat̰.pəšana-* adj. 'winning battles', *varəda.gaēθā-* 'increasing the world', *usərepaštāna-* 'cutting off life'. Likewise in nomina propria *haēcat̰.aspa-* 'Haecata-pa'.

2. Prepositional Adjective Compounds.
(Cf. Whitney, *Skt. Gram.* § 1310.)

§ 889. These are combinations in which the first member is a preposition (adverb) that governs the second member in meaning. The whole is equivalent to an adjective. Examples are:

Av. *āžnu-* 'reaching to the knee', cf. Skt. *abhijñu-* (Whitney, § 1310a); Av. *aiwi.daḣyu-* 'around the country', *aṇtarə.daḣyu-* 'within the country' (cf. Skt. *antarhastā*), Av. *uzdaḣyu-* 'out of the country'; Av. *upasma-* 'upon the earth' (*?nt-* § 152); Av. *parō.asna-* 'beyond the present' (i. e. *parō + azan-*) § 153, cf. Skt. *parōkṣa-*; Av. *tarō.yāra-* 'beyond a year', cf. Skt. *tirōahnya-*.

iv. Other Compound Forms.

§ 890. Beside the above regular compounds, in Av. as in Skt., there are also some other composite forms that require notice.

a. Numeral Compounds.
(Cf. Whitney, *Skt. Gram.* § 1312.)

§ 891. **Numeral Compounds** (Skt. Dvigu) are a species of determinative that have a numeral as prior member, and which are commonly, though not always, used as a singular collective noun in the neuter gender. Examples are:

Av. *θrigāya-* n. 'space of three steps', *θripada-* n. 'three feet, a yard', *nava.karšu-* n. 'the nine furrows', *nava.ḣšapara-* n. 'space of nine nights'. — Av. *paṇca.yaḣšti̥* (fem. acc. plu.) 'five twigs'. — Av. *haptōiriṇga* (masc. plur.) 'the Great Bear'.

b. Adverbial Compounds.
(Cf. Whitney, *Skt. Gram.* § 1313.)

§ 892. **Adverbial Compounds** (Skt. Avyayibhava) are composites made by the union of a preposition or a particle as prior member and a noun as final member, combined to form an indeclinable noun or rather neuter accusative used adverbially, cf. § 934. The class is quotable in an instance or two: Av. *āθritim* 'up to three times', cf. Skt. *ādvādaśam*; Av. *paityāpəm* 'against the stream, contrary' (§ 934) Ys. 65.6, Vd. 6.40 = Skt.

pratīpām (cf. Lanman, *Skt. Reader* p. 195); Av. *frā.āpəm, nyāpəm, upa.-āpəm* 'from out, down, to the water' Vd. 21.2.

c. Loose Compound Combinations.
(Cf. Whitney, *Skt. Gram.* § 1315.)

§ 893. One or two other points in regard to compounds and their formation may be noticed here.

1. The nomen propr. *nairyō.saŋha-* m. 'Nairyosangha' sometimes has its component elements separately declined, e. g. *nairyehe saŋhahe* Yt. 13.85, Vsp. 11.16, beside *nairyō.saŋhahe* Ny. 5.6. Similarly, the derivative *yavaēca.tāite* beside *yavaētāitaēca* 'for ever' Ys. 62.6, Yt. 13.50, cf. § 842. So in verbal derivatives, $z^d razdā$-, $z^d rasca$ *dāt*, etc.

2. Observe later such agglomerations, especially from initial words of chapters (cf. Te Deum), as Av. *kamnamaēzəm haitīm* 'the whither-to-turn Chapter' (*kām nəmōi zəm*) Ys. 46 end; *tat̰.pərəsā.pərəsa-* 'beginning with the words This-I-ask-Thee'. Likewise in nomina propria, resembling the Puritanical names, e. g. Av. *aṣəm.yeuhe.ruocā nąma* 'Bright-in-Righteousness by name' Yt. 13.120, et al.

§ 894. Long compounds are not common in Avesta; as examples merely may be quoted, Av. *frādat̰.vīspąm.-hujyāiti-* 'advancing all good life', *nairyąm.hąm.varətivant̰-* 'having manly courage', *pouru.sarədō.vīrō.vap̄wa* 'having a crowd of many kinds of male offspring' Vsp. 1.5.

Sandhi with Enclitics.
(Cf. Whitney, *Skt. Gram.* § 109 seq.)

§ 895. The principles of euphonic combination may be regarded as twofold: (1) as applied in the building up of a word from its elements; (2) in the union of words in a sentence. The former may be called **Internal Combination** or Word-Sandhi; the latter, though practically wanting in Av., is called **External Combination** or Sentence-Sandhi.

§ 896. The laws for the internal combination of formative elements and endings have been treated above under Phonology.

§ 897. Sentence-Sandhi, or the external combination of words in a sentence, is wanting in the Avesta (§ 4) except in the case of enclitics and in compounds, and there only conditionally. The words otherwise are written separately, each followed by a point. Thus, GAv. *yaþa ahū* Ys. 27.13; GAv. *yasca ātī* Ys. 39.3; YAv. *nī anəm* Ys. 9.17; YAv. *aipi imąm* Ys. 57.33, and countless others.

Note 1. In Geldner's *Metrik* pp. 54–57, numerous instances are collected where external sandhi is apparently to be accepted, but they are uncertain, and in the edition of the Avesta texts Geldner has rightly followed the MSS.

Note 2. Observe the MS. reading GAv. *zit* 'for indeed' (but in metre properly *zī tī*) Ys. 45.8. Conversely GAv. *yaþāiš* (so also according to metre, but better MS. authority for *yaþā āiš*, Geldner) Ys. 33.1.

Combination with Enclitics and Proclitics.

§ 898. Instances of Sandhi are common in the case of enclitics like *tū, hē, cit, ca* which form a unit with the preceding word and are often written together with it; but even here the manuscripts often preserve the usual law of keeping each word separate and unchanged. As examples:

YAv. *pairi.šē* 'round him' (combined like Skt *hi ṣaḥ* Whitney, *Skt. Gram.* § 188) Ys. 9.28 beside *nī hīm* (uncombined) Yt. 13.100. Again YAv. *skəndəm šē manō kərənāidi* 'make his brain cracked' Ys 9.28; GAv. *kas.tū* 'who to thee' Ys. 29.7; GAv. *kasnā* (cf. Germ. 'man') Ys. 44.4. So GAv. *saškəṇ-cā* (observe *ṇ*) Ys. 53.1 beside *usuhšyąn-ca* (observe *n*) Yt. 13.78.— Similarly with Sandhi after the manner of enclitics and proclitics. GAv. *huzəṇtuš² spəṇtō* Ys. 43.3; YAv. *havayas² tanvō* 'of his own self'; GAv. *vasas² ḫša-prahyā* Ys. 43.8; YAv. *yas² tahmō* 'I who am strong' Yt. 19.87; YAv. *uityaojanō* 'thus speaking', beside *uiti aojano*.

Note 1. In the MSS., enclitics and proclitics are frequently written together as a single word, e. g. GAv. *kāmanā* for *kā.m.nā* Ys. 50.1; *tāpwā* for *tā.pwā* Ys. 31.13; *t̰ŋgā* for *t̰ŋg.ā* Ys. 46.13; *nāiriva* for *nāri.vā* Ys. 41.2. Likewise YAv. *ātuī* and *ā.taī* Vd. 5.2, and many others.

Note 2. Observe that *-ca* 'que' is always written together with the preceding word; notice the difference of treatment of vowels and consonants before it. See *(-āca, -āca, -ica, -asca, -ās̄ca, -ɔ̄sca)* §§ 19, 26 Note, 120, 124, 129.

§ 899. Special attention may be drawn to the treatment of words before an enclitic beginning with *t*. In several instances, especially in the Gāthās, a word before a *t*-enclitic takes a sort of compromise form made by a mixture of the usual pause form and the grammatical Sandhi-form. Thus are to be explained:

GAv. *v̄stā* (compromise between *vas.tā* and *vā tā*, hence *ə, s*) Ys. 46.17; GAv. *yə̄ŋstā* (mixture of *yə̄ŋ tā* and *yas.tā*). Contrast GAv. *ākās-t̰ŋg* (= °*ās* + *t*) Ys. 50.2, with Av. *gaēpās-ca* (°*ās* + *c*). But GAv. *dō̄s-tā* Ys. 28.7, cf. § 124 above.

Note. Observe likewise YAv. *kas⁰.pwąm, yas⁰.pwā*, a compromise between *kū pwąm* and *kastvąm* etc. § 78 above.

§ 900. The laws of euphonic combination in Noun-Compounds and also in Verbal-Composition have been treated above §§ 753, 861 seq.; they require no further remark here.

(The Sketch of the Syntax and Metre follows in Part II.)

Indexes

to

Part I.

Order of Letters.

Vowels. Av. *a, ai, au, ae, ao — ā, āi, āu — i, ı — u, ŭ — ə, ə̄ — e, ē — o, ō — ω — q.*

Consonants. *k, h̬, g, ǰ — c, j — t, ṕ, ḍ, d, ṭ — p, f, b, w — v, ẏ, n, ŋ, m — y (i̯), r, v (u̯) — s, š, ṣ, ž, z, ẓ — h, ḣ, h̬.*

AVESTA-INDEX
(Grammatical Elements).

The references throughout are to the sections (§§).

Abbreviations are extensively used; but it is believed they will be readily recognized. For example, 'cpd.' is compound, 'cpsn.' composition; 'dcln.' means declension; 'endg.' ending; pronc.' pronunciation; 'primy.', 'scdry.' stand for primary, secondary; 'pdgm.' is paradigm; etc.

The Indexes are comparatively full, but if an element is not found under one of its letters look for it under one of its other letters, or under the appropriate head in the other Indexes. Remember that long and short vowels sometimes interchange in Avesta.

Av. = a.

a, pronc. 6; = Skt. a 15; for Skt. ā 17; interchanges with ā (ä) in MSS. 18 N., 472 N., 498; labialized to v 38, 39; strengthened or contracted 60; str. in causat. 685; lost after n, r, etc. in denom. 696 N.; loss of in scdry. deriv. 825 a; a-anaptyctic 72.

a-stems, dcln. 236; transfer of i-, u-stems to a-dcln. 256 N., 269.

a-, pronom. stem 422 seq., 431.

a-conjugation (themat.), in general 469-506; classification and formation 470; class (first) of verbs 470, 478-507; (sixth) 470, 479-507; (fourth ya) 470, 480-507; (tenth aya) 470, 481 till 507; transfer from root-class 529; transfer from redupl. class 563-5, 573; transfer from nu-,

u-class 574, 578, 582; transfer from intens. 707.

a-aorist (themat.), formation 648.

-a, primy. 761, scdry. 828.

a-inflection in cpds. 874; final in cpds. 865.

ai, aē, interchange in MSS. 193 N. 2.

-aiti, -aite (= -ɵti etc.) 452.

-aini, primy. 765.

-aini, scdry. 829.

aē, pronc. 7; = Skt. ē 54-5; strengthening of i 60; .for aya 64.

-aēna (-aēni), scdry. 829.

-aēm, for -ayam 494.

-aēvam (orig.) = Av. -ōyūm 62 N. 2.

ao, pronc. 7; = Skt. ō 54, 57; strengthening of u 60; for ava 64.

aoi, aon (āun), aor, for orig. avy, avn, avr 62.

-aona, scdry. 830.

-aom, -aon, for -avam 494.

-aoš (accent) = -ɒuš 265 (gen.).

-aka, sedry. 839.
-ac, see -aŋc.
-ata, primy. 786 N. 2.
-ate, in abl. sg. 222.
-af (- ...) 458.
-auk-, for orig. -as- 117-119; for old -ǫar- 126.
-anie, infin. 720.
an-stems, deln. 300; interchange with ai-stems 311; compar. of an-stems 365 N. 2; in epsn. 870.
-an, ptcpl. of roots in -an 711 (5).
-an, primy. 762, sedry. 831; treatment of -an in sedry. deriv. 825 c.
-ana (-ana) primy. 763, sedry. 832.
aŋc-stems, deln. 287.
-aŋe, -ac, sedry. 833.
aŋt-stems, deln. 291, treatment of in cpds. 869.
-aŋt, primy. 766.
ap-, see āp-.
|ʼap-, perf. ptcpl. 622.
-ay-, -av-, for -y-, -v- 68 N. 3; for -i-, -u- 828 N.
-aya-, -ava-, reduced to -aē-, -ao- 494.
aya- (tenth) class of verbs 470, 481 to 507.
-aya (suffix) 760; (for -ya) sedry. 852 N.
-aye (orig.) = Av. -je 66.
ar (r-vowel), rules for redupl. in verbs 465 b.
ar-stems, interchange with an-stems 311; deln. (radical) 329, deln. (neut.) 336-7; in composition 871.
-ar (-ara), primy. 767.
arə, for Skt. ṛ 47; interchanges with ərə in MSS. 47; for Skt. ir, ur, īr, ūr 48.
-arəta, -ərəta, in ptcpl. 711 (3).
-ava-, reduced to -ao- 64.

-ava-, in loc. sg. u-stem 295.
aṛy, aʼm, avr (orig.) = Av. aoi, aon (āoŋ), aor 62.
as (old), when it is retained in Av. 120 N.
ah, for Skt. aṣ 112-116.
ah-stems, deln 339; in epsn. 872.
|ʼah- 'to be', pdgm. 530 seq.; it forms periphrases 623, 724.
-ah, primy. 768.

Av. ā = ā.

ā, prone. 6 = Skt. ā 15; = Skt. ā 18, in contractions 51; for ā after y (i. e. yā = yo) 52 c; as strengthening of a 60.
ē, a, endg. instr. sg. 222.
ā-stems, deln. 243 seq.
-ā, in fem. formation 362; in 1st. pers. sg. 450, 456.
-ā, primy. 769.
-ā (final), how treated in cpds. 866.
-āaṭ, in abl. sg. 222.
āi, prone. 7; = Skt. āi 54, 59; for āyō 65; written for -aṇi 357 N. 2; = -ā(h)i 450, 462 N., 502.
-āiš, endg. instr. pl. 224.
āu, prone. 7; = Skt. āu 54, 59; for āva 65.
-āum, in acc. sg 265.
-āṭ, in abl. sg. lightened to -āṭ 19.
-āna, -āna, in perf mid. ptcpl. 715, 770.
-āna (-ani). sedry. 832.
-āhū, -ābhū, variants 354.
-ārəš, -ārə, endg. 455, 464.
ās 'was' 192 N.
āsu-, āsyaṇ-, compar. 365.
āh, = old ās 122.
āh-stems, deln. 352 seq.
|ʼāh- 'sit', in periphr. expressions 724.

I. Avesta-Index (Gram. Elements).—Reference to the §§. 253

Av. ᐧ *i*.

i, pronc. 6; = Skt. *ĭ* 15; = Skt. *ī* 21; long in vicinity of *r* 23; lengthened before final *m* 23; strengthened to *ae* 60; strengthened in caus. and sedry. deriv. 685, 825 b; stands for Av. *ə* (-*ən*, -*əm*) after palatal consonants 30; for orig. *ya* 63; interchanges with *ī* in opt. 552.

i, epenthetic 70; prothetic 71.

i-, pronominal stem, deln. 397.

i-, *ī*-stems, deln. 251 seq.

√*i*- 'to go', use in periphr. phrases 724.

i- primy. 771; sedry. 834; (final) in cpds. 867.

-*ika*, sedry. 839.

-*ita*, pass. ptcpl. 712; primy. 786 N.

-*iti*, suffix 789.

in-stems, deln. forms 316; -*in* for -*ən*, -*yən* 491-92.

-*in*, primy. 774; sedry. 835.

-*ina*, primy. 775; sedry 836.

-*inī*, primy. 766.

-*inti*, for -*ənti* 491.

-*ima*, pronom. stem 422 seq.

iy (orig.) Av. *y* (*i*) 68.

iv (Av.) = orig. *yv* 62.

iš-stems, deln. 358.

iš-Aorist 664.

-*iš*, primy. 776; -*išt* sedry. 777.

-*išta*, superl. adj. formation 365, 813.

Av. ᐧ *ī*.

ī, pronc. 6; = Skt. *ī* 15; = Skt. *ĭ* 20; in fem. formation 362; primy. 779; sedry. 837; (final) in cpds. 867.

īm 'this', pronoun nom sg. fem. 422.

-*īš*, -*ūš* as general plur. case 231.

Av. ᐧ *u*.

u, pronc. 6; = Skt. *u* 15; = Skt. *ū* 21; lengthened before epenthetic *i* 20; lengthened in acc. sg. before final *m* 23; strengthened to *ao* 60; strengthened in caus. 685; stands for orig. *va* 63; for Av. *v*, *w* (= orig. *uu*) 62 N. 3; stands for *ə* 193 N. 2.

u, epenthetic 70; prothetic 71; anaptyctic 72.

u-, *ū*-stems, deln. 262 seq.

u-(eighth) class of verbs 470; pdgm. 576-582.

-*u*, primy. 780; sedry. 838; (final) in cpds. 867.

-*un*-, for -*ran*- in verbs 493.

-*una*, primy. 802-3.

-*um*, acc. sg. of *va*-stem 63 N.

-*uy* = orig. *vy* 62 N. 3.

-*ura*, suffix 760; primy. 816.

urv = Skt. *vr* (*vl*) 191.

uv (orig.) = Av. *v* (*u*) 68.

uš-stems, deln. 358.

-*uš*, wk. form 349-50, 822; see *vah*.

-*uš*, like nom. in cpds. 867 N.

-*uš*, primy. 783.

-*ušī*, fem. to -*vah*-, see 362.

Av. ᐧ *ū*.

ū, pronc. 6; = Skt. *ū* 15; = Skt. *ŭ* 20; for *ū* after *y* 52 c.

ū-, *ū*-stems, deln. 262 seq.

-*ū*, primy. 784.

-*ūš*, as general plur. case 231.

Av. ᐧ *ə*.

ə, pronc. 6; = Skt. *a* before *m*, *n*, *v* 28-9; interchange with *a* in MSS. 29 N.; becomes *i* after palatals 30; stands sporadically for *u*, *i*

in GAv. 31, 193 N. 2; for -*i*-
(= *ya*) 63 N. 3.
ə, anaptyctic 72.
-*zuk*- = old -*ans*- 126.
-*əna* (-*ana*), primy. 703-4.
-*əṇt*, primy. 706.
-*əre*, pronc. 6; = Skt. *r* 47.
-*ərq*- = orig. *r* + *n* 49.

Av. | *ā*.

ā, pronc. 6; its character in GYAv.
28, 32; = orig. -*ans* (final) 32 N.;
stands for *an*, *ah*, *ā* before *b* 33;
anaptyctic 72.
ā (-*ās-ca*) = old -*ans* 129.
-*āe*, pronc. 7; (final) = -*aye* 66.
āu, pronc. 7; = Skt. *o* 54, 58.
-*āuš* = -*aoš* (accent) 265 genitive.
-*ång*-, *ǝngh*-, -*ǝn*- = old -*ans*- 128-9.

Av. ю *e*.

e, pronc. 6; = Skt. *ē* (final) 35;
= Skt. *a*, *ā* after *y* 28, 34;
= orig. *ya* (final) 67, 493, interchanges with *i*-final 35 N. 2.

Av. ஐ *ē*.

ē, pronc. 6; = Skt. *ē* (final) 36;
found chiefly in -*aē* 55.

Av. ͻ *o*.

o, pronc. 6; in -*a*- 37; stands for *a* 38.

Av. 7 *ō*.

ō, pronc. 6; = Skt. *āu* (final) 42;
stands for *a*, *ā* through labialization (rounding) 39; anaptyctic 72; = old -*as* 120; in dual 223, 240; for *āu* in cpds. 870.
ōi = Skt. *ē* 54. 56; (final) in 1st. sg. pres. 450.

-*āyām* = orig. -*avām* 63 N. 2.
-*ohu*, -*okva*, loc. pl. 342.

Av. ळ *ā̊*.

ā̊, pronc. 6; = Skt. *ās* 43, 124;
= Skt. *a* 44; interchanges with
-*ǎu*, -*aĕ* in MSS. 193 N. 2; = Skt.
-*ās* in dual 223.
ā̊wh = old *ās* 123, 224.
-*ā̊sč* = old -*ās* 124 N.

Av. ห *q*.

q, pronc. 6; = Skt. *a*, *q* with nasal 45-6.
-*q*, -*qm*, -*qm*, interchange in MSS. 193 N 1.
q(n), defective spelling in MSS. 45 N 2; pleonastic spelling 45 N. 3.
-*qn*, -*q* = old -*ans* 129.
-*qm*, dissyllabic gen. pl. 224; 3 sg. aor. imperat. 456, 627 N., 640.
-*qh* = old -*ans* 126-7.

Av. 9 *k*.

k, pronc. 8; general character 76;
= Skt. *k* 78; loss of *k* (*h*) 187 (5); interchange of *k/c* 76 N.
ka-, interrog. 406.
-*ka*, primy. 785, scdry. 839.
√*kar*- 'to make', plgm. 567 seq.;
perf. 606, aor. 637-40; pass. 680; intensive 705-6.
√*kar*- 'to cut', conjugation forms 555 seq., 565.
ki-, *ca*-, interrog. pron. 407.
√*kin*-, *ču*-, aor. 664.

Av. ௪ *q̌*.

q̌, pronc. 9; general character 77;
= Skt. *kh* 77, = Skt. *k* 77,
introduced before *ŗ* 77 N. 1, 188.

I. Avesta-Index (Gram. Elements).—Reference to the §§. 255

ḥt, in YAv. 90.
ḥd 77 N. 3.
-ḥtr- = orig. ktr 79.
ḥš = Skt. kṣ 158 N.
√ḥši-, aor. 649.
√ḥšnu-, aor. 664.

Av. ᚷ g.

g, pronc. 8; = Skt. g, gh 82-3.
√gam-, jam-, aor. 642-7.
√garw-, conjugation forms 584.
-gəd- 89.
gv (GAv.) = YAv. v 187 (1).

Av. ᛉ j.

j, pronc. 9; = Skt. g, gh 83.
jž, in GAv. 89.
jžar-, intensive 705-6.

Av. ᛈ c.

c, pronc. 8; general character 76; interchange of c/k 76 N.
-ca 'que', treatment of vowel and cons. before it 26 N., 124 N.
c/j, interchange in MSS. 193 N. 2.
√caṣ-, pdgm. perf. 622.
ci-, interrog. pron. 407.
√ci- 'to atone', conjugation forms 551.
√caš-, pdgm. 555.
cy (old) = Av. šy (š) 162.

Av. ᛄ j.

j, pronc. 8; general character 88; = Skt. j, h 88; = Skt. g 88 N. 2; = Skt. gh 88 N. 3; interchange of j/z, j/c in MSS. 193 N. 2.
√jam-, gam-, aor. 642-7.

Av. ᛏ t.

t, pronc. 8; general character 76; = Skt. t 78; loss of t 187 (6);

orig. t becomes Av. s 151; assumption of t after short root in deriv. 745 N. 1, 820; treatment of enclitics before t 899.
ta-, pronom. stem, dcln. 409.
-ta, ending pass. ptcpl. 681, 710; primy. 786; scdry. 840; becomes -da 786 N. 3.
√tan-, conj. forms 579-80.
tar-stems, dcln. 321.
-tar, primy. 787.
-tara, compar. adj. 363 seq., 841.
-tath, suffix 760.
-tāt, scdry. 842.
-ti, primy. 788; scdry. 843.
-tu, primy. 790.
-təm, 3 du. 454.
-təma, superl. adj. 363 seq.
-tǝe, -tayǝeca, infin. 720.
-tā (beside -pā), ending du. 448 N., 451.
ty, for -py- 79 N.
tr (Av.) = orig. tr 79 N.
-tra, -trā, primy. 791.
-prī, fem. to -tar 362.
tv (Av.) = Skt. tv 94.
-tva, -pwa, in gerundive 716; primy. 792.
ts (orig.) = Av. s 143.

Av. ᚦ p.

p, pronc. 9; general character 77; = Skt. th, t 77; = Skt. s 77 N. 2; stands for Av. d 86; interchange of p/d in MSS. 193 N. 2; stands for t in cpsn. 869 N.
-pa, primy. 793; scdry. 844.
-pi, -pu, primy. 794.
-pā (beside -tā), ending du. 448 N., 451.
pw = Skt. tv 94.

pwa- 'huus'; deln. 439.
-*pwa*, in gerundive 716; sedry. 846.
-*pwan*, see -*van* 820.
-*pwana*, sedry. 847.
-*pwant*, see -*vant* 821.
-*pra*, primy. 791.
-*pya*, sedry. 845.

Av. ᴅ *d*.

d, pronc. 8; = Skt. *d*, *dh* 82-3; internal *d* 85; dropped between consonants 187 (2).
-*da* (= -*ta*), primy. 786 N. 3.
dad-, *dap-*, interchange of stems 541-2, 553.
√*dar-* 'hold', perf. ptcpl. 618; aor. opt. 645.
√*dar-* 'tear', intens. 706.
√*dā-* 'give, place' = Skt. √*dā-, dhā-*, pres. pdgm. 540; aor. pdgm. 631 seq.; caus. forms 692; pass. ptcpl. 711 (2); in periphrases 724.
di-, pronom. deln. 396.
-*duye* = Skt. -*dhve* 452, 498.
dr = Skt. *dr* 85.
dv (orig.), treatment in Av. 96.

Av. ʟ *d*.

d, pronc. 9; = orig. *th* 77 N. 3; = Skt. *d*, *dh* 83; interchange of Av. *d*/*p* 86.
-*da* (= -*pa*), primy. 793.
-*dar* (= -*tar*), primy. 787.
dw (Av.) = orig. *dv*, *dhv* 96.
-*dwa* (= -*tva*), primy. 792.
-*dyāi*, -*dyāi*, infin. 720.
-*dra*, primy. 791.

Av. ℇ *f*.

f, pronc. 9, general character *fk*, *fb* etc. 81; in abl. sg. -*af*, -*āf* 222; in acc. sg. of neut. pron. 379.

Av. ᴜ *p*.

p, pronc. 8; general character 76; = Skt. *p* 78-9; as final in cpsn. 868.
√*par-*, conj. forms 588, 591.
ptr (orig.) = Av. *fadr* 79.
pv (orig.) = Av. *f* 95.
ps (orig.) = Av. *fš* (*fs*) 144, 161.

Av. ꝺ *f*.

f, pronc. 9; general character 77; = Skt. *p*, *ph* 77; = orig. *pv* 95.
fd (Av.) = orig. *pt* 77 N. 3.
fadr (Av.) = orig. *ptr* 79, 791.
fš (Av.) = orig. *ps* 144.
√*frī-*, conj. forms 584.

Av. ᴊ *b*.

b, pronc. 8; = Skt. *b*, *bh* 82-3; interchange of *b*/*w*, *v* 62 N.
√*bar-*, pdgm. 482 seq.
-*biš*, -*biš*, -*byā*, -*bya*, pada-endings 22, 85.
-*biš*, -*biš*, instr. ending 22, 224; as general plur. case 229.
√*bū-*, aor. 642-6; fut. ptcpl. 674.

Av. ᴡ *w*.

w, pronc. 9; = Skt. *b*, *bh* 83; Av. *w* becomes *v* 87.
-*wa* (in -*dwa*), primy. 819.
wš = Skt. -*ps*- 89, 180.

Av. ɪ, ᴜ *v*, *y*.

v, *y*, pronc. 10; general character 104.
vuh (Av.) = orig. -*sv*- 130.
vr = orig. -*sr*- 139.

I. Avesta-Index (Gram. Elements).—Reference to the §§.

vh, *iṿh*, interchange in MSS. 118 N.; = orig. *sy* 134, 135.
vhv (Av.) = orig. *sv* 130.

Av. ٢ *n*, ٣.

n, ṇ, pronc. 10; general character 102-3.
ngr (GAv.) = orig. -*sr*- 139 N.
ngh = orig. -*ns*- 128.
-*na*-, weak form in verbs 590.
-*na*, ending pass. ptcpl. 681, 713, 764; primy. 802; scdry. 848.
-*nah*, primy. 804.
nā-(ninth) class of verbs 470, 583-92.
-*ni*, primy. 805.
nu-(fifth) class of verbs 470, 566-74.
-*nu*, primy. 806.
ns (orig.) = Av. -*vh*- 125.
√*naṣ*-, *nas*-, aor. 658, 663.

Av. ٤ *m*.

m, pronc. 10; general character 105; = Skt. *sm* 140; instead of *n* in voc. sg. 193; interchange of final *m/n* in MSS. 193 N.; ending of acc. sg. 222.
-*ma*, primy. 808; scdry. 849.
-*maine*, infin. 720.
man-stems, dcln. 300.
√*man*-, aor. 656.
-*man*, primy. 809; scdry. (-*man*, -*mana*, -*mna*) 850.
-*mant*, scdry. 851.
√*mar*-, mid.-pass. 680.
√*mark*-(*marənc*-) conjugation forms 555-63.
√*mard*-, conjugation forms 564.
mā (= *md*), neg. in cpds. 366 N.
-*mi*, primy. 810.
marənc-, see √*mark*-.
mörənd-, see √*mard*- 564.

√*mrū*-, opp. Skt. √*brū*- 105 N. 1; pres. pdgm. 517 seq.; aor. 3 sg. 668.
-*mna (-māna)* = Skt. -*māna* 18 N. 2; primy. 811.

Av. ٢٠ (²⁰) *y* (ı̦).

y (ı̦), pronc. 11; for *i* by resolution 51; in reductions 61; vocalized to *i* 62; written by abbreviation for *iy* 68, 92 N. 1; *y* initial 91; *į* initial 91 N.; *į* internal 91; = Skt. *y* 92; = Skt. *v* (in Av. *nye*) 92 N. 2, 190; *y* lost after *s* 187 (3).
ya (orig.), becomes Av. -*i*- (-*ī*-) 63; becomes Av. -*e* (final) 67, 222 (instr.); is formative element in pass. 676-7.
ya-, rel. pron. dcln. 399 seq.
ya-(fourth) class of verbs 470, 480-507.
-*ya*, in gerundive and gerund 716, 718; primy. 812; scdry. (*aya*) 852; final in cpds. 865.
yah, compar. adj. dcln. 345-6, 365, 813.
-*yā*, primy. fem. 812.
ye, for -*ya*- in verbs 492.
-*yehī*, fem. compar. to -*yah* 363.
-*yu*, primy. 814.
yv (orig.) = Av. -*iv*- 62.

Av. ٦ *r*.

r, pronc. 11; *r*-vowel 60; = Skt. *r* (ļ) 100; = orig. *sr* 138; transposition 191.
r-stems, dcln. 333 seq.
-*ra*, primy. 815; scdry. 853.
√*ras*-, intens. forms 705 N.
-*ri*, primy. 817.
-*ru*, primy. 818.

17

-*ram*, secondary ending 3 pl. 455.
-*re*, 3 pl. pres. 452.
rt (orig.) = Av. š 163; = Av. *ərət*- 163 N.
-*rta* (orig.) = Av. -*ṣa* 786 N. 3.

Av. ю (v) = (u).

v (*u*), pronc. 11; for *u* by resolution 52; in reductions 61; vocalized to *u* 62; written by abbreviation for *uv* 68; = Skt. *iv, iv* 68 N. 2; = Skt. *bh* 87; for Av. *w* 87; = Skt. *v* 93; for *uv* 93 N. 1; combined with consonants 94; for *sv* 187 (1).
va-stems, have acc. sg. -*um* 63 N. 1.
-*va*, primy. 819; sedry. 854.
-*vairī*, fem. to -*van* 855.
√*vac*-, aor. 651, 668; fut. 672; pass. ptcpl. 711 (1).
√*van*-, aor. 658.
-*van*, primy. 820; sedry. 855.
-*vana*, sedry 856.
-*vant* (-*mant*), primy. 821; sedry. 857.
√*var*- 'choose', forms 567 seq.; 584.
-*var* (-*vara*), primy. 823.
√*varz*-, pres. 482 seq.; aor. 658.
√*vīd*-, perf. pdgm. 621.
vah-stems, deln. 348 seq.
-*vah*, ending perf. act. ptcpl. 714; primy. 822.
-*vɔ̄vh*, see -*vah*.
vy (orig.) = Av. -*uy*- 62.
-*vya*, sedry. 854 N.

Av. ɒ s.

s, pronc. 9; = orig. *s* 109 seq.; = orig. *sk₁*·142; = orig. *ts* 143; = older palatal *ś* 146; = orig. dental (+ *t*) 151; = orig. z (+ *m*) 152; = orig. z (+ *n*) 153; retained before -*ca* 189; ending of nom. sg. 222; = Skt. *ch* in inchoative 697; *s*-prefixes, how treated 754.
s-stems (orig.), deln. 338 seq.
s-, *sa*-, *siṣ*-aorist, see *h*.
-*sa*, 2d pers. sg = Skt. -*thā*: 453.
-*sa*, sedry. 827.
√*sand*-, *sa l*-, aor. 656.
st, origin 192.
√*stā*-, in periphrases 724.
sn = older *zn* 164 N. 1.
sp (Av.) = Skt. *śv* 97.
-*spa*, see -*va* 819.
sy (orig.), treatment in Av. 131.
sva (orig.), treatment in Av. 130.
-*sva*, -*iva*, imperat. 456.

Av. ʋ, ɯ, ʋ š, ṣ̌, ž.

š, ṣ̌, ž pronc. 9; general character 166 N., 154 seq.; *š* in Av. *fš* 147-9; = orig. *s* after *i, u, ḥ, r* 155-6; = Skt. *kṣ* 158; = older palatal *ś* (+ *t*, or + *n*) 159-60; = Skt. *rṭ* 163; in *šu* = older *zu* 164; *š* = older *zs* 165; = older *zš* (Skt. *sṭ*) 166; *š* in prefixes 745.
-*ša* (Av.) = orig. -*rta* 163, 786 N. 3.
-*šar* (Av.) = orig. -*rtar* 787 N. 1.
-*šam*, pronom. gen. plur. 380.
ši, as ligature 3; = Skt. *ṣṭ* 159.
šu = Skt. *ṣu* 160.
-*šna*, primy. 807.
žy (š) = older *cy* 162.
-*iva*, ending loc. pl. 224; sedry. 827.
šh, written in compounds 754.

Av. ʃ z.

z, pronc. 9; = Skt. *j, h* 88, 168, 169; = *s*-voiced 170, 872 N. 1.

√*zā-*, caus. 685 N. 2.
zd = Skt. *dh* 89, 171.
zn (orig.) = Av. *sn* 153.
zb = Skt. *hv* 99.
zm (orig.) = Av. *sm* 152.

Av. 𝐰 *ž.*

ž, pronc. 9; = Skt. *j*, *h* 88 N 1, 177, 178; in combination *jž*, *vž*, *žn* 89, 164 N. 2; = *ž*-voiced 179; = Skt. *kṣ* 181; = Skt. *ḍ*, *ḍh* 182-3.

Av. 𝐰, ष, 𝐡 *ḣ*, *ḣ*, *ḣ*.

h, ḣ, pronc. 12; general remark 184; = orig. *s* 110; = orig. *-sy-* 137; *h* (= *s*) dropped before *m* 187 (4).

h- (s) stems, deln. 338 seq.
h- (s) aorist, pdgm. 653 seq.
ha- (sa) aorist, forms 663.
-ha- (-vha-), in desiderative 699.
√ *harž-*, fut. 672-3.
hiš-aorist, formation 665.
√ *ha-* 'press', pres. forms 567, 588, 591.
-he = Skt. *-sya*, ending gen. sg. 222.
hm, as ligature 3; = orig. *-sm-* 141; element in pronom. deln. 379-81.
hy, ḣy = orig. *sy* 131-3.
-hyā, -hyā-ā, in gen. sg. 222.
ḣr, for *-r-* 100 N. 1.
ḣv, ḣv, as ligature 3; pronc. 12; = orig. *sv* 130.
-hva, -ǧva, ending loc. pl. 224, 736; ending 2 sg. imperat. 456.

II. AVESTA-INDEX
(Word-List).

Av. ⁓ a.
aēbi- f. 794.
aēwi-ǰac- 743.
aēpha 136.
aipya loc. sg. 281.
aiwyō dat. pl. 286 N.
airyaman- dcln. 300.
aēta- pron. stem, dcln. 417 seq.
aēm dcln. 422 seq.
aēna- dcln. 369.
aēṣa as nom. sg. m. 411, 418.
aēṣa- (aēta-) dcln. 417 seq.
aoi 62 N. 3.
aoim 369.
aohla 90.
aogǝdā 90.
aojā 527.
aojaite 526.
aojanu-, aojamna- 528.
aojō. aojō nom. sg. 341.
aojōs-ca pl. 343.
aka- 'bad' 365.
aciśta- 365.
apa°run- 313 N. 1.
advā nom. sg. 315.
adwan- 820.
afka- (aδka-) 81 N. 1.
aparǝse 484 N.
afstacinō 774.

avuhe dat. sg. 265.
ana- pron. stem 426.
antarǝ naēmāṱ 731 (4), 737.
aya- instr. 429.
aredus- dcln. 360, form 783.
arš- in cpds. 882.
ava- pronom. stem 432.
avaṅt- dcln. 441.
uvazaṇt- dcln. 442.
as, ās 'was' 453, 532.
asti- subst. 794.
astvaṇt- dcln. 291.
asrūšlǝm 638.
aṣ̌aoni- dcln. 257, fem. 362.
aṣ̌aoniš neut. pl. 315.
aṣ̌avan- dcln. 313. comparative 365 N. 3.
aṣ̌ahe 67.
aṣ̌āun- str. form 313, 315, 62 N. 1.
aṣ̌āṇnąm 62 N. 1.
aṣ̌āum voc. sg. 313.
aškarǝ 639.
aṣ̌jah-, aṣ̌ah- 347, 365.
acāhī 486.
azǝm dcln. 380.
azdbiš general pl. case 229.
ahe 137.

ahu nom. sg. 275.
ahmāka- 839.
ahmākǝm 440 N. 3.
ahmya loc. sg. 736.
ahyā reflex. 436 N. 5.

Av. ⁓ ā.
āaṱ 53, 731 (4).
āidi aor. pass. 668.
āhūirīm 375.
āhanš 77 N. 1, 889.
āṱ, āaṱ adv.bl. 731 (4).
ātar-, ātr-, āþr- dcln. 331.
āþravan- dcln. 313 N.
āþßitīm 375.
āp-, ap- dcln. 286.
ābǝrǝṱ- nom. sg. 281, formation 745 N. 1.
āfǝṇte 578.
ānuš̌hac- 754 (2).
ǝrǝi pf. 612.
ās 'was' 453, 532.
āsišta- 365.
āskǝiti- 789.

Av. ⁓ u.
uhta- 711 (1).
upasma- 876, 889.
uboibya 68 N. 1.
uruuaost 607.
uruvaduša 651 N. 2.

II. Avesta-Index (Word-List).—Reference to the §§. 261

ᵘrūdōyatā 685 N. 3.
ᵘrūpayeⁱŋtī 685 N. 3.
ᵘrvaēšta 694.
ᵘrvan-, ᵘrun- dcln. 314.
uvaēibya 68 N. 1.
usaⁱti 698 N.
ušāh-, ušah- dcln. 357.
ušąm, ušə̄uhəm 341.
uši.dąm 355 N.
uz, us euph. 750, 753 N. 2.

Av. ɪ ə.
ərənāvi 668 N.
ərə̄žncąm 3 sg. aor. imperat. 456, 627 N., 640.

Av. ɪ ʒ.
ənā̆hštā 607, 615.
əhmā 389.

Av. ↗ ō.
ōim, ōyum 369.

Av. ⁓ ō̆.
ō̄uha, pf. 539.
ō̄uhāⁱre 609.
ō̄uhāⁱre 503, 619.

Av. ⁊ q.
qsqsutā 651 N. 2.

Av. ᴈ k.
kaⁱnin-, dcln. 316, formation 774.
katārō, katārasciṭ 19.
karšvan-, dcln. 315, formation 820.
kuhžnvąna 465 N.
kərənāun 571.
kərənəntē 591.

Av. Ƌ ḫ.
hrafstrāⁱš 229.
hšapō, advl. 731 (5).
hštā 642.
hžmāvōya 390.
hžnaošəmina 663.
hžnəvišā 664.

Av. ℂ g.
gaⁱri-, form 48, dcln. 251.
guo-, gāu-, gava-, dcln. 278, in cpsn. 867 N. 2.
garənu- 806.
gava- see gao- 278.

Av. Ꞓ j.
jə̄nə̄m 84.
jžarvaṇt- 581.
jžōnvamna- 581.

Av. ᴘ c.
caⁱti 407.
caēšaētəm 484.
catuvrō 372.
caþwar-, dcln. 372.
caþwarəsatəm 374.
caþruš 375.
cašmə̄ng, °ąm, loc. sg. 305.
cāhrarə 606.
cikōitərəš 601, 614.
cina 407 N.
cinas 192, 557ˢ
civištī 664.
cōrəṭ 637.
cyavhaṭ 407 N.

Av. Ɛ j.
jaǰnaṭ 465, 619.
javhəntu, aor. 663.

jamaēte, du. subj. 451, 643.
jasaⁱti 142.
jiṭ 22.
jigərəzaṭ, 3 pl. 550.
jijižənti 701.

Av. ⱶ t.
tahma-, comparat. 365 N. 2.
taṭ, pronom. dcln. 409 seq.
taṭ-āpəm 81 N. 2.
tanuye 190.
tanūži, loc. sg. 360.
tanā-, dcln. 271.
tančišta- 365 N. 2.
tarasca, instr. advl. 287, 731.
tižar-, dcln. 371.
tūⁱrya- 374.
tātuhžva 745 N. 2.
tąm, dcln. 390.
təmavuhə̄, °uŋtəm 295.
tərəsaⁱti 698 N.
tvišī- 777.
-tō, advl. ending 728.
tušyah- 365 N. 2.

Av. Ƌ þ.
þwa- 435, 439.
-þwa, num. suffix 376.
þwaṭ, advl. 436 N. 4.
þwāvaṇt- 435.
þwōrəštāra, du. 39.
þri-, dcln. 371.
þrisata- 374.
þrižva 376, 827.
þrizafō̄, nom. sg. 315.
þrizafəm, voc. sg. 300.

Indexes to Part 1.

Av. ꝯ d.
duipiša, duidiša 463 N.
duidiš 550.
dnighu-, dahyu-, dcln. 269.
daēum, acc. sg. 63 N., 239.
dacuā-, dcln. 243.
dapušaṯ, abl. sg. 349.
daduše 350.
dadō, pf. 1 sg. 599.
dam-, dcln. 318 N. 2.
dayāf as pass. 678 N.
dareja- 48.
dasanąm 373.
dazde, pf. mid. du. 600, 606.
dahāka, duhākāca 19.
dātar-, dcln. 322.
nāmąm, °ąu 308.
°dāhīš 665.
cidaēm 607.
dīdarəšatā 701.
didrajtōduyē 498.
dižamna 660, 663.
duždar-, dužder- 787 N. 2.
duye 190, 370.
duš-, duš- in cpds. 882, 864.
duz-vacah-, dcln. 330.
dəbənaotā 569.
dəjit 22.
diṇg, dąm 318 N. 2.
dąnmahi 45 N. 3.
draonəbyō 307.
drīvī- 362, 779.
drəgvaṇt-, form 31, dcln 291.
drəgvātā 295.
drəgvāitē 18 N.

Avaode- 786 N. 3.
drvaṇt-, drvō 295.
dva-, dcln. 370.

Av. ẹ t.
ṯkaēšah-, ṯkaēšah- 81, 96 N.

Av. v p.
paitī.šmarəmna- 754 (1).
paityāpəm, advl. 892.
pairi.aētrānš, acc. plur. 327.
paiti.aṇharštə- 754 (3).
pairišhahta- 754 (2).
pasiryō 62 N. 2.
putar-, ptar-, dcln. 322.
paš-, dcln. 288, 310.
paṇcanąm 373.
paṇcasatōiš 374.
paṇca.yaḵštiš 891.
paṇtan-. paš-, dcln. 310.
poskāṯ 731.
fasne 735.
pərənavō, nom. sg. 295.
pərəniṇe, dat. sg. 316.
pərəsanyeiti 696 N.
pouruyō 62 N 2.
pāuhahe 661.

Av. ə f.
fədrō, f.trōi 322, 325.
fyauhuṇṯe 493, 582.
fracu, instr. advl. 287, 731.
frašṯu- 876.
frabda- 876.
fromrū 275.
frastərəta 711 (3).
frasrūta 694.
frāyərəyəṯ as pass. 678 N.

frąš, nom. sg. 287.
fryąmahi 45 N. 3.
fšuyaṇt-, dcln. 291.

Av. ꝑ b.
baēvarəbīš 336 N.
bajina 17.
baraiṯe, du. 451.
bājar- 787 N. 1.
buyata, buyama 463 N.
būiri-, dcln. 252.
bāšyauṯ-, fut. 672.
bərəhdē, nom. sg. fem. 245.
bərəzaṇt-, dcln. 295.
bəzvaṇt- 31.
brūtūirya- 191, 854 N. 1.
brvaṯəyąm 223.

Av. ⸾ n.
naēciš 408 N.
naēnižaiti 707.
naoma-, nāuma- 64.
nanā 17.
nar-, dcln. 332.
nase, imperat. 493.
nāidyah-, dcln. 346.
nāmənīš 229, 308.
nāmąm 308.
niṇre, 3 sg. 525.
nigrāire 452, 486, 521.
niš-, niš-, euph. 750, 753 N. 2.
nuruyō, nəruyō 62 N. 3, 332.
nərąš 49, 332 N. 1.
nərənš, acc. pl. 327.
nūaisā 612.
nōit 731.
nā» 389.

II. Avesta-Index (Word-List).—Reference to the §§.

nąsaṭ, redupl. aor. 651 N.
nmānaya, loc. sg. 239.

Av. 𑀫 m.

ma-, mavaṇt-, pronom.
 435, dcln. 438.
mainya, opt. 504.
mainyu-, dcln. 262.
magavan-, magāun- 313
 N. 1.
maδəma 63 N. 3.
mamnuš 350.
mas-, masyah- 365.
masyō, °avhō, sg. pl. 346.
mas-, compar. 365.
mazaṇt-, dcln. 298.
mazδnā, instr. 305.
mazdāh-, form 89, dcln. 356.
mazyah- 365.
mahrka- 100 N. 1, 785.
mā-ciš 408 N.
mātərąš-cā 49, 327.
māvōya 386.
mipakvacā 872 N. 2.
minaš 557.
mimarəhžavuha 701.
marəhgəduyā 556
mərąžyāṭ 560.
mruoi, 3 sg. aor. pass. 668.
mravī, 1 sg. pret. 519.
mravāire 452, 486, 521.
māh-, māuhō, dcln. 355.

Av. ɩo (ⁿ) y (i).

ya-, rel. dcln. 399.
yaēža (iaēže) 593 (4).
yaogəṭ 637.
yaoš, yauž 750 N.

yavaētāite 842, 893.
yasna-, dcln. 236 seq.
yāiš as general pl. 384.
yāhi, loc. sg. 353.
yṭaṭ 403.
yəm, voc. sg. 314 N. 1.
yuvan, yvan-, dcln. 314 N. 1.
yā-, dcln. 276.
yūšmākəm 440 N. 3.
yeṅhe, form 136, 399, m. for f. 383 N.
yeva (ieiu) 593 (4), 619.
yesnyata, instr. advl. 731.

Av. ᚱ r.

raē-, rāi-, dcln. 277.
raose, 2 sg. 518.
rapaēšta-, °ar, dcln. 249, 330, form 877, 881.
rarəš-, intens. 705 N.
raṅnvō, gen. instr. 265.
razura 816.
rəṇhavhōi 661.

Av. 𐬬 (v) v (w).

vainīṭ 637.
vaēδa, pdgm. 621.
vaēm 386.
vaoeātarə 613.
vaoeirəm 607, 616, 652 N. 2.
vakje-, dcln. 285.
vaḣyeite 672.
vacastaštivaṭ, advl. 730.
vacah-, dcln. 339.
vavhu-, compar. 365.
vavuhī-, fem. 362.
vavhō, vahyō 347.
varəš 637.
vastra-, dcln. 237.

vāxnuš 350.
vāci, 3 sg. aor. pass. 668.
vātōyōtā 39 N.
vārəprajni- 825 c.
vindita 560, 565.
vipuš-, wk. stem 349-50.
vipiži, loc. sg. 359.
vīδōyəm 63 N. 2.
vīdąm, imperative 456, 627 N., 640.
vīδōiþre, infin. 787 N. 3.
vilivah-, dcln. 349-50.
vīvəṅghatū 701.
vīs-, dcln. 279.
vīsaiti, num. 374.
vīspa-, dcln. 443.
vīspəm 20.
vīspāiš 229.
varəprajan-, dcln. 317, compar. 365 N. 3.
varəpravan-, comparat. 365 N. 3.
varənvaitē, du. 451, 568.
varəzyatəm 485.
və 'we' 389.
və 'you' 393.
vohu-, compar. 365.
vōijnāuyō 62 N. 3, 247.
vā 393.

Av. ꜱ s.

saēna- 187 (3).
sata 374.
sanaṭ 591.
sar-, dcln. 335.
saškən 607.
sāhīṭ 527, 637.
sūn- see spān- 314 N.
sōire 452, 526.
star-, dcln. 329.
stā, stō 531.

stāumi 525.
strjuš, acc. pl. 327-9.
span-, sūn-, deln. 314 N. 1.
spajiti- 789.
spašupa 578.
srvum 637.
snaipiš, deln. 359.
sjāvi, 3 sg. aor. 668.

Av. ϸ ſ.
ṣā̆iťm 162.
ṣ̌āvayoiṱ 162.
ṣ̌e, deln. 394-5.
ṣ̌ā, nom. fem. 250.

Av. m ſ.
ṣ̌yaoθnəm 162.
ṣ̌yeiṇti 162.

Av. ſ z.
zafar- 823.
ẏzan-, forms 553 N.
zam-, zəm-, deln. 318.
zaranaəmā 591.
zaranya- 48.
zi{{nāwhəmna- 465 N., 701.

zizanəṇti 553 N.
zizanən 652 N.
zā, nom. sg. 318 N.
zdi 533.
zyam- 'hiems', deln. 318 N. 2.
zraya, zrayāi, loc. sg. 341, 357 N. 2.
zrāne 314 N. 1.

Av. ϸ, ϧ, ψ h, h̤, h̟.
haurvaiti 582.
haom 440 N. 1.
haoyā 68 N. 3, 440 N. 1.
hakərəṱ 375, 730.
haḱi-, deln. 256.
haḱṣ̌aya, saṣ̌a 487.
hamaspaθmaēdaya 869 Note.
harəθre, infin. 787 N. 3.
hava- see hɪa- 440.
hazaura- 374.
hā as nom. sg. m. 411.
hā́iriti- 777.
hā̆u, pron. 432.
hātqm 18 N. 3.
hiþāuš, •qm 278 N.
hispəsmna- 405, 754.

hišmarəṇtō 465.
hu- in cpds. 882.
hudāh-, deln. 353.
huθriti- 31.
hūrō, gen. sg. 334.
hən 532.
hē̆, ǰē, deln. 394-5.
hō̆ (hvō) 416 N.
hō, kā, tat, deln. 409 seq.
hqm, hām, hiṇ- 753 N. 3.
hyaṱ 403.
hydrə, hyqn 455.
hyām, hyāṱ 535.
hva-, hva-, hava-, deln. 440.
hvaēpaiθe, instr. 239.
hvacah-, deln. 339.
hvatō, reflex. 436 N. 1.
hvavkārəm, acc. 325.
hvapā̆, •qm 357 N. 1.
hvar-, deln. 334.
harənu, instr. sg. 344.
harənavahā, •vṇtəm 295.
hvā̆ɪoya 436 N. 3.
hīsaṱ 698 N.
hōng, gen. sg. 334.
hɪqməhī 45 N. 3.
hɪo, hɪāvōya 398, 410, 436 N. 3.

III. GENERAL INDEX.

Ablative, the ending -āt lightened to -āt 19, 239; remarks on formation 222 seq.; advl. use of 731.
Abbreviation of final member of compound 876.
Absolutive (gerund) 718.
Accents, not written in Av. MSS. 2; effect of 265, 341, 885.
Accusative, formation 222 seq.; neut. sg. in pronouns 379; as infinitive 721; as adv. 731; in compounds 877, 881.
Active endings with passive force 678 N.
a-declension, transfer from cons. deln. 344; from vah stem 351; from āh-stem 355, 357 N. 3; from iṣ-stem 359 N. See also Transfer.
Adjective, deln. of adj. 219 seq.; pronominal deln. 443; comparat. degree 345-6, 363 seq.; adj. prefixes 747-8; formed by primy. and scdry. derivation 761 seq.; adj. denoting material 829; adjective cpds. 881-3, 887.
Adverbial prefixes 733; advl. uses of prep. phrase 737; adverbial cpds. 892.
Adverb, numeral 375; multiplicative 376; pronominal 436; formation of adv. 726-32; shows case-forms 731.
Agency, nouns of 787.

Agglomerations 893.
Aggregative compounds 879 N.
Alphabet, characters and transliteration 1.
Anaptyxis 2 N., 69, 72.
Anusvāra (Skt.), how represented in Av. 46.
Aorist-system, synopsis and formation 447-8, 624-68, radical aor. subjunct. 549; augment missing in aor. 626; has scdry. endings 626; modes of aor. 627; redupl. aor. 650-2; causative forms 652; sigmatic aor. 653 seq.; passive aor. 3 sg. 667-8.
Aspiration, pronunciation of h 12.
Aspirate mediae + t or + s 89.
Assimilation of consonants 185.
Augment, rules for in Av. 466; common omission of aug. 466, 626; restored for metre 466 N. 2.
Augmentless preterite as injunctive 466 N. 3.
a-vowel, contraction 60 seq.
Avyayībhāva (Skt.) compound in Av. 892.

Bartholomae's law, statement of, 89.

Cardinals — see Numerals.
Cases in declension 220 seq.; interchange 233; case-forms in adverbs 731; in cpsn. 877.

Causal signification without form 693; causal conjunctions 739.

Causative aorist 652; formation of causative 684-94, modes of caus. 686; inflection 687-8; aorist 689.

Comparative, adj. deln. 346; fem. form in -yehī 303; comparat. of *an*-stem 365 N. 3; in -*tara* 841.

Compound stems, in general 858-95; how written in MSS. 858 N.; union of members 861 seq.; hiatus in cpds. 861-2; treatment of orig. *s* after *i, u* in cpsn. 754; contraction in cpds. 862; sandhi in cpds. 863; case-forms in cpsn. 877; classes of cpds. 878-91; copulative cpds. 879; aggregative 879 N.; determinative 880-2; dependent 881; descriptive 882; sedry. adjective cpds. 883-9, possessive 884-6; participial adj. cpds. 888; prepositional adj. cpds. 889; numeral cpds. 891; adverbial cpds. 892; loose combinations and agglomerations 893; long cpds. not common in Av. 894.

Conjugation of verbs, in general 444 seq.; voice, mode, tense 445; infinitive 446, 719-20; participle 446; synopsis of conj. system 447-8; secondary conj. 447-8, 675-707; present-syst. 468-591; classes of verbs 469 seq.; thematic or *a*-conj. 469-507; transfer in conj. 471, 529, 553, 563, etc.

Conjunctions 738-9.

Consonants, how written in Av. 1; pronc. 6 seq.; general system 73 seq.; assimilation of 185; double cons. not allowed in Av. 186; dropping of 187-8; final cons. in Av. 192; interchange of cons. in MSS. 193 N. 2; rules for reduplicating cons. in verbs 465.

Contraction. of vowels 50 seq.; in cpds. 862.

Dative, dual -*we* for -*bya* 67; general remarks 222 seq.; as infin. 720; as adverb 731; in cpds. 877-81.

Declension, classes of 219 seq.; deln. of comparat. adj. 346; of stems in -*vah* 348 seq.; of stems in -*āh* (-*āt*) 352 seq.; of stems in -*iš, -uš* 358; of numerals 369 seq.; of pronouns 377 seq.; of pronominal adverbs 437 seq. See Stems.

Declinable stems, formation of 743 seq.

Demonstrative pronoun 409 seq.

Denominative verbs, formation and inflection 695-6.

Dentals, become *s* before dentals 215.

Dependent compounds 881.

Derivation, see Word-Formation 743 seq.

Derivatives, numeral 375; pronominal 436.

Desiderative, form 498; formation and inflection 699; pf. ptcpl. 701 N.

Descriptive compounds 882.

Determinative compounds 880-2.

Diphthongs, pronc. 7; their origin 53 seq.; by protraction 53; by reduction 53; proper diphthongs 54 seq.

Dissimilation of *n, i* to *a* 31.

Distributive force in pronoun 408.

Double consonants, not allowed in Av. 186.

Dual, its form in verbs 451 seq.

Dvandva (Skt.) compounds 879.

III. General Index.—Reference to the §§.

Enclitic forms of pronoun 386 seq.; sandhi with enclitics 895.
Endings, *pada*-endings in deln. 85; noun-endings 221-2; primy. and sedry. of verbs 448 seq.; of imperative 448 c, 456 seq.; of subjunctive 462; of opt. 464; of perfect 448 d, 597-600, of aorist 626; of passive 678.

Feminine, formation 362, 769, 779; comparat. *-yehī* 363: fem. and neut. forms interchange 232, 383.
Final consonants 192; member of compound 873 seq.
Future-system, synopsis 447-8; formation 669; modes 670; forms 671; fut. pass. ptcpl. (see gerundive) 682.

Gender, occasional difference from Skt. 220 N., 232, 283; distinction of gender in pronouns 384, 399.
General plur. case 228, 308, 315, 384.
Genitive, sg. *-ahe* for orig. *-asya* 67; gen. plur. of personal pronouns 440 N. 3; gen. in cpds. 877, 881.
Gerund, remark 718.
Gerundive 682; formation 716-17; form in *-ya* 812.
Gradation, see Stem-gradation.
Guṇa and Vṛddhi 60 seq.; give rise to diphthongs 53; in nouns 235; in verbs 481 N. 3, 509 seq.; in caus. 685; in intens. 702; in primy. derivation 757 seq.; in sedry. deriv. 825. See Strengthening.

Heavy syllable not strengthened 481 N. 3; form *-āna (-au)* 770.

Hiatus, in compounds 51 N., 52 N., 861-2.

Imperative, first person 447 N.; endings 448 c, 456 seq.; 3 sg. in *-ām* 456, 627 N.; mode-formation 460; of *a*-conj. 474, 500-1; of non-*a*-conj. 501.
Imperfect, see Secondary formation.
Improper subjunctive 445 N. 2. See Injunctive.
Inchoative, formation 697-8.
Increment, causes vowel-lightening 19.
Indeclinables 725-42.
Indefinite pronoun 408.
Indicative, of *a*-conj. 473, 496; of non-*a*-conj. 501, 525; of redupl. class 549-50; of perfect 612-16.
Infinitive 446; causal 694; formation and examples 719-21; in *-pre (-tar)* 787 N. 3.
Injunctive 445 N. 2, 466 N. 3.
Insertion of *ḷ* before *ṣ* 188; of nasal in 7th class 554; of *t* after root in derivation 745 N. 1.
Instrumental, general remarks 322 seq.; as adv. 731; in cpds. 881.
Intensive, formation and inflection 702-7.
Interjections 741-2.
Interrogative pronoun 406 seq.

Karmadhāraya (Skt.) compounds 882.

Labialization of *u (ū)* to *ō* 38, 39.
Lengthening, of *u (to ū)* before epenthetic *i* 20; of final vowels in monosyllables 24; of final vowels in GAv. 26; in causative 685 a; takes the place of strengthening 685 N. 3; lengthening before *-vaṇt* 857 N. 1.

Ligature, written in MSS. 3; *hm, hv, hv* 3, 13.
Liquid, pronc. of *r* 11; *l* wanting in Av. 11 N.; nature of *r* 100.
Locative, formation 222 seq.; loc. infinitive 721; as adverb 731; in compounds 877, 881.
Loss of a consonant 187-8.
Loose compound combination 893.

Material, formation of adj. denoting material 829.
Mediae (*g, d, b, j*), pronc. 8; character 82; med. aspirate $+t$ or $+s$ 89.
Members of compound 861-77.
Metathesis of *r* 191.
Metre, shows augment 466 N. 1; shows dropping of prefix 752 N. 1; shows Sandhi 753 N. 1, 897.
Middle voice 445 N. 1; with pass. force 676; mid. pass. ptcpl. 811.
Mode, in verbal inflection 445; formation 459 seq.; indic. 459; imperative 460; subjunct. 461-2; opt. 463-4; in *a*-conj. 473 seq.; in non-*a*-conj. 510 seq.; in perf. 603-4; in aorist 627; in future 670; in passive 679.
Monosyllables, long 24.

Nasals, pronc. 11; character 101; in 7th class of verbs 470, 554-65; in causative 685 N. 1.
Nasalization of *a* (*ā*) to *ą* 45, 46, 201.
Neuter, endings 225-7; acc. sg. of pronouns 379; form interchanges with fem. 232, 383.
Nomen proprium, formation 893.
Nominative, sg. fem. -*e* for orig. -*yā* 67; formation 222 seq.: in first member of cpd. 864, 867 N. 1.

Non-*a*-conjugation, formation 516-92.
Non-sigmatic aorist 628-52.
Noun-declension, 219 seq.; composition 859-95.
nu- (fifth) class of verbs 470, 566-74.
Number, remarks on 220.
Numerals 366-76; cardinals 366; formation 367-8, 374; num. adverbs 375; multiplicatives 376; in -*pa* 844; in -*ma* 849; numeral compounds 891.

Optative, mode-formation 463; endings 464; of *a*-conj. 476, 504-5; of non-*a*-conj. 514; of redupl. class 552.
Ordinals—see Numerals 366 seq.
Original *r*-sonant 47 seq.

Pada-endings, -*biš, -biš* 22, 85.
Palatal *š* = Av. *s, š,* ? 145 seq.
Palatalization of *ą* (*a*) to *i* 30, 491, 503 (1).
Participle, deln. pf. act. 348; general formation 446, 477, 709-15, 822; of *a*-conj. 475, 506-7; pf. pass. ptcpl. 681, 710 seq.; fut. pass. ptcpl. 682; causal 694; forms in -*ant, -mnu, -ana* 709, 811; passive in -*ta* 710-11, 780; -*ita* 712; -*na* 713, 802; participial adj. compounds 888.
Passive voice 445 N. 1; aor. 3 sg. pass. 667-8; form. and pdgm. 676-9; endings 678; pass. force with act. endings 678 N.; modes of the pass. 679; fut. pass. ptcpl. 681-2; pass. ptcpl. in -*ta, -na* 710-13, 786, 802.
Patronymics, formation 828-34; show vrddhi strengthening 834.

Perfect, act. ptcpl. deln. 348; perfect-system synopsis 447-8; personal endings 448 d, 597-600; of *ah-* 'to be' 539; perfect-system inflection 592-623; redupl. syllable 592-4; pluperfect 602; modes of the perf. 603 4; pdgm. 605 seq.; periphrastic form 623; perf pass. ptcpl. 681; perf. desid. 701 N.; act. ptcpl. in *-vah* 714, 822; mid. ptcpl. in *-āna, -ana* 715.
Periphrastic, perf. 623; verbal phrases 722-4.
Person in verbal inflections 447.
Personal pronoun 385 seq.; endings of verbs 448; of perf. 497-600.
Pluperfect 602.
Plural, general plur. case 228 seq.
Polysyllables, shorten final long vowels 25.
Possessive pronoun 434-5, 440 N. 3; cpds. 884-6.
Postposition of preposition 736.
Postpositive *a* in abl. and loc. 222-4, 379-80.
Precative, not quotable 666.
Predicate verb, used only once when prefix repeated 752 N. 2.
Prefixes, advl. 733; nominal 747-8; verbal 749-54; rules for connecting with verb 751; repeated 752; separated from verb 753.
Prepositions, in general 734-7; placed in postpositive position 736.
Prepositional adj. cpds. 889.
Present-system 468-591; causative 687. See Indicative.
Preterite, see pluperfect 602. See Indicative.
Primary, derivation 756-823; treatment of root 757 8.

Proclitics, see Sandhi 898.
Pronominal, deln. of adjs. 443; derivatives 857 N. 2.
Pronouns, synopsis 377 seq.; personal 385 seq.; relative 399 seq.; interrogative 406 seq.; indefinite 408; demonstrative 409 seq.; possess. 434-5, 440 N. 3; reflexive 435-6.
Pronunciation 6 seq.
Proper diphthongs 54 seq.
Prothesis 69, 71.
Protraction-diphthongs 53.
Punctuation, method in MSS. 5.

Quantity, agreement between Av. and Skt. 15; different from Skt. 16; rules for vowels 23 seq.

Radical syllable, in perfect 595-6; in intensive 704.
Reduction-diphthongs 53; reduction of *ya, va* to *i, u* 63; in verbal forms 493-4; of *ya* to *e* in compounds 865 N., cf. instr. 239.
Reduplication, general rules 465; redupl. class (third) of verbs 470, 540-53; redupl. syllable of perf. 592-4; absence of redupl. 620; redupl. in aorist 650-2; in desiderative 699-701; in intensive 703 in nouns 745 N. 2; redupl. of. orig. *s* 754 (2).
Reflexive use of personal pronouns 395; reflex. pronoun 435-6.
Relative pronoun 399 seq.
Relationship, nouns of 321, 787.
Repetition of same syllable avoided 194; of pronoun 408; of root in intensive 705; of prefix 752.
Résumá of Phonology 195 seq.
Resolution of vowels 52, 862.

Root-class (second), of verbs 470, 516-39; root aorist 629-47; root repeated in intensive 705; formation of root-words 744-5; root in primy. deriv. 757-8.

Samprasaraṇa 203.
Sandhi, occurrence in Av. 75; with prefixes 753; in cpds. 861 seq.; with enclitics 895-900; with proclitics 898.
Secondary conjs. 447-8, 675-707, 448 b; sedry. suffixes 826, 844-57. sedry. adj. compounds 883-9.
Semivowels, p. v 91-3.
Sentence-sandhi 897.
Shortening of vowels 25, 51.
Sibilants 106.
Simple a-aorist (thematic) 648-9.
Sigmatic aorist 653 seq.
Sonant, see Surd, Voiced.
Sonantizing of s to ṣ 170; of ʃ to š 179.
Spirants, pronc. 9; voiceless ḳ, ṗ, f 77; voiced ǧ, ḋ, w 82.
Stem-gradation 235, 284 seq., 290, 320, 595-6. See Strong and Weak.
Stems, deln. of stems in a 236 seq.; in ā 243-9; in i 257; strong and weak 284-8; in radical ī 261; in u, ū 262-75, in āi 277; in āu 278; in consonants 279 seq.; without suffix 279; in aṛe 287; in -aṇt, -maṇt, -vaṇt 289 seq.; in -an, -man, -van 299 seq.; in -in 316; in radical -n, -m 317; in orig. -r 319 seq., 333 seq.; in -tar, -ar 321; in orig. -s 338 seq.; in -ah 339; formation 743 seq.
Strengthening, in intensive 702; in derivation 825.

Strong and weak forms, in verbs 467, 509; in perf. 505-6. See Stem-gradation.
Subjunctive, improper subjunct. or injunct. 445 N. 2, 466 N. 3; mode-formation 461; first persons 462; endings 462; formation in a-conj. 475, 502-3; in non-a-conj. 512; in redupl. class 551.
Suffixes 755-857; primy. 756-823.
Suffixless formation 744-5
Superlative formation 363 seq.; in -tama 841.
Surd and sonant (voiceless and voiced) 74.

Tatpuruṣa (Skt.), cpds. 881.
Tense 445 seq.
Tenues (k, t, p, c), pronc. 8; character 76 seq.
Thematic vowel in verbs 461; thematic or a-conj. of verbs 469-507; a-aorist 648-9.
Transfer, in deln. 234 seq.; of i-stems to a-deln. 256 N.; of u-stems to a-deln. 269; of consonant stems to a-deln. 283 N., 297, 309, 313 N., 314 N. 2, 332 N. 2, 344, 351, 355, 357 N. 3, 359 N.; transfer of conj. classes and inflection 471, 529, 553, 563-5, 574, 604, 610, 707.
Transition, see Transfer.
Transposition, see Metathesis.

Union of members of cpds. 861 seq.
Unthematic conjugation 516-92.
u-stems, show trace of accent in genitive 265.

Verbs—see Conjugation.
Verbal system, synopsis 447-8; prefixes 749-54; composition 749

seq., 858; abstract forms (infin. ptcpl.) 708.
Vocalic *r*, how represented in Av. 47 seq.
Vocative of *an*-stems 193; formation 222-4.
Voice, in verbal inflection 445.
Voiced and voiceless 74; voiced spirants *j̇, ḋ, ẇ* 206; voiced and voiceless consonants in cpds. 863. See also Voiceless and Sonant.
Voiceless 74; voiceless spirants *ḳ, ṗ, f* 204; voiceless consonants 753 N. 2. See Voiced and Sonant.
Vowels, how written in Av. 1, 2; pronc. 6 seq.; system 14; agree in quality and quantity with Skt. 14; vowel-gradation 18 N. 2; higher and lower grades 18 N. 2; weakening through increment 19; long in vicinity of *v* 20; long and short fluctuate in MSS. 21; rules for quantity 23 seq.; preference for long in GAv. 24, 26; lengthened in monosyllables 24; shortened in polysyllables 25; treatment before -*ca* 26 N.; differ in quality from Skt. 28; concurrence of vowels 50; co-alesce 50 seq.;

contraction and resolution 50 seq.; short in contraction 51; strengthened 60 seq.; help-vowel (anaptyctic) 71; fluctuations in writing *ai, aē* 193 N. 2; vowel-variation 235, 467, 509 seq., 595-6; reduplication in verbs 465, 592-4; treatment in causatives 685.
Vowel-variation 235, 467, 509 seq., 595-6.
Vṛddhi, diphthongs 53; strengthening in patronymics 834. See also Guṇa.

Weak stem, -*uš* in perf. ptcpl. 350. See also Strong.
Word-formation 743 seq.; by prefixes 746-54; by suffixes 755-7.
Word-sandhi 895.
Writing, method in MSS. 2, 4; fluctuations in spelling between *a, ā* 18 N.; between *ə, a* in MSS. 29 N.; between *e, i* in MSS. 35 N. 2; between *ñ, ą* in MSS. 45 N. 1; defective (and pleonastic) writing of *ą (n)* 45 N. 1, 2; fluctuation between -*arə, -arə* in MSS. 47; manner of writing an older *iy, uv* 68 N. 2; -*ai* for -*ahi* 357 N. 2.

ADDITIONS AND CORRECTIONS.

a. Corrections.

A few obvious misprints are passed over without notice.

page vii (line 17) — for practise read practice.
" 1 (foot-note) — " *antarᵒ* read *antarⁱ*.
" 3 (§ 6 l. 14) — " fawing read fawning.
" 6 (§ 19 l. 9) — " *apāḫtaraṭ* read *afāḫtaraṭ*.
" 8 (§ 28 l. 1) — " *c* read *a*.
" 9 (§ 29 l. 6) — " *evīṭi* read *avisti*.
" 59 (§ 192 N.) — " 'thou didst promise' read 'he promised'.
" 117 (foot-note) — omit gen. sg. *tahe* and strike out foot-note.
" 125 (§ 440 l. 16) — for *yavāhi* read *yuvāhi*.
" 137 (§ 466 l. 13) — strike out Note 2.
" 148 (§ 505 l. 3) — for *vāᵗrᵒ* read *vāurᵒ*.
" 151 (§ 516 l. 12) — " *vås-ṭi* read *vås-ṭi*.
" 164 (§ 576 l. 1) — " eigth read eighth.
" 179 (§ 637 l. 5) — " *corᵒṭ* read *corᵒṭ*.
" 191 (§ 694 l. 4) — " Vs. read Yt.

b. Additions.

page 5 (§ 17 l. 5) — add: Av. *vāyu-* 'wind' = Skt. *vāyu-*.
" 10 (§ 32 l. 10) — " GAv. *iqm* 'her' Ys. 53.4 = Skt. *tām*.
" 15 (§ 51 l. 16) — " Note 4. In the Gāthās, as is shown by the metre, all contractions are to be resolved.
" 29 (§ 77 l. 9) — " Av. *vaḫšapa-* 'growth' = Skt. *vakṣátha-*.
" 38 (§ 95 l. 4) — " Av. *safur-, safan-*, cf. √*samb-*.
" 42 (§ 109 l. 9) — " Av *raocas.poirišta-*.
" 53 (§ 162 l. 10) — " So Av. *maraŋyāṭ* from *maraŋ-*.

Additions and Corrections. 273

page 57 (§ 183 l. 4) — add: So also Av. *vōiždišta-*, *vōišnu*, cf. Skt. *hid-*, *hed-*; Av. *vōiždayaṇt-*, *vōiždaṯ*, cf. Skt. *vid*.

„ 58 (§ 187 l. 4) — „ So also in Av. *yazāi* Yt. 10.14 = *yaza(h)i*.

„ 59 (§ 193 l. 14) — „ Orig. *pm* becomes Av. *hm*, cf. GAv. *hahmī (haf-ši)*, YAv. *vahmāi* (√*vap-*)—Geldner.

„ 59 (§ 193) — „ Note 3. Av. *u*, *ū* occasionally = Skt. *a* (derived from nasal sonants), e. g. Av. *vātō.šūta-* 'wind-riven' (cf. Skt. *ksa-tu-*), Av. *vayō.tāite* 'storm-bound' (√ *tan-*)—Paul Horn.

„ 75 (§ 254 abl.) — „ Observe abl. YAv. *aḫštaēš-a* 'in concord' (*aḫšti-*) Vd. 3.1.

„ 84 (§ 286 l. 2) — „ Dat. *āpe*, ZPhl. Gloss. p. 86.

„ 95 (§ 331 l. 4) — „ *ābrāṯ* (*a*-dcln.) Afr. 4.5.

„ 103 (§ 362 l. 10) — „ *maēša-* (m.) 'sheep, ram', *maēšī-* (f.) 'ewe'; *ḫšapra-* (m.) 'lord, king', *ḫšaprī-* (f.) 'mistress'.

„ 184 (§ 660 l. 1) — „ YAv. *vavhaṇt-* aor. act. ptcpl. with fut. meaning Yt. 13.155. See Justi s. v. √ *van-*.

www.ingramcontent.com/pod-product-compliance
Lightning Source LLC
Chambersburg PA
CBHW030117240426
43673CB00041B/1310